Angela Royston | How to get ahead in the

Armed & Civilian Forces

Raintree

www.raintreepublishers.co.uk
Visit our website to find out more information about **Raintree** books.

To order:
Phone 44 (0) 1865 888113
Send a fax to 44 (0) 1865 314091
Visit the Raintree bookshop at **www.raintreepublishers.co.uk** to browse our catalogue and order online.

First published in Great Britain by Raintree, Halley Court, Jordan Hill, Oxford OX2 8EJ, part of Harcourt Education.
Raintree is a registered trademark of Harcourt Education Ltd.

Editorial: Melanie Waldron, Lucy Beevor, and Kate Buckingham
Design: David Poole and Calcium
Illustrations: Geoff Ward
Picture Research: Ruth Blair and Maria Joannou
Production: Huseyin Sami

Originated by Chroma Graphics
Printed and bound in China by South China Printing Company

10 digit ISBN 1 406 20450 1
13 digit ISBN 978 1 4062 0450 6

11 10 09 08 07
10 9 8 7 6 5 4 3 2 1

British Library Cataloguing in Publication Data
Royston, Angela
Armed and Civilian Forces. -(How to get ahead in)
355'.002341
A full catalogue record for this book is available from the British Library.

Acknowledgements
The publishers would like to thank Julie Evans (Army), Phil Betts (RAF), Caroline Scott (RN), Emily Alleyne-Burchmore (police) and Mona Shah (Office of the Deputy Prime Minister) for their assistance in the preparation of this book.

The publishers would like to thank the following for permission to reproduce photographs: Alamy pp. **33** (David Stares), **36** (Photofusion); Angela Royston p.**29**; Corbis pp. **22** (Ashley Cooper), **11** (Creasource), **27** (Michelle Pedone/Zefa), **8** (Oleg Popov/Reuters); Crown Copyright/MOD pp. **4**, **9**, **10**, **13**, **14**, **15**, **17**, **18**, **21**, **24**, **26**, **28**, **29**; Empics pp. **35** (Andrew Milligan/PA Photos), **30** (Jordan Peter/PA Photos), **45** (Ockenden/PAPhoto); Firepix p.**41**; Getty Images p.**6** (Tom Stoddart); Report Digital pp. **47** (Duncan Philips), **5** (Paul Box), **31** (Shout); Rex Features pp.**42** (John Powell), **39** (Shout); Shout p.**19**.

Cover photograph of fighter pilot, reproduced with permission of Getty Images/Digital Vision.

Every effort has been made to contact copyright holders of any material reproduced in this book. Any omissions will be rectified in subsequent printings if notice is given to the publishers.

Disclaimer
All the Internet addresses (URLs) given in this book were valid at the time of going to press. However, due to the dynamic nature of the Internet, some addresses may have changed or ceased to exist since publication. While the author and publishers regret any inconvenience this may cause readers, no responsibility for any such changes can be accepted by either the author or the publishers.

Contents

Words appearing in the text in bold, **like this**, are explained in the glossary.

Chapter 1

An exciting and worthwhile career

So, you are thinking about joining the armed forces or the civilian forces. Is it the life of action and possible danger that attracts you? Or does the opportunity to serve your country or community appeal to you? Serving in the armed or civilian forces will certainly involve both of these.

What are the armed and civilian forces?

The armed forces – the Army, the Royal Navy, and the Royal Air Force (RAF) – protect the security of the United Kingdom. They defend the nation from attack and protect its interests abroad. They also take part in international peace-keeping and disaster relief. The Army operates mainly on land, the Navy at sea, and the RAF in the air. The civilian forces include the police, the fire and rescue service, **customs and excise**, and the prison service. Their role is to protect the security of the community.

below: *Being a soldier requires a lot of commitment and physical effort.*

It takes more than courage

To work in the armed or civilian forces you need to be fit and healthy. You must be able to accept discipline and obey rules and orders. But, don't worry – your basic training will help you to develop these abilities. It will also give you the confidence and knowledge to use your **initiative** and take split-second decisions. Everyone in the forces works with a team of highly trained people, so you need to be able to get on well with others.

above: *This policewoman is on patrol.*

Still interested? Read on...

The next few pages give you some basic information. They tell you about some of the conditions of work shared by all of the forces and whether you are eligible to apply. Each chapter then looks at a particular force. It tells you the qualifications you need to join at different levels and how to apply to join. It describes the basic training and the range of jobs available in each force. Then, at the end of the book, there are tips on how to present yourself well in an interview, examples of jobs in the armed forces, and where to find out more information.

HOW THE NUMBERS COMPARE

Force	Approximate number employed	Approximate starting salary
Army	109,000	£14,000
Royal Air Force	52,000	£14,500
Royal Navy	39,500	£12,000
Police	140,000	£20,000
Fire and Rescue service	39,000	£19,500
HM Prisons	47,000	£17,500

Conditions of work

Conditions of work include the time you are expected to start in the morning and the number of hours you work a day. They also cover the place where you work, the nature of your job, and things such as holidays. Fighting a war and protecting the nation or the community involves a particular set of conditions of work. Your hours of work, what you wear, and how much you are trained will be different from other jobs.

Irregular hours

When you join one of the armed or civilian forces do not expect your hours to be like those of your friends who are working in a nine-to-five office job. Instead you will often have to work in shifts and at weekends. You will sometimes be working in the evening and sometimes at night. If you work for the police or fire service, you may be called out to an emergency at any time. Most soldiers, however, work from 8 a.m. until 5 p.m. and have every weekend off, but not, of course, when they are on **operations**.

below: *Fire-fighting is dangerous work, but training helps to reduce the danger.*

Uniform and training

All the armed and civilian forces provide uniforms, which you must wear when you are on duty. You are expected to be neat and smart. Much of the work of the forces is out of doors and so the purpose of the uniform is to be practical as well as to identify you as a member of the force.

Whichever force you join, you will receive a thorough basic training. Further training continues throughout your career and many of the skills you learn will help you find a job when you leave the force.

Commitment

Both the armed forces and the civilian forces are looking for people who are committed to their jobs. The armed forces expect you to sign up for several years, although you can leave at the end of basic training if you change your mind. After that, you need to give a year's notice if you want to leave the Army.

EQUAL OPPORTUNITIES

All the armed and civilian forces have an equal opportunities policy – they are committed to employing women and men from all religions and ethnic groups.

OTHER BENEFITS

Pay: salaries are usually higher than for similar jobs in commercial companies.

Meals: food is usually provided and is cheaper than you would normally buy elsewhere.

Accommodation: housing is provided in the armed forces, although you can choose to live off the base.

Travel: in the armed forces you will have the opportunity to travel to many different parts of the world.

Are the armed forces right for you?

The armed forces accept a wide range of people and skills. The better your exam results, the more choice you will have in careers, but the main thing the armed forces are looking for is the right kind of person.

Personal qualities

To enjoy the armed forces and do well in them, you need to have the right attitude. You will be expected to do your best and to do it willingly. You will need to be well organized and self-disciplined and able to accept orders from others. At the same time you should be self-confident enough to think for yourself and to act quickly.

Physical qualities

You need to be physically fit and healthy to join the armed forces. Not all health conditions disqualify you from joining, so if you have a health condition, you should discuss it with someone at the recruitment centre. A large part of basic training is spent increasing your fitness, and the fitter you are before you start, the easier you will find it. Look at the "Get ahead!" box on page 11 for ways to increase your fitness.

above: *These soldiers are wearing special desert kit.*

Equal opportunities

The armed forces treat everyone equally, whatever their gender, religion or ethnic background. Vegetarian, **halal**, and **kosher** food can be provided, even on exercises and operations. Women play an important part in the forces, although there are some things that women are not allowed to do, such as fighting as soldiers on the **front line** or serving in submarines.

Sport and adventure

If you are good at sport, the armed forces give you a fantastic opportunity to develop your abilities, right up to Olympic standard. You can play football, rugby, basketball, hockey, and other sports. You can take up adventure challenges involving water sports, snow sports, mountaineering, and similar activities, and you will be sent on challenging training exercises in many parts of the world.

ARE YOU ELIGIBLE?

Age: you must be at least 16 years old to join up.
Nationality: you must have been a citizen of the United Kingdom or a Commonwealth country or the Republic of Ireland.
Academic qualifications: you can join with GCSEs, S-levels or no qualifications at all, but to join as an officer you need to have five GCSEs/S-grades including English and Maths, and the equivalent of three A-levels or three Highers.

above: *Working in the forces can often mean a posting to an exciting environment in a different country.*

Chapter 2

The British Army

The Army fulfils many roles. Apart from training exercises and fighting, its soldiers are often called upon to keep the peace in war-torn countries and to deliver aid to areas hit by an earthquake or other disaster. Such a complex organization involves different jobs, many of them similar to those in civilian organizations.

The Army groups its careers into seven main areas: combat; engineering; **logistics**; IT and communications; human resources, administration and finance; healthcare; and specialist jobs. For more about the jobs in each group see page 49.

ARMY WORDS

The Army is divided into different groupings and sub-groupings. A corps is associated with a particular job, such as the Royal Army Medical Corps or the Intelligence Corps. A battalion is a group of infantry soldiers or engineers. A **regiment** consists of one or two battalions. A brigade is a large group that includes several regiments and battalions.

left: *Cadets are allowed to fire rifles under the supervision of an army sergeant at an Army Cadet Force annual camp.*

Helping you decide

How can you tell which career to go for? An Armed Forces Careers Office (AFCO) will help – you can find the address of your nearest one in the telephone directory. You can talk to a recruitment advisor there and watch a video about the Army before you do the Army Entrance Test.

This test is done on a computer and your score will help the recruitment advisor tell you which careers are likely to suit you. You can also spend two days at an Army Selection Camp. There you can talk to recruits going through the basic training and get a real feel for Army life.

Applying to join

If you decide to apply, you will need to fill out an application form and be interviewed by an officer. The more effort you have made to find out about the Army, the better your interview is likely to go. You will also be given a medical examination, an **aptitude test**, and a physical fitness test. Only after all this do you finally decide if you want to sign up and join the Army.

Get ahead!

You can increase your fitness by working out every day. Running, press-ups, and sit-ups are the best ways of increasing your fitness. Start off by working out for about 20 minutes a day and increase it gradually. Make sure that you warm up before you work out and cool down afterwards. The physical fitness test will include a 2.4-km (1.5-mile) run. If you are male, you should aim to run this in less than 12 minutes and 20 seconds; if you are female, you should run this in less than 14 minutes and 35 seconds.

left: *Working out in a gym and running uphill will help you get fit.*

Basic training

Whatever career you follow, your life in the Army begins with basic training. Once you have passed Recruit Selection and joined up you will spend the first 12 weeks at an Army training camp. By the end of it, you will be physically much fitter and you will have learnt all the basic skills of handling weapons as well as first aid, map reading, and camouflage. You will probably be more confident and have made many good friends.

Fitness

As you progress through basic training you will become increasingly fit and more and more will be required of you. This is a real challenge, but if you begin to flag, your sergeant will be there to urge you on! By the end, you will be amazed at what you can achieve, including running with a heavy pack on your back. But it's not all hard work. You will also find yourself abseiling, kayaking, and taking part in other adventurous activities.

Discipline and initiative

The Army needs its soldiers to obey orders without question sometimes, but at the same time, soldiers have to be able to think for themselves and use their initiative. Sounds contradictory? It will all become clear during training. Knowing what you are doing and what is expected of you at all times is the key to success.

Get ahead!

Inspection tests check how tidy you keep yourself and your belongings. Get used to keeping your clothes clean and neat. Learn how to use an iron!

The next stage – specialist training

After basic training you have a few days off before you join your regiment and begin Phase 2 specialist training. Phase 2 training equips you for the particular career you have chosen in the Army. It may last a few weeks or up to 2 years.

BASIC TRAINING – THE LOWDOWN

Week	What happens
1	**Drill** practice, map-reading, first aid, and handling a rifle
2	Your first exercise, **fieldcraft** and night training, including camouflage techniques and building shelters
3	Computer-simulated rifle range – a bit like computer games but more real
4	Target practice on the live-firing range
5	Tests to prove your physical fitness, including a 2.4-kilometre (1.5-mile) run, and drill tests
6	A long weekend on home leave
7	Getting to grips with an obstacle course that includes a 3.5-metre (12-foot) wall and a river rope swing
8	Your second exercise, including live fire
9	Fitness test that includes a 6-mile march in full combat gear
10	Adventurous training, for example abseiling or canoeing
11	Test week in which you are assessed by a Section Commander
12	Final parade – called "passing out" – with your family and friends there to applaud you.

below: *This officer is leading recruits during basic training.*

Training for life

Every job the Army offers is a vital one. In Phase 2 training you learn the skills needed for the career you have chosen – skills that will give you one or more qualifications that will help you get a job when you leave the Army. If you work hard and do well, you will be given more responsibility and **promotion**.

Combat

Combat troops make up the largest group in the Army and include infantry soldiers, gunners, tank crew, and parachutists. Combat troops are trained not only to fight in different **terrains**, from jungles to deserts, they are also called on to deliver aid in disaster areas and for peace-keeping in war-torn countries.

Combat support

There are many job areas in combat support. Engineering covers a wide range of jobs from building bridges to laying mines and demolition. Engineering jobs include brick-laying and vehicle maintenance as well as mechanical and electrical engineering. The Army needs a constant supply of food, ammunition, and other goods, and it is the job of those who work in logistics to supply them. Sometimes delivery is by truck, at other times by helicopter drop or motorcycle.

below: *Working in combat support is a specialized job in the Army.*

above: *Army medical teams work in the field as well as in army hospitals.*

Receiving up-to-date information is as essential for a **platoon** of soldiers as it is for those planning the larger operation. Providing information is the job of IT and communications and includes signals and military intelligence.

Services

No part of the Army would run smoothly without the Adjutant General's Corps. It trains soldiers to be military clerks in administration, human resources, and finance. Other specialist jobs include doctors, dentists, nurses, dog trainers, military police, and musicians. The table on page 49 gives a few examples of the many jobs available in each career group. Most of the technical jobs in the Army require a GCSE in Maths and many also require Science and English. Grade D is the minimum but higher is better.

CASE STUDY

Michael is a fusilier in the Royal Regiment of Fusiliers.

I joined the Army when I was 18 because, although I had quite good GCSEs, my life was going nowhere. I was out of work, living on my own, and I thought the Army would give me some stability. Basic training was challenging. You have to be determined to get through it, but you're all in it together and help each other. You get an amazing sense of achievement when you complete it!

After basic training, I did advanced infantry training and my battalion is currently stationed in Cyprus. I'm 24 now and intend to stay in the Army – I feel I've grown up a lot and I see the world from a different perspective.

Officers

To be an officer in the armed forces you need to be a good leader. This means that you can communicate well with the soldiers you command. You have to be able to think clearly in difficult situations and make decisions quickly. You also need to relay those decisions clearly and quickly and give your soldiers the information they need to do their jobs.

Being an officer means that you need to win the trust and respect of your soldiers and, in turn, to trust and respect them. Officer training helps you acquire these qualities. You can choose one of three different routes to becoming an officer.

Commissioned officers

A **commissioned officer** is someone who commands other soldiers. Cadets aiming to become commissioned officers train at the Royal Military Academy Sandhurst in Surrey for 11 months. The training is designed to improve physical fitness and mental alertness. It includes learning about the Army and military tactics as well as how to use a rifle and survive in the field. Personal appearance is important and drills encourage teamwork and discipline.

Get ahead!

If you are between 12 and 18 years old, you can join the Army Cadet Force. Here you can develop leadership skills as well as take part in camps and adventurous activities. See page 52 for the website address.

At the end of the first term, officer cadets take part in a week's adventurous training. There are various challenging options including skiing, kayaking, and free-fall. At the end of the second term, cadets go on an adventurous training expedition (which could be in Britain or abroad) that puts all that they have learned to the test. After Sandhurst, commissioned officers train for the particular regiment they have chosen.

Professionally qualified officers

People with professional qualifications, such as lawyers, doctors, nurses, lawyers, and vets, also train at Sandhurst but their training is much shorter – just 4 weeks. During this time they improve their physical fitness and learn how to handle a weapon as well as basic military and fieldcraft skills, such as map-reading, first aid, and maintaining a vehicle.

Non-commissioned officers

You don't have to join the army as an officer cadet to become an officer. **Non-commissioned officers** (NCOs) are soldiers who have worked their way up through the ranks. Anyone who shows leadership potential will be encouraged and promoted. Some may go to Sandhurst as a Late Entry commission; others will take part in the Army's Command, Leadership and Management programme.

below: *These officer cadets are on their passing out parade at Sandhurst.*

Chapter 3

Royal Air Force

The Royal Air Force (also known as the RAF) defends the skies above Britain. It joins with other armed forces to protect British interests abroad and to bring peace to trouble spots around the world. Aircrews may also be called on to deliver aid to people left **destitute** by war or natural disasters, while helicopter crews are always on stand-by to rescue people in trouble in the mountains and on the seas around our coasts.

below: *The Eurofighter Typoon is one of the modern fighter aircraft.*

Career groups

Fighters, **reconnaissance**, and transport aircraft are the core of the RAF. Some of them are listed in the box opposite. The aircrews are the front-line forces in the air and they are supported on the ground by an array of trades – engineers, technicians, air traffic controllers, and flight operators. Yet other trades – catering, medical, personnel, and administrative staff – service the whole organization.

The RAF has its own regiment of soldiers too – gunners who defend air bases at home and abroad. You can find out more about these different careers on pages 22 and 23 and from any Armed Forces Careers Office (AFCO). Look in your local telephone directory to find the address of your nearest AFCO.

The selection process

The first step is to contact your nearest AFCO to get an information pack to help you decide which career you are interested in. You can also talk to a member of staff at AFCO who will answer your questions.

You will then fill in an application form and sit aptitude tests to see whether the career you have chosen is right for you. Then you will be interviewed. The interviewer wants to find out what sort of person you are and why you have chosen the career you have. The interview is followed by a fitness test, a medical test, and a final interview. If you want to join as an officer or aircrew, you will have to spend a few days at RAF Cranwell in Lincolnshire. All being well, you will then be given a formal offer of service. The whole selection process can take between 5 and 18 months.

above: *Part of the RAF's job is to rescue people in difficulty in remote parts of the UK and at sea.*

KNOW YOUR PLANES

Aircraft	Main use	No. in crew
Harrier jumpjet	fighter, air support for ground troops, flying from aircraft carriers, reconnaissance	1 or 2
Eurofigher Typhoon	fighter	1 or 2
Tornado GR4	bomber	2
Sentry	surveillance and airborne control centre	17
Nimrod	reconnaissance, search and rescue	13
Tornado GR4A	reconnaissance	2
Hercules	transport and troop carrier	3
Chinook helicopter	transport	2 to 4
Sea King helicopter	transport and search and rescue	4

Training in the RAF

Being selected and accepted as a recruit is an achievement in itself. It means that you have the potential to be self-disciplined, take responsibility, and play your part in a fast-moving, high-tech organization. Training helps you to realize those potentials. It also makes you more physically and mentally fit than you may have thought possible.

Get ahead!

If you are between 13 and 20 years old you can join the ATC – the Air Training Corps. This youth organization is sponsored by the RAF and is an excellent introduction to life in the service. It gives you plenty of opportunities for adventure and sport. Over half of all aircrew in the RAF were members of the ATC.

The training you do depends on whether you intend to join an RAF trade, become a non-commissioned member of an aircrew (NCA) or become an officer. Whichever route you take you will start with several weeks of military training.

Military training

All trades and NCA go first to RAF Halton in Buckinghamshire for 9 weeks of military training. Here you learn about the different aircraft and what they do. You will learn how to handle a rifle and to obey orders on parade-ground drills. At the same time you will become physically fitter as you meet ever greater challenges.

Get ahead!

The better your school exam results, the greater your choice of career in the RAF. Concentrate on getting the best results you can in maths, English language, science and technology subjects.

Trade training

Trade training begins at a number of RAF stations and can take up to 18 months. You will be posted to an RAF training station where you will learn your chosen trade from the experts. Worried about qualifications? Don't be. Different trades require different qualifications, from none through to GCSEs or S-grades to A-levels or Highers. You can find more about the qualifications needed for some of the trades on page 50. Furthermore, trade training gives you **National Vocational Qualification** (NVQ) or Modern Apprenticeship qualifications that will help you get a job when you leave the RAF.

NCA

Non-commissioned aircrew (NCA) are people whose job involves flying but who are not officers. After military training at RAF Halton, NCA go to RAF Cranwell in Lincolnshire for 10 weeks, during which time they learn about leadership, become more self-confident and able to take responsibility. The training involves a challenging field exercise that allows you to put into practice everything you have learnt. This is followed by training in the particular kind of weapons systems you will operate. You may, for example, learn how to use **radar** and **sonar** equipment to monitor ships.

Officers

Officers work throughout the RAF. All pilots are officers and are in charge of their aircrew. Elsewhere, officers lead teams of trades people, whole **squadrons**, right up to running the whole service. To join as an officer you need to have A-levels, Highers or a university degree. Training takes place at RAF Cranwell and lasts 24 weeks. It will test your physical fitness and includes military and leadership training.

below: *Hose running is part of the Defence Fire Service training at RAF Odiham.*

above: *These RAF pilots are flying a rescue helicopter over mountainous terrain.*

Careers for life

The RAF offers a wide range of careers, which all qualify you for similar work when you leave the service. Most aircraft are crewed by just one or two people, but all of them are supported on the ground by engineers, telecommunications experts, administrators, caterers, health workers, and so on. People who work hard get plenty of opportunity for further training and promotion. They will leave the RAF with qualifications – from NVQs to university degrees – that are recognized by commercial companies.

Aircrew

After training, pilots may find themselves flying supersonic jets, large transport planes or helicopters. Whatever plane they fly they will leave with the skills required to fly commercial aircraft or helicopters or become a pilot trainer. Weapons systems include missiles, radar, radio, and systems that hunt for submarines or monitor ships. Weapons systems operators also include those who operate the winch in a rescue helicopter and those who look after troops on a transport plane. Weapons systems operators gain special skills in, for example, telecommunications or foreign languages.

Engineering and IT

If you are technically minded, you will find plenty of scope in the RAF. There are two large groups of engineers: **avionics** engineers maintain the aircraft and all the on-board systems and general technicians look after all the machinery and systems used on the ground.

People who work in Air Operations use the latest IT and communications systems to produce flight plans and control air traffic. They know exactly where each aircraft is at any time. Communications specialists operate and maintain equipment such as radar and radio aerials and antennae. Intelligence analysts monitor, collect, and analyse information on other forces.

Administration and others

Managing and running the day-to-day activities of the RAF is a major challenge. Spare parts have to be supplied, equipment has to be transported from one place to another and accounted for, thousands of hungry mouths have to be fed. The organization uses all the same skills and careers as companies to look after their finances and their staff. But not many companies also employ musicians, photographers, and sports trainers, let alone their own police force and regiment. The RAF does!

CASE STUDY

Phil is a chief technician in the RAF.

I hadn't thought about the RAF until I went to an AFCO with a friend who was thinking of joining up. He didn't, but I did! At first I found it hard to get used to obeying orders but I enjoyed the camaraderie of basic training. I trained as an avionics technician, gaining a BTEC level 3 in Aerospace Systems Studies. My job was maintaining Tornado GR4s, Canberras, and VC10s. I worked my way up to senior NCO, and I'm now working in the RAF's career service.

Chapter 4

Royal Navy

The Royal Navy defends the seas around our coasts and helps to police the world's oceans to stop international drug smuggling and terrorism. Like the other armed services, the Royal Navy also brings aid to countries devastated by wars and natural disasters. The Navy is not just a fleet of highly specialized fighting ships and submarines. It has its own fleet of fighter aircraft and helicopters, the Fleet Air Arm, and its own crack troops (most highly trained soldiers), the Royal Marines. Some staff work in shore bases around the world, providing the rest of the service with technical and administrative support.

below: *This Royal Navy ship is decked out with flags to celebrate the 200-year anniversary of the Battle of Trafalgar.*

Many careers to choose from

Ships, planes, the Royal Marines, and shore bases – each offer many careers with different starting qualifications. You can join the Navy with no qualifications or you can join with GCSEs/S-grades, A-levels or Highers, and even with a university degree or professional training. How do you decide which is for you? Having read this chapter, the next step is to visit your local Armed Forces Careers Office (AFCO).

At the AFCO you can ask a member of staff any questions about the Navy before filling out a questionnaire. If you want to join as a **rating**, you will be tested in English language, mathematics, **reasoning**, and mechanical comprehension. If you pass these tests you will be invited back for an interview with a careers officer, a pre-joining fitness test, and a medical examination.

If you want to join as an officer, you need to have five GCSEs or S-grades including English and Maths, and the equivalent of three A-levels (D, D, and E) or three Highers (grade C). The selection process takes place over 2 days at the Admiralty Interview Board. It involves written tests, leadership tasks, a planning exercise, and an interview, as well as fitness and medical tests. Royal Marines have to complete the Potential Officers Course at the Commando Training Centre Royal Marines in Devon before attending the Admiralty Interview Board.

Get acquainted

If you want to join as a rating and would like to find out more, you can attend a Royal Navy Acquaint Centre Course on HMS *Caledonia* in Scotland. Here you will get a taste of life in the Navy and help in deciding which career to choose.

Get ahead!

Browse the Royal Navy's website (www.royal-navy.mod.uk) to find out all you can about the Royal Navy. It also gives information on individual careers and the qualifications needed for each. You can join the Sea Cadets or the Combined Cadet Force, if there is one in your area.

Worried about seasickness?

Don't worry – everyone gets seasick from time to time. You may feel queasy at first but you will soon get your sea legs. After several weeks at sea, your main problem will be adjusting to firm ground for the first few days back on shore!

Training

Once you have been selected as a rating you will begin basic training at HMS *Raleigh* in Cornwall. Basic training lasts 8 weeks and, once you have signed the enrolment form, you must stay for at least 4 weeks. During basic training you will learn about the Royal Navy, first aid, and fire-fighting. You will also learn about a warship and its weapons systems and practise parade-ground drills.

Improving your fitness is an important part of basic training for all recruits. By the time you have finished basic training you should be able to run 2.4 km (1.5 miles) in less than 12 minutes 20 seconds if you are male, and less than 14 minutes 35 seconds if you are female.

below: *This Royal Navy recruit is practising camouflage techniques.*

Officers

To train as an officer, you go to Britannia Royal Naval College in Dartmouth, Devon. The training takes between 28 and 49 weeks. The first 14 weeks are spent developing leadership and communication skills and learning how to handle a boat on the River Dart. You then spend 7 weeks on an operational warship before returning to college for strategic studies and more academic work. This is followed by another stint on a warship to learn about all the different branches of the Navy, before continuing professional training in a particular area of the service.

Royal Marines

The Royal Marine Commandos are an **amphibious** fighting force. They can launch an assault by land, sea or air at short notice anywhere in the world – in mountains, deserts, jungles, or the Arctic. They are often the soldiers who spearhead an attack, the first front-line troops to engage in battle. Training at the Commando Training Centre in Lympstone, Devon, lasts 32 weeks and, if you are fit enough and determined enough, you should be successful.

Get ahead!

Get as physically fit as you can (see page 11 for some tips). Learn to swim before you start training. One of the basic fitness tests is to swim 40 metres (130 feet) with clothes on. And get used to washing and ironing your clothes – the Royal Navy is very particular about how you look after yourself and your uniform.

above: *Being able to swim is essential if you are thinking of joining the Royal Navy.*

KNOW YOUR SHIPS

Ship	Main function	No. in ship's company
Aircraft carrier	Carries fighter jets and helicopters	685 + 386 aircrew
Assault ship	Carries troops and helicopters for fighting on land	325 or 285
Destroyer	Provides anti-air defence to protect groups of ships	287
Frigate	Anti-submarine and multi-purpose fighting ships	250 or 185
Submarine	Carries torpedoes and/or missiles	135 or 130
Minehunter	Keeps Britain's coasts free of mines	45 or 34
Patrol boat	Protects Britain's fishing fleet and offshore gas and oil rigs	45 or 30

Careers in the Royal Navy

Careers in the Royal Navy are more varied than in any of the other services. In the Navy you can work below the sea as a diver or submariner, on the sea in a ship, in the air in the Fleet Air Arm, or as a Royal Marine Commando. For most jobs, ratings do not need academic qualifications; instead you have to pass selection tests and interviews to be accepted for particular jobs.

Surface ships

The Royal Navy has more than 70 surface ships. Some of them are shown in the box on page 27. All carry weapons and have state-of-the-art technology and communications systems, plus engineers, technicians, and IT specialists to operate them. In addition they employ administrative staff, chefs, and healthcare specialists – doctors, nurses, and dentists.

below: *A navy rating may operate radar equipment on board a ship.*

Submarines

The Royal Navy has 15 nuclear-powered submarines, some of which carry nuclear weapons. Submarines stay at sea for many weeks at a time, so to join a submarine you have to be able to live in a confined space for long periods. Jobs for ratings include operating the machinery and systems and collecting information on which the captain and officers base their decisions.

MEN ONLY

Not all jobs in the Royal Navy are open to women. Royal Marine Commandos fight on the front line and so, in keeping with the **Geneva Convention**, are not open to women. Women cannot work on submarines or do mine-clearance diving because these could harm their health.

above: *These aircraft handlers are refuelling an aircraft on the flight deck of an aircraft carrier.*

Fleet Air Arm

The naval air stations are at Yeovilton in Somerset and Culdrose in Cornwall. The Harrier is the Navy's **fixed-wing** fighter jet – it can take off and land on a short airstrip, often on the deck of an aircraft carrier. Jobs on board aircraft carriers and on air stations include maintaining the aircraft and helicopters and managing them during take-off and landing.

CASE STUDY

Dawn is a leading writer in the Navy.

I joined the Navy when I was 21. The training on HMS Raleigh was hard work for me, particularly the physical fitness, but finishing it gave me such a sense of pride. My job is as a leading ***writer*** *dealing with pay, leave requests, and travel. I work on shore bases and on ships – I spent 2 and a half years at sea on the aircraft carrier HMS Invincible. What I enjoy most about the Navy is all the friends I've made and the places I've been, particularly the 3 months I spent in the US on a training exercise. I am already a middle manager and aim to become a petty officer.*

Chapter 5

The police force

Police work involves a lot more than chasing and arresting suspected criminals. As a police officer you have to be able to communicate well in many different situations: talking to members of the public, writing up crime reports, and presenting evidence in court. Police officers also spend a lot of time trying to prevent crime and educating the public on how to avoid crime.

below: *The police force is keen to recruit people from all ethnic groups.*

Police forces

Each region in Britain has its own police force. You do not need any specific academic qualifications to become a police officer, but you do need to have a good general education to pass the selection process. Each force has an equal opportunities policy – they employ both women and men and, particularly in large cities, are keen to recruit people from different ethnic groups.

Applying to become a police officer

The first step is to fill out an application form. It will be checked and, if your application is accepted, you will be sent an information pack and invited to an Assessment Centre. Read the information pack carefully – it explains exactly what will happen at the centre. Some police forces even offer to help you to prepare for the assessment process.

The assessment process involves written tests, role plays, and an interview. One of the written tests, Verbal Logical Reasoning, assesses how well you can analyse facts and evidence. The role plays give you the chance to show how well you communicate and handle different kinds of situations.

If your tests and interview are successful, you will have a medical test, an eye test, and a fitness test. Take note – most people who fail to get in to the police force do so because they are not fit enough. You do not have to be as fit as people applying for the armed forces, but you do need to have a good level of general fitness. The police will also do various security checks to see, for example, whether you have a criminal record, and other background checks. All being well, you will be sent a letter offering you a place.

below: *Police divers have to search rivers and other waters for evidence.*

Get ahead!

It will help your application if you can show that you are a responsible member of the community. You could become a police cadet, for example, learn first aid or help out at a youth club.

DO YOU QUALIFY?

To join the police force you need to:

- be at least 18
- be physically fit
- meet the required eyesight standards
- be a UK citizen, a Commonwealth citizen, or member of the **EU** or **EEA**, or a foreign national with unrestricted residency.

How tall you are is not a factor!

Training

Anything can happen to police officers on the beat. They need to be able to handle a wide range of situations, from administering emergency first aid, or helping an elderly person who cannot remember where they live, to stopping a fight, helping victims and witnesses of crime, and arresting suspect criminals.

Recruit training

Each police force trains its own recruits, either at its headquarters or at its own training centres. Training of recruits varies from force to force, but includes lectures in the classroom and practical exercises. Together they teach you all the skills you need to be an effective police officer, particularly the ability to make quick decisions, communicate with the public, and treat them fairly. Hendon Police Training College in North London trains recruits for London's Metropolitan Police Service and has its own police station and a mock courtroom where recruits can practise for the real thing.

Get ahead!

Visit the website www.police-information.co.uk or www.policecouldyou.co.uk to find out about courses and home learning that will help you at all stages of your training.

During recruit training you will learn a lot about the law and about correct police procedures. As a police officer you must be above suspicion, so you will be expected to maintain the highest professional standards and levels of **integrity**. Training also teaches you self-defence and emergency first aid and improves your physical fitness. You have to pass every part of the course to carry on to the next stage as a **probationer**.

Probationer training

Training doesn't stop when you become a probationer. For the next 2 years you will pound the beat as an independent police officer, putting everything you have learned into practice. At the same time you will be carefully assessed and supervised by a training officer.

CASE STUDY

Will Taylor, a police officer, explains why he joined the police.

I decided to join the police because of a personal experience. I was attacked and mugged by three youths, but luckily a police car happened to drive by about 30 seconds later, so I flagged it down. They caught all three of the muggers and arrested them. It made such a difference to me that I wanted to do the same for someone else. I completed my 2 years as a probationer a few months ago. One of the really good things about the police is the range of specialisms. When I'm ready, I'd like to train as a dog handler.

above: *Probationary officers work with experienced officers when they are on the beat.*

A choice of careers

After 2 years on patrol as a probationary officer, what then? Many police officers decide to stay on the beat and perhaps be promoted through the ranks to sergeant, inspector, and so on. Other officers decide to train and specialize in one particular aspect of policing.

Specialist branches vary from region to region but are likely to include rapid response officers, scene of crime officers, dog handlers, neighbourhood police officers, traffic police, and a firearms unit. Competition for specialist jobs is fierce and you need to show an aptitude for a particular specialism before you will be chosen to train in it.

Dealing with crime

Rapid response officers are usually the first on the scene of an incident. Officers are trained to assess situations fast and take appropriate action. If firearms are involved, they may call in the firearms unit. They are trained to use weapons, but only as a last resort. Scene of crime officers take photographs and fingerprints, and collect **forensic evidence**, such as hairs, clothing fibres, and blood samples. The evidence is then examined in a laboratory by forensic scientists who check **DNA** and fingerprints and look for incriminating chemicals.

CID

The Criminal Investigation Department (CID) is staffed by detectives. They investigate serious crimes, including murder, assault, rape, **fraud**, and robbery. They work closely with scene of crime officers and forensic scientists, and use the huge police database to check details of known suspects. Experienced CID officers may go on to work in the Fraud Squad, the Drug Squad or the Crime Squad.

above: *Police horses are trained to remain calm whatever the situation.*

Other specialisms

Traffic police make our roads safer by trying to prevent motoring offences as well as catching and prosecuting law-breakers. Most forces have a helicopter and air support unit, which they use to track people, get officers to crime scenes quickly, and to rescue casualties.

Most forces also have dog handlers, who each work with a particular dog. A dog's sense of smell is much better than a human's, so dogs are useful for sniffing out drugs and explosives. Many forces also have specialist units for dealing with crime within the family. Some officers focus on child protection and others on domestic violence, but they are all trained to deal sensitively with very vulnerable people.

Neighbourhood policing

Neighbourhood police officers specialize in preventing crime. They get to know people in a particular community and are often the first to receive information about crimes. Police community support officers work alongside police officers, although they do not have as many powers as police officers. Neighbourhood policing means working mainly out of doors and spending a lot of time on your feet, walking around. Police officers and community support officers usually work in pairs.

Neighbourhood police officers

Neighbourhood officers work closely with community leaders and local community groups. Some officers may specialize in **youth intervention**. They visit schools as part of the school curriculum. They may also set up anti-bullying services and advise children on how to avoid dangerous or confrontational situations.

above: *Police community support officers get to know people in the community.*

Police community support officers

Police Community Support Officers (PCSOs) provide a visible presence and help to reassure people who are worried about crime. They can give out some fixed penalty notices and can detain suspects until a police officer arrives.

To qualify as a PCSO you need to fulfil the same conditions as a police officer. You have to fill in an application form and complete an assessment process similar to that used for police officers. You do not need academic qualifications, but you need to be able to write up reports. More importantly, you need to be good at dealing with the public and making quick, confident decisions. The training is shorter than for police officers and covers the law, first aid, and patrolling skills.

Parking enforcement

Making sure that drivers had parked correctly used to be the job of traffic wardens and was a responsibility of the police force. Now, however, local authorities (town councils and county councils) are taking over responsibility for parking. Parking in the wrong place stops the traffic flowing well, so drivers who do not keep to the rules are given fixed penalty fines. Traffic wardens, also called parking attendants, check whether motorists have paid the correct parking fees. Parking offences are not crimes, but dealing with angry motorists is not easy and is sometimes dangerous.

You do not need to have academic qualifications to be a parking attendant but you do need to be able to speak and write English. You also have to be calm and tactful and good at handling difficult situations. Your training will help you do this.

Chapter 6

Fire and rescue service

The fire and rescue service deals not only with the serious job of fire-fighting but with much more besides. Fire-fighters are called out whenever there is a major incident, such as a rail or air crash, a major road accident, or a terrorist bomb. They are also called out to more minor accidents, such as people stuck in a lift, or to a flood in a basement. As well as answering emergency calls, fire-fighters educate the public about fire safety and clean and maintain their fire engines and equipment.

Get ahead!

If you are aged between 13 and 19, find out if your local fire service runs a LIFE course (LIFE stands for Local Intervention Fire Education). The course lasts a week, during which experienced fire-fighters teach you some fire-fighting skills. You can also help to prepare yourself for the selection tests by doing a **BTEC** qualification in Public Services. Even better, City of Wolverhampton College run a Fire Service Pre-Recruitment Access Course.

Organization

Britain does not have a national fire service. Instead, there are 47 regional fire and rescue services. Although there are some differences, they all select and train new recruits in much the same way. Most fire and rescue services employ retained fire-fighters as well as full-time fire-fighters. Retained fire-fighters are men and women who live or work near the fire station. They may be builders, shop-keepers, typists or technicians, for example, but, when the "bleeper" goes, they drop what they are doing and become part of the fire-fighting team.

Qualities of a good fire-fighter

You have to be at least 18 years old and physically fit to become a fire-fighter, and you need to have the right qualities. Do you have a good head for heights? You need to if you want to be a fire-fighter! You need determination and courage and you have to be able to think clearly and act quickly in confusing circumstances. You also need good stamina so that you can keep working in, for example, smoke-filled buildings.

But the fire service does much more than fire-fighting. A large part of their work involves educating the community about fire safety, so fire-fighters also need good communication skills. You do not, however, need to have academic qualifications – the only way to get into the fire service is to pass the selection test.

COMMUNITY FIRE SAFETY

The aim of community fire safety is to reduce the risk of fire. Fire-fighters educate the public about smoke alarms and tell them how to avoid kitchen fires and fires caused by smoking cigarettes. They inspect hotels and public buildings to make sure they reach fire safety standards.

above: *These fire-fighters are rescuing people trapped in a car after a road accident.*

The selection process

The fire and rescue services insist that there are no short cuts to getting in. Everyone, whether they are university graduates or have no academic qualifications, has to go through the same selection process. You have to apply to a particular fire and rescue service and it will only take you on if it has a vacancy. Vacancies are hotly contested!

Get ahead!

The best way to do well in the selection process is to prepare well. Browse the website www.fireservice.co.uk – it tells you what to expect and is full of tips and hints. Read the application pack carefully and make sure you are physically fit before you apply. Before your interview find out everything you can about the fire and rescue service and the particular job you are applying for.

How do I apply?

The first step is to contact a fire and rescue service and, if they are recruiting, they will send you an application pack. Make sure you fill in the application form correctly – see page 48 for tips on how to fill in application forms. Provided your application form is accepted, you will be invited to a training centre for selection tests. These include written tests and physical fitness tests. The tests are followed up by an interview and a medical test.

Written tests

The written tests assess how well you can take in information and how accurately you can remember it. For the numerical tests you have to calculate numbers in your head. Observation tests assess how well you can observe and weigh up a situation. Mechanical tests find out how practical and mechanically minded you are. Several books have been written on different types of tests so that you can practise them in advance (see page 53).

New selection tests are brought in from time to time. Read your selection pack carefully!

Fitness tests

The physical tests are challenging, mentally as well as physically. The actual tests vary from one region to another but will probably include the "bleeb test". For this you have to run 20 metres (65 feet) back and forth on a track to the sound of a bleep. You hear a bleep when you start and a bleep at the end of each 20 metres. The problem is the bleeps get closer together, so that the run gets harder, not easier. You can find out more about the bleep test on the website *www.fireservice.co.uk*.

Other physical tests include running out hoses, for example running out six 25-metre (82-foot) hoses in 8 minutes, and climbing ladders – to make sure that you are comfortable with heights. To see if you can work in confined spaces, you will have to find your way in the dark through a crawling alley wearing full breathing gear.

left: *These recruits are learning how to pitch a ladder.*

Training

Basic training for full-time fire-fighters takes place at the fire and rescue service and lasts from 13 to 20 weeks. It is hard work – about 70 per cent of it is practical and 30 per cent is theoretical – and you are constantly assessed. Retained fire-fighters do a basic training course followed by sessions at their local stations at the weekends and in the evenings.

above: *Fire-fighters on a training exercise.*

The first phase

Basic training is also called Phase 1 training. First, you learn fire-fighting skills, such as handling hoses, pumps and ladders. You also learn about health and safety – although fire-fighters work in dangerous conditions they know how to avoid unnecessary risks and hazards.

Then you are taught how to use breathing apparatus and how to rescue people from confined places. You learn how to deal with incidents such as traffic accidents, air, and rail crashes. Such incidents often involve using powerful cutting equipment to rescue people, administering first aid, and dealing with serious trauma injuries.

Phase 2 training

Phase 2 covers the first two years of your career in the fire station. You will be regularly assessed as you put what you have learned in Phase 1 into practice. You also add to your theoretical knowledge through further learning modules.

Further prospects

New equipment and procedures are constantly being introduced, so training and assessment continue throughout your career. You can also apply for promotion or for specialist training in, for example, community fire protection, driving a fire engine, or operating a turntable ladder. As a child you may have dreamed of driving a flashing, wailing fire engine through busy streets – the reality takes many months of special training!

CASE STUDY

Elisabeth explains why she became a fire-fighter.

I wanted to join the fire service because I'm an active, sporty sort of person and I wanted to help the community. The selection and training were physically challenging but, with the help of the trainers and the other people on the course, I was able to achieve all the required standards. Fire-fighting is not just about strength, though – it's also about good communication skills, relaying information, and calming people involved in an incident. Every day and every incident is slightly different – I'm always learning something new. Best of all, I am making a real difference to other people's lives.

KNOW YOUR ENGINES

Fire appliance	What it does
Pump ladder	Carries crew, hoses, ladder, and equipment
Turntable ladder platform	Has extra-long extendable ladder for reaching people in high buildings, but no hoses or equipment
Foam tender	Specialist vehicle for dealing with chemical fires
Incident Response Unit	Carries special equipment, such as decontamination equipment, for dealing with terrorist incidents

Chapter 7

Other civilian services

Apart from the police and fire service – the main civilian forces – there are smaller forces who are concerned with the security of the nation. They include customs and excise, immigration, and the prison service. They also include coastguards and Trinity House, who look after the safety of ships around the coasts. Most coastguard stations are in remote areas and are staffed by people who have retired from the Royal Navy.

Customs and excise

The main work of customs and excise officers is to stop smuggling, particularly drugs and other illegal items. Smugglers are also people who try to avoid paying duty or tax on, for example, imported cigarettes. Customs officers work closely with the police and most of their work goes on behind the scenes. You may, however, have seen a customs officer at an international airport, searching someone's luggage.

Excise officers inspect import companies and **distilleries** to make sure that the correct duty is being paid, while VAT officers check whether companies are paying the correct levels of Value Added Tax (VAT) to the Government.

To join the service as a junior manager, you need to have five GCSEs (grades A–C) or five S-grades (grades 1–3) and two A-levels, Highers or the equivalent. If you have at least two GCSEs (grades A–C) or two S-grades (grades 1–3) you can apply to join the service lower down and work your way up. If you are accepted, you will be trained and may eventually be promoted to customs officer or excise officer.

above: *Customs officers often use dogs to sniff out illegal items at international airports.*

Immigration

Immigration officers work at airports, ports, and at the Channel Tunnel. Their job is to make sure that everyone who enters the country has the correct passport, **visas** or work permits. They have to assess whether people are telling the truth about their reasons for coming to Britain. Immigration officers have to be well organized and good at keeping written records. To apply to be an immigration officer you need to have the equivalent of two A-levels, but you can join as an immigration assistant with five GCSEs (grades A–C). You must be a UK national and have lived in Britain for the last 5 years. Your basic training will be at Heathrow or Gatwick airports or at Dover, and you must be willing to work in different parts of the country.

Get ahead!

To be an immigration officer you need to have a GCSE in English language and it helps if you can speak another language.

The prison service

Prison officers supervise people who have broken the law and have been sent to prison or who are in prison awaiting trial. They also supervise young offenders in remand centres and other institutions. Their job is not just to keep prisoners in order, but to support and care for them, too. You have to do shift work, often through the night, and spend most of the time indoors, inside a prison.

Qualities of a good prison officer

The prison service is looking for people who can work in a disciplined environment, with many rules and regulations, and, at the same time, empathize with prisoners. You have to be able to keep order, on the one hand, and win prisoners' trust and confidence, on the other hand. You have to be committed to helping people who are in a difficult situation.

Qualifications and training

Scotland, England and Wales, and Northern Ireland each have their own prison service with their own rules about age and qualifications. In England you have to pass an entry test and interview, while in Scotland you must have five S-grades (grades 1–3) or have worked for three years managing people.

Basic training lasts several weeks. It includes role playing in various situations and specialist training for those who are going to work with young people. The training continues for the whole of the first year, during which time you are supervised and supported by an experienced member of staff.

DO YOU QUALIFY?

To join the prison service in England and Wales, you need to:

- be at least 18 and a half years old
- be a British or Commonwealth citizen or a member of the EU
- have been living in Britain for at least the last three years
- pass medical, eye, and fitness tests
- not belong to any organization that the prison service considers to be racist.

Specialist jobs

There are several different specialist jobs within prisons. Some involve working directly with prisoners, such as a nurse or instructor. Instructors teach trade skills, such as woodwork, engineering, and tailoring. Other officers specialize in jobs to do with running the prison, such as administration, catering, driving, gardening, and so on.

above: *Prison officers can specialize in gardening and work in the prison garden.*

What have you already done that is relevant to the service or job you are applying for? Have you, for example, ever had to take responsibility, or give or take orders? Are you a school prefect or leader of a youth group? Why do you want to join the service? What are you hoping to get out of it?

Application forms

Your application form is the first impression that the recruitment officer or employer will have of you. Read the form carefully and think about your answers before you fill it in. It is a good idea to photocopy the blank form and practise on it. Once you are satisfied with all your answers, copy them carefully onto the proper form.

Interviews

The best way to do well at an interview is to prepare well. Find out everything you can about the force you are interested in. If you are applying for one of the armed forces, read up about any ongoing military situation, such as Iraq, and find out about the current situation in Northern Ireland. All the armed and civilian forces are committed to treating everyone equally, whatever their gender, religion or race. Make sure you know the policy and what it means, especially if you are applying for the police.

Good luck!

DOS AND DON'TS FOR INTERVIEWS

- Arrive early. Being late makes a very bad impression.
- Dress smartly and look business-like. Don't wear the kind of clothes you would wear for a night out with your friends.
- For the armed forces, cut your hair short if you are male.
- Don't wear body piercings.
- Make sure your shoes and finger nails are clean.
- Be confident. Look the interviewer in the eye and answer questions clearly.

BRITISH ARMY

Examples of jobs for privates	Main qualifications needed to get in	Some of the qualifications you can achieve	Possible regiments
COMBAT			
men only: Infantry Soldier; Tank Crew; **men or women:** Gunner	No academic qualifications	Full driving licence; NVQs in, for example, training and development	Any of 32 infantry battalions; Royal Armoured Corps
COMBAT SUPPORT			
Engineering			
Signals Electrician; Vehicle Mechanic; Heating and Plumbing Engineer; Combat Engineer	GCSEs in Maths, Science, and English or equivalent trades qualifications	LGV trailer licence; City & Guilds engineering qualifications; BTEC diploma in engineering	Royal Corps of Signals; Royal Electrical and Mechanical Engineers; Royal Engineers
IT and Communications			
Signals Electrician; Radio Systems Operator; Electronics Technician; Operator Military Intelligence	GCSEs in Maths, Science, and English or equivalent NVQ and BTEC qualifications	City & Guilds Engineering qualifications; BTEC National Certificate in Engineering	Royal Corps of Signals; Royal Engineers; Intelligence Corps
Logistics			
Technical Storeperson; Chef; Driver; Postal Courier Operator	Some jobs require no academic qualifications; others require GCSEs in English and Maths	NVQ in Food Preparation and Cooking; Department of Transport licences; NVQs	Royal Logistic Corps; Royal Artillery; Army Air Corps; Royal Corps of Signals
SERVICES			
Administration			
Military Clerk	GCSEs in English and Maths	NVQ in Business Administration	Adjutant General's Corps
Healthcare			
Healthcare Assistant; Veterinary Technician	Good education; GCSEs; appropriate BTEC or nursing qualifications	Recognized professional qualifications	Royal Army Medical Corps; Royal Army Veterinary Corps
Specialist			
Dog Trainer; Musician; Royal Military Police	Qualifications vary with job	Qualifications recognized by civilian equivalents	Royal Army Veterinary Corps; Corps of Army Music

ROYAL AIR FORCE

Examples of jobs for aircrew and trades	Main qualifications needed to get in	Some of the qualifications you can achieve	Civilian equivalent
AIRCREW			
Weapons Systems Operator	5 GCSEs/S-grades, including English Language, Maths, and Physics	BTEC and other qualifications recognized by civilian aviation companies	Navigation specialist or other specialist job
ENGINEER			
Aircraft Technician; General Technician; Weapon Technician	3 GCSEs/S-grades in Maths, English Language and an approved Science or Technology subject	City & Guilds Aeronautical Engineering; Engineering Maintenance	Electrical or mechanical engineering technician
IT and COMMUNICATIONS			
Air Traffic Control Assistant; Aerospace Systems Operator; Flight Operations Assistant	2 GCSEs/S-grades in English Language and Maths; none	Apprenticeship in Information Technology	Air Traffic Controller
Communications and Information Systems Specialist	3 GCSEs/S-grades in English Language, Maths, and Science	Advanced Apprenticeship	Telecommunications Technician
ADMINISTRATION			
Personnel Administrator; Physical Training Instructor; Mechanical Transport Driver	none; GCSE/S-grades in English Language; none	NVQ in Business Administration; Coaching; NVQ in Handling Air Passengers	Office manager; Sports Coach; Courier
Catering			
Chef; Air Steward	None	Apprenticeship in Hospitality	Chef, Caterer; Air Steward, Food Manager
Healthcare			
Medical Assistant; Dental Technician	none; BTEC in Dental Technology	Recognized qualifications in Medical Assistance	Paramedic; Dental Surgery Assistant
Security			
Regiment Gunner; RAF Police; Fire-fighter	None	NVQ in Security; Advanced Apprenticeship in Firefighting	Security Guard, Police Officer, Fire-Fighter

ROYAL NAVY

Examples of jobs for ratings	Qualifications needed
WARFARE	
Communications and Information Specialist working with communications equipment;	GCSEs/S-grades
Mine Warfare Specialist operating sonar equipment;	GCSEs/S-grades
Mine Clearance Diver	none
SUBMARINE	
Warfare Rating (Submariner);	none
Engineering Technician (Marine Engineering Submariner);	GCSEs/S-grades
Chef	none
FLEET AIR ARM	
Naval Airman (Aircraft Handler) preparing and controlling the flight deck;	none
Naval Airman (Survival Equipment) involved in training aircrew in survival techniques	none
ENGINEERING	
Air Engineering Technician maintaining fixed-wing aircraft and helicopters;	none
Engineering Technician (Weapons Engineering) responsible for weapons, radars, and sonars;	GCSEs/S-grades
Engineering Technician (Marine Engineering) responsible for the ships' engines	GCSEs/S-grades
ADMINISTRATION	
Stores Accountant;	none
Steward;	none
Chef;	none
Writer responsible for administrative and clerical duties	none
HEALTHCARE	
Medical Assistant;	none
Dental Surgery Assistant;	GCSEs/S-grades
Naval Nurse	GCSEs/S-grades

Websites

General

- how2become Ltd (*www.how2become.co.uk*) – This website has tips about applying to join each of the armed and civilian forces. It also sells CDs that contain lots of information on each of the forces, including their selection processes, tests, and interview questions.
- Learndirect (*www.learndirectadvice.co.uk/helpwithyourcareer/jobprofiles/profiles/*) – Go to "Security Services and Uniformed" for job profiles for the armed and civilian forces.

British Army

- The Army Cadet Force (*www.armycadets.com*) – This is the official ACF website.
- The British Army (*www.army.mod.uk*) – This is the official website for the Army. It includes profiles of the different jobs. It also allows you to chat to a recruitment officer online and to download a copy of the Army's fitness programme.
- My camouflage (*www.mycamouflage.co.uk*) – This is a website for 13 to 17-year-olds, with games and information about Army life and about sponsorship by the Army for further education.

Royal Air Force

- Air Cadet Organization (*www.aircadets.org*) – This is the official ACO website, with information about target shooting, flying, and other ACO activities.
- Royal Air Force (*www.raf.mod.uk*) – This is the official website for the RAF, providing information about the aircraft, training, and different jobs available. It also has links to information about sponsorship.
- Royal Air Force Careers (*www.rafcareers.com*) – Go to this RAF website for more information on careers: the qualifications you need to apply, the qualifications you can gain, and much more.

Royal Navy

- Royal Navy (*www.royal-navy.mod.uk*) – This is the official website of the Royal Navy, with information about the ships and submarines, Fleet Air Arm, and Royal Marines. You will find everything you could want to know about the Royal Navy on this site.
- Sea Cadets (*www.sea-cadets.org*) – This is the official website for the Sea Cadets.

Police

- Metropolitan Police (*www.metcareers.co.uk*) – This is the official website for London's Metropolitan Police.
- Police careers (*www.policecouldyou.co.uk*) – This website has information to help you decide whether you could be a police officer and how to apply.
- Police information (*www.policeinformation.co.uk/Docs/policetrainingcourses/directory/index.html*) – This website tells you about police training courses and courses that will help you pass the police selection test.
- UK Police Service (*www.police.uk*) – You can access all the regional police forces and non-geographical forces from this official site.

Fire and Rescue service

- Apprenticeships (*www.apprenticeships.org.uk/youngpeople/*) – This website tells you about apprenticeships that are available for the fire service.
- Fire service information (*www.fireservice.co.uk*) – This is an unofficial but useful website for the fire service. Go to "Recruitment" for information and tips on the application process.

Books

General

- Corfield, Rebecca. *Preparing Your Own CV* (Kogan Page, 2003)
- Corfield, Rebecca. *Successful Interview Skills* (Kogan Page, 2006)
- Parkinson, Mark. *How to Master Psychometric Testing* (Kogan Page, 2004)
- Smith, Heidi. *How to Pass Numerical Reasoning Tests* (Kogan Page, 2003)
- Tolley, Harry and Ken Thomas. *How to Pass Verbal Reasoning Tests* (Kogan Page, 2000)

Armed and civilian forces

- Bryon, Mike. *How to Pass the Firefighter Selection Process* (Kogan Page, 2004)
- Higgins, Nick. *Real Life Guide to The Armed Forces* (Trotman, 2004)
- Hindle, Fiona. *Getting into The Armed Forces* (Trotman, 2002)
- Pilgrim, Dee. *Real Life Guide to The Police Force* (Trotman, 2004)
- Tolley, Catherine, Ken Thomas and Harry Tolley. *How to Pass the New Police Selection System* (Kogan Page, 2004)

Glossary

amphibious able to go on land and in water

aptitude test test that measures whether someone has the ability to learn particular skills

avionics electronics used in aviation

BTEC Business and Technician Education Council. The qualifications it awards include the Higher National Certificate (HNC) and Higher National Diploma (HND).

commissioned officer officer whose rank is from second lieutenant to field marshall. Commissioned officers are of higher rank than non-commissioned officers (NCOs) and they have to have completed commissioned officer training.

customs and excise Government department that collects taxes on imports and exports and certain other goods, such as alcohol

destitute without a home, food or enough money to support yourself

distilleries factories where strong alcoholic drinks, such as whisky, are made

DNA deoxyribonucleic acid, the complex molecule that carries genetic information in living things

drills repeated exercises used in training

EEA European Economic Area. Its members are the 25 countries of the European Union plus Norway, Iceland, and Liechtenstein.

EU European Union, a group of 25 European countries that have agreed to work more closely together to maintain a peaceful and financially successful Europe

fieldcraft skills needed to operate and survive on active service

fixed wing type of aircraft wing that does not move

forensic evidence objects or substances that relate to a crime. Forensic evidence includes fingerprints, poisons found in the stomach, and drops of blood.

fraud obtaining money by deception

front line zone of battle where two sides in a war confront each other

Geneva Convention agreement accepted by most countries that sets standards of reasonable treatment of victims of war, prisoners of war, and troops

halal meat from an animal that has been prepared according to Muslim law

initiative ability to make your own decisions

integrity honesty and keeping to high moral standards

kosher meat that has been prepared according to Jewish law

logistics successful organization of a large and complex operation

Modern Apprenticeship Scottish apprenticeship, lasts for 4 years

National Vocational Qualification (NVQ) in England and Wales, a work-related, competence-based qualification that shows you have the knowledge and skills to do a job effectively. NVQs represent standards that are recognized by employers throughout the UK.

non-commissioned officer (NCO), officer in the Army whose rank is from lance corporal to staff sergeant or colour sergeant; petty officer in the Royal Navy

operations action that involves several people working together

platoon group of about 28 soldiers within a regiment or corps

probationer recently qualified person in their first year or two of service

promotion being raised to a higher rank or more responsible job

radar system that uses radio waves to detect the position of aircraft, ships or objects that are too far away to be seen

rating sailor in the Royal Navy who is not a commissioned officer

reasoning ability to think logically about facts and reach a conclusion

reconnaissance observation of enemy territory or military forces to obtain information

regiment large group of soldiers

sonar system for detecting objects or ships under the sea using sound waves

squadron group of aircraft, ships or troops of soldiers

terrain area of land, often with particular natural features, such as a desert or mountain

visa entry in a passport showing that the holder of the passport is allowed to enter the country and the length of time they are allowed to stay

writer Royal Navy term for someone who works in administration

youth intervention work undertaken with young people to reduce the possibility of their becoming criminals or victims of crime

Index

Titles in the *How to get ahead in* series include:

Hardback 978 1 4062 0450 6

Hardback 978 1 4062 0448 3

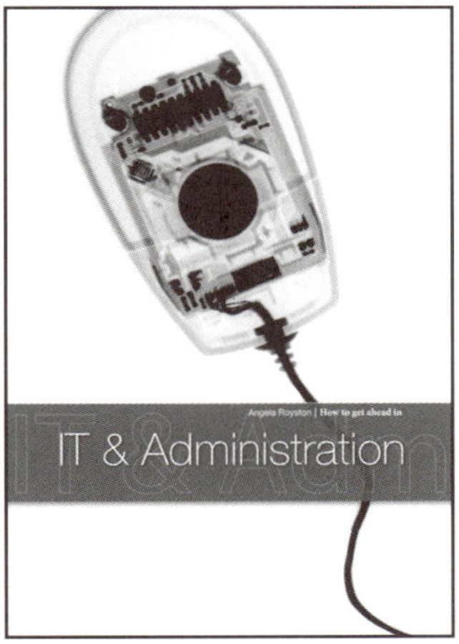

Hardback 978 1 4062 0449 0

Hardback 978 1 4062 0447 6

Hardback 978 1 4062 0446 9

Other titles available:

Beauty	Hardback 978 1 4062 0442 1
Catering	Hardback 978 1 4062 0443 8
Construction	Hardback 978 1 4062 0440 7
Engineering and Design	Hardback 978 1 4062 0441 4
Healthcare	Hardback 978 1 4062 0444 5

Find out about the other titles in this series on our website at www.raintreepublishers.co.uk

Edited by Fox Proof Editing
Cover design by Ashes and Vellichor

RHAPSODY
ASH AND THE BASILISKS
2
HOLLY BLOOM

one

. . .

Ash

I can't breathe. My heart skips a beat as time slows down. Lights and cameras flash, my vision blurs, and loud music plays, but it sounds like I'm trapped underwater and gasping for air.

Everything else falls away until all I can see is the three of them. *Levi. Damon. Zach.* But now I see them for who they really are. *Venom. Ripper. Zed.*

How is this even possible? I don't understand. It makes no sense. They can't be the Basilisks. I don't want to accept it, I…

"Ash?" Cookie takes my arm to steady me. She shoots an apologetic glance at the Lionhearts and lets out a nervous laugh as my eyes stay locked on Venom. "Ash is just shocked, that's all."

The Lionhearts, the Basilisks… What the fuck am I supposed to call them now?

"Levi," Zach addresses his bandmate firmly—or should I call him Zed? He grabs Venom's shoulder to turn him around, breaking our gaze, but his magnetic green eyes will be permanently seared into my soul. They are the

same eyes I've looked into before but hidden behind different lenses.

How could they have lied to me? We've been around each other all summer, but they never said a word. They had plenty of opportunities to share their secret with me.

Zed nudges his head in the opposite direction. He doesn't look at me as he says, "We have to go. The car's waiting. We can't miss our flight."

I look at Damon—Ripper—who watches me with an intenseness that makes my inner thighs tingle. How could I have been so blind? I missed all the signs.

My mind flips through my summer memories like I'm rewinding a movie in my head. Images whoosh past in quick snapshots, but I can't take them in properly.

"We'll see you soon, Ash," Ripper says in a low, seductive rumble, then he adds, "on the set of Popstarz."

"Take care of yourself," Venom says. He's dropped a bombshell and is leaving me to deal with the aftermath alone. The fucker. Who does that? Not giving me an explanation is worse than fucking me without telling me who they are.

When we were on Buggy, I didn't care about their identities. I wanted them to keep their masks on. I told them their music was all that mattered, but that was before I knew the truth. The truth changes everything…

I stay rooted to the spot, suspended in shock and disbelief. Even without the stage of people surrounding us, I still wouldn't be able to demand answers. They've rendered the girl who always has an answer to everything speechless.

The three men I spent the entire summer avoiding are the same people I craved to see again. The same men who

I looked up to for years. The same men I believed were the best thing to ever happen to me.

"Ash." Cookie nudges me in the ribs with more urgency this time. I still can't speak, so she talks for me. "She'll see you soon."

"Yes," Zed says with an air of finality, "she will."

With that, the three of them hurry away. Zed leads the band, striding to the waiting limo. His broad shoulders flex as he walks. Broad shoulders that I've stroked. From his walk, I can't tell whether Zed knows what Venom revealed. If he did, he has damn good composure. The Zed I spent the night with would protect their privacy with his life, and he'd be furious about their biggest secret being uncovered.

Ripper casts one final lingering look in our direction before getting into the car. His jaw tenses, like he's holding himself back.

I turn away from them.

Fuck. How could I have allowed myself to believe the Basilisks were my soul mates? This revelation only proves how different our worlds are.

Nausea bubbles in the pit of my stomach. Have I been a joke to them? They came into my life and flipped my world on its head. With camp ending, getting my phone back and building up the courage to text Ripper has been the thing I've looked forward to the most, but it will never be the same now. Knowing their real identities dashed any lofty hopes I had. We'd never work.

Millions of girls want to climb into bed with the Lionhearts, but not me. The Lionhearts represent everything I hate about the music industry. How can the jingle-writing pop stars be the same people who make the music that

tears my heart open and makes it sing? It doesn't make sense.

"Are you okay, Ash? You look pale." Conor's voice drags me back to the present moment. He frowns and puts his hand on my shoulder, turning to the others to say, "She looks like she's gonna pass out."

I don't know how I haven't already. I'm not sure whether I want to cry or punch someone.

Conflicting thoughts and scenarios race through my mind as I try to process everything.

Is their double life a joke to them? Is being the Basilisks something they do for fun? How can I ever believe what we shared was real and not based on another bigger lie?

"I…" My voice trails off as their limousine door slams in the distance. I gulp. "I'm fine."

"See? She's fine," Leila reiterates. She's beaming and hugs me again. "You're going to be on Popstarz, Ash! Everyone is going to know your name!"

Finding out who the Basilisks are is enough to process without the added pressure of performing on live television in front of millions of viewers.

My hijacked performance of *Bring Me to Life* didn't unleash my full-on metal scream, but it was alternative enough to show the judges a glimpse of the artist I aspire to be. There's no place for someone like me on a show like Popstarz.

Cookie points to the left. "Look who it is!"

Two familiar figures are weaving their way through the crowd of campers, alumni, and parents.

"Ash!" Brick yells. He punches the air in a way that would look terrible if it was anyone else. Somehow, he makes everything look effortlessly cool. "You did it."

My dad is grinning by his side and gives a double thumbs-up. That's a big deal for him.

I smile meekly, filled with relief at seeing them. While my world has flipped on its head, the two of them remind me of home, and I try to clutch onto that sense of normalcy. I'll need it to get me through the next few hours until I can be alone.

"Let's go see them," Cookie says, dragging me off the stage to join them. Leila and the twins traipse after us, still buzzing with excitement over pulling off the plan. Like Cookie, none of their parents could make the final show either.

We pass Jacqueline and the other judges, who are still sitting at their table. They are whispering in urgent tones, and Jacqueline is smiling, but it looks like she's baring her teeth instead. Unlike her, McCallister isn't trying to hide his discontent. His round face grows redder by the second, no doubt infuriated by my performance and ruining the show's finale. Jacinta Vickers, one of the Popstarz judges, smiles in my direction and raises her hand to wave, but she drops it just as fast as Jacqueline's head swivels in my direction, and Yu Jin's eyes flick over to me in curiosity.

Jacqueline has threatened me before. She wants to be the puppeteer. The person pulling the strings and responsible for creating the stars of tomorrow. She may have insisted on me getting a solo in the final show, but she didn't expect it to happen this way. After my blatant disregard for her rules, a niggling feeling in my gut tells me she and Starnote will be out for my blood.

But I have no time to address the encroaching dread taking hold of me as Brick lunges and picks me up like I'm a child. His arms squeeze tightly around me, and he spins in a circle.

"You killed it, Smash," he says. His spinning is not helping with my dizziness. "You're going to be on Popstarz."

"Holy shit," Leila lowers her voice but is still loud enough for everyone to hear. "He's hot."

When Brick puts me down, his ears turn pink, forgetting we're in public. He steps back in an awkward shuffle, remembering that we're not kids anymore, and it's only been a few months since I rejected him.

Brick clears his throat and introduces himself to my Camp Harmony friends. "It's great to meet you, I'm Brick."

Everyone is welcoming, but I can't hold back a snicker as Conor grips Brick's hand a little too tightly. Leila quickly kisses Conor on the cheek, and his smile relaxes. They shouldn't have waited so long to get together. They're both glowing.

Dad grins sheepishly. He stands at the edge of the group like he doesn't know what to do with himself, but his eyes shine with proud tears.

"He's right, kid," Dad says, sniffing. "You did good, but I never doubted you for a second. Your mom would have been proud of you up there."

"Thanks, Dad," I murmur.

His words mean a lot, and he's right. I spent many hours speaking to Mom about my dreams. I only wish she could have been here to see me. Wherever she is, I hope she's looking down on me and that I've made her proud.

"So, what's next?" Dad asks, clearing his throat. "When will you be flying to the big city?"

Out of nowhere, Jacqueline swoops in like a hungry vampire, ready to take over the conversation.

"You must be Mr. Cooper," she gushes, holding out her hand. "It's wonderful to meet you."

"Sheriff Cooper," Dad corrects her, straightening up. He looks at her hand for a few seconds, leaving her hanging, before shaking it reluctantly out of politeness. "You must be Jacqueline. The one who took Ash's phone away."

I snort but disguise it with a cough. Dad is into grunge bands like Nirvana and doesn't listen outside of the genre. He is oblivious to the fact he's facing off with one of the most successful people in the music industry. His cop instincts let him see straight through her act. He likes to avoid confrontation, but he won't kiss her ass like other parents.

Cookie's eyes widen as Jacqueline laughs in a high-pitched way, trying to glaze over his comment by saying, "And it's a good thing I did. I may have unconventional methods, Sheriff Cooper, but as you've seen tonight, our methods have made your daughter a star." She turns to address me. "We have returned your phone to your cabin alongside your other belongings. You have two weeks before rehearsals start."

"I can't wait," I reply in a fake jovial tone, meeting her gaze and trying to muster some of my dad's strength.

Performing on Popstarz was never the end goal. I wanted to show Tiffany that crushing the competition wasn't the only way to become successful. She couldn't get away with what she did to Riley, and when the "little people" stood together, we were more powerful than she could ever imagine.

"I'll get Amber to send over the details, and the show's producers will be in touch," Jacqueline says. Her icy stare strays behind me and scans my row of friends. Her chipper tone drips with sarcasm. "I know I have all of you

to thank for Ashley's very special performance this evening. I'm sure I'll find a way to thank you for all the passion you have shown."

Leila crosses her arms, but Cookie shrinks by my side. I can't let my actions compromise their futures, too.

"It was my idea," I say hastily. "I thought Riley should get the recognition she deserved, considering she didn't get to perform last year."

Jacqueline presses her lips into a disapproving line. "I'll see you again soon, Ashley."

She walks away, leaving us reeling and surrounded by the scent of her distinct perfume.

Brick lets out a low whistle. "Damn, she needs to get laid…"

Dad clears his throat.

"Sorry, Sheriff Cooper," Brick says quickly.

"I'll leave you kids to hang out," Dad says.

I start to argue. "But—"

"It's fine, Ash," he says. He ruffles my hair and winks. "They have a good buffet."

I spot Claudia over his shoulder and wave her over. She's been working all day and must have finally gotten a chance to take a break.

"Claudie." Cookie gives her a huge hug as she approaches. "I'm going to miss you."

"I'll miss you guys next year too." Claudia smiles. "Despite all the trouble you've caused me."

"Sorry about that," Leila says.

"Thank you for everything," I say to her, hoping she'll sense the added gratitude behind my words. "We couldn't have done it without you."

"You were amazing, Ash," Claudia says, "all of you were. What you pulled off will go down in Camp

Harmony history… and probably lead to added security next year."

Conor grins. "We can't help causing trouble wherever we go."

"We're Irish." Declan claps him on the back. "It's in our nature."

"I hope we'll see you again," Cookie says. "How are we going to survive without your cooking?"

"I'm sure we'll see each other again," Claudia says with a smile. "But I have to head back to the kitchen now. I only have a short break and wanted to make sure I said goodbye."

We all exchange hugs, and it hits me that camp is ending.

"Dad, this is Claudia," I say quickly, catching him before he sneaks away. "The woman behind that amazing buffet you were just about to visit."

"We'll walk back up together," Claudia offers with a bright smile. "I can tell you all about my secret recipes."

"Good luck," I say. "Cooking's not exactly his forte."

"But he's good at ordering pizza," Brick chips in to defend him, and I roll my eyes.

"I'll see you back at your cabin in an hour," Dad says. "Then we gotta hit the road."

I nod. "See you soon."

The two of them set off. It was hard for him to get time off with the station being short-staffed, so we'll be driving home all night to make sure he can make his shift tomorrow. I don't mind. I know I won't be able to sleep anyway —not when Venom's green eyes are all I can see every time I blink.

Stop it. I push it from my mind. I refuse to let myself think about it until I'm alone.

"Urgh," Leila sighs, rolling her eyes and gesturing toward Tiffany's entourage. "They're pathetic."

They are busy gushing over her and Rita Lockhart, Tiffany's celebrity mom. Rita plays it up for the crowd, but I detect an underlying crazy lurking behind her fake smile as she shoots a resentful glare in my direction. After overhearing Rita's outburst earlier this summer, it's clear she isn't happy about her daughter having to share the spotlight with a nobody. If Tiffany wasn't a bitch willing to do anything to succeed, I'd feel sorry for her.

"I can't believe it," Cookie says as we all head back to Accommodation Village. "We pulled it off."

"You didn't have to say that to Jacqueline, Ash," Declan says. "We all helped and did it together."

"It's fine," I reply with a shrug. "Jacqueline already hates me. I don't want to drag you guys down with me. We all know I'm going to go out during the first round of Popstarz anyway."

"I wouldn't be so sure," Cookie says, swiping her phone wildly. "You're trending on Twitter."

Leila snorts. "Tiffany will love that."

"You're stealing her big moment, Ash," Conor adds with a grin.

"Yeah, well, she shouldn't have led me into a lake where I could have drowned unless..."

Unless the Lionhearts—Basilisks—saved me. I swallow the lump in my throat. It's bad enough they lied to me, but I also have to be grateful for the fact they saved my life.

"She did what?" Brick interrupts. His expression turns stormy. He doesn't get mad often, but he looks like he'll lose his shit over this.

"It's a long story," I say, shooting a warning look at the

others to keep their mouths shut. He doesn't need to know the details. "But I'm fine."

I don't need him to cause a scene. Tiffany will already be furious with me for stealing her big moment, but I still have to compete against her in Popstarz, which means we'll be seeing more of each other. She's done a great job of trying to make my life miserable at Camp Harmony. Can she maintain that level of contempt when we compete on a national level under the scrutiny of cameras?

"Oh my gosh," Cookie squeals, waving her phone in the air. "It's Riley."

"What?" Leila takes the phone from her hands and hits play. We all crowd around the screen to see a video of a pretty girl. It's only a brief clip, but Riley congratulates me on my win and performance in the final show. She doesn't mention Tiffany. Leila's expression softens and her eyes mist over as she says, "That's why we did this."

"It's what she deserved," Conor says. His arm is draped over Leila's shoulder, and he holds her tighter. "She got her recognition."

"If only she didn't have to sign a stupid NDA, we could out Tiffany for what she did," Leila says, then grins at me. "All you gotta do now is win Popstarz."

I laugh nervously as the others talk about their summer plans. I nod as we walk along the tree-lined path. Campers who haven't looked in my direction all summer are suddenly waving at me and smiling like we're old friends, wishing me good luck on the show. Fucking leeches.

Brick nudges me in the ribs playfully. "It doesn't look like everyone hates you, Ash," he teases.

I scowl as my black hair falls in front of my eyes and mutter, "Appearances can be deceiving."

It's easy to be nice to someone when you think they're going to be famous.

I stay quiet, listening to the other's conversations. Leila will be going on tour. She has a string of festivals lined up all over Europe—England, Spain, Germany, all places I'd love to visit one day. Conor and Declan don't have firm plans yet, but they're looking to go their separate ways to "find themselves" for a while. Conor is considering joining Leila on her tour. I hope he does. Their adventurous sides will bring out the best in each other. Cookie hopes to get a job straight away; she's waiting to see if any internship offers come her way after the show.

"Someone approached me earlier," Cookie says. "It's for a small and upcoming label. They're not mainstream yet, but it'd be a great experience, and I could make a real impact."

"You deserve it," I tell her. Relieved to hear she isn't considering working for Starnote and her involvement in my performance hasn't killed her chances.

Cookie has been my rock this summer. Without her, I wouldn't have gotten through it. Whatever she does, I know she'll make something of herself in the music world.

We reach our David Bowie cabin, and I stare at it, trying to commit the image to memory. Around us, most campers are getting ready to leave with their parents. Some will already be counting down the days until they return.

I will miss this place despite the last three months being a whirlwind. Being here made it easy to forget about the real world, but now I have no choice but to face the music… quite literally.

Having Brick by my side only makes the end of camp feel more real. His support means the world, but his pres-

ence only amplifies the loss I feel over the Basilisks… and how I won't be able to get away from them.

During Popstarz, I'll have to spend more time with Tiffany, a group of fame-hungry hopefuls, and worse, the three guys I fucked without knowing who they were underneath their masks.

"Ash," Brick says gently. He hangs back, putting some distance between us and the others. "Are you sure you're alright? You know you don't have to do Popstarz. You can come home." Part of him sounds hopeful that I'll return to Meadow Springs, but we both know there is no choice here. I'd be stupid to pass up on this opportunity. It's what my mom would have wanted, too.

"I'm just tired," I say, although his frown tells me he isn't buying it. I feign a smile that hurts my cheeks. "It's been a long day."

"Ash, come on." Cookie hurries me. "We need to help you pack."

The others are leaving in the morning. The twins and Leila will be driving home, and Cookie's parents are flying in to pick her up.

For the last time, I look around the cabin-filled street and the lights of the main stage on the horizon. When I first arrived, I thought the stage looked big and grand, the place that would make my dreams come true. I imagined how it would feel to perform here, but now that I have, why does my heart feel so empty?

Camp Harmony may have been my dream, but this summer has taken a turn I never expected… and it won't be long until I have to face the consequences.

two

. . .

Zed | Zach

I slam the limo door behind us, curling my fingers into fists and holding onto my fury. I bite down on my tongue to stop myself from unleashing the insults I want to hurl at Venom.

What happened to our agreement to never share our identities? We vowed to take our biggest secret to the grave.

Venom may have thought we couldn't hear what he said, or understand what his cryptic clue meant, but we aren't stupid.

If we weren't being watched by cameras, campers, and Starnote scum, my reaction wouldn't have been to plaster on a smile and act like everything was normal. I'd have punched him in the jaw as soon as I realized what he was about to do.

What did he think would happen when he told Ash? That she would fall into his arms and profess her undying love for us? We're not in a fucking fairytale. We know that better than anyone, considering we're living most people's idea of a dream, which is more like a living hell.

The morning after we fucked, Ash made it clear it was a one-night thing, but Venom and Ripper caught feelings they can't seem to shake.

I shouldn't have let it go on for this long. I should have taken Ash's lyric book off him. Venom spent hours poring over her words during the last few weeks, thinking he was growing closer to her. But he was only growing closer to an imaginary woman who would never want him—us—back.

Realization crossing over Ash's face only confirmed my suspicions and everything I feared. Her beautiful eyes widened in confusion, then turned to hurt… betrayal… anger… the same feelings that are coursing through my shaking body right now.

I take a deep breath in and hold it, counting to eight. I can't lose my shit in front of the limousine driver who is listening to our every word. He'll be looking for any hint of a story to sell to the papers to make more than his yearly salary. That's the problem when you're a Lionheart. You can't trust anyone. The Lionhearts aren't people. They are a product forced to perform like dancing monkeys to fill Starnote's fucking pockets.

What do we do next?

Ripper and Venom are the only two people in the world I thought I could trust. We disagreed on many things, but keeping our secret is what we valued above all else, but Ash broke that. She came along and ruined everything.

What if she shared our secret? Our careers would be over, and I'd never be able to wear a mask again. The best part of being a Basilisk is our music, of course, but also how no one knows who we are. When you've lived your life under the spotlight in the shadows of a famous family

with lofty expectations, being able to put on a mask and live life how you choose is powerful.

Doesn't Venom realize the gravity of the situation? He's put us all at risk. He hasn't only threatened our identities, but also our entire future.

"Drink anyone?" Ripper says. He uncorks a bottle of champagne and swigs from the bottle. His knees are jumping around, and he's tapping his feet the way he always does when he's on edge. "It's the best."

Ripper is the most attached to Ash. His obsessive nature means he's made Ash his world, even if he doesn't fully realize it yet. But he didn't miss the look of horror on her face when she realized who we were. I've imagined the situation happening, but it sure as hell didn't play out like that. Seeing her blatant disgust cut through my chest like a fucking knife.

I thought Ash was better than that. I thought she understood and wanted to get to know the real us. She never wanted to see under our masks, but now she can't see past the Starnote fucking package.

"I'm not thirsty," I snarl through gritted teeth. My eyes burn into Venom's, hoping he can read what I'm thinking.

Venom crosses his arms over his chest and shakes his head. He avoids looking in my direction and averts his gaze out of the window at the trees rushing past. Good fucking riddance.

"What a show, huh?" Ripper says, continuing to drink from the bottle. "And the ending..." He wipes his mouth with the back of his hand, "that was something else."

"Not now," I snap, then soften my voice for the benefit of the eavesdropping driver. He could be a spy from Starnote. It wouldn't be the first time they've planted

people to watch our every move. "Why don't we appreciate the scenery? It's the last time we'll be back here."

I'll make sure of it too. We've fulfilled our bullshit contract to Jacqueline by returning to Camp Harmony once, and I never want to return.

None of us speak as we head down the highway. We have a packed schedule until Popstarz filming starts: a few days of photoshoots, a week on location for a Lionheart music video, and several signings on the road.

I can't help my mind straying to Ash and what she'll be thinking, wondering what her next move is going to be, and what the hell she's going to do when she sees us again.

three

. . .

Ash

"Ash!" Dad knocks impatiently at my door. He's excited to have me back home and more attentive than he has been my entire life, which is sweet but suffocating. He keeps telling people his daughter will be on Popstarz—not that he needs to. That's all our small town is talking about. "Are you coming down?"

"Soon," I groan.

In the two-week gap before Popstarz starts, I've locked myself in the garage, pounding beats on my drums.

Whenever I go for a walk outside, journalists and kids who didn't look my way in high school accost me with questions or autograph requests. Sunglasses and a hood don't help when people hang around on your street waiting for you to leave. I can see why celebrities go to Harmony Resort for a break.

Brick's been busy at work too, so I haven't spent a lot of time with him. Although, he finally told me he was dating Jade, the new intern at his dad's business. I haven't met her properly, aside from a quick video call when I was

at camp, but he's asked me over for pizza tonight, so we can meet properly.

I'm not in the mood to meet new people and socialize, but at least Jade won't be in a mask pretending to be someone she's not.

The emptiness and bitter pangs of betrayal at discovering the Basilisk's identities are still raw. After getting my phone back, there were some messages from Ripper. I only saw the blurry outline of the message preview through my tears before I hit delete on all of them and erased his number.

What he has to say doesn't matter.

The more I think about my time at Camp Harmony, the more I see the signs. Zach was there when I lost my shit on a drum kit, and he knew how to give me expert advice. Damon pulled me from the water and saved my life, as well as gave me advice during our mentoring session to warn me of the dangers of life in the spotlight. Levi had my back when McCallister singled me out and shared his lyrics with me, even performing the song with my suggestions at an open mic. Despite all those signs, I ask myself whether I would have had sex with them if I knew.

One of the hardest things about Venom revealing their secret was how I struggled to listen to their music without being reminded of them. When they were a mystery, their music made me feel better. After Mom died and my mental health hit rock bottom, they guided me through the tough times, but now I'm lost without their music to lean on. Suspended in perpetual silence and torn between what I'll do when I see them again.

I jump as my cell vibrates and roll over in bed to check it, expecting it to be another update from Cookie about her

internship. As suspected, she's already hunting for fresh talent.

Instead of seeing her name and photo, I see an unknown number. I blink twice as I open it to read:

Unknown: How are you? Nice job at the final show.

I know who it is instantly, and it infuriates me. He infuriates me. Damon fucking Archer has an air of superiority and a huge fucking chip on his shoulder. I recall his smug grin when I caught him smoking a joint in the forest on one of my first nights at camp. The Lionhearts may think they're entitled to everything, but they're not having me… again.

Damon used to date Alexa Frost. Why would he be interested in someone like me when he has Victoria's Secret models dropping to their knees?

Spending a night with the Basilisks meant everything to me, even if I played it down to them the next morning. It was better to play it cool than to get rejected. It would have been easier to have never seen them again than to learn the truth about who they are.

My fingers are already flying over the keypad before I can stop them.

Me: Are you going to pretend like nothing happened? You know I know.

My phone vibrates seconds later in my shaking hands.

Unknown: Are you going to keep our secret?

Is their fucking secret all he cares about? Where is his apology for lying to me for weeks on end? He knew who I was from the start. He should have never given me his number.

I fling the phone away from me with an exasperated sigh and choose to ignore his message. He can think about what he's said a little longer.

I'm not going to out the Basilisks, not just because I'm embarrassed about what happened between us, but also because I don't want any of their fans to go through the same process I did.

Imagine finding out that the people you look up to most in the world are also the people who represent everything you hate.

"Ash," Dad calls up the stairs from the living room, where I'm guessing he's sitting by the window and watching the street like a hawk. "Aren't you going to Brick's? I see the pizza guy going in."

Dad's been even more protective than usual since my return. He's fearful of some crazy person breaking into our house. Popstarz is a huge show, as is the fan hysteria that goes along with it, but I still never imagined the scale to be as big as it is. Being a nobody all my life makes me want to shrink into the wall with all the questions and people wanting to know more about me. Sometimes I wonder whether I'd have been better off staying in Meadow Springs after all…

"I'm coming," I shout back, heaving myself up and throwing on my black hoodie. That and leggings are all I've been living in. "Two minutes!"

Pizza won't take away my irritation at Ripper's attempt to get in contact, but it'll certainly help.

I pop my head in to say goodbye to Dad. "I'll bring you back a slice," I promise.

"Have a fun time," he says, only half paying attention as he's taking a painfully long time to text something on his phone. He's been glued to that thing recently to stay up to date on the latest news, and I like making fun of his slow speed. "It's good you're getting out of the house."

I roll my eyes and head to the backdoor. Instead of crossing the front yard, where I know there's a chance of people waiting around and speculating about whatever is going on, I hop the fence between our houses at the back. Brick is already waiting on the other side as I tumble over and land clumsily.

"Nice try, Smash," he comments.

"Where's the pizza?" I mutter back.

"Hi." From behind him, Jade steps out. She's got an over-eager smile, but her eyes scan over me as if she's assessing whether I'm someone she should worry about. She's even prettier in person. They would have made a great prom king and queen.

"Hey," I say, putting on my friendliest voice, which differs from my regular sarcastic mumble. "You must be Jade. It's great to finally meet you."

It's not the first time I've faced awkwardness from girls who want to date Brick. It comes with the territory of having him as a BFF.

"Come inside," Brick says, then winks, "before you make front-page news."

"I think everyone's got better things to do than read about me going to eat pizza," I reply.

We head into the living room. Usually, I sit next to Brick on the sofa, but I make a point of sitting on the

armchair furthest away from him in the hopes it'll put Jade at ease.

"So, how do you like working at the yard?" I ask Jade. I roll my eyes to tease her. "Lotta fun counting parts and collecting deliveries, huh?"

"It's great," she says. "Brick's great. He's shown me how everything works. I was thinking about getting a job in the city, but now I think I'm gonna stay here. I love it so much… and with Brick and I getting so close." She rubs his arm, and he flinches slightly. "It makes sense, right babe?"

"Sure," he shrugs, leaning forward to open the pizza boxes, caring more about the food than what she's saying.

From where I'm sitting, it's clear Jade's into him, but I'm not sure how he feels about her.

"So, Ash," Jade says, "are you excited about going on Popstarz?"

"It'll be fun," I lie.

"You'd better not forget about me when you get famous," Brick jokes as Jade tenses. Fuck, he can be so dense sometimes.

"What about the Lionhearts?" Jade asks.

I freeze in my tracks, dropping the slice of pizza I was about to pick up. "What about them?"

"What are they like?" Jade asks. "I mean, I shouldn't say this…" She chuckles. "But I've had a crush on Zach for, like, ever."

"Who hasn't?" I mutter.

"You've never liked them, have you, Ash?" Brick says, coming to my defense, and maybe also because he's jealous of another guy getting Jade's attention.

"I'm not a fan of their music," I say.

"You must have spoken to them at camp," Jade

continues to push, something I expected, but now find myself getting annoyed by. They are the last people I want to talk about. "Are they as nice as they seem?"

"I didn't speak to them much," I lie. "They do a lot of stuff for the cameras. In reality, they weren't around a lot. They had better things to do. You can imagine what their schedule is like."

I'd love to know what Jade would think if I told her I'd fucked the three of them. The thought makes me internally chuckle.

"That's a shame," Jade says. "Maybe you'll get to know them more on the show. Could you get me an autograph?"

"Maybe," I reply noncommittally, knowing there's no way over my dead body that I'll give them the satisfaction of asking that.

"Come on, Ash," Brick teases. "You'll be best friends with them soon."

"They're fucking assholes, okay?" I say, unable to keep the resentment out of my tone and taking them aback. I can't help myself.

"Okay," Brick says, trying to smooth over the tension in the room. "How about we put on a movie? What do you want to watch, Ash?"

"Jade can decide," I say, relieved that we don't have to talk anymore.

All the while, my thoughts stray to Ripper's message, wondering what the guys are up to.

Are they thinking of me as much as I'm thinking of them?

four

. . .

Venom | Levi

The atmosphere fizzes with tension. When Zed has a problem, it lives under his skin like a wild animal. He needs to unleash it to function and, so far, he hasn't had the chance, which means trouble. I can almost hear his temper bubbling like a volcano close to an eruption underneath the calm exterior.

He smiles for the cameras, and graciously thanks the swooning girls who are shooting our music video, but I catch his malice-filled side-glances out of the corner of my eye when no one's looking.

He's furious with me. Ripper is too, but I suspect he's relieved it's me who Zed is directing anger at… and a small part of him may also be grateful for the fact I told Ash instead of him. Perhaps it's even what he wanted.

I didn't intend for it to happen. I watched her give the performance of a lifetime on that stage, proving to the world, and to me, how strong she is. She was brave enough to do what we weren't able to. Ash bared her soul and exposed her vulnerability for the world to see.

She didn't scream or roar like I'd heard her before, but

the song choice was perfect. *Bring Me to Life* captured the essence of Riley's story. Yet again, she proved her musical talent. She isn't in the industry for money, fame, or glory. She makes music because it's in her blood, and it keeps her heart beating. Music is her life, and on the stage, it fucking shows.

After being moved by her performance and facing her, all I could think of were her lyrics. Her words rose to the surface from the depths of my subconscious. The perfect lines to symbolize the journey she's been on:

> Split your heart open,
> Invite the darkness in,
> Let it make you whole again.

I blurted them out before I could stop them. She looked at me like I'd gone crazy, and then, for a split second, she saw me. Really saw me. Not Levi York, a Lionheart, or even Venom, part of the Basilisks, but the real me. Her eyes saw straight into my soul and made me want to pull her into my arms. When I'm around her, it feels like she's holding me together.

A cameraman interrupts my reverie, snapping the clapperboard. "That's a wrap."

We're on a beach in California. The sprawling white sand and sparkling sea may look like paradise, but spending hours dancing and miming a song that none of us wrote was exhausting. Tonight, we have to appear at a celebrity birthday party. They are a movie star everyone has heard of, but I've never spoken to them. Not that it matters. They don't care about making conversation, they only want us there for the kudos of having the Lionhearts attend.

"Your car is waiting," Hayley says in her usual clipped, snippy tone. Hayley is our new chaperone for work trips, a.k.a Jacqueline's eyes and ears. Her head is stuck so far up Jacqui's ass that it's a wonder she can see. She's hardly let us out of her sight the entire trip, working us from morning until dusk. "You have a few hours to get ready before the party—"

"Yeah, we know," Ripper snaps, unable to contain his irritation. He can get away with being a diva. It's something he's known for.

"Thanks, Hayley," Zed smooths Ripper's abruptness and overcompensates his rudeness with politeness like he always does. "You're perfectly organized as ever."

She blushes at his compliment, and I roll my eyes behind my sunglasses.

Ash wouldn't be as easily impressed. That's why she's so captivating. She isn't like any of the other girls we've met on our travels, the ones who are so eager to fuck a famous pop star that they only spread their legs to tell their friends. The "Hearties" want to use the Lionhearts' cocks as dildos.

Ripper never complained about the female attention, though. He was well aware gorgeous women only wanted to sleep with him for a story, but he figured, why the hell not? There had to be some perks to being the monsters we've had to become. But Zed was more inconspicuous. He made sure whoever he screwed signed an NDA before leaving his bed in the morning. If a sex tape of him leaked, he'd have to face his mom's wrath. And me? Ash is the first girl I've been with in years. It's not that it hasn't tempted me, but sex means more to me than that. My scars were off-putting, and I never found someone I wanted to share my true self with before.

I wish I told her that before we left Camp Harmony. Waiting until the last moment to tell her who we are wasn't my best move. Would it have turned out differently if I shared our secret before then? Or would she have still looked repulsed?

"What're you waiting for?" Ripper calls over to me as I watch the sun casting reflections over the water. "We need to go."

"Coming," I reply.

We trudge through the hot sand. I'm sweaty and exhausted from having to wear a long-sleeved sweater all day. As well as hiding my scars, it hid my tattoos too.

"Let's enter the feeding frenzy," Ripper grumbles.

A crowd swarms around our car, stopping us from getting inside, which I suspect isn't an accident. Hayley planned it. She likes to give the public what they want. Selling us piece by piece. If we shit in a bucket, she'd probably try to sell that, too.

I keep my gaze fixed on the ground and ignore the flashes. Thankfully, no one expects me to speak. Being known as the quiet Lionheart has its advantages.

"Thanks, everyone." Zed steps into his role naturally. "We don't have time to sign autographs right now."

"Please," a teenage girl screams, her voice coarse as she's on the verge of tears at the prospect of not getting us to scribble on the paper she's clutching to her chest.

"Okay, fine," Zed relents, raising his hands and shooting them a dazzling smile. A few girls squeal and others sway on their feet like they're about to pass out. If only they knew what Zed was really like. "Maybe we have time for a few."

I sign objects thrust in my face without saying a word. A hat. A T-shirt. A receipt from Burger King. They push

phones in my direction as people beg for photographs. I don't respond.

"That's all we have time for today," Zed says finally. We may as well be animals in a fucking zoo. "Thanks for coming to see us. We appreciate your support."

Ripper opens the car door and gets in first. I follow close behind while Zed continues to bid farewell to our doting fans.

"You got a sunburn," Ripper comments, looking at my nose.

"Great," I murmur, crossing my arms and slouching back in a moody sulk. I watch through the tinted windows as Zed continues to sign their shit. "It looks like we're not going anywhere soon."

We'll be here for another twenty minutes at least. Zed's family trained him from birth to deal with fans and the press. He manages situations well, which is amazing for Starnote and for making the Lionhearts the biggest boy band of all time, but it doesn't make it any less depressing to live through.

"Are you excited about the party?" Ripper asks.

The atmosphere is strained between us. Unsaid words hang in the air. He opens his mouth like he wants to say more, then shuts it again. He doesn't know where to start.

"You bet," I lie. My tone drips with the sarcasm of someone who'd rather scoop their eyeballs out than go to another party. "I love parties."

The fans play some of our smash hits on their phone outside the window. Over the top of their hysterical squealing, the driver can't hear a word we're saying.

Ripper steals a look at the driver to be safe, then drops his voice and leans in closer. "I haven't heard from her."

The makeup under Ripper's eyes has smudged to

reveal dark circles. He hasn't slept in days, relying on ridiculous amounts of caffeine and energy drinks. Like my sudden bout of insomnia, I'm sure working too hard isn't the reason for his tiredness.

"What?" I ask, wanting him to repeat it to make sure I heard him right.

"She should have her phone back now," Ripper says, trying not to move his lips for fear of someone lip-reading, "she hasn't replied to any of my texts from before."

I'm not sure why I expected anything else, but having it confirmed feels like I've fallen from a height, and my heart has been left behind.

Back in Camp Harmony, Jacqueline took Ash's phone away from her after the video of her performing with us went viral. Until we found out they confiscated it, Ripper sent her countless text messages, and we assumed she was avoiding us.

I thought she may have reached out to Ripper again after my revelation. A string of angry insults, probing questions, or threats to expose us would have been more welcome than her silence. Silence is the worst thing of all.

What is she thinking?

I run my hand through my hair. "Fuck."

"I thought…" Ripper's voice trails off.

He doesn't need to finish his sentence before I reply, "Me too… and I'm sorry… you know… for what I did."

Exposing our identities was selfish. I didn't think about the consequences when it felt right at the moment. It wasn't only my relationship with Ash that I compromised, but Ripper and Zed's too. It sucks to see Ripper in pain, knowing it's all my fault.

I ping the elastic band on my wrist to distract me from

sinking into a well of self-hatred that I won't be able to pull myself out of.

Ripper notices the angry red mark on my wrist and says, "Hey, it's not your fault."

I raise an eyebrow. "Isn't it?"

Trying to make me feel better doesn't change the facts.

"I'm glad you did it," Ripper says. "I wanted to tell her too."

I nod at Zed outside. "How mad is he?"

Ripper grins. It's the first genuine smile I've seen from him since we left Camp Harmony. I never thought we'd be sad about leaving that place after dreading going back there for so long.

"Mighty pissed," Ripper says, then claps me on the shoulder, "rather you than me, brother."

The door opens, releasing a tremendous roar of screams until Zed shuts it again. His clothes are disheveled, and his red hair is windswept like he's just completed a parachute jump.

"Drive," Zed barks at the driver. His patience has finally reached a breaking point. He realizes his mistake and softens his voice, then says, "We don't want to be late for the party."

It takes fifteen minutes to exit the parking lot. Despite the tinted windows, I get a great view of boogers from the many noses pressed against the glass. The driver goes extra slow, navigating awkward maneuvers when people are peering to look inside. One woman even kisses the window multiple times, leaving smeared pink lipstick marks behind.

"That was fun," Zed says wryly as we finally head back to the hotel where we've been staying for the past few days.

"I've got a headache," I lie, hoping if I sow the seed, I can get out of the party. It's not like anyone will miss me. All I'll do is slink away with a drink and sit in a quiet corner until Ripper or Zed tells me it's time to leave. The perk of going to parties in a celebrities' house is that they're so big, it's easy to hide out. Security is kept to a minimum once you're inside. No one wants to risk any leaks about the drugs, orgies, or the other crazy shit going down.

Zed sees straight through my bullshit and narrows his eyes. "I'm sure you'll live."

I can't remember when Zed took the leadership role in the band. I guess it was a natural fit and suited his personality. His taking charge is something I've always been happy with. After all, he came from a famous family and knew how to navigate the celebrity world. It made sense for him to make the big decisions. But Zed wasn't happy that I made a decision without him for the first time. He's a giant control freak who likes to have his way.

I catch Ripper's eye and watch his lips twitch at the edges. Usually, it's the two of them who have underlying tension, and I have to play mediator.

No one speaks again on the ride back to the hotel. We pull in at the back, where staff wait to smuggle us inside. You'd think staying at the world's most exclusive hotels would go to our heads, but when you're sneaking through the kitchens and laundry rooms to avoid crowds, you're constantly reminded of the hard work going on behind the scenes. Our life isn't as glamorous as it appears.

As soon as we reach our room and the door shuts behind us, I know we're heading for trouble. Zed's rising frustration is apparent as he stretches his arms and his muscles tense.

"Zed, we need to talk about it," Ripper says, daring to voice what we've all been avoiding. "I still haven't heard from her."

Zed doesn't need to ask who he's speaking about.

"What did you expect?" Zed snarls. His eyes burn into mine like he's trying to scorch a hole through my skull. "Did you think she'd be interested in us if she knew the truth?"

"I…" I begin, trying to form words, but nothing sounds right to say out loud. That's why I prefer writing lyrics. It's easier to express myself through words on the page. Eventually, I feebly say, "It just happened, okay?"

"It just happened?" Zed mocks. He scowls and turns his back on me. His hands wrap around an expensive-looking vase. A second later, he hurls it across the room with a crash. The small pieces scatter across the shiny floor.

Ripper jumps, looking from the broken vase to Zed, who is shaking in fury.

"Zed?" Ripper steps forward. He puts his hands up, afraid that he's going to get another piece of modern art thrown at his head. "It'll be okay."

Usually, it's Zed or me talking Ripper down from one of his episodes. Zed is always in control. I've never seen him like this before.

"I'm sorry," I say, but an apology won't be good enough to fix the mess I've made.

Zed's murderous glare signals I'm not even close to being forgiven. "Do you realize she could ruin everything we've built? This could be the end of the Basilisks."

I hang my head. I want to argue and tell him that Ash would never do that to us. She understands our music,

understands us. But I can't bring myself to say it after seeing her expression when I told her the truth.

Reading Ash's lyric book lulled me into a false sense of security. I thought I knew her. Maybe I romanticized her in my head, thinking she was the girl who could complete us. But it's also possible I've made the biggest mistake of my life.

"I know," I say, deciding it best to address Zed's worries head-on. "I shouldn't have told her."

"No," Zed rebuffs in agreement, "you shouldn't have."

"Venom knows he made a mistake," Ripper says, "but what's done is done, right? She hasn't told anyone yet. That's a good sign, isn't it?"

"We don't know that for sure," Zed snaps. "She could be biding her time, waiting until we're on Popstarz. She could already be in conversations with the press, auctioning our secret off to the highest bidder."

Suddenly, what felt like the right decision at the time was becoming more and more blurred. I've been holding onto hope that Ash might get in touch again, but finding out she ignored all of Ripper's messages means my hope is fading fast.

What the fuck have I done?

"I told you she'd ruin everything," Zed says, then looks down at the remains of the vase. "You two can clean it up."

Zed stalks away, leaving Ripper and me alone.

Ripper exhales, letting out the breath he's been holding. "Well, shit… I've never seen him so worked up before."

"Me neither," I admit.

"He's right though," Ripper says. "She'll ruin everything if we let her."

Ripper takes out his phone and texts wildly. His jaw sets in a determined expression as he hits send then flips the screen around to show me.

"There," he declares. Ash's name is on the screen. "We're done waiting around."

five

. . .

Zed | Zach

Fuck!

My body shakes, rattling with inner fury. An angry mosh pit of thoughts rage inside my mind, conflicting and slamming into each other with zero order to the chaos. They are a string of nonsensical threads that don't fit together because all I can see is her: her voice, her face, her fucking eyes… they're all I can think about. She's consuming me from the inside, and I don't know how to handle it.

I count, forcing my mind to form a list of what we've got coming up, ticking items off as I run through my mental itinerary that I have control over. It doesn't work. My thoughts stray back to her. How am I supposed to concentrate when nagging doubt is gnawing away at my insides, screaming that everything I've built could fall apart at any moment?

I shouldn't have thrown the ugly vase at the wall. It's not like me. I'll have to make an excuse about a clumsy fall to the hotel staff tomorrow.

I'm usually good at controlling my temper. I refuse to

let it rule me. Underneath the persona I portray to the world, there is a caged monster. And, even though Ash isn't around, she's unleashing my fucking beast.

She knows who I am—who we are—and not knowing what she's thinking is driving me insane. She's derailed our lives, and I despise her for it, but I hate her even more because I can't get her out of my damn head.

When I close my eyes, I remember her soft skin under my fingertips, how her breathy moans sent goosebumps racing over my arms and blood shooting down to my cock.

Being a Basilisk has given me a reason to live for all these years. Performing our songs is my favorite thing to do, and having Ash sing at my side took it to another level. It gave me an adrenaline rush like jumping out of an airplane. That addictive feeling is what I keep coming back to. She stood onstage with us like it was where she belonged—only she didn't. Did she?

My mind automatically conjures the worst-case scenario, while my rational reasoning sides with Ripper. No news is good news.

Before I can dwell on it further, my cell vibrates. My brother's smiling face fills the screen, and I groan inwardly. I consider not answering it, but he'd provide a welcome distraction from my well of self-pity.

"Hello?" I answer.

Elliot only calls when he wants something. Thankfully, I keep myself busy. Being on the road means I don't see my family often, and that's by choice rather than design. But it's harder to avoid him when we're staying in the same city.

"Bro!" His overexcited voice calls down the line. I can tell instantly that he's high. Taking drugs is his preferred

way to pass the time. A few years ago, Elliot's acting debut in a blockbuster hit catapulted him to fame. He was nominated to win an Oscar—much to our mother's delight. When he didn't win, the crushing disappointment sent him down a path of self-destruction. Even after many stints in rehab on my dime, unbeknownst to our mother, he still spent most nights snorting whatever junk he could get his hands on. "Are you going to the party tonight?"

I'd rather release my frustration in the recording studio, but I have no choice. Jacqueline's instructions and expectations were clear. She wants us to go to the party to promote Popstarz and sweet-talk some big-name stars in attendance into making a guest appearance on the show. Jacqueline could do that herself, or she could get one of her many minions to do it, but she prefers letting us get our hands dirty. That's how the bitch got her power.

"Yeah," I reply reluctantly. "We'll drop by."

"Sweet," he says. "Can I swing by before? I'm in the neighborhood."

"You know where we're staying?" I raise an eyebrow, then realize it's a stupid question. Paparazzi and fans have camped outside our hotel for hours. We can't go anywhere without an entourage. "Fine, but come in the back entrance."

"I'm on the way," he answers. "I'll see you in a few."

The line cuts off. Fucking brilliant. It won't be the first time Elliot has entered this hotel the secret way. He's well-known for hosting huge, wild parties that end in drug-fueled orgies. Elliot is a douche, but he's also my brother, and I can't blame him for how he turned out with a mom like ours. My siblings and I never stood a chance. We're all fucked up.

I hop into the shower, and just as I finish getting dry,

there's a crash and loud footsteps in the hall. I throw on a shirt and pants. I don't need to call to ask what the commotion is. Elliot has arrived.

"You didn't tell us Elliot was coming," Ripper says as I leave the bathroom with my shirt open. Ripper raises his eyebrows, wrapping his arm around my brother's shoulder to keep him standing.

Venom emerges from his room, watching on anxiously. Elliot makes him uneasy. He's unpredictable. You can never tell what he's going to do next.

"I thought we could all go to the party together," Elliot says, still swaying on his feet. His giant pupils absorb most of his irises. If he's this fucked now, he won't last the night. We'd be better off putting him in a cab and sending him to bed before he can embarrass himself, or Mom, further.

Elliot and I look alike. We're both redheads, like my sister, Lacy. But Elliot's slightly shorter than me, with more muscles and defined cheekbones that make him look like he belongs in a magazine. It's a shame his personality doesn't match.

Venom joins us, looking from me to Elliot. "Are you sure you wanna go?"

My relationship with my family is strange. We all know it, but it's nothing the band speaks about.

"Of course," I snap, more because I know it'll annoy Venom more to go along with my brother. I still haven't forgiven him fully yet.

"Sweet." Elliot slaps my back, slurring his words. "Let's get outta here. Rock and roll, baby."

He leads the way out of the hotel room with Venom hot on his tail. He owes me after spilling our secret to Ash, so I hope he's going to play the role of babysitter for the night. That'll be a fitting punishment.

Ripper reaches out to me, resting his hand on my forearm and making my skin tingle. I shake him off and spin around in accusation. "What?"

Ripper's face falls.

"Nothing," he answers hastily, biting his tongue.

He looks good tonight in ripped jeans and a faux leather jacket that would look weird on anyone else. He's the only one of us who can get away with wearing somewhat alternative clothes in public. Venom has made zero effort with his appearance as usual. He dresses like a computer programmer in a hoodie and jeans. Couldn't he at least try to make an effort?

Elliot stumbles and Venom catches him, shooting a look at me over his shoulder to ask if we should be taking him.

"Move," I snarl through gritted teeth. "We'll be late."

"Oh my gosh!" A cleaner, carrying a stack of freshly washed towels, almost drops them as we approach. "It's the Lionhearts!"

Ripper winks, and her face flushes like she's going to pass out. Her blush reminds me of Ash, and I see a flashback to the night on the bus. How the pink glow spread over Ash's skin when her lips parted, and she moaned our names.

I feign a smile to the cleaner, hoping she doesn't faint—it wouldn't be the first time—so we don't have to stick around to make sure she's okay.

We slink past and get straight into the waiting car. As soon as we're inside, my cell vibrates in my pocket like clockwork. I know who it is, and I'm not surprised when I check it to see a text from Amber—Jacqueline's number-one follower—asking whether we're going to the party and reminding us to keep her updated.

I ignore it, hitting delete on the text. We've been Starnote's puppets all day. We deserve to blow off steam, regardless of whether we're on a special mission of Jacqueline's.

Elliot fills the silence, chatting about which models he's hooked up with lately, while Ripper encourages him and asks questions at regular intervals. Venom catches my gaze, searching for something in it, but I look away. He's apologized, but I'm still pissed at him. Until I know Ash doesn't pose a threat, I'll hold a grudge.

We drive for thirty minutes to a gated community. An area packed with lavish mansions, home to the richest and most pretentious celebrities in the city. Security guards at the gate take one look at us and let us drive straight through. That's one of the few perks of everyone knowing your name.

We hear the party before we can see it. Music carries in the night air, and sports cars line the street. Everything from Maseratis to classic cars. I've visited this community since I was a kid staying with my parent's friends. It's a playground for vapid famous people whose personalities are empty, and they fill the space with all the material possessions money can buy.

Before my parents divorced and Dad moved to Switzerland on a whim, they worked away from home a lot. They brought us up in the hands of the best nannies in the business, although they struggled to manage the three of us. We'd learned the art of manipulation by watching our parent's toxic relationship crumble over the years. The only times I remember them not arguing were when they hosted similar parties to this one.

Elliot bounds out of the limo like an enthusiastic puppy. "It's party time."

He stumbles on the first step.

"I'll watch him," Ripper promises, racing after him to catch a potential fall.

Venom hesitates, shooting me a pleading look. "Can't I just wait here until you're done?"

"No," I say. "Let's go."

We follow the others up the steps leading into the mansion. Venom trudges reluctantly a few steps behind.

"Zach!" A shrill-voiced blonde greets me as soon as I step into the vast foyer. Our recently divorced party host has an appetite for pretty young girls, and he would offer to pay their college tuition to look after his guests' every—and I mean, *every*—need for the evening. That kinda thing is normal. It happens all the time. "It's so great to see you."

From a glance around and a rough calculation, there must be enough girls for every guy in the room. Attending wives and girlfriends cling to their partner's arms like they're too scared of being replaced to let go.

A brunette takes Venom's arm, making him flinch. Her face falls, but I have no time to smooth over the situation and massage her ego tonight. I have one eye on Elliot. We can't afford for him to cause any more trouble for our family. Two girls hang off his arms, giggling at whatever nonsense he's saying as he steers them straight to the nearest bathroom. No surprises there.

"What's your name?" I ask the blonde, feigning interest when all I can think about is how she and all the other girls look the same.

Fake tits, blown-up lips, and makeup that makes her cheeks look unnaturally sculpted. She's beautiful, but she's not what I want.

"Rachel," she replies.

"Why don't you grab us a drink, Rachel?" I say. "I'll wait here."

"Sure, I'll be right back." She paces away excitedly to a bar, which I know will be many rooms and a sea of people away. With any luck, she won't be able to find me again.

I set off in pursuit of Elliot, leaving Venom behind. I roll my eyes as I overhear him mumbling excuses about getting some air, even though we've just stepped inside.

No one pays me any attention as I swan into the gigantic living area where the main party is taking place. It's the size of a small club with all of the furniture removed. The shiny marble floors reflect the multi-colored light from the strobe system.

The one good thing about these parties is that everyone is famous. Unlike a night out at a regular bar, where everyone stares at you or begs for photographs and autographs, everyone here doesn't care about your status—apart from the well-paid escorts, of course.

It's not the first time I've been to the Lockhart mansion. It's not the only house the Lockhart family has, but I remember visiting when I was a child. Our parents were close until Tiffany's dad fucked our au pair, and communication became frosty.

"Zach!" I hear her coming before I see her and groan inwardly. It was bad enough to endure her tailing me all summer at Camp Harmony. "I thought it was you."

I plaster a fake smile and turn to address her. "It's good to see you again, Tiffany."

She beams, flicking her long hair over her shoulder. When we were young, everyone made jokes about how Tiffany and I would end up married. She seems to have taken those jokes to heart, expecting me to succumb to her flirtations and advances, which is never going to happen.

I clench my fists, remembering what Tiffany did to Ash. If it wasn't for Ripper pulling Ash out of the lake, she could be dead. I used to believe Tiffany was harmless—simply starved of attention and eager to please, but desperation has turned her into a monster.

"I'm so excited for Popstarz," Tiffany exclaims, slurring her words slightly. Despite being under twenty-one, it isn't hard to sneak bottles of champagne when you're the host's daughter. If she hadn't turned into a psychopath, I'd almost feel sorry for her having to watch her dad hook up with models her age. "I'm so happy you'll be a judge, Zach. You'll put in a good word for me with the other judges, won't you?"

I smile but don't answer and change the subject. "Have you seen Damon or Elliot?"

"No." She twirls a blonde curl around her finger. In the dim lighting, she could easily be mistaken for the girl who disappeared to get me a drink. Another clone in this colorless world. "But you can hang out with me. Dad got a new jacuzzi installed in the pool house. Do you want to see it?"

"Maybe another time," I lie, scanning the crowd and glimpsing Ripper's head towering above them. "I'll speak to you soon."

She pouts but doesn't argue as I move around her to make my way across the room to follow Ripper's retreating figure.

I find him leaning cross-armed outside a bathroom, where I can hear giggling from inside.

I raise my eyebrows and shake my head. "Coke break?"

"Sure is," Ripper replies.

"Fuck…" I stand next to him, pressing my back against the wall to stop myself from hammering on the door and

causing a scene. "I thought he was getting better. He wanted to make a go of it this time."

"He'll get there," Ripper says, then grimaces, "one day."

"It's inevitable when you're part of this world," I say, gesturing around.

No one can hear our conversation over the sound of the booming bass of house music that makes my ear drums want to bleed.

"Z…" Ripper leans closer. His breath tickles my neck and my body tenses at the sensation. "You don't have to be strong for everyone all the time. It's okay for things to not be okay. With Ash—"

"I don't want to talk about her," I snap, shutting him down.

At that moment, the bathroom door bursts open and two women spill out. One pulls her dress back down, adjusting it, while the other tries to pat away the lipstick smudged across her cheek.

I overhear one commenting, "What a jerk," as they hurry past.

Ripper and I exchange an unenthusiastic glance before heading into the bathroom to find Elliot slumped by the toilet, cradling its base like his life depends on it.

"Elliot?" I say cautiously, knowing better than to approach him outright.

He desperately tries to snort the remnants of who the fuck knows what off of the seat.

"She wants to cut me off," Elliot mutters. I'm unsure whether he's talking to us or himself until he looks up. His eyes have a glassy, dead appearance.

I shut the door behind us gently and lock it. There are

enough damn bathrooms in this place that we won't be disturbed.

"Who?" I question.

"Mom," he groans. "Mom wants to cut me off. She says I'm a failure. That I'll never amount to anything. I never won that Oscar. Since then…" His bottom lip trembles, and I'm reminded of how he used to follow me around when we were young, constantly seeking my approval.

I sigh. Addiction issues and crippling self-doubt go hand-in-hand.

"She doesn't mean it," I tell him. It's something she enjoys threatening. "She's just saying it because she wants you to get better, okay?"

"You didn't hear her," Elliot argues. A wail comes from the back of his throat as he sobs.

It's disconcerting to watch a grown man cry, and Ripper shifts on his feet, unsure whether he should be here, but I shoot him a glare to tell him to stay where he is. Elliot needs me, and I… well, I need him—not that I'd tell him that.

"Text Ve—Levi," I correct myself quickly, forgetting myself in the heat of the moment. "Tell him to meet us here."

"She means it, Zach. I know she does," Elliot cries, bringing his knees up to his chest and rocking back and forth while snot drips down his face. "Just look at me! I'm a failure, next to you… the golden boy…" He wipes his nose and narrows his eyes, turning vicious. "Her precious Lionheart son can do no wrong. No one measures up next to you. How am I supposed to compare?"

If Mom knew about my secret double life, her opinion of me would transform. A son who sings in a heavy metal

band would be more devastating to her than the thought of Botox being outlawed.

"It's not a competition," I try to remind him. "She loves you."

Our family has always battled trying to meet Mom's impossibly high standards. Elliot always struggled to find his place in the Royal family. Perhaps it was inevitable he turned out this way, and I can't help but wonder whether that could have been me.

Before I met Ripper and Venom, I was heading for a life of reckless partying. With a family destiny to fulfill, living under constant pressure takes its toll. While Elliot took drugs for a release, I turned to music and created another version of myself. The real me. Zed. The person I've always wanted to be.

There's a knock at the door.

I hold my hand out for my brother to take. "Levi is going to take you back to the hotel, okay?"

I'm in damage-control mode. If Mom is threatening to cut Elliot off, hearing rumors about how he embarrassed himself at a Lockhart party wouldn't do him any favors.

"No," Elliot objects, batting my hand away like an impetuous toddler. "I want to stay! It's a party."

I kneel until I'm at his eye level. My precious brother. So fucking broken. This is what fame and expectations do to people. A dream turned into a nightmare.

"If you don't leave," I say, hating myself for having to bargain this way but knowing it'll be for the best, "I'll call Mom."

The color drains from his face as he whispers, "You wouldn't."

"Wouldn't I?" I ask, holding out my hand again. "Do you want to take the risk?"

He staggers to his feet without assistance but lets Ripper steady him.

"Fine," Elliot hisses. "I'll leave."

We open the door to see Venom waiting.

"You get your wish," I say to him, nudging my head for Ripper to pass over Elliot like a piece of luggage. "Take Elliot back to the hotel. Make sure he doesn't speak to anyone else on the way out, and don't let him out of your sight, understand?"

Venom nods. "Got it."

I watch him and my brother disappear into the darkness and strobe lights.

"Zed," Ripper says, grabbing my hand and pulling me back into the bathroom. He corners me against the wall, surrounding me with the smell of his cologne. He smells good. Too fucking good. "I'm sorry about Elliot, I—"

I don't want to talk. I kiss him hard, pushing him back against the door. Ripper responds hungrily, matching my kiss with equal hunger as his stubble tickles against my freshly shaven face. Shit. His cock hardens in his pants, and his thick erection rubs against mine. His hot mouth and tongue fill the emptiness in my soul and the guilt that threatens to consume me.

Ripper pulls away from our kiss and asks with swollen lips, "Zed, are you sure you're okay?"

His eyes, wide with concern, irritate me.

"I don't want your fucking sympathy," I growl back, grabbing his hair with my hand to pull his head back. "I want to forget."

"Then I'll make you forget," Ripper purrs.

His hands slide over the bulge in my jeans, teasing my hard-on. We've never hooked up in public before. It's a risk, but I can't help myself. I need this. I need him.

I grab his throat, but he resists and comes at me. His hands slide under my shirt as our tongues fight each other in a battle he'll lose. I push for control, and he's on the verge of submitting, ready to take my pain away. I force him back into the sink.

"Turn around," I growl.

He does as I ask, and I watch our reflections in the mirror. I'd never been attracted to guys until Ripper. Before that, I was certain I was 100 percent hetero, but Ripper made me want to bend him over and do things straight guys would never dream of. He's the only man that's ever had that effect on me.

"Zed," he groans, his voice thick with lust and desire I want to quench.

I know what he's going to say, and I yank open the nearby bathroom cupboard.

I find what I'm looking for. There's always a bottle of lube lying around at these parties. When they're not working, celebrities have little else to do but fuck people they shouldn't.

I balance the lube on the sink. Ripper's pupils grow as he watches me in the mirror. He arches his back and pushes his ass against me. He wants this as much as I do.

I know he's been pining over Ash. Ripper is the type of man who usually fucks a different girl every night, but he hasn't shown an interest in anyone else since sleeping with Ash. But there's only so long he can jerk off over the memories without having to fuck.

I yank his pants down to his knees, taking a second to admire his perfectly tight ass, then pull a condom out of my pocket. I wasn't expecting to use it tonight, but it never hurts to be prepared.

His ass isn't as round as Ash's, but it'll do. I take my

cock out and drop my pants to my ankles. Fuck, I need something to take me away from here, remind me that there's more to life than this, and make me forget.

Outside the bathroom, the music is still booming. We won't be heard, and I'll be quick. I squirt lube down his ass and massage it around his asshole. His hot, tight hole that's just begging to be fucked. We don't have long, but I'll be quick. I tease him with my thumb, circling gently, then slide it inside him. A groan escapes his mouth, a deep growly moan that makes me even harder.

"Quiet," I warn him. The party may be loud, but anyone could be listening.

He nods, biting his lip. Fuck, he looks sexy as hell in his reflection as I pump my thumb in and out of him. My cock strains from desire, but I resist, working him to make sure he'll be ready.

I squirt more lube over him, massaging it in, then slather my shaft with it.

"Give me what I want, Zed," Ripper murmurs, clutching the sink tightly as his skin stretches over his knuckles. "I fucking need you."

I'm done waiting. I angle my cock, edging in slowly. First, the tip, enjoying the sensation of him opening for me. Ripper's shoulders tense, and he moans, sending vibrations racing through my body and making my balls tighten.

I want to bury myself inside him in a single thrust, but I have to control myself. I'm too big to do that, but we don't have long. My sharper thrusts become more aggressive as his ass widens to accommodate me. He takes me like the good boy he is.

"Fuck," Ripper moans as I grab his hair and yank his head back. "We both fucking needed this."

"Shut up," I hiss, releasing my grip and watching our reflection as he jerks forward from the force of another inch inside him.

I shut my eyes and think of the night I can't forget. Sharing Ash's body with my bandmates. How her moans were the sweetest melody as we took our pleasure and stole it from her—even fucking Ripper can't erase her from my mind.

Ripper bucks against me suddenly. The sudden movement takes me by surprise. I grunt and release, then withdraw. I needed that.

I pull out, remove the slippery condom, and flush it down the toilet. Fuck the environment. We made enough donations to charity, and one condom won't kill the ocean while oil companies are dumping into it. Maybe that could be the subject of a new Basilisk song.

"Zed…" Ripper spins around. There are tears in his eyes, and instantly, guilt swells from the pit of my stomach. Had I been too rough with him?

"Are you hurt?" I ask.

"No, baby," he says with a smile, running a finger along my cheekbone. "Are you?"

Usually, I put a stop to his sentimental bullshit. What happens between us is based on sex and primal instinct. We're there for each other when we're horny, and no one else is around to satisfy us. Yet, I don't push him off this time.

My mouth is dry and my voice is a pitch higher than usual. "Ripper…"

"You don't need to say anything," he says, pulling his pants up. His cock is still gloriously hard for me, but he has zero expectations for anything more. Instead, he wraps his muscular arms around me and squeezes tightly.

I don't struggle to free myself; I let him hold me. I sigh and think about the life I wished we had. A life where we don't have to be different people caught between two worlds.

"What do you say to a one-off Basilisk show?" Ripper asks. "I can get Ted to set it up. It's been a while since we played in the city, and we fucking need this."

I'm usually opposed to something this risky, especially now that the world is watching the Lionhearts more closely because of Popstarz. But if we don't let loose again soon, there's no way I'd make it through the next month of filming without doing something stupid.

"Do it," I growl. "Set it up."

The Basilisks are coming to town for one night only.

six

. . .

Ash

Dad's words rang through my head during the five-hour flight.

"Are you sure you'll be okay?"

It's the first time I've flown alone. If Dad had his way, he'd have driven me all the way, but it would have taken too long, and he couldn't get the days off work. Besides, Popstarz was happy to cover the bill for me to travel business class. When would I get the opportunity again?

Flying is strange. It reminds you of how small you are. We're nothing but a tiny dot on a huge planet. Up in the sky, I forgot about Popstarz, the Lionhearts, and the Basilisks—well, for a few minutes at least.

After waiting around for ages and struggling to find my luggage, I head out of the airport and see a limousine waiting. Everyone in the vicinity turns to stare as I stride past them. Some people take photographs on their cell phones as I stagger to the driver holding a sign with my name on it.

I thought a few journalists in Meadow Springs were

bad, but at least in a small place, they still saw me as Ash Cooper, the Sheriff's daughter.

I never stopped to think about how it would feel to have people recognize me. I know the final Camp Harmony show had an impact, and viral videos circulated the internet all summer, but it still doesn't make it any less strange. Millions of people watched me and knew my name, but they didn't know anything else about me.

"Hi," I stammer, keeping my gaze fixed on the ground, trying to avoid attention.

"Ashley," the driver says in greeting, tipping his hat. "Welcome."

A young girl runs over to us. She looks around twelve and has clip-in purple streaks in her hair, reminding me a little of myself at that age.

"Ashley," she calls, ignoring her parents who are trying to call her back. "Ashley!"

I turn around. "Um... Hi?"

"Can I have your autograph?" she asks.

"My autograph?"

"Yes." The girl giggles like I've said a joke and thrusts a napkin and pen under my face. "You were my favorite in the final show."

I scrawl my name—a total mess—and hand it back, mumbling, "Here you go."

Her whole face lights up. "Thanks, Ashley."

Her enthusiasm is contagious, and I wink. "You can call me Ash."

She squeals as her parents arrive to apologize. With firm hands on the girl's shoulders, they steer her in the opposite direction.

Wow. This is... fucking surreal. Is this something I should come to expect when I'm in the city? If a random

kid in the airport stopped me, how crazy are things going to get when Popstarz airs?

Doubt creeps in, making my palms sweat, as a voice in the back of my head wonders whether this is something I want.

Am I prepared for what's coming? I'm a small-town girl. A nobody. Just like Zach's mom said. Will Popstarz swallow me whole, and is that what Jacqueline intends?

"Come on," the driver says. He takes my luggage from me and opens the door. "I want to beat the traffic."

I'm in a daze as I climb inside. The limo is plush with black seats that make me feel like I'm about to slip right off of them. I'd have been more at home in Dad's old truck.

I press my nose against the tinted glass to watch the city move by. I've never visited a city this big before. The streets are living, breathing entities with a flow of their own. Everyone moves in their own way to create a symphony. Lights dazzle my eyes as tourists rush down the sidewalk, taking photos and pointing at items in stores with bright window displays. The beeping of cars, street vendors, and cabs weaving through traffic are overwhelming like stepping straight onto a movie set.

My driver doesn't speak to me. Maybe that's something I should get used to. A conversation I had with Damon—Ripper—at Camp Harmony comes back to me. At a mentoring session, he said that fame comes at a cost.

Goosebumps run up my arms, making me pull my denim jacket closer around my body like a cloak for protection. My fingers fly to the patch stitching and stroke the embroidered sentence. *Illegitimi non carborundum.*

After crawling through slow traffic, we finally come to a stop outside a red brick hotel. It's taller than any building in Meadow Springs, and security guards stand

by its entrance, which only adds to the intimidating effect.

"We're here," the driver declares. He huffs in agitation and checks the clock pointedly to hurry me when I don't move. "I'll follow with your luggage."

"Thanks," I stammer. I can't hide forever. A couple of photographers milling around start heading in our direction like piranhas getting the first scent of blood. They must have found out that this is the location where the Popstarz contestants are staying for the show's duration.

Flashes of white light blind me as I step out of the limo. I thought celebrities wore sunglasses as a disguise, but now I know differently. Somehow, despite the lights in my vision, I stagger past them and find refuge in the foyer.

I blink twice to shake away the blurs from my vision.

"Ashley." Amber, who I recognize as being Jacqueline's assistant from Camp Harmony, hurries to greet me. She must have been waiting. I stand like a mannequin as she drops an air kiss on both of my cheeks like we're old friends. Has she forgotten how she marched me through the mess hall to Jacqueline's office to be reprimanded the last time we saw each other? "It's great to see you again."

"You too," I reply in a voice that implies the opposite.

"Let's check you in," Amber says, overlooking my sullen response. "Jacqueline thought it may be nice for you to see a friendly face when you got here."

A friendly face? Yeah, right. More like she wants someone to spy on me already.

"Great," I reply, feigning a yawn. "I'm pretty tired. It was a long flight."

"Of course you are." Amber smiles, but it doesn't meet her eyes. "Let's get you your key, and I'll show you to your room."

She escorts me to the front desk and swipes the keycard from the concierge's hands before he can say a word.

"This way," she says.

Her signature heels clack against the marble floor as she leads me to the elevator. A giant crystal chandelier casts a soft light over us, while the sound of a piano playing in the background creates a grand ambiance. This is far from home.

We step inside, and she presses the button for the twelfth floor. There are fifteen in total. Hiring out the entire hotel for the duration of the show must have cost an eye-watering amount.

I cringe at my reflection in the mirrored elevator. It gives me a fantastic three-hundred-and-sixty-degree view of how shitty I look. Red-faced. Greasy hair. Dark circles under my eyes.

"You're the last person to arrive," Amber says. "All the other contestants showed up yesterday. All of you, the judges, and the Lionhearts are staying here for the duration of the competition. It makes it easier for logistics. There are a lot of photo ops and early starts. There's also plenty of rehearsal space here. They've even changed the basement into a dance studio." I struggle to pay attention as Amber drones on, listing the hotel's other facilities when all I can think about is going to sleep. "There are eight other contestants, plus two bands. But we all know bands never win Popstarz, even if they become more successful afterward..." The elevator pings as we climb higher, but Amber talks at double speed to compensate and ensure she covers everything in the quick journey. "You'll be meeting the others soon, which I'm sure you're excited about."

"Yeah," I say with the enthusiasm of a mourner at a funeral. "I'm super pumped."

If Tiffany and the Lockets are anything to go by, I'm not exactly brimming with enthusiasm at the thought of meeting my fellow contestants. Maybe Popstarz will be different. Camp Harmony is competitive, but you have to go there—unless you're like me, a rare unicorn who gets a scholarship. On the contrary, anyone can apply to Popstarz. Auditions are aired, then they invite the finalists straight to the live shows. They used to include a boot camp element, but they scrapped that a few years back. They prefer to jump straight into the shows after viewing numbers took a dip.

The elevator pings, making me breathe a sigh of relief. I step out into an impeccable hallway. Tall black doors are spaced out along the hall, and each of them has a plaque with a golden number and name.

"You're at the end here," Amber says, leading the way.

I grimace at the sight of Tiffany's name on the door next to mine and hope I can sneak past without running into her.

"Thanks for showing me to my room," I say, swiping my keycard to open it, hoping Amber will take the hint.

Instead, Amber does the opposite. She steps right on in without an invitation. Rude much? If only she was a vampire and needed my permission to cross the threshold…

"I'll show you around," she volunteers, trying to be helpful, but I don't trust her. She's Jacqueline's foot soldier, and she'll have an ulterior motive hidden behind her perfectly styled hair.

"I think I'll be fine," I reply, but she's already halfway across the room.

It's more than a room. It's basically an entire apartment with an open-plan design and wooden floors. On the right, a kitchen area is minimal in design, with a sleek stove and white cupboards without handles. How are you supposed to open them?

Beyond that is a marble table with four white chairs that look like they belong in a spaceship. Past those is a living room area with a long white sofa, candles nestled atop a fireplace, and a giant window that takes up most of the exposed wall.

"Before I leave you," Amber says, standing at the table where papers are neatly placed. She picks one up. "I need you to sign another contract."

I already had to sign multiple contracts before arriving. Thankfully, Dad knows good lawyers who owe him a favor and looked over them before signing. The agreements covered what you'd expect for any television show: outlining terms and conditions, agreeing you understood that the show would be edited at the producer's discretion, outlining various stipulations for what would happen if you won the prize… not that I expect to get that far.

The prize is the same every year. Eight contestants—well, nine after my last-minute addition—battle it out to win half a million dollars in cash and a coveted record deal with Starnote.

"What's this?" I frown as I skim over the document. After a long flight and staying awake for hours on end, the text swims before my eyes.

"It outlines the accepted conduct for contestants while you're living here," Amber says, thrusting a shiny pen into my hands. "All you have to do is sign right here." She points at the dotted line.

"I'll look in the morning," I say firmly, putting the

paper down and crossing my arms over my chest. I'm not as naïve as I was at the start of the summer. Camp Harmony showed me the lengths people will go to get what they want, and I'm not putting my name on anything until a lawyer reads it first.

Amber's smile sours like she's sucked a lemon.

"Fine," she says, turning up her nose. "I'll be back in the morning to get your signature." She sniffs, nodding at the big stack of remaining papers on the table. "You can read through those, too. They explain your schedule for the next few weeks. You can have your manager look it over."

My mouth goes dry. "My manager?"

"Don't you have one?" She laughs, then adds, "I guess there may not be a point if you don't get far. We can always assign someone to you from Starnote."

"I'll be fine," I say hastily, feeling the urge to whack Amber over the head with the stack of papers. I mirror her fake smile and chime, "Thanks, Amber."

Her lip curls. "I'll see you tomorrow."

She saunters away. My shoulders sag in relief as soon as the door clicks behind her.

I walk around, awe-struck, even extending my arms and twirling a few times. Holy shit. This place is beautiful, straight from the pages of a glossy magazine. It's sophisticated and worlds apart from my childhood bedroom with band posters plastered across the walls, or the cozy cabin draped with wall hangings that Cookie and I shared during camp.

I slip my sneakers off, terrified to make a mess, and shuffle over to shut the blinds. The view looks onto another row of buildings and gives a good view of the street below. I'm at the back of the hotel, so I don't see the

tree-lined entrance, but a bird's-eye view of the dumpsters and delivery trucks pulling in reminds me that I'm still in the real world.

I saunter toward an adjoining door that leads to a corridor. Two rooms are leading off it. I step into the first one. Damn, I don't think I've ever seen a bed so big. The crisp linen is bright white, almost blinding me, and the pillows are perfectly plumped. There's a dressing table, complete with light bulbs around its edges, and an entire wall is a sliding wardrobe.

I want to sink into the freshly laundered sheets and pass out, but I need to wash the grime off me. I leave the bedroom and enter through a second door to a bathroom. There are rows of shampoo, body lotion, and soaps lined up. Brands I haven't heard of, but judging by their understated luxurious packaging, I can tell the price of them would make my eyes water.

"Oh!" I gasp as I step onto the tiles in my socks and jump back. I gingerly hold my toe out, taken aback by the toasty heat on the soles of my feet. Nice. Now that is something I could get used to.

Thick towels are expertly stacked, and the bath is big enough to fit three people. If soaking in the tub isn't your thing, there's a separate shower with a fancy waterfall head. I doubt I'll be competing in Popstarz for long, but while I'm here, I'm going to make the most of it.

If my room is this incredible, I can't imagine how flashy the judges' rooms are… or the three men I'll have to face sooner or later.

Despite sleeping on a mattress that feels like you're suspended on a fluffy cloud, I didn't sleep well. I tossed and turned, unsettled by being in a strange place.

I wake to texts from Dad, Brick, and Cookie—all asking how I'm doing. Cookie demands pictures of the hotel and asks whether I've met any of the other contestants yet.

I decide to reply to them after I've had a caffeine hit. It takes ten minutes to figure out how the machine on the kitchen counter works, but it's worth it. While I wait, I grab my laptop and send over copies of the contract to Dad for his lawyer friend to look over.

It doesn't look legally binding, but I want to be sure. There are pages outlining codes of conduct: no drugs, no unsanctioned media interviews, magazine appearances, or photoshoots while the show is airing. I recognize many clauses from my Camp Harmony contract. It seems Jacqueline, and Starnote, are the real puppet masters behind Popstarz. There are other documents to look through among the big stack Amber left. Schedules for rehearsals, mealtimes… blah… blah… who knew I'd be swapping one prison for another?

Footsteps in the corridor make me freeze, followed by a shuffling noise as someone slides a golden envelope underneath my room door.

I tip-toe over to it, press my ears to the door, and wait until the footsteps disappear before moving again.

My name is written on the front in cursive font. If it were from the Basilisks, they'd call me Ash—wouldn't they? Stop being ridiculous, Ash. As if they're going to be writing to you.

I tear it open and slide out an invitation.

You are invited to the first Popstarz opening mixer.

All contestants and judges are required to meet in the
dining room at 7 p.m. for dinner.
Dress code - formal attire.
Wardrobe and makeup will be sent to your rooms at 3 p.m.

Before I have time to consider the implications and fully breathe a sigh of relief that I'll not have to wear any of the clothes I've brought from home, my phone buzzes again.

Instead of Cookie pestering me for photographs, I swallow hard as I see a text flash over the screen.

Unknown: You can't avoid me forever.

The wardrobe department arrives on the dot, along with an army of three makeup and hair wizards. A hipster stylist with tortoiseshell glasses wheels a rack of designer dresses inside.

"Well?" he asks in a thick Italian accent, tapping his foot impatiently and sniffing in disgust at my loungewear attire as I dare to approach the rack. I gingerly flick through a few of the choices. "What do you like? What calls out to you?"

"You can choose," I reply. His hand hovers over a bright pink dress, making me add hastily, "but maybe something dark. I don't do bright."

He huffily whooshes through and selects a purple dress. His lips curl into a smile as he holds it out against me.

"Yes," he declares. "Perfect."

The makeup and hair team nod with enthusiastic agreement. Am I supposed to say something? I err on the side of caution and say nothing.

"Wear this one," he orders.

I regard it cautiously. It's not something I'd usually wear, but I don't argue with the shrewd fashionista. The dress has a tight-fitting top half with a flippy skater skirt. The stylist is already searching through a shelf on the bottom of the rack filled with shoes. He chooses a chunky pair of black boots. Now those are more my style.

"Pair it with these," he says in a bored tone, thrusting them into my hands along with a pair of silver earrings. "We'll leave you to change. Enjoy the evening."

I don't question how he knows my size as he disappears out of the room, wheeling the clothes away, moving on to save his next victim of a fashion crime.

"Let's get your hair sorted," a woman says. "Do you ever do anything with it?"

The three of them gather around me like a flock of fussing birds and move me over to the dining table without having to push. I plop myself into a chair, suddenly feeling very self-conscious of my bare face next to the gorgeous women who look ready for the catwalk.

"You must be excited," one says as she gets to work, plugging in a curling iron. I almost tell her to give up as curls usually fall out of my straight hair but decide against it. "Everyone can't wait for the next series of Popstarz to start."

"Yeah," I say unconvincingly, "it's gonna be great…"

The makeup artist puts two fingers under my chin, lifts it, and turns my face at all angles. I squirm under her scrutiny. She's looking at me, but she isn't really seeing me. My features are just another blank canvas for her to work her magic.

"Why don't we put some music on, hm?" she suggests, sauntering to the television and putting on MTV. The Lionhearts' faces fill the screen, and I flinch, looking away.

"You're so lucky to get to work with the Lionhearts. I've heard they're great guys."

"They're okay, I guess," I mumble as she turns up the volume, and I grind my teeth. I guess it beats small talk though, right? She lines up various products, so many that it almost covers the entire surface of the table. She starts by massaging an orange-smelling lotion into my skin. "Are you sure all of this is necessary?"

They all laugh like I've told a funny joke. Isn't this all a bit much for a simple dinner at the hotel?

I only say a few words for the rest of the transformation process. My nails dig into my skin as I ball my hands into fists and fight my instincts to escape from their clutches, scrub my face clean, and hide from the world.

I expected to feel out of my depth when the competition started, but I hadn't considered everything else happening outside of rehearsals and live shows. Being on Popstarz is like becoming an A-list celebrity overnight. Everyone is watching your every move, and there is no room for slip-ups.

"Close your eyes," they say. Despite the layers of makeup on my face, it doesn't feel heavy like it often does when I apply my own. I do as they ask as they mist my face with a setting spray. A few seconds later, she declares, "Perfect. We're done."

They spin me around in the chair so fast I almost get whiplash and shove a mirror under my nose.

Is that really me? I have to blink twice to check. It's the first time I've had my makeup professionally done, and I look like me… but better. Just like when Bella turned into a vampire in *Twilight.*

My winged eyeliner is flawless, and my smokey eyes are perfectly blended with subtle purple hints that match

my dress. A light non-sticky gloss and plum liner give my lips an extra plump look, and the dusting of blush over my cheekbones makes me look just the right level of alive.

"Thanks," I say. "You've done a great job."

"We know," the makeup artist chirps with a smug smirk. "Enjoy your evening."

They pack up their suitcases and trot away. They really are wizards. I check the time—only ten minutes until I have to be downstairs. I decide to head down early.

If I'm going to see the Basilisks again, this is how I want to look when I do it.

I wait for the elevator, relieved not to be greeted by Tiffany. Instead, another woman joins me. She looks just as glamorous as me, so I assume she's another contestant. Her curly hair bounces around her chin, and she reminds me of a red-haired Marilyn Monroe. She looks older than me—early thirties, I'd guess. Her gold, sequin dress hugs her curvy figure and gives her an impressive cleavage that makes it hard to look away.

"Umm… Hi," I say, deciding to make conversation.

Her eyes widen in surprise, then her face breaks into a wide, friendly grin.

"You're Ashley Cooper," she says, holding out her hand. "I'm Meredith Rayne."

"Meredith," I repeat, shaking her hand. "It's great to meet you. You can call me Ash. Everyone else does."

She twists her ankle to draw my attention to her six-inch heels and screws up her face. "I don't know why they gave me these. I won't be able to walk in them."

There's a warmness about her. After the lack of welcome I received at Camp Harmony, I assumed it would be the same atmosphere here. Perhaps it won't be so bad after all.

"You'll be fine," I try to reassure her. "You can always hold on to my arm, and you look amazing."

"Thanks," she says, but casts a lingering look at my flat boots enviously. "Gosh, they look so comfortable."

"A perk of being tall," I say with a shrug, then wink. "They don't want me towering over everyone else."

The elevator pings and we get inside. Entering the party with someone else will help put my nerves at ease.

"Have you met anyone else here yet?" Meredith asks. "I guess you already know Tiffany Lockhart. Then again, who doesn't? That girl is basically a celebrity already."

"Yep, I know Tiffany," I reply wryly, refraining from calling her a bitch. "But I haven't met anyone else yet."

"Same," she says, barely stopping to take a breath. "I work as a wedding singer normally. That's where I was scouted for the show. I never thought I'd get on it..." She's the kind of person who talks a lot when she's nervous. She'll be a good ally to have when my instinct is to go quiet. Her chatter helps distract me from the knots tightening in my stomach as we get closer to the ground floor. The shrill ding makes me jump. "I guess this is us."

I take a deep breath and step out after her. Amber is waiting in the foyer, directing people to an adjoining bar and restaurant area.

"It's nice the two of you could finally make it," Amber says with a tinkling laugh that makes me instantly feel like a five-year-old. "Where is your signed contract, Ashley?"

"My lawyer sent it this morning," I say. After a quick call with Dad, he got it checked. As much as they want to try to control every aspect of our lives when we're here, there is nothing binding in there. The behavior clause is basically a glorified recommendation. "Didn't you receive it?"

"I'll check." She sniffs in disapproval, swiping her phone screen with her talons. "It all looks in order." She nods. "This way."

"I thought we were early," Meredith whispers under her breath as we follow her.

"Welcome to Popstarz," I mutter.

"This is..."

Even Meredith can't find the words. The space looks like it could fit over a hundred people, but it's eerily empty, with one long table set for thirteen. Classical music plays, multiple chandeliers twinkle across the wooden floor, and each place setting has more cutlery than I know what to do with. Waiting staff hold drinks on trays around the room. There are more of them than there are guests.

My eyes dart around. The Lionhearts—or should I say, the Basilisks—haven't arrived yet.

No one has sat down yet. They mill around near the table, sipping from champagne flutes. Jacqueline is deep in conversation with the other judges, Jacinta Vickers, and Yu Jin, while Tessa Pope, the cheery show host, stands nearby. Tiffany hovers, trying to inject herself into their conversations. She looks more gorgeous than ever in a startling emerald floor-length dress.

Other contestants float around. A group of four men stand in a huddle formation, looking like a boy band. There's a group of three girls, talking behind their hands and giggling while checking out the boy band, who I assume are in a band of their own from their coordinated outfits.

Popstarz normally has two bands and six soloists, but there are seven this year because of my last-minute addition. The first in Popstarz's history.

Another woman with a black bob stands alone in a

corner, yawning and looking bored. I catch her eye and smile, but she looks away instantly. A soloist who prefers to be alone.

There are three other men: a skinny guy who looks like he's still a freshman, a sharply dressed muscular man with a well-groomed beard who gives off easy-going vibes, and a darkly handsome maverick who is busy checking out Tiffany's ass.

Jacqueline notices Meredith and me entering, and she clears her throat. She chimes her glass to catch everyone's attention, and silence descends over the room. In her all-white suit, she looks like a powerful scientist ready to take over the world.

"Welcome, everyone," Jacqueline says. The boy band claps and whoops but promptly stops after receiving one of her withering glares. She continues, ignoring their interruption. "Congratulations for making it onto Popstarz. Tonight is an opportunity to get to know your fellow contestants before practice starts ahead of the first live show in a week. One of you standing here," she pauses for dramatic effect, "will win half a million dollars and a recording contract with Starnote. You've beaten thousands of people to be here today." Her stare lands on me. "Don't blow the chance you've been given." She claps her hands to signal the end of her speech and holds her arms out. "Now take a seat next to your place card."

"I hope we're sitting together," Meredith says hopefully, but she can't help staring at the gorgeous bearded guy with the smoothest-looking mahogany skin and glittering amber eyes. She drops her voice. "Or maybe I can deal with sitting next to him."

I cast a glance at the name card where Meredith's crush sits. "Next to Marcus."

"Marcus," she repeats, practically drooling, then lets out a tiny squeal to see her name next to him. "See ya later."

I groan as I circle the table. Meredith is lucky to be next to Marcus and surrounded by the girls from the band. Unfortunately, I'm on the opposite end of the table next to Tiffany and Jacqueline—right where she can keep her eye on me.

"Nice to see you again, Ashley," Tiffany simpers, shooting me a fake smile. Her pretending to be nice doesn't fool me.

"Shame I can't say the same for you," I reply under my breath, quiet enough that only she can hear me.

Tiffany's lip curls. What did she expect? The bitch could have killed me. After I discovered what happened to Riley and how she could be partially responsible for the accident, I'm definitely not going to start kissing her ass now. I'll act civil for the cameras, but I won't be fake.

Tiffany turns away from me and asks Jacqueline, "Aren't the Lionhearts coming tonight?"

When everyone sits down, the table is full.

"They couldn't make it," Jacqueline answers. "They have other commitments, but they'll be here tomorrow."

There is a collective sigh from all the other girls around the table, particularly the band. I pour myself a glass of water, wishing it was vodka.

"I saw Zach a few days ago," Tiffany croons, attracting the attention of the table and lapping up every second. She isn't famous in her own right yet, but everyone knows who she is. She flicks her hair over her shoulder, relishing how everyone is hanging onto her words. I bite down on my back teeth, but I have no right to be annoyed. I liked Zed from the Basilisks, but I never

signed up to date Zach Royal. "Zach is just so excited to be here."

"What's he like?" a girl asks.

"We're super close," Tiffany says, narrowing her eyes in a look that says, *He's mine, bitch.* Pathetic. Oh, how I'd love to wipe the smirk off her face and tell her about what happened that night on Buggy, but that'd also mean accepting Zed and Zach were the same fucking person. "Our families have known each other forever. I know he's so stoked to spend more time with me. With them being mentors at Camp Harmony too, it's like they can't stay away."

"You must know them too then, Ash?" Meredith chips in and receives a death glare from Tiffany. Unfortunately for her, a chance conversation with me in an elevator has secured her a place in Tiffany's bad books. I should have warned her.

"They're great," I reply with a flat voice, then allow the rest of the conversation to flow without me as our food arrives. At least eating gives me something to focus on. I watch the judges carefully select the right spoon for the soup and copy them.

I learn that the other female soloist is called Priya. Aside from introducing herself, she remains silent and clicks her tongue impatiently at Tiffany's bragging remarks—unlike the girl band, who call themselves Candy Kisses.

The boy band, United, talks among themselves at the end of the table with the youngest guy who calls himself Spark. The other soloist who has spent most of the dinner ogling Tiffany is called Theo. He keeps trying to interject into Tiffany's conversations but keeps being rebuffed. The

guy is handsome, but he's too eager. Someone needs to tell him to take a hint.

I nod along to conversations I'm only half paying attention to and hope the main course won't be long. As Tiffany leans around me to chat with Jacqueline, Jacinta Vickers shoots me an apologetic smile. I've noticed she doesn't say a lot, but whenever she does, people pay attention. Yu Jin's hands are glued to his phone, and he doesn't look up from the screen. He even leaves the table to take a call.

Tiffany and Jacqueline discuss how the rest of the competition will work. There's a show at the end of each week. All contestants will get allocated a judges' team, and a different Lionheart mentor will support each team. After the live shows, the public gets to vote on who they want to keep in the competition.

Jacqueline stays tight-lipped when questioned about what the theme for the first show will be, or what teams we're on, but we'll find out tomorrow after rehearsals start.

We'll have dance rehearsals and work with vocal coaches for several hours a day. Our grueling schedules will have a mix of free time, plus other Popstarz activities.

I excuse myself from the table after the main course before dessert arrives. The portions are tiny, and I make a mental note to find out where the best food joints are in the neighborhood. How can I perform when I'm hungry?

I slink away to the nearest bathroom. When I'm safely inside the stall, I steady my breathing.

Remember why you're doing this, Ash. I'm here because I want a music career. This is giving me a platform to do that.

I quickly text Cookie to let her know that Jacqueline and Tiffany are just as unbearable away from Camp

Harmony when an alert pops up on my screen, making me almost drop my phone in the toilet.

"Fuck," I curse, grateful that I'm alone.

Although I've tried to ignore the latest news from the Basilisks, old habits are hard to let go, and I still receive alerts from their Wiki page.

A bright red banner flashes over the screen. *Surprise tour!*

Their updates have been very infrequent since their short tour ended. Their next album doesn't have an official release date yet. An album I know will be fucking amazing after hearing them rehearse.

My hands are shaking as I click on their website to find out more. I'm not sure whether to be angry, annoyed, or downright impressed that those bastards skipped out on the Popstarz opening dinner to perform a surprise Basilisk's gig. So much for Starnote business…

I know it's only a matter of time before I see them again, but it'll be hard to speak to them under Jacqueline's scrutiny. This could be the best chance I have of talking to them alone.

Fuck it.

If those assholes are going to bail on dinner, then I will too. I leave the bathroom to be accosted immediately by a "helpful" member of staff. Their attentiveness makes me uneasy.

"Is everything okay?"

"Sorry," I say, holding my head like I'm in pain. "Can you send my apologies for the rest of dinner? I'm not feeling so good… I think I have to lie down."

"No problem, Ms. Cooper. I'll share the message," the guy bows his head like I'm royalty. "Is there anything else I can do for you?"

"Not right now," I say, then change my mind. "Actually, is there a more inconspicuous way to leave the building? You know, for future reference."

He beams, pleased to help, and says, "Our celebrity clients choose to use the back entrance, including the Lionhearts." He continues to explain how to get out without having to step onto the main street.

"Thank you," I reply. "You've been really helpful."

He hurries away to deliver my message. His chest puffs out with pride at having a purpose, and it gives me an opening.

I take the elevator back to my room, knowing I've got a limited window to get out without anyone noticing.

As soon as I slam the door to my room behind me, I turn my suitcase upside down and search through it until I find an oversized hoodie. I put it over my dress and zip it up. It covers the dress entirely. I shove my hair up into a ponytail, then put a beanie hat on. With that and my sunglasses, I should be able to get to the Basilisks show without being recognized.

Jacqueline would be pissed if she discovered I snuck out of the hotel on the first night, but I'm a grown freaking adult. There's nothing in the contract I signed about staying here all the time. Besides, I'll make sure I'm not caught.

I text Cookie again, letting her know where I'm heading and linking her to the webpage. I may be doing something stupid, but she's the only person I can trust with this. She's the only one who knows about my date with the Basilisks.

Me: I'm sneaking out to see the Basilisks. They're performing here…

Cookie: Are you sure that's a good idea?

Hell fucking no, it isn't a good idea, but I need to see them again as the guys I thought they were. I have to see them in their true form again.

Me: I'll let you know when I get home.

eight

. . .

Ash

No one pays any attention as I slip past the chefs who are applying carefully considered garnishes to tiny chocolate pots. They look delicious, but my sugar craving is superseded by something else… my hunger for answers.

I only have to walk a short distance up the block to hail a cab. The driver doesn't look twice as I give him the address and we speed away into the night.

It takes an hour to reach the venue, a shady-looking underground club. The Basilisks are smart not to perform on the hotel's doorstep.

Pulsing bass and smashing drums make the walls vibrate and remind me of the last time we performed together. I thought that singing with them was the best moment of my life until I learned the truth.

The show will finish soon, so I decide to look for Buggy. They'll have parked their bus close by. They don't go anywhere without it—unless they want to risk being seen without their disguises.

I stroll through the empty streets, hugging my hoodie tighter around my body to keep out the cool night breeze.

Passersby give me a strange look for wearing sunglasses in the dark, but I have to be sure no one will recognize me. I can't risk having another viral video disaster.

Just as I'm considering turning around and storming into the club, I spot a familiar figure leaning against the wall and smoking a cigarette. Ted. The Basilisks manager.

I stomp over to him and demand, "Where's Buggy?"

"Nice try, sweetheart," he says, blowing a cloud of smoke in my face and making me scowl. I lower my sunglasses. "Oh, it's you…" He chuckles. "Congratulations on getting on Popstarz. I didn't think I'd see you around here again."

I cross my arms. "I need to speak to the Basilisks."

He raises his eyebrow, inhaling deeply. "So do all the other fans. We don't all get what we want."

"They want to speak to me too," I say with confidence.

Well, I assume they do. Why else would Ripper text me?

"No can do," Ted says. "No one gets past me. The Basilisks didn't tell me they invited you. Zed would have my head if I let someone hang out on Buggy without them there."

"I'm not asking to hang out there," I say, glowering at him. He's enjoying being an asshole. "All I want to do is wait there until they get back."

He sighs. "You're not gonna give up, are you?"

I incline my chin defiantly and reply, "Nope."

We stare each other down. Neither of us wants to back down or look away. It's starting to drizzle. A few water droplets hit my forehead and bounce off, but I don't blink.

"Shit," Ted curses as the rain comes down heavier and extinguishes his cigarette.

I grin as he breaks his stare. I win.

"You're not going to let me stand out here in the rain, are you?" I ask.

"Fine," he grumbles, "but you're taking the fall for this."

"Sure," I reply.

We weave through the backstreets together. I take off my glasses, pulling my hoodie up over my head further. No one will recognize me in streets this dim.

"We've parked her in storage. Buggy needs some work done before the next tour season," Ted explains as we take a turn. I avoid pointing out his questionable use of the word "her" for fear of him changing his mind. I need him if I don't want to get lost—these streets are like a maze. "It's time for her to get an upgrade, you know."

"How long will it be until the show ends?" I ask, hoping to cut him off before he launches into a lecture about cars.

We're halfway down the street of large storage units, so large that they look like they could store a bus. He pauses at a shutter. On the wall, he presses buttons on a keypad, and the shutter rolls up with a shriek.

"The show should be finished now," he says, checking his watch. "They don't want to hang around tonight. They'll be back soon."

"I'll just wait here," I say.

"Don't think I'm letting you inside alone, Ashley Cooper," he says, wagging his finger. "Not without them around. Who knows what you'll do?"

"What do you think I'll do?" I narrow my eyes. "Trash the place?"

"After what you did at the Camp Harmony show, who knows what you're capable of." He shrugs. "It was a ballsy move, but reckless."

"You watched it then?" I ask.

"I guess." He checks his cell and groans. "I need to make a call. Just wait here, okay? Don't touch anything."

"I won't," I reply with a sly smile, stepping inside as soon as he starts talking to his mom.

Buggy fills most of the space. The space is almost as tall as it is wide. I follow the flame lines with my eyes, trying to forget about what happened the last time I was on the bus.

As voices approach, I freeze. I'd been intent on coming here, but I haven't thought about what I'll say when I see them again. I press my back against the wall to hide from view.

"Where were you, man?" Ripper asks Ted, who is busy looking around, trying to find me in the darkness.

He clears his throat nervously, then says, "You have a visitor."

"A visitor?" Zed snaps.

The Basilisks step out of the rain as I move out of the shadows.

They are still in costume. Zed dons a full-length trench coat with black feathers at its edges. He looks like the king of hell with a thorny crown on his head, and a pointed metallic mask covering his face.

Next to him, Ripper wears full leather and a bug-like silver mask with enormous eyes that look like they'll change colors under different lights.

Venom lurks behind them both. His favorite pumpkin mask covers his face. A ragged black jumper trails down at his knees, making him resemble a terrifying scarecrow.

All of them stop when they see me. I look into their masks with zero fear, not caring that my hair is stuck to my forehead and mascara is running down my cheeks.

I try to sound braver than I feel and say, "We need to talk."

Zed turns to Ted in accusation and growls, "You let her in?"

Now I know what he sounds like without the voice changer. I try to pick out intonations that could give his identity away, but it's a struggle. Their deception has taken years of practice and skill to pull off.

"Hey man." Ted raises his hands. "She insisted!"

"We can talk inside, Ash," Ripper says, first to break from the line-up.

He swaggers toward me with confidence. A walk I recognize as being Damon Archer's. How did I miss that? Was I so star-struck by seeing the men I idolized for the first time in the flesh?

"Fine," I snap, marching over to Buggy's door. "That works."

"Why don't you come back later, Ted?" Ripper suggests.

"Fine by me," Ted replies, scuttling away, pleased to be free from Zed's furious, red-eyed glare. The bold contacts make it look like he's shooting lasers through his mask.

Ripper opens the door to Buggy and bows slightly. "After you."

The lights come on automatically as I climb the steps. I focus on putting one foot in front of the other to contain my rising panic. We need to have this conversation. It's better we're in a place where we won't be disturbed and don't have Starnote or the media breathing down our necks.

I drag my gaze from the floor and sofas, where I'd writhed and moaned as the three of them took turns fucking me.

Ripper follows behind, then Zed strides in, and Venom shuffles along after them, bowing his head like he's committed a crime. Venom spilling their secret must have resulted in Zed giving him a tough time, but I'm glad he told me—at least one of them is honest.

The door shuts behind us, followed by a drawn-out, awkward silence. Ripper goes to take his mask off.

"Keep it on," I insist, stopping him.

It will be easier to say what I need to without seeing their faces.

Ripper drops his hands to his sides, while Zed crosses his arms, and I can't tell where Venom is looking behind his pumpkin head.

"Why are you here?" Zed asks, his echoing voice booming.

Zach Royal is someone who can command a stage. He's known for his hospitable nature and how well he treats his fans. The man in front of me is a different person.

"Because you lied to me," I say. I have to know the truth. "How can you pretend to be someone you're not?"

"You never asked us who we were," Ripper reminds me.

"Smart ass," I reply. "That was before I knew you were the Lionhearts." My chest flushes with anger. I've imagined this moment millions of times over the last few weeks, but now my mouth is dry, and Ripper's growly voice is having an entirely different effect on me. "How can you—"

Zed tilts his head to the side and asks, "Are you trying to ask how we can be the nation's sweethearts and the metal band who screwed your brains out?"

I sputter as blood races to my cheeks. I never expected

him to be so candid. He's probably smirking underneath his mask at my reaction, and that only makes me angrier.

"How did you do it?" I demand. "How have you gotten away with it for so long? How has no one found out about who you are?"

There are so many questions I want to ask, and these are only the start.

"It hasn't been easy," Ripper replies with a nonchalant shrug. He heads to the bar and cracks open a beer. "Does anyone else want one?"

"No," I growl.

"We became the Basilisks when we were in Camp Harmony," Venom murmurs. To my surprise, he isn't wearing a voice changer, and I recognize his voice instantly. "Being the Basilisks is the only chance we get to be free. It all began when we snuck out and played at shows in disguise. It was fun at the start, but then it spiraled… and then… we couldn't be the Basilisks anymore. Everything changed when we got signed by Starnote."

"So, you sold out?" I ask.

Zed scoffs. "Isn't that what you did by coming to Camp Harmony?"

"We're not talking about me, Zach."

He flinches at my use of his real name.

"What?" I mock. "Shouldn't I call you that?"

"I know you're upset," Ripper steps in to reason with me, but I don't want to listen to his bullshit. "You don't understand everything yet. Zed comes from a different world. Would Vanessa Royal want her son to form a metal band? Of course not. We needed to survive, and it was the only way we could. Venom and I don't come from money.

Being a Lionheart allowed us to pursue what we wanted to do. The Basilisks are in our fucking blood."

"Does anyone else know who you are?" I ask.

"No." Venom shakes his head. "Only you."

I nod, trying to take it all in. As angry as I am, I can't help but feel special that I'm the only person to be privy to their secret.

"We're careful," Zed says, stepping closer. "We cover our tracks. We've spent years disguising our voices, changing how we walk, juggling our commitments, and covering Venom's tattoos and scars when we perform as the Lionhearts. And we all agreed to stick to one rule. One rule that was more important than anything else—tell no one who we are. Until Venom broke it."

Building tension simmers in the air between them. At one time, causing a rift between my favorite band would have been my worst nightmare. The Basilisks have meant the fucking world to me, and now they appeared to be crumbling… because of me.

"I'm glad he told me," I reply.

"But I shouldn't have told you like that," Venom says, shifting his weight from one foot to the other. "It wasn't fair."

"No," I agree, "it wasn't."

Ripper puts a straw in the beer bottle, pokes it through the hole in his mask, and sips loudly. The slurping stops abruptly, and he asks, "Why have you been ignoring my texts?"

I laugh. Is he for fucking real?

"Have you told anyone?" Zed asks, straight back to his interrogation. Of course that's all he cares about. Their precious fucking secret. Hasn't he stopped to think about how I feel after he used me for a night?

"No, and I'll keep your secret," I say, "but only because I don't want anyone else to feel the disappointment I did when I found out that you're fucking imposters."

"Don't pretend you're any better than us, Ash," Zed sneers. "You act self-righteous, but the truth is, we all know you wouldn't have been interested in us if you knew who we were."

I step back like he's slapped me. A cop car's siren doesn't drown out the thudding of my heart.

"Go on," Zed continues, "tell me I'm wrong."

I say nothing.

Zed laughs and gestures to Ripper and Venom. "These two actually thought you cared about us. They thought you understood and wanted to know the real us. So, answer this question, Ash... If you knew who we were under our masks, would you have come back to our tour bus that night?"

My mouth opens and closes. I wipe my clammy hands against my hoodie, refusing to look at Ripper and Venom, whose stares are burning into me, waiting.

"Answer his question, Ash," Ripper says. His tone isn't filled with malice but laced with a lingering hope for an answer I can't give.

"No," I answer. "I wouldn't have come back to the tour bus if I knew who you really were. How could I ever get close to people who are living a lie? How can I trust a single word you say?"

"You're the one that's lying to yourself, Ash," Zed snarls. "You think you're so much better than us. You think you can have the best of both worlds, but you can't. That's not our fucking reality, and it's not yours."

"I thought you weren't like the rest of them," Ripper

mumbles, shaking his head and backing away. Fuck, I've hurt him. "I thought you got the real us."

"I—"

Nothing I say will change anything. The damage has been done.

"I think it's time you go, Ash," Venom says, opening the door for me to leave. "You don't want them to find out you're gone."

I nod shakily. Zed grabs my arm as I pass him. Burning infernos blaze through the holes in his mask and make me squirm.

"You're not a Lionheart fan," Zed says, his fingers digging into my skin, "but you're no better than those fans you look down your nose at. You're nothing but a Basilisk fucking groupie."

"Fuck you," I spit, shaking myself out of his grasp and charging away.

I don't look back. Hot tears spill from my eyes and sting my cheeks in the chilly breeze.

Maybe Zed is right.

Am I no better than the shallow assholes that I condemn?

nine

. . .

Ripper | Damon

"See?" Zed declares. He's so fucking proud to be proven right, just like he always is. "I told you."

For once, I wanted him to be wrong. I thought I was right about Ash. I had met other girls, but she seemed different. She saw through me. She didn't want to see under our masks. She blindly accepted us, seeing the depth behind our music…

How can Ash be the same as the mindless clones who see us like products you can buy off a shelf in the store? I can't accept it. I won't.

Venom doesn't say a word. He slumps in a chair, wringing his hands in his lap.

"Well done, Zed," I yell. I take off my mask and hurl it at the wall. I can't stop the words from coming. "You shouldn't have called her a groupie. You're just happy to be right because you don't want to be fucking happy."

"But it's true," Zed hisses. When he's upset, his vindictive side comes out. A trait he learned from his mom, who is one of the world's best manipulators. "Ash is just

another one in a long line of girls wanting to fuck us. She admitted it."

I whirl around, grab the neck of the beer bottle, and throw it on the floor. It shatters into small pieces, just like my heart being smashed to smithereens.

We all felt a connection to Ash—regardless of whether Zed wants to admit it. A connection we didn't want to break but has been ruined because of the one thing continually ruining our lives. The Lionhearts.

"She isn't who we thought she was," Zed says definitively. He wants to wipe Ash Cooper from our lives completely. "That's it. It's done."

How can we be over when we didn't even begin?

I don't want it to be over.

It can't be, yet she was so convincing…

She wanted us to stay masked like she was too afraid to face us. She couldn't stand looking at us, and that fucking killed me. I want her to see past the Damon Archer bullshit and get to know the real me.

When Ash performed with us on stage, it felt fated. But since she walked into our lives, the Basilisks were being torn apart. She changed everything.

"Fuck," I roar, punching Buggy's wall. I don't do any damage, but it stings like a bitch.

"Ripper," Venom approaches gingerly, but my head jerking around sends him jumping back. He knows better than to stand in my way when I lose my temper. "She..."

I think of her. How her lips pout when she's mad. How her smoldering eyes hide an untamed wildness. How I want to pull her close, hold her in my arms, and stop her from walking out of this fucking bus.

Goddammit.

I collapse onto the sofa, panting, and bury my head in my hands, trying to breathe through my fury. It's not only anger I'm feeling, but crippling sadness.

Will people like us ever find happiness?

"It can't be over," I say to myself again and again. A renewed sense of calmness washes over me the more I say it. "I won't let it."

I jump as my cell vibrates in my pocket. Venom notices, peering over my shoulder. We're both thinking the same thing.

Is it Ash? Does she want to tell us she made a huge mistake? Even Zed, although he'll deny it, cranes his neck to get a look at my screen.

Then I see her name, and my hope extinguishes.

Jacqueline: Come to the penthouse when you get back to the hotel.

"Fuck," I groan, then throw my phone out of reach. It bounces, undamaged, taunting me.

Zed picks it up. I sense the fury emanating from beneath his mask.

"You need to go," Zed says. "We have to play the game."

I look at Venom, hoping he'll say something else. Suggest going to find Ash and tell her Zed didn't mean it. I know he feels the same way about her as I do.

Instead, Venom sighs. His cold and emotionless exterior is as frustrating as it is enviable. Regret drips from his words as he mutters, "Zed's right. We should go back. We have no choice."

Having no choice is the story of my fucking life. It all

started when I arrived at Camp Harmony. I believed it was going to be a dream come true. If I could turn back the clock, I'd take back every single minute to return to being a nobody again.

"Easy for you to say," I retort indignantly. "You're not the one she wants to fuck."

Zed removes his mask. His hair is slick with sweat from exertion, but his eyes soften. We are our true selves in masks, but when we talk like this, we're exposing our souls to each other.

"Hey," Zed lowers his voice to a soothing melody and kneels in front of me. Even when he's talking, the bastard has impressive vocal range. "Look at me, Ripper."

He looks strange with burning red eyes, but it matches how I feel inside.

"Why?" I demand.

"You're never gonna fuck her again, okay?" Zed says gently. "We're not gonna let that happen. Just see what she wants."

I run my hands through my hair. My skin crawls like someone has let loose hundreds of ants. I want to itch. Rid my body of them. Scratch. Take it all away.

"We can make a stop at the changeover point," Zed continues. He's talking about another secondary hotel where we've checked in under fake names. "We can change there, leave in another disguise, and get a car to pick us up from there, then meet our limousine at another location." It's exhausting having to live double lives. How can Ash think this is what we want? "If we leave soon, we'll be back in an hour. You can see Jacqueline, then it'll be done, okay?"

Zed places his hand over mine. He isn't affectionate.

I'm usually the one who comforts him, but I appreciate the gesture.

"You're not on your own," he says, but I'm unsure whether he is talking to me or himself. "We've got each other."

Zed's plan works perfectly, and we return to the hotel undetected. The others pause before entering our room, but my night isn't over yet.

"Good luck," Venom says.

"Remember what I said," Zed says, "In and out, okay?"

I nod, gritting my teeth.

"Don't draw any attention," he reminds me as I turn to leave.

I scowl. "No fucking shit."

What did he expect me to do? Break out into a scream ballad and wake up the Popstarz contestants sleeping below us? My stomach flips. Ash is somewhere in the building. Part of me wants to knock on every door until I find her, but Zed would kill me…

I head along the corridor and start climbing the short flight of stairs. Jacqueline's room is on the floor above. She has the entire penthouse to herself—only the best for the queen of the music industry.

I knock on the door once, hoping she won't hear it. Unfortunately, it flies open instantly.

"Damon, it's so good to see you." She greets me with a smile that makes my stomach churn. She's wearing a black kimono and opens the door wider. "Come inside."

I clench my fists as I step into the room. I've been in

many extravagant hotel suites, but this one tops them all. It's full of glittering crystals and chandeliers, polished tables, and so many fresh flowers that it tickles to breathe through my nose.

"Nice place," I say with zero enthusiasm.

"Isn't it?" she says in her tinkling, entertaining voice. "Make yourself at home."

Jacqueline used to impress me. She came from humble beginnings and worked her ass off to get to where she was. That kind of hard work is something I used to respect and admire. But with her success came power. A power for her to abuse and exploit.

She wanders around, trailing her fingers over the side of a sofa with golden edges. It looks uncomfortable to sit on, favoring art over function.

"What did you want to talk about?" I ask.

She waggles her finger at me and wanders to her minibar.

"Oops." She giggles as her kimono slips open to show her upper thigh. Her seduction attempts won't work on me. Not anymore. "I'm sure I can tempt you with a fine scotch."

"Why am I here, Jacqui?"

"I wanted the company," she replies, pouring our drinks. She slides one across the bar toward me. "Take a seat."

I stand, downing the scotch. The burning in my throat only further ignites the ache in my chest from Ash's rejection.

"It's been a while since we've spoken," Jacqueline says, watching me out of the corner of her eye. "I'm sorry to hear about you and Alexa."

"I'm not," I snap.

She leans forward to trail her fingers up my forearm. I remember the first time it happened. The words she said to me.

I can make you a star, Damon.

To a teenager, the attention of an older and successful woman was the highest form of flattery.

You just need to do something for me first.

I didn't see it as a problem. Screwing her was fine. Heck, I screwed half the girls in Camp Harmony. I embraced the lifestyle. Work hard, play harder.

Fucking Jacqueline was a secret. If she could open doors for me and the Lionhearts, it was a small price to pay… until I realized the true cost and the hold she wanted to have over us. Over me.

It was supposed to be fun. No strings attached. That's what I thought, anyway. Until sleeping with her became an obligation. An expectation. Something I had to do to secure the contract, to secure the front page, to secure the perfect photographer. Privileges were earned, not guaranteed. When we finally signed the Starnote contract, it was the best and worst day of my life.

The best because I no longer had to fuck her to get what we needed. And the worst because we were now tied to her with no escape.

When Zed and Venom found out what happened, they were furious. They both try to make sure I spend as little time with her as possible, but she can be hard to avoid.

A shrink would say the experience has made me distrust women. I don't do relationships, keeping people at arm's length. Sex is nothing more than an exchange. I didn't let anyone get close enough to hurt me. Casual sex was fine. I thought I'd be happy with that… until Ash

came along. She's the only girl I've ever wanted anything more with.

"It's getting late," I say, slamming the glass down.

I have no time for Jacqueline's games.

"You can stay, if you like?" she suggests hopefully. Her eyes narrow in threat, but desperation hides behind her baby blues. Her youth is slipping away, and so is her relevance. No one can remain at the top forever, and she fucking knows it.

"It's been a long day," I say firmly. "I'll see you around."

"Fine," she snaps. "If that's the way you want to be. If you don't mind photographs of you high making great headlines."

I laugh bitterly.

Years ago, her threats terrified me. In the early days, we needed the income to be the Basilisks, so we couldn't afford any mistakes.

Now, the Lionhearts are an unstoppable machine. Starnote used to prop us up, but now it's the other way around. A story about me snorting coke would make front-page news and damage my reputation, but it'd cause more destruction to the Starnote brand.

"Do it, Jacqui," I challenge. "Unless you want me to tell the press how you fucked a teenager and blackmailed them."

"You wouldn't."

"Wouldn't I?" I shoot her my most charming grin. "Try me."

I walk out, leaving her agape.

Zed wanted me to keep her sweet because it would make his mother happy, but fuck her. She needs to understand that Starnote doesn't own us. We own them.

And even if Ash doesn't want to know who I am under the mask, I'm going to stick around long enough to stop her from getting swallowed up by a monster machine. A psycho like Tiffany could cope in that world, but not Ash.

Whatever her feelings are toward us, I can't sit back and watch her become destroyed by them… just like I had.

ten

. . .

Ash

Returning to the hotel undetected was easy, but why is catching my breath so hard?

In.

Out.

In... and out.

I can't believe I said those things. Confronting them was supposed to make things better, not worse. They are the ones who lied to me, but now I'm left feeling like I'm in the wrong.

I hop in the shower, trying to wash the nasty feeling away. It has no effect. I turn the water from hot to freezing. I gasp but don't move, concentrating on the chilling wave. My head aches, but the water dulls the pain, allowing me to just take a pause and stop thinking. It's the reason why I started cutting.

Cutting gave me relief. It gave me something physical to focus on over the chaos raging inside my head. The ability to control something when everything else was falling apart. But I can't go back to that again... I won't.

Shivering, I turn off the water and wrap myself in a towel that covers me properly.

My teeth chatter as I grab a bathrobe and return to the warm living room. It's almost 4 a.m. but I won't be able to sleep.

The television is on, and I flick mindlessly through the channels. Nothing but reruns of episodes of comedies I've seen a thousand times. The canned laughter leaves a bitter taste in my mouth, but I turn up the volume, hoping it'll drown out the guilt.

Fuck.

I jump at a noise, thinking my mind is playing tricks on me.

A knock.

It happens again.

Would the Basilisks risk speaking to me here? I didn't think so, but an unexpected flutter of hope takes me by surprise.

I rise cautiously, aware that I'm wearing nothing but a giant robe. I peer through the peephole.

A voice comes from the other side. "Let me in."

"Cookie?"

I open the door to be assaulted by a ball of brightly colored locs barreling toward me. She almost winds me from the force as her arms wrap around me.

"Cookie?" I stagger, steadying myself. "What are you doing here?"

"You didn't reply to my text," she says, taking out her phone and waving it in my face. She's wearing a duck-patterned pajama set with a fluffy pink jacket and has a backpack slung over her shoulder. "I had to check that you were okay when I didn't hear from you."

"I'm fine," I say. "I didn't realize you were in the city."

"About that..." She smiles sheepishly. "I've got nowhere to stay right now. Would you mind if—"

"You can stay here," I finish her sentence as a giant smile breaks over my face. It makes my cheeks hurt after all my scowling.

Having Cookie around as a positive influence will stop me from spiraling into the pit of depression that's always a constant threat. It hovers on the edges of my consciousness like the Grim Reaper waiting for the perfect moment to claim me.

"If you're sure," she bites her lip, twirling a loc around her finger, "I'm supposed to be sofa-surfing, but the place I found on the internet didn't look so great after I arrived. I wanted to surprise you later this week."

"But why are you even here?" I ask, adding hastily, "not that I'm unhappy to see you."

"I thought this would be a great place to search for talent," she says, then winks. "Besides, telling people my new BFF is the badass crushing it on Popstarz will help."

Even though I've blown it with the Basilisks, at least I can do some good tonight.

"Anyway!" Cookie pushes past and lets out a low whistle as she checks out the room. "Holy shit, this is better than our Bowie cabin."

"You're telling me," I say.

The white walls that were closing in on me moments ago shrink back once more. Cookie is a ray of light and familiarity, blasting away the cobwebs. Unlike the vultures and paparazzi, she knows and cares about me.

"Is that all you've brought with you?" I check out the silver backpack she's carrying that makes her resemble a silver turtle. "You don't pack light."

"I left everything behind when you didn't text back,"

she says. "I had to make sure you got back safe. Either that or hear from you to say you're spending another night on that fiery-painted tour bus."

My heart sinks as Cookie wiggles her eyebrows suggestively. The last thing I want to do is remember how the Basilisks gave me multiple orgasms. Cookie notices my body tense, and her expression changes entirely.

"Oh, Ash…" she says, putting her arm around my shoulders. "What happened?"

"It doesn't matter," I say, keeping the promise I made to the Lionhearts about their secret identities. "All that matters is what I thought we had wasn't real." I ignore the giant lump in my throat as I say definitively, "It's over."

Cookie nods. Her uncanny ability to know when not to ask any more questions is like a sixth sense. She strides to the room service telephone and picks it up.

I frown. "What're you doing?"

"We need ice cream," she says, pressing a load of buttons, then pauses. "You have no limits, right?"

"They never mentioned it." Having her around will be good for me. In the new world that I'm about to descend into, she'll help anchor me to reality. "And I skipped dessert…"

"That's settled then," she says. "Now, you can tell me all about the other contestants."

eleven

. . .

Ash

Contestants huddle in an anxious horde in the dining room for breakfast. I've barely slept and feel like warmed-up shit while everyone else is glowing.

"Are you sure you're okay?" Meredith asks. I'm grateful she's sitting next to me, and I don't have to listen to Tiffany blowing smoke up her ass while we eat. "You don't look so good."

"I'm fine," I reply, playing with my cereal.

Suddenly, there's squealing from the Candy Kisses.

"Oh my gosh," Meredith says, dropping her toast. "It's the Lionhearts!"

I bow my head, letting my hair fall over my face and spot through the small gap—goddamn my thin hair—three figures walking past our table.

"I can't believe it's them," Meredith whispers, practically giddy.

I grip my spoon so tight that my hands shake. None of the guys look in my direction. The three judges follow behind them. All of them gather at a separate table, sitting in a row. It reminds me of a wedding day with a top table

for the most important guests. The Lionhearts take a seat, leaving a vacant chair beside each of them for a judge.

Jacqueline enters last, followed by four cameras who are documenting the moment. Now I wish I had stayed in bed.

"Can I have your attention?" Jacqueline says. She didn't need to ask seeing as everyone's eyes are stuck on her. "You'll be finding out which group you're in today."

By group, she means which judge will be our mentor. As well as having to fight against each other, the judges have an ongoing rivalry too. They work closely with each of their acts and want to be the group leader of the next budding star.

"We will be recording this announcement," Jacqueline says. Her lip curls in disapproval as she looks me over, deciding I'm not camera-ready. She addresses the crew. "Just take a few pans of the room."

"I'm so nervous," Meredith whispers in my ear.

"Me too," I reply dryly, crossing my fingers under the table and hoping I don't get Jacqueline.

"We will allocate each contestant to a judge's group. Each group will have a Lionheart mentor," Jacqueline explains. "Think of it like your own small team."

I cross my toes too, hoping that Tiffany isn't in mine.

"Jacinta Vickers will be paired with Levi York. Yu Jin will be with Zach Royal, and whoever is lucky enough to be in my group will be with Damon Archer."

I glance at Damon. He crosses his arms as a stormy expression rolls over his features. I yank my gaze away to stop myself from wondering what he's thinking about.

"Now for what you're waiting for," Jacqueline says. She pulls a scroll from her suit jacket that's bound with a ribbon. She unwraps it and rolls it out, prolonging the

process. Fucking theatrics. "We have randomly allocated groups."

Randomly allocated my ass. We all know it's a fix.

Not Jacqueline, I chant in my head, not Jacqueline.

"Ashley Cooper!" Her voice goes straight through me like the piercing cry of an untuned guitar string. Everyone turns and the camera zooms in while I keep my facial expression neutral. After a dramatic pause, she calls, "Jacinta Vickers."

I breathe a sigh of relief as Jacinta's twinkling eyes meet mine and she smiles. Jacinta seems nice, someone who cares about music. I avoid looking at the table where the Lionhearts are sitting.

Jacqueline continues down her list, reading off names one after the other. United, the boy band, is also in my group, and Marcus, the hottie Meredith was checking out.

Meredith nudges me. "You'll have to put in a good word for me."

Meredith is in Yu's group and, unsurprisingly, Tiffany almost jumps out of her chair in delight when she joins Jacqueline's group.

"Now that's out of the way," Jacqueline says, brushing her hands together, "the producers will start filming your intro videos ahead of the first live show."

It was only a matter of days before they plastered my face over every television in the US

"And one last thing," Jacqueline says, just when we think she's done. "The first theme of the show will be the nineties. The producers and crew will join us after breakfast to introduce themselves, then you'll get started with your schedules. Good luck."

"Let the fun begin," I murmur under my breath as if we're about to enter the Hunger Games.

"You'll be fine," Cookie reassures from the sofa. "It's only an intro video. Your voice will do the real talking."

I pace back and forth. It's been three days since I saw the Basilisks at Jacqueline's breakfast announcement. Rehearsals are in full swing, and the schedule is intense.

I worried about having to fend off bitchy competitors and dealing with Tiffany's snide remarks, but none of us have time for drama.

They've converted two large rooms in the hotel into dance studios. A Starnote recording studio is across the street where we will rehearse songs too.

I've spent a little time with the others in my group and had vocal lessons with Jacinta, but Levi has been absent.

My first song is *Zombie* by The Cranberries, which works for me. My style differs from the other artists who competed in the past, and Jacinta is happier to lean into more alternative songs. It's far from my preferred style, but it beats Taylor Swift. While Jacinta attends some of my rehearsals, I'm mainly supported by singing coaches hired by Starnote. Most of them make McCallister seem like a pussycat.

I've heard from Meredith, who is fast becoming a friend, that other contestants are planning to put on a giant spectacle. Thankfully, I don't have to remember a full choreography routine. Our dance teacher has been having a hard enough time trying to get me to sway. Who knew that there was a correct way to sway?

Despite all of that, I'm more nervous about filming my introduction video than the live show.

"I don't know if I can do it," I say for the hundredth time this morning.

"You're Ash fucking Cooper," Cookie says. "You killed the Camp Harmony final show. This will be easy."

While I've been rehearsing, Cookie has been working from the room, doing administration work and handling client bookings for the label she's interning at. She's been waving the long hours off as good experience and rationalizing that most people have to start out doing shitty jobs, but her sparkle is fading. The only time it lights up is when she's helping me prepare for rehearsals.

"I don't know…"

"Look," Cookie jumps up, ready to give me a briefing, "all you've got to do is be yourself. People will like you. You're a small-town girl who made it big because of a stroke of luck. You're like them. People will like that."

I roll my eyes sarcastically. "So, I'm the underdog."

"You can sing, Ash," Cookie says. "Sure, Popstarz isn't the place to sing metal, but at least they're not making you sing what McCallister did."

"Yet," I groan. "I don't know what I'd do without you, Cookie. You should be my manager."

"Seriously?" Cookie asks, almost tripping and knocking over a pile of binders she's neatly stacked. "Do you mean it?"

I laugh at her shock. "Of course I do. Don't you remember the deal we made at Camp Harmony?"

"But you'll have loads of people wanting to represent you, Ash," she says. "I'm… no one."

"No, you're not," I tell her, then wink. "You're Ash Cooper's new manager."

Cookie squeals and runs over to hug me. "I won't let you down, Ash."

"Consider a free place to stay as payment," I say, bemused by her reaction.

"If I'm your manager," she says, "I'll be able to come to rehearsals with you. I can help you on set today with the video."

"But Cookie..." My voice trails off, guilt hitting me. "You have a job."

"Fuck the job," Cookie says. "They're getting me to do all the work that they'll take credit for. I'm getting paid little to nothing and have free rent for a while. I want to help you do this."

"But you said you need the experience," I say. "I don't want you to blow your prospects by thinking I'm going to make it. What if I don't? There are plenty of people who make it onto Popstarz and are forgotten a few years later."

"I believe in you, Ash," Cookie says with conviction, then she shrugs. "Besides, if it doesn't work, I'm a Camp Harmony alum. That means something. I'm not the only one who would have taken a sabbatical after graduation."

I bite my lip. "Only if you're sure."

"I'm positive." She beams and takes a step back. She looks me over and frowns. "We need to get hair and makeup in here pronto, then you can practice what you're gonna say with me for this video."

I gulp, hoping I've not made the wrong decision here...

We head into a meeting room in the hotel. It has a neutral background and is rigged for the shoot.

"Friends aren't allowed on the set," Amber points out in her snide tone as we arrive.

"I'm her manager," Cookie says with an air of entitlement that makes Amber scowl. I wish I had a camera to

document her sour face. "I'll be staying with Ash throughout the shoot."

Amber sniffs, looking at Cookie's vibrant dress in disgust. It's a paisley purple pattern and matches her locs of varying blue shades.

"I didn't realize you found representation, Ashley," she snipes.

"Well, I have," I reply, then nudge Cookie. "And I've picked the best."

Amber presses her lips together. "The production crew is waiting for you inside," she says. "Go on."

Cookie leads the way. She recognizes a few of the camera operators and speaks to them like they're old friends. Many of them used to attend Camp Harmony.

Two armchairs are carefully arranged in the center of the set, with cameras and fluffy speakers positioned to catch every word.

A crew member beckons me over. "You can take a seat here, Ashley."

"She prefers Ash," Cookie interjects smoothly.

"Sorry," the guy clears his throat and corrects himself, "Ash."

I take a seat and smooth down my hair. The hotel's shampoo has made it extra shiny. After the hair and makeup wizards did their magic, you'd never guess I hadn't slept.

The host of Popstarz, Tessa Pope, strides onto the set. She is your typical gorgeous blonde, but Cookie told me how she's made her real money through property investments. She's smart as well as pretty.

She comes over to introduce herself and says hello. I mumble something incoherent back. I don't know if I'll ever get used to being around people who I've only seen

on television. I want to poke them to check that they're made of more than pixels.

"This will just be a simple interview," she tells me as crew members fuss around us, clipping on microphones and checking the audio. "I'll be asking you a few questions about why you came to be on the show. A bit about your background. That kinda thing."

"My background?"

She ignores my question but senses my fear from my rabbit-in-the-headlights expression. She tries to dismiss my worries with a wave of her hand. "It's all standard stuff. You'll do great and, besides, it'll all be edited."

Cookie appears by my side and thrusts a cup of water into my hands.

"Just breathe, Ash," she whispers. "If it wasn't for the bronzer, you'd look like you were about to pass out. You're going to smash it, okay? I'll be right over there."

The water helps. I take a drink and nod, hoping I can get over this quickly.

"Everyone ready to start?" someone asks as Tessa takes her seat next to me. "Ash?"

I nod.

Let's get this over with…

twelve

. . .

Venom | Levi

I've been avoiding the contestants all week. Jacinta bought my lie about being unwell and having to rest to make sure I'm recovered enough to appear in the show. Starnote needs their performing monkeys to be in perfect health. Although, I couldn't miss Ash's interview.

I don't stand in the foreground. I lurk at the back of the room, out of sight and away from the cameras.

I'm surprised to see Ash's friend, Cookie, directing the production crew. That makes me feel better, knowing she has someone to look out for her. After the show airs, she's going to need it.

The interview is underway. I know how these work, but Ash is nervous. She's clasping her hands so hard that her nails dig into her skin, making me want to take her hands in mine and tell her it'll be okay.

She looks different, still beautiful, but her makeup changes her appearance. I prefer her face bare when I can see the pretty blush on her cheeks.

Tessa launches into the first question, asking Ash about where she grew up. For someone who is newly internet

famous, there's not a lot of information about her. I should know. I've tried looking. All I know is that she grew up in a small town called Meadow Springs.

"You must have been surprised when your name was called out on the Camp Harmony stage," Tessa says. "How did you feel at that moment?"

"Um…" Ash stalls. My stomach drops. Is she thinking about my revelation, and how I ruined the moment for her? "I couldn't believe it."

"Was it a dream come true?" Tessa presses for more, knowing exactly how the editor is going to want to cut the scene.

Ash is trying, but she's not comfortable in front of the cameras. Like me, she prefers to let her music do the talking.

"I guess," she replies, then murmurs in disbelief, "I can't believe I'm here."

"Everyone knows you from the viral video," Tessa talks like they're old friends. "How did it happen?"

"My best friend uploaded it without me knowing," Ash says. "I didn't expect the video to take off."

"Is this Brick Langford you're talking about?" Tessa probes, fishing for information.

My skin prickles at the mention of his name. I assume he's the guy who looks like a model and watched her at the final show.

Ash's eyebrows raise in surprise. She'll soon get used to everyone knowing her business.

"How long have you known each other?"

"Since we were in kindergarten," Ash says, relaxing more, "I wouldn't have got into Camp Harmony without him, so I owe all of this to him."

"The video Brick uploaded was recorded at your

mom's funeral, wasn't it?" she asks, putting her hand on Ash's arm, pretending to give a shit. "I'm so sorry for your loss."

They will edit out her pushiness to make her sound caring and compassionate.

Ash freezes and bows her head, hiding behind her hair. "Yeah."

"Losing your mom at a young age must have been hard," Tessa says. "I'm guessing you two were close?"

Ash nods.

"What do you think she'd say if she could see you now?"

I want to storm onto the set and tell Tessa to stick her questions up her ass, but I flick the band on my wrist, leaving an angry red mark behind.

"I think she'd be proud of me," Ash says with a small smile as her eyes glaze over slightly. "She was always my biggest supporter."

Tessa continues with the line of questioning for another half an hour. Ash answers where she can, but I can tell her mind is elsewhere.

When the interrogation finally ends, I linger in the shadows as Cookie fusses around Ash, and the camera crew packs away their equipment. Then, her head turns, looking past the crew as if she senses I'm watching.

Her eyes meet mine across the room. I don't look away, holding her gaze and hoping she can understand what I'm trying to say.

I'm sorry, Ash...

She turns her head and looks away.

thirteen

. . .

Ash

The buzz of the crowd only intensifies my nerves.

"How do you feel, Ash?" Cookie asks as I play with my hair nervously.

As we sit backstage, others rush around us in the green room, running to complete final sound checks and putting the last touches on hair and makeup.

"I'm terrified," I admit.

"You and me both," Meredith agrees, taking a seat opposite us. Other contestants, including Tiffany, are singing scales to warm up. The girls from Candy Kisses are having an argument, which doesn't bode well.

"You'll be great," I tell Meredith. It's easier to reassure her than worry about myself. She looks beautiful in a tight red dress that clings to her gorgeous curves.

The green room doors swing open. The judges and the Lionhearts enter. I haven't spoken to any of the guys since our confrontation. I've tried to avoid seeing them too, even though Venom watched my video interview. His intense stare made my skin prickle as unsaid words hung in the air between us.

"Good luck tonight everyone," Jacqueline says. From her brisk tone, it sounds more like a threat. "We know you're all going to make us proud."

"We'll see you out there," Jacinta says. "Have fun and enjoy yourselves, you won't get this moment again."

Jin nods sharply. "Let the show begin."

Jacqueline pauses. "Do you have anything to say to the contestants, Lionhearts?"

It's not a suggestion, but an order. Zed steps forward as I become more interested in my newly manicured nails. They're painted matte black, and the color changes to purple in the light.

"It's an amazing feeling to be on the stage," Zed says. "This will be a moment you'll never forget. Take it, and don't worry about anything else. Let the music speak to you."

"Thanks, Zach," Tiffany croons in response, batting her eyelashes. She looks angelic in a silver dress. She's covering a Britney song with a unique twist. After overhearing her dress rehearsal, I begrudgingly prefer her version.

The Popstarz crew bustles in to hurry the judges along. I'm fourth in the show's line-up, which suits me fine. No one wants to go first, and my nerves would be shot if I went last. I'm only holding it together because Cookie is distracting me with photographs on Leila's social media feed.

After camp finished, Leila began the festival season. She's having an amazing time. Conor went out to join her, and they've been posting snapshots of festival crowds, idyllic cafes, and pretty scenery while they explore Europe together. They're currently in Paris, eating croissants and posing in front of the Eiffel tower.

"Leila and Conor are going to be streaming Popstarz on her phone," Cookie says. "They won't miss it."

"No pressure then," I groan, wishing the show was over so I could see Brick already.

To celebrate the first show, all contestants could invite two guests to an exclusive after-show party. Dad couldn't make it with his work schedule, but Brick managed to get away. He and the other contestants' guests are watching the live show from the party location on a large-screen television.

Brick is also texting Cookie about the snacks available —as usual, food is his top priority. Popstarz paid for him to fly out business class and stay in a hotel for the night—not the same one as the crew and contestants, but a nice one a few blocks away. For a guy who never wanted to leave Meadow Springs, traveling is a big deal to him.

"Ash!" A runner comes to get me. "You're up next."

I take a deep breath, fighting the urge to vomit.

"You're going to kill it out there," Cookie says in her best calming voice, "I'll be waiting right here."

I nod shakily, then follow the runner through the twisted corridors. I know what to expect after our rehearsals, but it doesn't make it any easier.

Different people fuss around like buzzing flies, adjusting my hair, and checking my microphone is working. We've cut to an ad break, but we'll be back soon.

How is this my life?

If someone told me a year ago I'd be here, I would have never believed them. Adrenaline makes me want to run, but I stay rooted to the spot, listening to my heart thudding in my ears.

I've rehearsed my songs so many times they feel like second nature, but it doesn't stop the irrational fear of

me forgetting my words from flooding through my brain.

"Are you ready?" a voice asks.

I nod, hearing Tessa give me an introduction from the stage.

"That's your cue." A hand gives me a small push. "Go."

I step onto the dark stage, and the spotlight follows me as I stride to the middle of the stage, trying not to trip as I go. The stark white light is so bright that I squint, and the audience plummets into darkness, helping me forget where I am.

The music starts, and my body takes over. I know what to do. When I start to sing, everything falls away. I start rocky, nerves causing me to stumble over words, but as soon as I pass the first few lines, the song flows through me. I close my eyes and channel the emotion behind the song.

My voice echoes around the studio hauntingly as purple smoke floats around my knees. I'm not sure what overall effect it's creating for the audience, but it transports me to somewhere else, and before I know it, I'm building to a high note.

I throw my head back and let a whisper of a raspy roar peek through my words. Only a hint of what I'm capable of, but it gives the song a raw edge. An extra punch to the lyrics.

Before I know it, the music fades. I step back and bow my head, then the thunderous applause starts.

Applause doesn't mean they liked it. They're given cues on screens to tell them how to react, but the clapping still gives me a rush.

When the audience quietens, Tessa joins me. She hugs me like we're old friends.

"Well, Ashley… I have goosebumps," she declares.

She keeps talking, but I struggle to pay attention. I fix my eyes on the illuminated judge's table. It's surreal to be seeing something I've only seen in pixels.

Mom and I used to watch Popstarz when I was young, but I stopped tuning in when I hit my teenage years. I scowled whenever I heard the catchy opening sequence, but Mom still watched it every week. Now I wish I could watch it with her and point to myself on the screen. She'd have liked that.

"Now, over to the judges," Tessa announces. "Let's see what they thought of your performance, Ash."

I nod, trying to stop swaying from how much my legs are shaking.

"Ashley," Jacinta declares, clapping her hands. "What can I say? You were magnificent. Your emotions came through in that song. It was a perfect fit for your voice."

"You would say that… you picked it," Jin remarks playfully. He rarely shows emotion off camera, but he knows how to act.

"I have good taste," Jacinta replies, "and if I were the other judges, I'd be intimidated after that song."

"Jin, any comments?" Tessa prompts.

"It wasn't flawless," he says, followed by boos from the audience. "You had a slow start, but it could have been nerves. Next time, I'd like you to come onto the stage with confidence. You have a good voice, but do you have star quality? I'm not sure."

I nod along with a fake smile, accepting their comments graciously as I've watched many others do over the years.

"Jacqueline?" Tessa continues along the row.

Jacqueline smiles. "Can I just say how amazing it is to see a Camp Harmony star up on this stage?" The audience cheers. "Ashley, it was a good song choice, but I'd like to see more from you," she pauses to build tension. "I feel like you're holding back."

Holding back? If I let loose, I'd scream the whole fucking studio down. Me being restrained is best for everyone.

"Thank you, judges," Tessa says. The cameras swivel and point in our direction, likely zooming in on my awkward smile that's making my cheeks hurt. "If you enjoyed Ashley's performance and want her to be our next Popstar, she needs your vote to stay in the competition. All you've gotta do is follow the instructions on the screen—call, text, or cast your vote online. Next up, we'll be having another Camp Harmony star join us."

After her spiel, we cut to commercials. The production team swarms around Tessa to fix her hair, while I'm ushered from the stage into the post-show room to join the other contestants who have finished their performances.

Theo, Tiffany's admirer, puffs out his chest, brimming with confidence.

"Great job!" Cookie bounds over and pulls me into a hug. "You were amazing."

I shrug. "The judge's opinions were mixed."

"Don't beat yourself up about it, kid. You were brilliant," I hear Marcus—Meredith's crush—say as he pats the back of the young kid who went first. His voice is a warm honey-filled drawl, and he looks up at me and smiles. "Great job, Ash."

"Thanks," I reply, then look at Cookie quizzically. "What happened?"

"Spark forgot the lines," Cookie whispers.

Poor kid. Marcus's words don't seem to help as Spark buries his head in his hands. The pressure is real.

"I'm just glad it's over," I say, collapsing into a chair and wondering how the fuck I'm going to do that again if I get through to the next round.

United, the other act who already performed, crowd around a laptop, checking how many followers they're gaining. Their hands will ache from the high-fives and fist bumps soon.

I check the clock and ask, "How long do we have to go until we can go to the after-party?"

"Only another four hours," Cookie answers apologetically, then hands back my cell. "You're blowing up with messages."

I see a string of names: Brick, Leila, Claudia—even Dad! Then… fuck.

"Looks like someone hasn't forgotten about you," Cookie teases as she peers over my shoulder to see a text from an unknown number.

"I'll be right back," I mutter, heading to the drinks table before opening the message.

Unknown: Great job, Ash… but it was no Basilisks show.

I recognize the number instantly. *Ripper.* I snort, then curse myself. He's funny. Damn it. I grudgingly re-add him as a contact.

Me: Can't you take a hint?

Ripper: I don't give up that easily…

Is the post-show adrenaline messing with my head? As much as I'm confused and hurt, a small part of me can't help feeling pleased he enjoyed the show, and that maybe... just maybe... whatever happened between us isn't over.

Me: We'll see about that.

Am I flirting? Fuck.

I'm playing a dangerous game, but I know one thing for sure. Performing live in front of millions of viewers didn't come close to giving me the same buzz as singing with the Basilisks in a dingy warehouse.

Without them, would I ever feel truly alive again?

"I think I'm going to throw up," Meredith says as the production crew beckons us out of the room.

"Me too," Spark mumbles behind her.

The public has been voting for a tense two hours, and we're about to return to the stage to hear our fate.

We line up into groups, then head out to stand beside our group leaders in a designated area.

"Good luck everyone," Jacinta says. "You all did great."

No one gets to reply as the team counts us back in to signal we're going live again.

Tessa dives straight into the introduction for the second part of the show. "We've had some amazing performances tonight. Everyone here has already become a member of the Popstarz family, and we'll be sad to see one of our acts go."

All that's running through my mind is how this might be the end of my music career. Finished before it started. On one hand, I'd be pleased to leave Jacqueline and Starnote's bullshit, but I don't feel like I'm done with the city yet—or the Basilisks.

"The first name of the person going through to next week's show is... Tiffany!"

Predictable. Tiffany squeals. Then the spotlight above her head goes out.

Tessa continues down the list, calling out names,

"Meredith!"

"Candy Kisses!"

"Priya!"

"Spark!"

The kid collapses to his knees in a prayer position. He's been breathing into a paper bag all night backstage, so hopefully, this will give him confidence.

"Marcus!"

I prepare for the worst. It's going to be me. My performance wasn't as flashy as some of the other contestants. People expect a show on Popstarz, and all I did was stand and sing.

"Ashley!"

My hands fly to my mouth in shock as I'm thrust into darkness, leaving only two acts: the egotistical boy band and Theo. I hope Theo leaves. I'm tired of seeing him drool over Tiffany.

"The act with the fewest number of votes who is leaving us this week is..." Tense music plays in the background. "United."

Strobes flash around the studio as they hug each other.

Tessa goes to join them, thrusting a microphone in their faces. "How are you feeling?"

What a stupid question.

The bravest of the group steps forward and says, "We're disappointed to be going this early, but this won't be the last you'll hear of United."

"I'm sure it won't be," Tessa agrees politely. She closes out the show as everyone gathers around United to say their goodbyes.

Although I've made it through week one, I'm not sure how many more lives I have left…

fourteen

. . .

Ash

After the announcements, they bundle the contestants into cars and whisk us to an exclusive venue a few blocks away. Unluckily for me, Tiffany's in the same car. I bite my tongue as I listen to her high-pitched critiques of other people's performances.

"I think it's clear who the real Camp Harmony winner was," Theo says, agreeing with everything she says.

"Exactly," Tiffany says. "She just got the sympathy vote."

Marcus, on my left side, smiles apologetically and mimes, "Ignore them."

"Don't worry," I mumble, "I'm used to it."

When we arrive at the venue, my hands sweat at the sight of a red carpet and paparazzi. This is supposed to be a party, not a movie premiere.

Among the many contracts I signed upon arrival, there were clauses about making appearances at events. There was no getting out of it, even if I wanted to. Being on Popstarz is about more than your voice, it's about creating

hype around the show by appearing in newspapers. It catapults all contestants into the public eye overnight.

Priya—the quiet, moody woman with the perfect bob—crushed her performance. She poses for the cameras effortlessly, oozing coolness. Behind her, I walk like Bambi on ice. After smiling a few times, and getting blinded by flashes, I hurry into the venue to meet my friends.

Brick is easy to see straight away. He's standing near the bar and towers above everyone else. He looks like a model in a plain white shirt and black jeans.

"Smash!" His face lights up as I approach. He scoops me up into his arms and spins me around like he used to do when we were kids. "You did great."

"Put me down, Brick," I hiss in his ear. "People are staring."

"Oh, that must be him," someone says from behind us. "The guy who got her into the show. Aren't they so cute together?"

I ignore their speculations. It's not the first time Brick and I have been mistaken for a couple. Although looking at the pair of us side by side, I can't see why they think we'd be a good match. An alternative goth-looking girl and the athlete aren't a natural pairing on paper.

Cookie joins us, flanked by a journalist. We all have to speak to the press, and she's tracked down the best among a bad bunch.

"Ash, this is Dee from *Edge* magazine," Cookie says. Dee is a hipster, out of place among the glossy magazines hounding other contestants. *Edge* is an up-and-coming new music magazine that has a hipster edge. "I thought you could have a chat."

"Sure," I say, despite wanting to return to the hotel room and hibernate.

"I loved your performance, Ash," the woman says, pushing her thick-rimmed glasses up her nose. They're too big for her face but suit her. "I've got a few questions for you..."

She fires off a few generic questions that I'm able to answer easily—when I started singing, what it means to me, and what the reaction was from Meadow Springs when they found out I'd won the Camp Harmony final show. She's angling for a rags-to-riches Cinderella-vibe story.

"It's good the two of you are here," she says after I think the interview is over. I frown in confusion, not sure who she's talking about until she grins at Brick. "A lot of our readers want to know what the story is between you two after watching your video, Ash. Is he your Prince Charming?"

My mouth falls open, but Brick clears his throat.

"We've known each other for years," Brick says, then winks, "but never say never."

"How about a picture of the two of you together?" Dee's eyes sparkle as she waves over a photographer. "It would look great alongside the article."

"Sure," Brick agrees, not giving me a chance to answer. He drapes his arm over my shoulder and smiles like it's school picture day.

I smile, but it turns into more of a grimace.

"Perfect." Dee checks the photograph. "You'd make a cute couple."

Before I can jump in to correct her, Cookie steps in to end the interview.

"Thanks so much, Dee. I think that's all we have time for right now," Cookie says, sliding her business card into Dee's hands. When did she get those babies printed? The

girl never sleeps. "You can get in touch with me if you have any more questions for Ash."

"Thanks," Dee says, then drops her voice, "and off the record, you're my favorite."

"Um… thanks," I mumble.

Dee disappears into the crowd, and I spin to face Cookie and Brick in accusation.

"What the hell was that?" I demand.

Brick squirms under my stare, looking at Cookie for help. She stays quiet, biting her lip with a guilty expression all over her face.

"I'm only doing what I was told to do by your manager," Brick says, throwing her under the bus and absolving himself of all responsibility. "I'm just gonna head over there and leave you to talk…"

"Smart move, Langford." I scowl, crossing my arms over my chest. "Why do I get the sense there's something you're not telling me, Cookie?"

"Ohhhh… about that…" she says, fiddling with her necklace. "Don't hate me, but there may have been some edits to your video intro. It might have made it sound like you and Brick are star-crossed lovers."

"What?" I can't believe it. "Why didn't you tell me before?"

"Because I knew you'd be mad," she says, "and because you didn't want to watch the video back."

I got the option to watch my intro video, but the thought made me cringe, so I asked Cookie to screen it for me in advance and trusted her judgment.

"But you know that's not true," I say. I cast a glance over at Brick and whisper, "He's dating someone else."

"I spoke to Brick about it first," Cookie says. "He was cool with it. Look, I know it's not ideal, but as

your manager, you asked me to make a call. The public loves a good romance story. It doesn't matter if it's true or not, and it might just keep you in the competition."

I exhale slowly. "It's one thing spinning stories about me, but bringing Brick into it seems a step too far…"

"He said he didn't mind," Cookie insists, "and he didn't have to come tonight. But he'll do anything to support you, Ash."

"That's the problem," I mutter.

I don't want to give him the wrong impression. We're now at a point where our friendship is just recovering after he confessed his feelings for me at the start of the summer. Jade would be angry about this. She's not exactly my number-one fan.

"Hey," a deep voice says from behind us. I freeze. "Can I have a word with Ash for a second?"

"Sure, Levi." Cookie grins at Venom and then glares at me to be polite. She knows how I feel about the Lionhearts, but she has no clue how complicated this is.

Levi looks like he's ready for a cozy evening in wearing an oversized hoodie and jeans. His floppy hair falls over his face as his sparkling green eyes draw me in.

"What do you want?" I snap.

"I've been asked to speak to all the acts in Jacinta's group," he replies, stepping closer. I edge away, getting a hint of his cologne that makes my knees go weak. "I wanted to say congratulations."

I raise my eyebrows. "No more bombshells to drop on me this time around?"

He grins sheepishly, burying his hands in his pockets, then says, "You already know everything there is to know about me, Ash."

"Really?" I say, dropping my voice, "Because I don't feel like I know you, any of you, at all."

Levi advances, leaning in to be heard over the loud music. His breath tickles my neck and makes my skin tingle. I remember how his lips felt on mine, how his body… fuck, stop.

"We may have lied about who we are, but you saw the real us that night," Levi says. "Zed shouldn't have said what he did to you on the bus. You're more than a groupie to me, Ash."

I flinch. Zed's words stung, and I've been replaying them in my head. I was quick to judge them for hiding who they were. But by turning away from them, who does that make me? Am I just as bad?

"V—" I stop myself, "Levi, we shouldn't be talking about this here."

"Another time then," Venom says. "How about tomorrow? I have something I need to return to you."

I hesitate. I should stay away. I can't trust him, but I also want my lyric book back.

"Fine," I relent. "But only because of the book."

He nods abruptly in a business-like fashion. "I'll text you the address."

"I'll see you then," I quip.

His fingers brush against my arm for a second too long. "I look forward to it."

His husky tone sends shivers down my spine, then he turns and disappears into the crowd, leaving me with more questions than answers.

The night is in full swing. The contestants who are old enough to drink legally are loosening up, but I'm pleased to be sober.

Brick, Cookie, Meredith, and I stand together, chatting about how the show went. We're interrupted at various points by journalists to answer questions. The constant talking is exhausting, and my energy is draining. Introvert problems, right?

"These are amazing," Brick says, grabbing another mini pizza and popping it into his mouth. Servers circle with canapés, and one particular girl keeps looping around to return to him. As ever, he's oblivious to her interest.

"How is Jade?" I ask him.

"Things are okay." He shrugs. "We're just casual, nothing serious."

I nod, although I think to myself that I'm sure Jade doesn't feel the same way. Her protectiveness over him was obvious when I met her. Guys can be so fucking dense.

To our right, Tiffany giggles loudly. Loud enough to draw my attention.

"Oh my gosh, look." Cookie's eyes dart in Tiffany's direction. "It seems like Tiffany is trying to make her move."

I follow her gaze to see Tiffany and Zed sitting in a booth. Her legs are almost sprawled all over his lap.

She touches his arm like he's told the world's funniest joke. The man hiding underneath Zach's persona is not someone who tells funny jokes. Zed is a serious control freak who despises the pretense he puts on.

"They look good together," Meredith says, "although she's trying too hard."

"You should have seen her at Camp Harmony," Cookie says. "She followed him around the whole time."

"They're basically made for each other," I say, more bitterly than I intended. "They are both from famous families."

"You're probably right," Meredith agrees. "Can you imagine what their kids would look like?"

Perfect beautiful babies that would make the Royal and Lockhart families happy. I'm not sure why the idea turns my stomach so much. Isn't that how the world is supposed to work? Guys like Zach date girls like Tiffany, but Zach doesn't exist…

Zed doesn't push her away or fend off her advances. A pang of jealousy stabs at my chest. I can't look away. His eyes tear away from Tiffany for a second to meet mine. A slight smile crosses his lips like he knows I'm watching. What game is he playing? And, worse, why am I falling for it?

"Urgh." Cookie rolls her eyes and makes a gagging noise. "Just more of the Tiffany show. Does anyone want to dance?" A song I don't know comes on, and Meredith instantly volunteers. I politely decline as they head to the dance floor together, leaving Brick and me alone.

Tiffany's hysterical laughter makes my teeth grind together. Why do they have to make it so obvious? No one wants to see them draped all over each other.

"So…" Brick begins. "Pretty weird that people want us to be a couple, right?"

"Yeah," I reply, "but I guess it's good for the competition, as Cookie says. I don't want to upset Jade, though."

"Honestly," he says, running his hand through his hair, "I think I'm gonna call things off with her. It doesn't feel right. Things are just intense with her, you know?"

"Uh-huh," I say, only half paying attention and keeping one eye on Tiffany and Zed. "You should do what's right for you."

"The stuff you said in the video," Brick says, moving to stand in front of me and blocking my view of the blossoming connection on the other side of the room that makes me want to push pins into my eyes. "Did you mean it?"

I rack my brain to recall what I said. I talked about how we were good friends, how he's always been there for me, and how I couldn't imagine life without him.

"Sure I did," I reply. "You know how much you mean to me, Brick. If it wasn't for you, I wouldn't be here."

"You did this all on your own," Brick says. "Your mom would have been proud."

My eyes fill up as I whisper, "Thanks, Brick."

He pulls me into a half-hug. Around us, I hear whispers.

"People are like vultures," I whisper in his ear.

"Let's give them what they want for a little longer," he says playfully, hanging on.

I laugh louder than I usually would. Zed isn't the only one who can play games. Having to pretend to like Brick romantically is off-putting, but if Zed wants to act like this, then I'm not above being childish either.

Brick and I go to take a seat at a table and chat about the past few years: how things have changed, how he always knew I'd make it…

"Thanks," I say. "You know I meant it when I said that I couldn't do any of this without you."

"I was thinking," he says, having to lean in closer. "Coming to the city, seeing you in the show, it's opened

my eyes. I've even been thinking about traveling and leaving town."

"What?" My eyes widen in surprise. "Are you for real?"

"Don't sound so surprised."

"This is huge, Brick," I say, almost jumping up in my seat. "What would your dad say?"

"I haven't told him yet," he says. His cheerful expression turns glum. "The business isn't doing so well. Things have dried up."

"Oh, Brick…" My face falls. "Is there anything I can do to help? I'm sure it's just a phase. Your dad's always done well."

"You've got an eyelash on your cheek," he says, changing the subject. He reaches out to brush it away. "There."

I smile. "Thanks."

At that moment, an angry figure storms past. They knock through the crowd, tearing a divide through groups of people, and slam the door to the club closed behind them.

"Wow," Brick comments with a low whistle. "Damon Archer isn't in a good mood."

Is that because of me?

"Do you want to take a walk outside?" I ask, suddenly feeling flush.

"Sure," he agrees.

We slink out of a fire escape onto a backstreet, leaning against the building wall.

"Tonight's been pretty crazy, huh?" I say, then grin mischievously. "But the biggest bombshell of the night is Brick Langford wanting to leave Meadow Springs."

He rolls his eyes. "I'm a changed man…" he pauses

hopefully, "but there is one good thing that could come from it."

I tilt my head to the side. "You mean apart from seeing more of the world? Or, the fact you can be the hottest guy in another place?"

"Us," he says. The vibe between us changes instantly. "Things wouldn't have worked before because we wanted different things. Maybe it would be different now?"

"Brick, I..." I stammer.

We've had a great evening, but pretending to flirt for the press may have given him mixed signals. My heart sinks.

"You said all those things in the video," Brick says. "It sounded like you wanted to try—"

"I haven't seen the video yet," I cut him off. "I thought Cookie told you it was edited."

"She did, but the way you were acting tonight..." He shakes his head. "Fuck, Ash. I thought we could just be friends. I really did, but coming here, seeing the video, and everyone acting like we're a couple... it's too much, okay?"

"I never wanted you to get pulled into this."

"Well, I have," he says. "I'm being followed around by journalists in Meadow Springs, too. They're driving business away. You may have gotten everything you ever wanted and found a whole new life, but it's affected me. I'm a person with real fucking feelings. I'm good enough to pretend to be your boyfriend for the cameras, but then you just want to drop me."

"I never asked for that to happen," I desperately try to reason with him. "You don't have to pretend to be my boyfriend."

"And harm your chances on the show? I won't do

that," he says. "I've always been there for you, Ash. But what about me? Do you think it's easy for me to pretend?"

"I..."

I can't think of anything to say. I haven't even stopped to consider the sacrifices he's made for me.

"Just forget it, Ash," he whispers. "I'm gonna leave."

I don't stop him.

I've already done enough.

fifteen

. . .

Ripper | Damon

"Don't do it," Venom urges. "You need to keep your cool."

I yank my arm out of his grasp. "How can you say that?"

Not everyone can keep their emotions in check like him.

We both saw his fingers stroking her cheek, and my whole world ruptured. She replied to my text earlier. I thought that was progress. She was angry, but she'd seen the light. I knew it. I could feel it deep in my fucking bones, until…

Fuck.

Fuck.

Fuck!

The pretty boy quarterback swooped in. I drain my drink but need something stronger. I push through the crowd, craving fresh air before I explode.

I storm out of the after-party and don't look back. Jacqueline will be mad, but who gives a shit? I can't watch Ash get with someone else in front of me. It'd fucking destroy me.

I've been watching her all evening. Laughing around with the guy who America is hailing the "perfect boy next door." Her childhood sweetheart. The man who changed her life. I spit on the ground as I stalk through the streets to find my car. I always have a driver waiting. You never know when you'll need to make a hasty exit.

Zed will be furious too, but he's too busy fulfilling his family obligations to realize I'm gone.

"Club Seventy-Four," I bark at the driver.

It's an exclusive members-only club with a waiting list years long to get into, but I'm let in without hesitation every time.

It's time to let fucking loose. Damon Archer, the party boy, is back.

We get to the club—an unassuming building that doesn't attract attention from the outside. I've heard rumors that it used to host secret society meetings and be a whore house for global leaders. Either way, it's the hottest location in the city.

A bulky security guard blocks the entrance, "Password?"

"Fuck you," I spit.

"Mr. Archer," a hostess moves around the guard to greet me, ignoring my lack of password. They know how much I spend behind the bar. "It's been too long since we saw you."

"Yes," I reply, "it has."

I descend the stairs into the red light of the basement. Through the revelers, I spot Zed's brother. It's the perfect place for someone like him—lost, broken, and filling the emptiness inside with something else.

"Damon," Elliot calls from a high-backed chair where

two escorts sit on his knees. They're the high-class kind who cost thousands to fuck. "Good to see you, man."

I nod in his direction to acknowledge him but don't stop to chat. I need liquor, and I need it fast. I order the most expensive vodka—it's super smooth and doesn't sting like the cheap shit. I don't care about the expense. I want to go back to a time before I met Ash fucking Cooper.

I should give up on her. That would be the sensible thing to do. I should leave her to live her life. I barely know the girl, but she's buried herself so deep under my fucking skin that I can't forget her, no matter how hard I try.

"On the house," the bartender says, sliding a bag of coke toward me, hidden under his glass.

I thank him, slipping it into my jacket pocket. It's been months since I partied hard, and I need to let loose.

I head to the busy bathroom. It's more like a hotel suite with individual cubicles, a line of sinks in the middle, and a beautiful topless girl lying on a table with a line of coke between her breasts.

I pay her fake tits no attention as I push to the front of the line, snort a free line from her, and leave again.

The thudding music rattles my bones as I go to the center of the dance floor. Strobe lights make the evening pass like a series of snapshots, but I can't see anything but another man touching Ash's face.

What're they doing now?

A woman sidles up to my side, writhing her hips and grinding against me.

"Damon," a familiar voice says. Alexa Frost is as stunning as ever. "Long time no see."

Considering she sold me out to the press for cash and

branded me as a cheating asshole, she looks happy to see me.

As if reading my mind, she says, "No hard feelings, right?"

She slides her hand down my chest, pushing her body closer. The heat of her against my skin makes it crawl. "Have you missed me?"

I catch her wrist and spin her around. Her ass presses into my groin, making my cock shrink. I lean in and whisper in her ear, "I wouldn't fuck you if you were the last woman on earth."

She jumps and spins around. Her beautiful face contorts, exposing the ugliness lurking under her harsh bone structure and fleshy lips.

"You're a fucking asshole," she snaps.

I smirk. "So what if I am?"

She flounces off in a huff to join her model friends. They're not real friends considering I fucked two of them while Alexa and I were fake dating.

"Damn…" Elliot joins me, checking out Alexa's retreating figure. "I'd tap that."

"You're welcome to her," I say, then nudge my head. "Bathroom?"

Elliot's eyes light up. Zed will be pissed that I'm leading his brother astray, but judging by the size of Elliot's pupils and how his whole body is buzzing, it's not gonna be the first load of drugs he's taken tonight.

We weave through the throng of dancers. They're all beautiful people who belong in magazines. Beautiful people with empty fucking souls who all look the same. People who are so broken by this cut-throat world that they spend their nights trying to forget. Fame is a bitch.

"Hey." A firm hand grips my shoulder. I ball my fists,

ready to break their nose. I used to get into fights a lot. Zed got pissed at trying to cover them up for the media's benefit. "Where are you going?"

Zed catches my fist in his hand as I make a clumsy swing. His jaw clenches as he hisses at his brother, "Get out of here, Elliot, unless you want me to tell Mom about how you're spending your night."

Elliot scampers away, terrified of being cut off.

Zed's disapproving glare makes me feel like a child. Venom stands behind him.

"How did you know where to find me?" I ask them.

"How doesn't matter," Zed snaps. "We're leaving now."

"You can't tell me what to do," I snarl. "The party isn't over yet."

It won't be over until I'm so fucked up that I can't remember Ash's name, or how mine sounded on her lips when my cock was deep inside her.

"The party is over when I say it is," Zed threatens ominously, firmly planting his hands on my shoulders. "We're leaving."

"Come on, dude," Venom says. "It's for the best."

I push past Zed, bumping his shoulder as I head for the exit. Venom falls into step beside me. He couldn't stop me if I tried to run. I'm stronger and faster.

"You shouldn't have come," I sneer at Venom as he opens the door to a waiting car like a cop ready to transport a prisoner.

"You left us with no choice," Zed says.

"Fuck you," I say as I get into the vehicle.

Venom gives the driver directions. To my surprise, we aren't heading to the hotel. The cab drops us off at the

corner of a quiet road, a few streets away from where Buggy is stored.

It's a risky move for us to be out in the open like this, but I can't think properly.

"Thanks for the ride." Zed tips him generously and retrieves his backpack from the floorboard.

As soon as we're out of the car, Zed opens it and hands us glasses and baseball caps to wear. He's like a grandma handing out supplies.

We keep our heads down and don't say a word, but simmering resentment exudes from every pore in Zed's body.

When we get closer to the garage, Zed pauses and rummages in the bag for balaclavas. "Swap out for these."

The street is covered by a few cameras. Although we trust Ted to manage the Basilisks, we don't trust him with our real identities—not only because he could have the same reaction as Ash, but because the guy has been saving to move out of his mom's basement for years. Would he stay loyal when tempted by a stack of cash?

We head inside Buggy in silence. When the doors close behind us, Zed pulls off his balaclava.

"You look better with it on," I retort.

"What the fuck are you doing, Ripper?" Zed pushes me. "You caused a massive fucking scene storming out like that. What happened?"

"You didn't see her, did you?" I say. "She was fawning all over Captain fucking America."

"Oh boy…" Venom says, heading to the bar to get a drink. "She's not interested in him."

"You didn't see the way he looked at her," I spit. I saw how his eyes never strayed from her and how delicately his fingers brushed her cheeks. The guy is in love with her.

Everyone could see it. My voice cracks slightly. "I thought she was… the one."

"It doesn't matter," Zed explodes. He refuses to let me dwell in self-pity. "You have no control over what Ash does. Her moving on is a good thing. It's the best thing for us, for everyone."

"How can you even say that?" I demand. I take out my phone and show him the message. "She fucking replied to me." I wave it in his face to prove my point. "It's not over, Zed. At least I didn't think it was until I saw *his* hands all over her…"

"I'm meeting her tomorrow," Venom mumbles. He speaks softly so I have to strain to hear him, but he may as well have screamed in my ear.

Both Zed and I freeze.

"What?" we exclaim in unison.

"I'm her mentor and," Venom shrugs like it's nothing, "I have to give her lyric book back."

"Unbelievable." Zed's cheeks flush like he's about to have an aneurysm, shaking his head wildly in disapproval. He turns on Venom, "Why the fuck didn't you say anything?"

"Because of this," Venom answers, gesturing at Zed who is shaking in anger, "because I knew you'd act like this. You turned her away by calling her a groupie, Zed. You know she's more than that. Ripper is right. It's not over."

"You two are fucking delusional!" Zed's nostrils flare like a bull ready to charge. "It won't work. It can't."

"Maybe it can," Venom says. "If she wanted us out of her life, she'd have revealed us to the press, ignored Ripper's message, and refused to speak to me. Whether

Ash wants to admit it or not, I think she feels the same way we do."

"We have to win her back," I say.

"You two are fucking insane," Zed says, but I see the cogs in his mind turning. He's considering all the possibilities and what could go wrong. "It won't work."

"We don't know unless we try," I say, already starting to feel better even though my come-down is beginning.

There is hope.

sixteen

. . .

Ash

After sending a string of ignored texts to Brick, I groan and hug my knees against my chest.

"He's still ignoring you, huh?" Cookie asks from the other end of the sofa. She holds out a plate, offering a slice of peanut butter toast. "You should eat before rehearsals."

"I'm not hungry." I sigh, then release the word vomit from the thoughts racing through my mind, "I don't want to hurt him. We were just getting back to being friends, then this whole publicity stunt gave him the wrong impression. He said he would break up with his girlfriend too."

Cookie raises an eyebrow. "He said they weren't dating."

"That's not the point," I reply, snatching a piece of toast in frustration. None of this is Jade's fault. "Brick thought we weren't right for each other because we wanted different things. He wanted to stay in Meadow Springs, and I wanted to leave. Him wanting to see the world doesn't change anything."

I huff and bite into the toast. It's dry and scratchy in my throat when I swallow.

"You're not the only one who had a rough night," Cookie says. She went out early to buy a stack of papers and magazines and is flicking through them to see what they have reported about the show. "Look at Damon Archer."

She passes me a paper and points at a photograph of Damon in a club with his gorgeous ex hanging off his arm.

"I don't know why she's giving him another chance," Cookie says, shaking her head. "He'll only break her heart again."

"Mhmm," I mumble.

I have no right to be mad. He can do and see whoever the fuck he likes, but why would he text me then do that? I can't tell which of their identities is real. A part of me wants to believe that Damon, the Lionheart playboy who screws around, is the fake exterior for the kind and sensitive member of the Basilisks. Things just don't add up.

"You have a meeting with Levi today, right?" Cookie asks, bringing up my schedule on her phone. "It'll be good to get the low-down from him on what's going on in the other groups."

"Oh… that," I say, as if it'd slipped my mind when it's all I've been thinking about since I woke up. "Sure, I'll see what he says."

"You seem distracted," she says, then adds softly, "I'm sorry about how you left things with Brick, okay? If I knew it was going to cause a row, I'd have tried to get them to cut the video differently."

I force a half-smile. "Both of us know the more you object, the more likely it'll be put in."

"Probably," she agrees, "but he'll come around. It will be okay."

"We'll see," I say, then pick up a copy of *Edge* magazine. "Articles like this aren't going to help, though."

A picture of Brick and me at the party is on the front page. He looks as gorgeous as ever and the title says, "High School Sweethearts Reunited." Rejecting him once was bad enough, but having to do it twice was even worse. Being reminded that we're a happy couple by the press won't help the situation either.

"Meeting Levi can take your mind off it," Cookie says, checking her watch. "You better go."

I drag my legs up from the sofa and into the bathroom to change. I look like a mess in an oversized T and leggings with slashes over my thighs. My hair is tied in two messy braids that I slept in. I dot spots of concealer over blemishes and put on a thin smudge of tinted lip balm to make my lips look a different color than the rest of my face. That'll have to do.

Levi and I are meeting at the studio next door. He has to meet every contestant in Jacinta's group, now just me and Marcus, so I'm nothing special.

"I know you don't like the Lionhearts," Cookie calls over her shoulder as I turn the handle to leave, "but try to be nice."

She doesn't know just how nice I've been to those three men…

The studio is quiet apart from a few Starnote employees bustling around the reception desk. During Popstarz, we have free rein of the place.

To my surprise, Levi is already waiting and jumps up when he sees me.

"Ashley." He nods in greeting, almost formally, and I fight the urge to laugh. "I thought we could go for a coffee first?"

"A coffee?" I raise my eyebrows. "Sure."

I could do with the caffeine hit. He draws his hood and we leave together.

"My favorite coffee shop isn't far from here," he says, holding open a door to a nearby car for me. "But I'd rather not walk through a crowd of journalists."

A wise choice.

We don't speak on the ride. Everyone knows who Zach Royal and Damon Archer are, but people forget about Levi York. He tries to blend into the background and doesn't speak a lot. With his hood up, no one gives us a second glance as we enter the coffee shop.

It's quiet. The barista recognizes us but acts discreetly, showing us to a private room in the back.

"That's why I like this place," he says with a grin as soon as we're alone. "We tip well."

I take a seat opposite him. It's a nice place with vibrant prints covering the white walls and rustic furniture that doesn't match.

I cross my arms. "Why did you bring me here?"

We've only just sat down when the barista hurries in and places steaming mugs in front of us. Black coffee. It smells divine—chocolatey, almost.

"They make the best black coffee," he says. "I thought you'd like it. I ordered in advance."

"How did you know what I'd want?"

"We spent a summer at Camp Harmony together," he

replies with a bemused smile. "Don't you think I noticed how you took your coffee in McCallister's class?"

I'm tempted to say something about how he's a coffee stalker, but I press my lips together.

"So…" my voice trails off.

"So…" he repeats, dragging one syllable like he wants me to speak first.

"Why did you bring me here, Ve—" Crap. "Levi." Correcting myself is hard. "Is that what you'd prefer I call you?"

"No." Venom scowls. "Of course not, but you should when we're in public."

"I don't know how you don't slip up."

He smiles sadly. "Years of practice."

"You didn't bring me here to talk about music, did you?" I ask, narrowing my eyes suspiciously.

"We can talk about whatever you want, Ash," Venom replies. He ducks down to retrieve my battered lyric book and pushes it over the table. "There you go."

I run my hands over the cover affectionately, then snatch it up into my arms and hug it to my chest.

I narrow my eyes at him. "You shouldn't have read it."

It's like peeking at someone else's diary. Music is how I express my emotions, and I bore my fucking soul into those pages. Words that I never wanted to share.

"What I did was wrong," Venom admits, hanging his head. "I should have stopped reading as soon as I realized what it was."

"Yes," I say. "You should have."

"Your songs are amazing, Ash," he says. The compliment makes my heart flutter, but I keep my face impassive. His eyes probe mine, searching for an answer he won't find. "Your words tell a story. They captivate me."

If I was sitting across from a masked Venom, I'd tell him the feeling was mutual. I'd talk about how his lyrics pulled me from the darkest pit of hell and struck a chord inside me that made me feel understood. But I say nothing.

"I can tell from your lyrics that you're like me," Venom pauses, scrunching his nose like he's deciding what words should come next. "I find it easier to write music than talk to people."

"I get that," I mumble.

I've felt that way too.

Venom bends down again and pulls another notebook out of his backpack. I recognize it from the afternoon at Camp Harmony when I found him writing. "This is for you."

I look from him to the beaten cover. "What do you mean?"

"I want you to take it," he says, although the sadness in his eyes tells me he's struggling to let go. "It's only fair."

I push it away. "You don't have to do this."

"I do," he insists, unwavering in his decision. His tone is commanding when he reiterates, "I want you to have it, Ash."

"Thank you," I say, picking it up carefully like it's a precious artifact. Its pages hold his deepest thoughts and need to be handled delicately. "I'll take care of it."

He shrugs, looking pained. "I want you to know me as well as I know you."

My thoughts stray to the scars hidden under his baggy clothes. The many white slashes over his skin. A stab wound. The secret and hurt he doesn't show the world. When I look at him, I don't see an entitled pop star; I see a lost and troubled guy who doesn't know where he fits in.

"What happened to you?" I blurt out.

His eyes widen at my subject change. Most people would be confused about what I'm asking, but he knows exactly what I'm talking about from the tensing of his shoulders.

"Sorry," I say. What the fuck came over me? How would I feel if it was the other way around? "I shouldn't have said anything... it was wrong... it's none of my business."

seventeen

. . .

Venom | Levi

It's uncomfortable to be alone with her, but it's not because of her presence. Being in her company is amazing, but there's an invisible wall between us.

When she didn't know who we were, she let her guard down. She trusted the Basilisks. She let us in. But now, she's cautious, more guarded. I sense it from the way she shuffles around in her chair, playing with the rings on her fingers, and bouncing her knees under the table. Her restlessness is contagious.

I hadn't planned to give her my notebook, but it felt right. Just like when I told her our secret. It's only fair. I've seen the deepest parts of her soul through reading her words, and I need her to see the real me too, even if exposing my vulnerability split me open more than any blade could.

If I didn't, how could she ever trust me again?

Ash stares into my eyes, searching for something. They pierce through the veil I hide behind and look past the bullshit, and it's fucking terrifying.

"What happened to you?" she asks. Blood rushes to my

head as she shakes her head and starts mumbling an apology, but I'm glad she asked.

It shows she wants to get to know me, doesn't it? But I'm not sure where to start.

Does she want to hear about how I was the poor kid with absent parents who made money from busking? Does she want me to tell her I was a teenager who never fit in at school and got bullied for being an outcast? Will it change anything for her to discover that the first time I found the courage to chase my dreams turned into something awful?

"I should go." She gets up to leave, sending the chair screeching back, but I grab her wrist to stop her. Electricity shoots from my fingertips and up my body. She jerks, and I know she feels it too. A connection.

"No," I say. "Please. Don't go."

Her eyes dart to the door, but she doesn't argue and takes a seat again.

"If you read my notebook," I say, "you'll know all there is to know about me."

She frowns, biting her lip. Shit, she's stunning. Last night they painted her face and changed how she looked, but this version of her, the raw and real version is my favorite. Ash isn't like us. She doesn't need to cover her face with a mask.

"I don't want to read about it," she insists. "I want to hear it from you."

I gulp. I took her to the coffee shop where I had an agreement with the owner that guaranteed my privacy, but I never expected our conversation would take this turn.

My mouth and tongue feel like sandpaper in my mouth as I croak, "What do you want to know?"

"Why don't you sing?"

I provide backing vocals as a Lionheart, but that's not singing to me.

I hadn't sung in years until we were in the recording studio in Wilderton over the summer. Ash's encouragement unlocked something I've kept tethered for too long. It's a story I don't like to tell, but she deserves to know. It's the least I can do.

"When we were younger," I say, my voice barely above a whisper, "I thought I could be a soloist. There was a metal open-mic night. I invited Zed and Ripper to come with me right after our first summer at Camp Harmony."

I remember the excitement when we arrived at the venue. A sketchy dive bar with broken windows. Not long before that, the three of us got drunk and listened to metal together for the first time. It was a bonding experience that changed the course of the rest of our lives.

The open mic was meant to be fun. We dressed up—wobbly eyeliner and black paint smeared over our cheeks. I wanted to surprise them by singing onstage and sharing my new songs.

"You don't have to tell me," Ash murmurs, bringing me back to the present. Her voice is calm and reassuring, giving me the strength to keep going.

"I was one of the last to perform. It was a surprise for the guys, something I thought would make me look cool." I roll my eyes. I should have known I'd never look cool. I take a deep breath and continue, replaying it in my mind as I go. "I got on the stage and started to play. The guitar was in the wrong key, but I didn't mind. I was super psyched to play something that I'd written…"

My adrenaline was pumping. Ripper stood in the back, giving me a wolf whistle when my hands closed around the mic, then it all fell apart…

"The next thing I knew," I say, wincing as smashes and screams rattle through my mind, "the bar was raided. I'm not sure why. Maybe the guys who owned it upset the wrong people. Maybe the people thought we were all freaks..."

Ash's eyes widen, hanging on my every word as my voice trails off.

"A fight broke out," I say matter-of-factly, playing it down. A fight was an understatement. A gang charged in with guns. Thankfully, Ripper and Zed were at the back and able to get away, dodging the rush of the stampede, desperately trying to reach the exit. Five people died that night. Five innocent people. "People got hurt. Some people died, and all I could do was stand on that stage and watch..."

I close my eyes for a second, then open them to rid myself of the images I still have nightmares over.

"I didn't get away unscathed," I say, my hand jumping to the scar on my stomach. It's a reminder of that night and how I was lucky to get out alive.

"Venom," Ash whispers, forgetting where we are, but it's what I need to hear. I need to hear my name coming from her lips. "I'm so sorry."

"It was a long time ago." I take a sip of my now cold coffee. "But that's why I don't sing with the Basilisks. I freeze and can't get the words out... or, I couldn't, until that day at the recording studio with you."

eighteen

. . .

Ash

Venom's body almost falls in on itself, a part of himself shutting down as he tells his story. I see the sadness and feel his pain. It consumes him. The rage, the anger, the hopelessness… and I understand it because I've been there.

Images from my own nightmares surface. Blood-stained sheets… split skin… white skin… open eyes… slack mouth… Mom.

No, I push those images away, finding inner strength and resolve. This isn't about me.

I reach across the table, unable to stop myself from taking his shaking hands.

"I'm so sorry for what happened," I say. I am. I really fucking am. "You have a beautiful voice. A voice I love to hear."

A ghost of a smile lurks on his lips, then it vanishes as he pulls his hands out of my grasp.

"I'm sorry for not telling you about us sooner, Ash." He avoids my gaze. "Keeping it from you was wrong, but I need you to understand it's only because we wanted to

get to know you. We wanted you to see us for who we are, not for who we have to pretend to be for everyone else."

Whenever I used to listen to the Basilisks, I thought they wrote their songs for me. Venom's words strike a chord. I can relate to that, having to smile for the world when you're falling apart on the inside.

"Thank you for telling me that," I say, finally believing I'm seeing the real him for the first time. Venom wears a mask, but now he isn't hiding anymore. He's been through shit, and so have I. "You didn't have to, and you didn't have to apologize either. I'm glad you told me the truth."

"I wanted you to know because of what happened that night..." He clears his throat as my cheeks heat, and I squeeze my thighs together. "It meant something to me. It wasn't just a one-night thing. I don't want it to end. None of us do."

My heartbeat quickens. From the intenseness of his glare, I don't question that he believes what he's saying.

"You can speak for yourself," I say, remembering this morning's headlines, "but you can't speak for the others. Haven't you seen the papers?"

Venom laughs, taking me by surprise. "Are you talking about Ripper?"

"We've all seen the papers," I mutter, unable to keep the annoyance out of my voice.

"You don't get it, Ash." Venom reaches across the table and slips his fingers through mine, stroking my skin with his calloused thumb. His touch makes everything else fall away. "Ripper only went partying because of what he read about you, and what he saw last night with your friend."

"You mean Brick?" I scoff at the ridiculousness of it. "We've known each other since we were kids. We're just friends."

He raises his eyebrows and mimics me, “Have you seen the papers?”

I don’t know whether I’m more irritated or impressed. I raise my chin stubbornly, refusing to back down. “The headlines about me are bullshit.”

“And so is what you saw about Ripper,” Venom says, then smirks at having made his point. He may be right, but I won’t admit it. “Look, the whole thing with you is eating Ripper up inside. You need to talk to him.”

“He doesn’t want to talk to me.”

“He does,” Venom says, squeezing my hand. “You need to go to him. He needs you right now.” His green eyes twinkle, drawing me in like he’s a hypnotist casting a spell on me. “We all do, even if it doesn’t seem like it.”

As much as I don’t want to admit it, maybe a part of me needs them too…

nineteen

. . .

Ripper | Damon

"What do you want?" I call, slurring my words slightly. "I told you I'm not going anywhere."

Buggy is spinning, but that's what happens when it's morning and you're still drinking. I'm lying on the sofa in my boxers, and empty bottles are strewn on the surrounding floor.

I clutch my head. Fuck, it's like someone is hammering on drums in there.

"Hey," I yell as the shutters close. "Zed, you…" I can't think of an insult. "I'm staying here."

The bus door opens, letting light stream in and burn my retinas. I squint.

"Rough night, huh?" a soft voice asks.

The leftover coke in my system combined with alcohol isn't a good mix. My eyelids flicker as a female figure steps closer. Am I seeing shit, or have I finally overdosed after a bender? I've taken more drugs before and lived to tell the tale, so the latter didn't seem likely. At one point, drugs were the only thing that could get me through the day.

"Ash?" I ask. "Is that you?"

Yes, there's no mistaking her long legs and swishy black hair. Venom strides in behind her.

"What're you doing here?" I snarl at him.

"You two need to talk," he says. This is a first. He's not one for staging interventions, that's usually Zed's jurisdiction. "You're not leaving the bus until you've figured this out."

"Wait!" Ash turns in accusation. Fuck, she's sexy when she's angry. "That wasn't part of our deal."

"I'll be back soon," he promises, already one foot out of the door.

He shuts it, leaving the two of us alone. She stands awkwardly, surveying the damage. She crosses her arms, lips curling in disapproval, and it makes me grin.

"Doesn't look like you've had much sleep," she comments.

I stand up and stretch, yawning. "Yeah, something like that."

Her cheeks flush, and I smirk. She's checking me out. What's she thinking? Is she remembering how we fucked her until she screamed our names in the spot she's standing in?

"What's wrong, Ash?" I tease, feeling sober for the first time in hours. "Don't you recognize me without the mask?"

"That's not funny," she says, although her lips twitch.

She walks through the bus, studying our Basilisk paraphernalia. It's a mess. Dishes are piled up by the sink along with empty pizza boxes.

She wrinkles her nose. "You guys live like pigs."

"That's rock 'n' roll, baby," I say, although I reach for a nearby hoodie. I don't want her to think I'm a complete

animal. Now I wish I'd taken Zed's advice and had that shower.

I run my hand through my hair and steal a glance at my reflection in the mirror. My dark hair is a mess, and I reek of booze. This isn't how I imagined my next conversation with Ash going.

"Can I get you a drink or something?" I ask. My palms tingle from nerves. I'm usually confident talking to girls, but that's because I don't give a shit about what they think. But I want Ash to like me.

"I'm good," she declines, then points at a mask on the wall. "Is this from your first tour?"

"Uh-huh." I hunt around a nearby cupboard to find our accompanying photo album and thrust it into her hands while holding my breath. I step away before saying, "You might like this."

Her jaw drops as she opens it. "Woah."

It's filled with polaroids of us. Venom went through a phase of wanting to document what we did. He had lofty ambitions of putting them together in a book for the fans, but the idea went nowhere.

"I'll be right back," I say, making a hasty dash to the bathroom to splash my face with water and brush my teeth.

When I return, Ash is trying the door handle with the book tucked under her arm. She sighs, realizing she's stuck. Venom wasn't kidding about locking us in. There's a spare key on the bus, but I say nothing.

"What's wrong, Ash?" I ask. She freezes, knowing I've caught her. "Do you want to get back to your boyfriend?"

"Brick isn't my boyfriend," she says, narrowing her eyes.

I scowl. "That's not what it looked like last night."

"What about you?" She turns my question around. "Are you and Alexa Frost back together again?"

"No!"

"See? Not everything is as it appears," she says. She's never afraid to say what she's thinking. Something I've always admired about her. Ash moves some of my dirty clothes off the sofa, takes a seat, and opens the album. "If I'm stuck here, you may as well tell me about your time on tour."

I sit next to her. All I can focus on is how close her body is to mine and how warmth is radiating from her skin.

"It was crazy," I say, trying to get my shit together. I point to a few pictures of us in masks. "That's the first time Venom wore the pumpkin mask for the fans."

"It's his favorite." Her eyes light up, and I see the girl we met in Wilderton. The one who saw our music as works of art and didn't care who was behind it.

"Sure is," I say. "He likes that one because it gives him more room to breathe."

She gasps like I've divulged an enormous secret. "What?"

"Why are you shocked?" I ask, reclining back.

"I mean, that's it? That's the reason he wears the pumpkin mask?"

I laugh, remembering how she used to stalk us on the Basilisks Wiki and how cute I found it. The fans like to obsess over the smallest detail and why Venom always wears a pumpkin mask is a popular topic.

"Sorry to disappoint." I wink. "It's not a big conspiracy. He can get claustrophobic. Prosthetics are hot."

She laughs. A genuine laugh. It makes me smile to know I made her smile. Usually, she scowls at me without

a mask, and I'm surprised at how fucking good it feels. It's making my come-down bearable.

"Fans would lose their shit if they found out," she says.

My voice dips to a low, dangerous growl. "Can you keep a secret?"

She bites her lip, drawing my eyes down her face. She has no idea how badly I want to catch her bottom lip between my teeth and suck on it to draw a delicious moan from her.

My unanswered question hangs in the air. The question is about more than a mask. She swallows hard, and her pupils dilate. Fuck, she's attracted to me. She might wish she wasn't, but she can't deny her instincts.

She murmurs in a husky tone, "Yes."

I lean in, closer and closer, tipping my face to meet hers. I'm being cautious. I don't want to scare her off when we're finally making progress. She doesn't back away. Our noses are almost touching, then my lips brush against hers. So softly it's like we're not touching at all.

I pull away slightly, just enough that my lips are still tingling. I watch her chest and her breathing quicken, but she doesn't back away. This time, I lean in again without hesitation.

I kiss her gently, and she responds. My hands cup her face, and she shuffles closer. Our kiss becomes more urgent and hungry.

My cock hardens. I feel like a teenager again, making out before my parents come home. It's the same rush of excitement. She makes it feel like the first time.

BANG!

Suddenly, the door bursts open, and we spring apart.

If looks could kill, Venom would be dead.

"Shit," she says breathlessly through swollen lips.

Venom raises his eyebrows, bemused. "I came to check you hadn't killed each other," he says, "but it looks like you've been just fine."

"I should go," Ash mumbles, turning scarlet. "I have to get back for rehearsals."

"Ash!" I catch her wrist, already seeking my next hit. I need her. "When can we see you again?"

She looks torn, pausing for a few seconds before saying, "Soon."

Soon.

Never has one word sounded so fucking good.

twenty

. . .

Venom | Levi

I lead Ash to the waiting car a few blocks over and don't say a word.

"I—" she begins.

"No," I interrupt before she can say any more. "You don't need to explain."

"Aren't you—"

"Mad? Jealous? No," I say. I never thought I'd be able to share the girl I liked, but seeing Ripper almost lose himself again made me realize how much he needs her. How much we need her. "Thanks for speaking to him. He needed to see you."

She nods. "I have one question, though."

"Go on," I say.

"Is your pumpkin mask your favorite because you're claustrophobic?"

"Is that what he told you?" I grin and shake my head, holding the cab door open for her. "It's not a lie. I get claustrophobic, but that's not why that one means the most to me."

Her face lights up, hanging on my every word. "Now you have to tell me."

"Maybe I will," I say. "But you'll have to wait until our next date to hear it."

"A date?"

I shrug like it's nothing but hope she'll say yes. "If you like."

"I don't know how we could..." Her voice trails off, thinking about what would happen if we got caught together.

"Don't worry, I've had years of practice," I say. Sneaking around is something we're professionals at. The cab driver coughs to hurry us along, but I'm not joining her. "Have a nice day, Ash. Take the cab back. I'll see you around."

twenty-one

. . .

Ash

My stomach is still fluttering from my conversation with Venom. A date? He didn't seem to care at all that he walked in on me kissing his bandmate.

My lips tingle when I think about Ripper's kiss. I don't know how it happened. He has serious bad-boy vibes, and while I shouldn't like him, it's impossible not to. Being around him makes me lose my self-control. Kissing him felt natural, and holy fucking shit it was good.

But he has a vulnerable side too. His eyes were filled with crushing disappointment when I got up to leave. There's more to him than his rebellious rule-breaking exterior, and it intrigues me.

When I return to the hotel room, Cookie is busy liaising with the wardrobe department. Picking outfits is my least favorite task, and she's amazing at it.

"How were your rehearsals?" she asks, looking up from the rack.

"Great," I reply.

After spending the morning with Venom and Ripper, I went straight to the studio and crushed my vocals

The next Popstarz show theme is around pop, and I have a surprise planned. It was Jacinta's idea and, despite my initial resistance, I've come around to it. I'm giving a Lionheart song an original twist that also doubled as an apology for my acting like an ass.

I haven't forgiven them fully yet. I still don't know what's going on between us, but it isn't the end. Kissing Ripper and spending time with Venom proved that. We can't avoid each other, and I've never felt more understood or alive than when I'm around the Basilisks, so I want to see where things go… even if it comes with risks and secrecy.

"What's the special occasion?" I ask, noticing the outfits Cookie's flipping through are cocktail dresses.

"It's another contestant dinner tonight, remember?" she prompts. "I thought it'd be good to find you something to wear from wardrobe."

She's right. I own nothing appropriate.

"Perfect." Cookie picks a slinky dress. Red, simple, understated. I prefer black, but Cookie keeps insisting I branch out of my comfort zone. Paired with my black hair, smokey eyes, and matte nail polish, I'd look like a vampire. The stylist smiles as Cookie thanks her and disappears. "What do you think?"

I groan, despite the gorgeous dress. "Are you sure I can't get out of it?"

"Nope," she replies, "it's in your contract." Cookie winks. "I'll be thinking of you when I'm grabbing ramen at that new place everyone's raving about."

"That sounds like bliss," I grumble. "That contract is like signing our souls away."

"You'll have a great time," Cookie says, then adds

hopefully "or at least you can pretend to. By the way, I missed a call from Brick earlier. Did he reach you?"

"Weird." I check my cell and see no texts or voicemails. "I haven't heard from him."

She shrugs. "Must have been a pocket dial." She spins the dress around on its hanger. "Let's get you dressed up."

I roll my eyes as she switches on dance music. There's no getting out of it.

———

I pull the sides of my dress down. It didn't look short until I put it on, riding high and leaving me worrying about flashing my ass if I lean over.

"Looking good, Ashley," Theo, the sleazeball, comments as I enter the dining room.

Yep, this is definitely the last time I wear this dress.

Dinner is another painfully formal affair with the same set-up as before. I head to the bar where pre-poured drinks are waiting. I grab an orange juice, wishing I was old enough to drink the champagne to help me get through the evening.

Ripper is standing nearby, casually leaning against the wall. He looks me over hungrily and runs his tongue over his lips. Everyone else is gathered around the table as he approaches me, and my cheeks heat.

He arches one eyebrow and asks, "Are you looking forward to tonight?"

I mutter sarcastically, "Oh yeah, I can't wait."

He takes his cell out of his pocket. I'm about to tell him it's rude to text mid-conversation when my clutch vibrates. I turn away from him and check the message flashing over the screen.

Ripper: You look beautiful.

"It's true," he says.

I tuck my phone away with fumbling fingers, pretending I didn't hear him.

Music is playing, so no one can hear what we're saying, but my heart races. If we want to continue whatever this is, I need to learn to be around him without blushing like a schoolgirl—or maybe that'll help make it more convincing. That's the normal reaction when in the company of a boy band most girls have a crush on.

"Thanks." I'm not used to compliments. "I should sit down."

This time, I'm lucky to be placed at the end of the table with my group—Jacinta, Venom, and Marcus.

Zed sits next to Tiffany at the center of the table. She paws his arm, and he doesn't look in my direction, but his back straightens when I sit down. He's noticed me but doesn't want to show it.

Does he know I've spoken to Venom? Has he heard what happened with Ripper?

It's easier to tell what Venom and Ripper are thinking, but Zed is impossible to read… all I'm sure of is that he thinks I'm a threat who will expose them.

"How was practice, Ash?" Marcus asks, making polite conversation.

I answer nonchalantly, then flip the question around, giving him time to talk, which is a welcome distraction.

They bring the first courses out. Mushroom pâté on sourdough. If Dad saw the size of these portions, he'd be asking where the rest of the food was.

Venom catches my eye across the table and smiles, then it vanishes so fast I think I've imagined it.

Jacqueline tapping against her glass makes the table descend into silence, and we all turn to face her. Her pristine white dress is tailored to her figure, and her hair is styled in an elegant updo that emphasizes her sharp cheekbones.

"Congratulations on making it to the second week," she says. "Tonight is our opportunity to celebrate. Tiffany has also asked to say a few words."

"Thank you, Jacqueline," Tiffany simpers, rising in her chair. Jacqueline better prepare herself for an ass licking. "Going into the next show, I want to recognize that this isn't easy for anyone. But I would like to extend my heartfelt support to my dear Camp Harmony friend, Ashley."

Hearing my name jolts me out of a daydream of what my date with Venom might look like.

"Ashley doesn't want to say anything, but I'm sure we've all seen the most recent headlines," she says. What is she talking about? "Being here without your mom must be tough, Ashley. When I heard the show will donate funds to a charity, I had to put forward Suicide Awareness. For those of you who don't know, Ash lost her mom to suicide a few years ago, as well as trying to take her own life herself..."

Panic rises in my chest, catching in my throat and making me want to cough. Tiffany continues to talk, words that I can't hear because it feels like I'm submerged in water.

Everyone in Meadow Springs knew my mom was ill. Her untimely death was tragic, but not a surprise—although some people were disapproving when they discovered she took her life to spare us from watching her decline. That information would have been easy for journalists to find by asking the locals, but how did they find

out about me? Aside from the hospital staff, Dad, and my therapist, there's only one other person who knows I swallowed those pills. One person who I never thought would betray my trust.

"Tiffany," Zed's steely tone brings me back to the present. His voice makes the hairs on the back of my neck stand on end. It's dark, foreboding almost—a tone I've never heard him use as Zach. "That's enough."

"But it's such an important cause," Tiffany says. The bitch doesn't know when to quit. "All I want to do is show Ashley that she has our support."

The only "support" Tiffany has given me is when she dragged me into a freezing lake where I could have drowned. I'm sure she'd be happy to tip more pills down my throat if it meant increasing her chances of winning Popstarz.

"That's enough," Zed snaps, slamming his fists on the table and making her squeak in surprise.

"Ahem." Jacqueline coughs, realizing dinner is veering dramatically out of her control. She glowers at the Lionheart frontman as she says, "Thank you, Tiffany. I'm sure Ashley is very grateful. Now let's talk about…"

The other contestants' pitying looks make my skin crawl. Venom tries to catch my eye, but I don't look back.

I have to get out.

I need to be on my own.

My heart pounds.

My breath grows shallow.

I need relief. I need to…

I stand, hitting my knee on the wooden table as I do. My shaking legs feel like they're about to collapse, but I will my body to move—at least until I'm out of there.

I don't care that I'm making a scene. A small group

finding out about my past is bad enough, but my story is being blasted around the entire fucking world like my life is nothing more than a gossip column.

"Ashley," Jacinta calls after me, but I don't listen. I storm past the servers and start climbing the stairs, taking two at a time.

I want to scream.

I want to claw at Tiffany's perfect eyes and go crazy on a drum kit until my arms ache from the force.

Pent-up rage, frustration, and sadness want to swallow me, and I'm helpless to stop them from taking over.

Zed's voice follows me. "Ash."

I don't look back.

My thoughts blur and tears distort my vision.

Mom's gray face was motionless. Weeping wrists. Blood, dripping in a pool, tapping against the wooden floor. Red sheets, wet and destroyed, bunched around her lifeless body. My piercing scream. A row of pills, promising to take the pain away. Dark clouds rolling in…

"Ashley." Zed's voice is closer now. His firm hand grabs my shoulder. "Come with me."

I want to resist and try to wrestle out of his grasp, but I can't. Silent, ugly tears fall as I struggle to catch my breath.

"This way." He takes my arm and steers me to the elevator. "Just breathe slowly. In and out."

The elevator walls close in. Why would Brick sell me out like this? He's supposed to be my best friend.

"Come on, Ash," Zed murmurs as we reach our destination. I'm not sure where we're heading. He uses a keycard to let us into a room I don't recognize. "Sit down over here."

I do as he asks, perching on the edge of a cream sofa. Zed kneels in front of me and takes my hands. His grip

anchors me to the present to stop my consciousness from floating away.

"You need to breathe with me, okay?" His voice is calm, cutting through the chaos. "You're having a panic attack. Just follow my breathing."

I count in my head with him.

In. One. Two. Three. Four.

Hold. One. Two. Three. Four.

Out. One. Two. Three. Four.

I don't know how long we sit there. Whenever I think I have my breathing under control, a rising panic creeps in, and I'm gulping for air again, but Zed stays where he is. He keeps counting, pulling me back.

Slowly, my tears dry up. Our surroundings fade to nothingness. I concentrate on his hands and our synchronized breathing.

"There," he says finally. "How does that feel?"

I sniff and mumble, "Better."

I'm not having palpitations anymore, but that doesn't mean I'm okay.

"I'm sorry about what Tiffany did down there," Zed says, moving to sit by my side. "She shouldn't have done that."

Tiffany enjoyed breaking the news, but she didn't put the story into the public realm.

"I feel," I struggle to find the word, "violated."

"I get it," he says. "The press are like vultures. People you think you can trust sell your stories. It's what happens in our world. It doesn't get easier, but you get used to it."

"I don't know if I can do this," I confess. "This life, the cameras, the press, having to watch over your shoulder constantly."

"You're one of the bravest people I've ever met, Ash," Zed says. "You can do this."

"Yeah, right," I say, unconvinced. I don't want his fucking sympathy. "You've already told me what you think of me. A groupie whore, remember?"

He flinches. "I should never have said that. I was hurt, and sometimes, I just lose it." He hangs his head. "But I mean it when I say that you're one of the bravest people I know. At Camp Harmony, you took on Tiffany Lockhart. You stole the final show and stood up for what was right. You act with integrity, happy to fight for what you believe in and the people you care about."

I stare at the weird-looking statue on a nearby shelf, unsure how to take his compliments and whether he's being sincere.

"You don't have to say that to make me feel better," I say. "I don't need your pity."

"I don't pity you, Ash," Zed says. "I understand you. I've been where you are now. I've been watched my whole fucking life. My family has expectations of who they want me to be. I've grown up under a fucking lens, and…" He sighs and runs his hand through his red hair. "That's why I was so mad when Venom told you our secret because I can't lose that. Being a Basilisk is the only shred of privacy I have left. It's my only way to live a normal life."

I thought I'd understood why they wanted to keep their identities a secret, but I get it more now. My story coming out is a one-off incident. How would it have felt for Zed to have his every move watched, tracked, and written about?

"I meant what I said the other day," I say, wanting to give him more reassurance. It's all I can do. "I promise I won't tell your secret, Zed."

"That doesn't matter now," he dismisses. "All I want is for you to be okay. You don't have to go on this journey alone. We're here for you. I'm here for you."

I nod as a weight I didn't know I was holding lifts from my shoulders. Then I remember what Brick did, and it crashes down on me again.

"Apart from my dad, the hospital, and my therapist, no one knows what I tried to do except for Brick," I admit. I bite my bottom lip to stop it from trembling. "I thought he was my best friend."

"I can track him down." Zed's jaw clenches. His features transform into a mask of pure fury. "I'll fix it."

"No," I say, fearing he'll hurt him. He has money and connections. "I'll handle it. I just..."

I've never opened up to anyone properly about what happened that night before. Sure, I touched on it with the therapist, but I didn't feel comfortable with her. But now I have the urge to tell Zed about it. Being in his company makes me feel safe like I can tell him anything, and he won't judge me for it.

"I hate the way people look at you after something happens. The look of pity. It's how everyone used to look at me in Meadow Springs after my mom died," I say. "I took those pills because I couldn't deal with it anymore. I missed my mom. When she died, everything fell apart. Nothing was the same, and I wanted it all to stop. Everything was too much. The sympathy. The pain. Now it's going to happen all over again. When people look at me, all they'll see is the girl with the dead mom who tried to kill herself."

Zed takes my hand again. I don't pull away as his fingers stroke my knuckles.

"That's not how I see you, Ash," he says. "It's not how

any of us see you. We see a strong, beautiful woman who looks at the world differently than other people."

I roll my eyes. "Please, you don't have to—"

"I mean it." Zed squeezes my hand tightly. "We haven't known each other long, and I'm not going to pretend I know everything about you, but you make us want to be better. Since we met you, the Basilisks haven't been the same."

How do I respond to that? My heart rate speeds up again, but not from panic.

"You're not on your own, Ash," Zed says. "If anything gets too much for you, you call us. Anytime. We're here for you. We'll always be here for you."

I look into his eyes: blue, sparkling, troubled. On the outside, he's a pop star living the Hollywood dream. He commands the cameras, putting on an act, but he's hurting on the inside too.

Zed's gaze strays to my lips. Despite their lying and his harsh words, I can tell he's sorry. He hasn't said it—apologies don't come easy to him—but I sense it from the intense way he watches me like he'll jump in front of a bullet to protect me.

"I want to kiss you," he says, "but I won't… not yet. I need to be sure that you want this."

"Zed…"

He puts a finger to my lips.

"Ripper and Venom are happy just to be around you, but if I kiss you, I need you to be ours." His tone is deep and rumbly, igniting a fire in between my legs. The Basilisk is stirring under the surface and begging to be free. I realize I want to see that side of him again. "I can't have another fling. That's not something I want with you. You mean more to me than that, and I don't want to ruin

this by moving too fast if you're not sure what you want."

"I-I-I—" I stammer.

"I need you to be sure you want us, Ash," Zed purrs. "We don't live a conventional life. It'd be easier if you found a nice guy who didn't have to hide behind a mask and didn't come with extra complications. You've seen for yourself tonight the damage the press can do. I can't ask you to live a life of secrecy for us. I need you to think about it first. This is about more than just me. I have to know whether you're ready to be with the three of us and accept everything that comes with it. I'll give you time to think about your answer and, if you want out, we'll respect that."

Is he saying what I think he is? Before I can answer, a knock at the door makes us jump. I'm reeling from his omission as he goes to answer it.

Cookie looks past Zed and barrels inside without waiting for an invitation. She was supposed to be out with friends tonight.

"Ash." She's panting, doubled over, clutching her phone in her hand. "I've been looking for you everywhere. I saw…" She stops to catch her breath. "I saw the news, and I had to come straight… away… to see if you were okay."

"I see you'll be in excellent hands now, Ashley," Zed says, returning to his usual cool and collected self.

I stand, taking that as my cue to leave. I catch Zed's eye, hoping to convey that, even though my head is a scrambled mess, I think I know what I want, but all I can say is, "Thank you for everything."

"Anytime," he replies, but there's a loaded meaning behind his words.

Cookie looks between us, frowning, then dismissing whatever she's thinking.

"You already know?" she asks as we reach the elevator. "How? I came as soon as I heard."

"Tiffany broke the news to the entire table at dinner," I explain. "Ze—Zach wanted to make sure I was okay. I was a little… upset."

"That bitch," Cookie rages. "How could she do that?"

"It's okay," I try to calm her down. "Well, it's not okay, but I wouldn't expect anything less from her."

"I'm so sorry, Ash," she says again as we reach our room. We both collapse onto the sofa. A million thoughts flit around my head. "I've already rung your dad and told him about it."

"How is he on a rating of one, totally fine, to ten, driving all the way here to check on me?" I groan.

"I told him I'll be with you, and he doesn't need to come," she says, "but he was looking at flights until I talked him down."

Typical Dad.

"Thanks," I say. "I know what he's like when he goes into super protective mode."

"Are you sure you're okay though?" Cookie asks. She already knows about my mom from our conversations, but I've never shared my mental health struggles with her. "It can't have been easy to sit there while Tiffany said a load of bullshit."

"I'll be fine," I reply as Zed's words come back to me. I'm not alone. The Basilisks are behind me. At one time, listening to their music was enough to motivate me to get out of bed and go to school. Now I know the guys behind the masks. Things are crazier than I ever expected, but

their presence brings me comfort. They believe in me. “Speaking to Zach helped.”

“Look at you making friends with a Lionheart,” Cookie says. “I never thought I’d see the day.”

“I guess they’re not all that bad,” I say with a shrug. “Have you read the stories?”

“Do you want me to show you them?”

I shake my head. “I don’t need to, but it’d be good to know what they say, in case I need to set the record straight.”

“I can give you a quick run-down,” she volunteers, adding quickly, “but only if you want to hear it.”

“I have to.”

“If you want me to stop at any time, just say the word, okay?” Cookie says, “I’ll give it to you straight, then we don’t have to talk about it again if you don’t want to.”

I brace myself and nod.

“They say that your mom was ill, and she took her life, and you were…” Cookie takes a deep breath. This is hard for her to relay, but she pushes on. “You were the one who found her. There’s a lot around mental health and depression. They say you overdosed. Basically, it paints it as a tragedy and that you’ve had a,” she uses her fingers as quotation marks, “troubled few years.”

Hearing her rattle off the points is like ripping off a Band-Aid.

“Is there anything you want to contest or tell your side of the story?” Cookie asks. She puts down her phone. “We don’t have to do this now, you know. This can wait.”

“No,” I insist. “I want to.”

Her eyes soften. “If you’re sure…”

“It’s all correct,” I say, and it only confirms my suspicions. Apart from Dad and those on the emergency call,

Brick is the only person who knows I found her. "Brick had to have told them. No one else knows those details."

Cookie gasps, almost falling off the sofa. "But why would he do that? He's your best friend."

"Yeah," I reply, numb and devoid of emotion. Our strong friendship has fallen apart like a tumbling house of cards. "I thought so too."

"I didn't think he'd do something like that..."

His betrayal hurts more than knowing the entire country is pitying me.

"Neither did I," I say. He may be hurting after my second rejection, but this is a total betrayal. Things will never be the same again. "I need to call him."

"I can give you time alone. I'll go and wait downstairs since I've got work to do anyway. Text me as soon as you're done?"

I nod.

Cookie pauses as she reaches the door and turns back to say, "If you ever wanna talk, you know I'm here. Or if you ever don't wanna talk and want to sit and binge through hours of Netflix together, I'm your girl."

"Thanks, Cookie," I smile. "I'll text you."

Now, I have to figure out why my best friend betrayed me.

twenty-two

. . .

Ash

I find Brick's number and hit dial. I don't know what I'm going to say yet, but my earlier panic has given way to a wave of simmering anger. He answers on the second ring as if he's been waiting for my call.

"Ash." Brick's voice is higher than usual, completely different from his natural chilled manner. "I wanted to call you—"

"Why?" I ask. "So you can tell me why you went to the press and told them stories about me?"

"Ash," his voice breaks, "please let me explain."

"Is this because of what happened last night?" I snarl, not leaving time for him to respond. "Did you do it because I rejected you? I thought we were friends, Brick. I thought our friendship meant something to you, or have you been waiting to hook up with me for years and aren't interested now because you know it's never gonna happen?"

"I know why you're angry. I get it, I do." His voice is desperate, pleading. "But I didn't realize I was talking to a journalist. I'd never have done that to you. After our fight

I went to a bar nearby. No one checked my ID, so I started drinking. I was upset, okay? A woman sat next to me, buying me more drinks, and we got talking. She never told me who she was."

"And you told this random woman my fucking story?" I blast. We're from a small town, but he isn't a total moron. "You know your picture is all over the papers, right? People are calling us America's fucking sweethearts! I'm on Popstarz. Didn't you stop to think that I'm not someone you should talk about?"

"I know, I know..." He's choked up, but it's hard to find sympathy when it's your story splashed over the pages of every tabloid. Brick may not have acted with malicious intent, but actions have consequences. "Things just came out. I was telling her how I'd been there for you through tough times, and she asked me a few questions about it. It didn't come out in the way she wrote it. I said a bunch of other stuff. She must have just put it all together and twisted my words."

"And shared my darkest moments with the entire world," I say. "This is even worse than when you shared the video of me singing at Mom's funeral. I know you were upset, but it isn't an excuse. You can't take it back."

Brick has an annoying habit of trying to act in my best interest to my detriment. His uploading my video may have gotten me into Camp Harmony, but, yet again, it showed me breaking down mid-song.

"I know," he says. "Your dad's already come around, and he's furious. I tried to stop her from leaking the story when she called me this morning. It turns out I gave her my number at the bar. She said there was nothing she could do. It was coming out anyway, and she offered to give me money for it. A lot of money." He

pauses for too long. "Enough money to save the family business."

"And you took it?" My stomach turns. "You profited from it?"

"Look, Ash..." He's fucking unbelievable. "She was going to print the story anyway. I know it sounds bad, and I'll give you the—"

"It doesn't just sound bad, it sounds fucking terrible." My hands shake with fury. "You took the money."

"You can have it," he offers. "When Dad cashes the check, I'll tell him to transfer it to you—"

"I don't want it," I snap.

"I tried to call Cookie earlier," he says. "I wanted to give you a heads-up, but what choice did I have, Ash? The story was coming out anyway, and the money can save the business. I panicked. It was wrong. I shouldn't have taken the money, but my family—"

I always knew fame would come at a price. Hell, it's something the Lionhearts warned me about. But I never predicted my best friend would do this.

"Fuck you, Brick," I say. "Don't call me again."

I don't realize until after I've hung up that I'm crying. Fuck. I knew Popstarz would change my life, but I never expected it to take a turn so quickly.

Everything I thought I knew is falling apart.

twenty-three

. . .

Zed | Zach

The torturous dinner party has finally ended, and we return to our suite.

"We can't let him get away with it," Ripper rages. His anger is taking over as he prowls around like a predator. "Didn't you see her face when Tiffany said those things? What happened broke her."

"Ash is strong," I say, although I'm just as furious about Ash's secrets being exposed, I have to stay measured, despite my instincts wanting to track Brick Langford down. "She'll be okay."

"That's not the point." Ripper picks up a cushion and throws it. It doesn't have the same effect as the vase I smashed. If anything, it's kinda cute, and Venom disguises a laugh behind a cough. When Ripper gets riled, it's best to let him get it out of his system. "He needs to pay."

"We don't know the full story," Venom intervenes. He's spent the most time with Ash recently. "They're close. We know better than anyone how manipulative the media can be."

Ripper scowls, unwilling to listen to reason, and hisses, "If he cared about her, he'd never have done that."

"He's not from our world," I remind him. "We've made mistakes in our past, remember?"

Ripper stops pacing and turns to face me. "So, what happened?"

"What do you mean?" I respond, although I know perfectly well what he's asking.

"What did she say when you followed her?" Ripper presses.

Venom is paying full attention now, too. He should have been the one who followed her. But when he rose from the table, I was already halfway across the room in pursuit. It was stupid of me. Venom is her mentor. He should be the one comforting her, but my feelings overwhelmed me.

I couldn't stand to see her hurt, knowing what she was going through.

"Tiffany wasn't happy," Venom says. "She looked like she was about to cry."

"Fuck Tiffany," Ripper snarls.

It wasn't my best move to have snubbed Tiffany. My mother and hers are working on plans to shine even more attention on our families. Mom hasn't divulged the full details yet, but I suspect it'll involve a fake relationship, which I know Tiffany will be happy to go along with. Me disagreeing with her publicly won't do our "couple goals" image any favors.

"Jacqueline understood my reasons," I say. After I returned from comforting Ash to join them for dessert, I spoke to her and she bought my lies. "I've got the most experience in handling the press. It's fitting that I offered advice."

"How was she?" Venom asks, chewing on his lip in concern.

I opt not to tell them about Ash's full-blown panic attack because that'd be all the ammunition Ripper needs to go to Meadow Springs and handle Brick himself.

Instead, I go for a half-truth. "She's been better, but she'll be okay."

"Jacqueline will love this," Venom says. "It'll be more attention for her perfect show."

"It won't be the only story that leaks about the contestants either," I say. Before I rejoined the dinner, I contacted a few journalist friends I'd made over the years. Not all journalists are bad, and if we had to be written about, I've always liked to control a story. "Another story is coming out about Meredith's teenage pregnancy, Theo cheating on his ex-girlfriend, and something about drug addiction for another one. They're going all-out with digging up the dirt for this series."

"Starnote will love their viewer numbers," Venom comments wryly. He turns to a seething Ripper, who is sitting in a large high-backed chair. "Have you heard from Jacqueline?"

I pinch the bridge of my nose. Being stuck in a hotel with the girl we like, the older woman who kick-started our careers and wants to use Ripper's dick like her personal dildo, and the girl my mom wants to set me up with is difficult to juggle.

"Since she tried to proposition me in her room?" Ripper laughs coldly. He doesn't like to show it, but he hates himself for what happened between them. I hate myself for it too. He did it for us. She manipulated and used him. "She's sent a few messages asking to meet, but

I've ignored them. But she can't find out about Ash. After earlier—"

My head snaps up. "What happened earlier?"

The two of them exchange a guilty look. What am I missing?

Venom squirms under my glare and says, "I may have taken Ash to Buggy to see Ripper during our mentoring session."

A week ago, I'd have lost my shit over his recklessness, but I don't have it in me. After sharing my feelings with Ash, how can I be mad? The two of them are as crazy about her as I am.

"And?" I prompt him to continue. "What happened?"

A small smile crosses Ripper's face, dissipating some of his rage. He doesn't need to say anything. I can read his expressions well enough to know it was a good meeting.

"We need to be more careful," I say.

Venom's mouth falls open. "Aren't you going to lecture us for not telling you?"

"I'm mad you didn't tell me," I say, "but it doesn't change the fact it's going to keep happening. No matter how much we try to stay away from Ash, it's not working."

"What're you saying, Zed?" Ripper pushes, wanting to hear me say it. The bastard.

"If Ash wants to make this work," I say, "and that's a big if, we have to be careful. After what happened tonight, she might not want to be part of our lives. If she wants to pursue whatever this is between us, then we have to be careful. We can't afford any fuck-ups, for our sake or hers."

They nod in agreement.

"I told her she needs to think about what she wants," I

say. "If she wants out, we have to respect that." My eyes rest on Ripper in particular. "All of us have to respect that. Agreed?"

"Agreed," they say in unison, despite initial hesitation.

"I told her to think about her answer," I say.

Now it's a waiting game. We've left the decision in Ash's hands. As much as I don't want her to walk away or think about it being a possibility, I'd understand if that's what she wanted. Who would want to be with us and all the baggage that comes with it?

I always thought that the Basilisks would be enough for me. It was better than anything I could have hoped for. A creative outlet. A life where I got to make my own decisions. But, for the first time, I'm questioning whether that would be enough for us without Ash by our side. If she didn't want to pursue our connection, would there be a permanent void in the Basilisks forever?

twenty-four

. . .

Ripper | Damon

The show drags on. A spectacle that makes me want to stuff cotton balls into my ears and has me checking my watch under the judge's table.

It's an ad break. Jacqueline, who is sitting by my side, leans in. Her wall of perfume hits me and catches in the back of my throat. Her custom-made fragrance could double as a bug exterminator.

"Are you enjoying your night, Damon?" she asks in a low, sultry voice as her hand slides over my thigh. "I'm looking forward to an early night. Are you?"

I don't react. How can I when we're being watched by a live audience behind us and surrounded by my band-mates and the other judges?

I bite my tongue and clench my fists, hoping she'll take the hint. Her hand slips toward my shrinking cock before pausing.

"What do you think, Damon?" Her predatory stare burns into my skin, scorching it. "You have to sample the newest wine I ordered from France. A mature red." She flutters her eyelashes. "I know you'll like it."

"I'm sober," I snap.

She withdraws her hand, her lip curling. "That's not what it looked like at Club Seventy-Four last week."

"Times change," I snarl, no longer afraid of her wrath.

I think of Ash somewhere backstage, who will be nervous about her upcoming performance.

There have been more articles published since the story about her broke. Most people feel sorry for her, which she'll hate. If anything, it's made her more popular with the public. Everyone roots for the underdog.

"Places, everyone," the crew calls, signaling the end of the break. "We're back on in five… four…"

I look to the left. Venom tilts his head as if to ask whether everything is okay. I nod sharply. Not as okay as I want it to be, but I'll live.

We have another Basilisks show lined up in two days. Being cooped up in one place is enough to drive anyone insane.

Tessa walks across the stage to the audience's cheers. She acts like the perfect host, but she's coked up ahead of time to keep herself going. It won't be long until they discover her habit and she loses all of her presenter jobs—hopefully, her property investments should see her through any rough times ahead.

"Next up, we have Ashley Cooper," Tessa declares in a highly animated fashion. "Ashley's story has melted hearts across America this week. You can donate to a cause dear to Ashley's heart by dialing the number on your screen now. Ashley will be singing…"

Tessa pauses and puts her finger to her earpiece as if she's getting a message. I sit up straighter in my seat. Is Ash going to bail?

"I'm hearing there is a last-minute song change," Tessa

says. "Let's welcome Ashley singing *Hold Me Tightly* by the Lionhearts."

Jacqueline's head swishes around to throw daggers at Jacinta. Even though she, Jacinta, and Jin are supposed to have equal say, Jacqueline gets the final decision on song choices. She'll be furious they dared deviate from her rules. If Jacinta notices, she doesn't react and claps wildly. What could Jacqueline do? She can't reprimand her on the air.

Starnote drama doesn't matter to me, though. Ash picked one of our songs. That has to mean something, right?

The stage catapults into darkness, then a lone spotlight shines over Ash sitting on a stool with a guitar.

It's pop week. All the other contestant's performances have dancing, but yet again, our girl isn't afraid of being different.

Ash is beautiful in black jeans and a tight white T-shirt with jewelry she would have never picked out on her own. It's a smart choice. It plays into her girl-next-door vibe.

Ash starts to play. *Hold Me Tightly* is upbeat with a catchy tune. Ash's version is slow and haunting. It changes the meaning of the song and reflects the week she's had.

Her voice is soft and melodic, more gentle than I've ever heard it before. It's a direct contrast to her gravelly growl that I've grown to love so much. She sings delicately, every note perfectly hit, tugging at my heart and taking my breath away.

I'm captivated and awe-struck at her ability to give a Lionheart song emotional depth.

She sings:

"Hold on tightly,
Don't look down,
With you by my side, there's no turning back…"

I turn my expression into an unreadable blank canvas, knowing the cameras will be watching. Everyone loves to see an artist's reaction when someone covers their work.

Is this Ash's way of giving us the answer we've been waiting for?

When she finishes, I stand alongside Zed and Venom. The entire studio erupts. Ash looks up from the guitar with wide eyes, stunned at the reaction she's getting. She doesn't know how talented she is.

Tessa returns to the stage and joins her. She puts her arm around Ash's shoulder. "This must have been a hard week for you, Ashley."

"It has been," Ash answers honestly, "which is why I wanted to do a twist on a modern pop song. It seemed more fitting."

"And what a twist it was," Tessa says. "Why don't we hear what the Lionhearts thought of your cover?"

Cameras zip along the line, getting a close-up of our faces.

Zed answers, "I'm sure I speak for all of us when I say that we loved it. You did a better job of our song than we did."

Ash beams, making my chest ache like someone has grabbed my heart and squeezed it tight.

Tessa points the microphone at Ash and says, "How does it feel to get that feedback from the Lionhearts?"

"Great," she replies. "I never expected it."

Her eyes stray across the studio to meet mine with an

underlying fire, and I fucking know what her answer is going to be.

My cock stirs in my pants, and I'm thankful Jacqueline's dirty paws are off me.

The girl standing on stage who captured the nation's hearts has also stolen mine.

twenty-five

. . .

Ash

After everything that happened this week, I don't want to prance around the stage like a show pony. I want to make people fucking feel something.

When Jacinta suggested I cover a Lionheart song, I almost spilled coffee over my sheet music. Their songs are catchy and mindless, but when Jacinta played *Hold Me Tightly*, I heard something else. Sure, it was about love, but it mixed something else in. Between the lyrics, I could see through their veil of pretending to be who they really are.

I made it my own by adding an acoustic spin, but I didn't know whether the public would like it. It didn't fit with the other performances, but if I had to leave, at least I would know that I'd given my all.

Before Tessa announces the results, we have to endure a performance from a singer who I only know from their dating history that's always splashed over magazine covers.

"Good luck," Meredith mimes as we file back onto the stage to hear our fate.

When we stand there like lab rats under a light, it

doesn't feel like any time has passed since last week. Tessa drones on to build tension.

When she calls the first name, I'm stunned and almost fall over.

"Ashley."

Tiffany smiles politely and claps along with everyone else, but her facade drops for a split second. She's furious —perhaps she's still sulking after Zed took my side at dinner.

This may not be the type of music I live for, but I'm grateful to have had an opportunity to make a song my own. It gives me more freedom than I had at Camp Harmony, and maybe, for now, that's enough…

Other names are called out until Marcus, the hunky guy Meredith has been lusting over and the only other survivor apart from me in Jacinta's group, is revealed to be the leaving contestant. Everyone is shocked, including the audience. His good looks placed him as a favorite to win. Poor Meredith. It's a blow to Jacinta, but it will please Jacqueline that it's not one of her acts.

After we gather to say goodbye to Marcus, we're all escorted to waiting cars to whisk us off to an after-party at a nearby club. Even though Tiffany and I are under twenty-one, they have made an exception to let us in—much to my dismay. It's another photo opportunity I can't get out of, but it beats what happened after last week's show.

The Basilisks stand by the bar, surrounded by women fawning for autographs. I look away from their polite smiles and feign interest in a cocktail menu of drinks I can't have. Unfortunately, my solitude doesn't last long.

"Ashley," Tiffany simpers. She positions herself to be directly in Zed's view. "I wanted to congratulate you on

such a great show. You did an amazing job under the circumstances."

Can't she say something nice without adding a snide quip at the end?

"Thanks, Tiffany," I say, not buying her bullshit but refusing to lower myself to her level. "You too."

"After what happened," she continues, looking over my shoulder while she talks. "I'm surprised you could hold the last note. The last-minute song change helped the audience sympathize with you."

"I'm not playing the sympathy card," I say, trying to stop myself from losing my cool. "I'm trying to make people feel something through my music. Maybe you should try it next time?"

"Yes," she says, nodding, not paying attention to what I'm saying. She laughs suddenly, making me jump in surprise. "Oh, Ashley. You're so funny."

I raise my eyebrows. "Do you think acting like we're friends is going to impress him?"

"You know nothing," she hisses, then wriggles her fingers in Zed's direction. "I know what I'm doing. Don't say anything. He's coming over."

Although I promised I'd never share their secret, I'd love to see Tiffany's reaction if she found out who the guy she's gushing over really is.

"Tiffany," Zed joins us and greets her, then gives me a curt nod. "Ash."

"I was just saying to Ashley that she did an amazing job covering your song," Tiffany says, putting her hand on his arm. He stiffens at her touch, but she's oblivious. "*Hold me Tightly* is one of my favorite Lionheart songs. Although, I prefer your version."

If she wasn't such a bitch and her attempts to seduce

him weren't so pathetic, I may have felt threatened. Instead, I stifle a laugh at her desperation.

"You're right. She did a great job with the cover," Zed agrees. He turns to me. "Ash, can I borrow you for a second? A photographer wants to take a picture of the four of us."

If only the photograph captured the look of sheer devastation on Tiffany's face.

I hesitate, then nod. "Sure."

I trudge after him to the others. My arrival makes the cooing fan girls scowl, but I ignore them as the photographer barks orders at us. He positions me between Zed and Ripper. My cheeks heat, thinking of the other ways they have wedged me between them. Ripper rests his hand on the small of my back. The warmth of his palm radiates through my shirt, and I wriggle, but Zed's arm around my shoulders pins me in place.

We smile at the camera, and a series of flashes blind me temporarily.

"Nice song choice," Ripper comments as the photographer scurries away into the crowd. "I didn't think you were a Lionheart fan."

"I'm not," I reply, "but I like that song."

"Ash—"

"Not here," Zed interrupts him, putting an end to our situation. He keeps his eyes fixed on Ripper so anyone watching would think he's speaking to him. "We'll go to the usual place after this." Zed looks at me, searching my stare to make sure I've picked up his hint. "I hope to see you soon, Ash."

I don't drop eye contact and say, "I'm sure you will."

twenty-six

. . .

Ash

After making my excuses to leave early, I climb into a car and ask the driver to take me to an area close to Buggy, hoping I'm not making a massive mistake by misreading Zed's signals.

"Are you sure?" the driver asks nervously. "You don't want to be around that area when it's dark."

"I have a friend that lives around here," I lie. "I'm meeting her and staying the night."

My explanation seems to satisfy him because he doesn't push for answers. I wipe my clammy hands on my jeans. Real fucking sexy, Ash. I have to control my nerves.

Am I mad to be meeting the Basilisks again? It's like I can't help myself. No matter how hard I try, I can't deny how they draw me in.

The Basilisks accepted me for who I am—can I do the same for them? Zed asked me to decide whether I wanted to be part of their life. The past few weeks have given me insight into their world but… are they worth the sacrifice? My body buzzes from nervous, excited energy, confirming I'm making the right decision.

I wait until the cab leaves before I start walking. From memory, Buggy is only a few streets away. I pull my jacket tighter around me. The streets are dimly lit, making it hard to see what or who may be hiding in the corridors.

Behind me, I'm aware of a man following close behind. I quicken my pace.

"Hey," the man in pursuit calls. "Where are you going so fast, pretty lady?"

My hands jump to my purse, and I curse, realizing I left my pepper spray behind. I can almost hear Dad's voice lecturing me on personal safety, but I ignore the man and keep going. He is quicker than I am.

"Don't walk away when I'm talking to you," the man yells, speeding up. I smell dried sweat and liquor before he grabs my shoulder. He's built like a fucking house and grins down at me. "I said, I want to talk."

I raise my knee, readying to kick him in the balls, when someone launches at him from behind. I take a second to realize it's Ripper.

The monster staggers backward, blinking in disbelief at Ripper, whose hood has fallen in the struggle, and asks, "Aren't you the guy from—"

Before he finishes his sentence, Ripper's fist smashes into his face, breaking his nose. The man howls and cups his bleeding face like a baby.

"Come on," Ripper says, grabbing my hand. "We gotta go."

We break into a run. The wind rushes through my hair as Ripper pulls me through the dark streets after him.

"I know a shortcut," he says.

We race past a row of dumpsters, then cut down an empty street to the left, making a few sharp turns. The cab

driver was right. This isn't a place anyone should visit alone at night.

We come to a stop to catch our breath. Ripper's knuckles are covered in blood. I don't condone violence, but that fucker was asking for it.

"Thank you," I say, panting, "for… you know."

Ripper grins. A wild, crazy look stirs behind his eyes. This is the real him. The one who thuds on the drums and screams his heart out.

"I didn't think you'd come, but you did," he says, stroking my cheekbone. "Why didn't you get dropped off closer?"

"I didn't want to draw any attention," I say, then it dawns on me that he found me conveniently fast. "How did you find me?"

He shrugs. "I may have followed your car."

"Ripper—"

His lips are on mine. There is no mask. Just him and me. A desperate longing consumes me as he catches my lip between his teeth and teases out a moan from me. My body crumbles. I've tried to resist him, but I can't.

"Fuck, Ash…" He pulls away reluctantly, even though he's looking at me like he wants to devour me in the alleyway. He's fucking hot. "We need to get to Buggy."

I nod, unable to form words. I'm dizzy from what may be one of the best kisses of my life. He puts his jacket hood up and puts his arm around my waist protectively as we head to the garage.

When we get there, we're not alone. As soon as the shutter door slides up, another figure steps from the darkness. Zed is waiting. His eyes dart from Ripper's bloody knuckles to my swollen lips. He misses nothing.

"Where the hell have you been?" Zed asks. "What did you do?"

"We're fine," I say. "There was just a guy that was getting handsy with me in the street."

His lips press into a disapproving line as he looks to Ripper for more details. "What's the damage?"

"Nothing you wouldn't have done in the same circumstances," Ripper replies.

"Did he see who you were?" Zed continues his interrogation. If he wanted a career change, he'd make a good cop. "Did anyone else see you?"

"No," I answer for him. Regardless of what the man thought he saw, there's no way anyone would believe that Damon Archer had broken his nose. I add hastily, "The guy was wasted, anyway."

Zed doesn't look convinced. This is a potential risk, and risks are what he wants to avoid.

"Fine," Zed says after a long pause, deciding to let it go. "We all need to talk."

I follow him into Buggy. Venom is waiting for us on the bus. Like Zed, he notices Ripper's knuckles right away.

"What hap—"

"It's nothing," I snap, shooting him a warning glare.

"You should see the other guy," Ripper jokes. "I'm gonna clean myself up."

I've always been the girl who rolls her eyes at damsels in distress in movies. I've never wanted a guy to step in and save me, but still… I couldn't help finding it sexy as hell how Ripper defended me.

"Congratulations, by the way," Venom says. He must notice my confused expression as he adds, "on getting through to the next round of Popstarz."

"Oh… that."

"It's a big deal," Venom says. "You should be proud of yourself."

"It was an interesting song choice," Ripper smirks, returning from the bathroom with clean, uninjured hands. "How did you like becoming a Lionheart for a night?"

The atmosphere changes. We all feel it. An underlying tension is simmering, but no one wants to be the first to address it.

"I…" I start, then stop. I know what I want to say, but I can't find the words.

The three of them wait patiently for me to continue. Many women dream about having a group of handsome guys hanging on their every word, but reality doesn't live up to the hype—especially for someone shy like me.

My eyes are drawn to the masquerade-style mask hanging on the wall. It's crow-like with black, shiny feathers fanning from its center.

I walk over to it, noticing Ripper not so subtly check out my ass as I pass, and take the mask off its hook.

They watch as I put it on and tie it around the back of my head before facing them again. It's easier this way. Our roles have been reversed.

"I've been thinking about what you said, Zed," I begin. I've not rehearsed this, but I let my emotions speak for me. "Although I was angry when I found out your true identities, it hasn't changed the facts. That night when we all sang together, and we…" I gulp, thinking about the toe-curling orgasm they gave me that rocked my core. "I know that being a Lionheart comes with strings attached. Your lives aren't normal, but mine isn't either. I've been thrust under the spotlight and, honestly, without having you guys over the past few weeks, I don't think I'd have gotten through it."

Zed steps closer, and his voice drops to a low rumble, "Do you realize what you're saying, Ash?"

"Yes," I say.

"Do you understand what you're getting yourself into?" Zed presses, sending goosebumps down my spine. "It won't be easy."

His warning only makes me more sure that I'm making the right decision.

"I know it won't be easy," I reply, refusing to be intimidated as he towers over me, "but I'm willing to take that chance."

"Ash—"

"No," I stand firm, cutting him off before he can spout any more excuses. "I've made my decision."

"You know you can't take it back," Zed says, standing so close that I can smell his cologne. "This is your last chance to get out."

"I know," I reply, "and I'm not going anywhere."

I look at the three of them. There's Ripper—effortlessly cool, tall, dark, and handsome. The rebel with a wild streak who will do anything to mask his hidden vulnerability. He has a dark side and a deep-rooted anger that comes from a place he tries to run from and forget.

Then Venom. He tries to shrink into the shadows and hopes the walls will swallow him up, but he's been pushed under the light. He doesn't see that he belongs there. The scars covering his skin tell a story of hurt and pain, but they also speak of someone who has come back stronger… stronger than he knows.

Finally, there's Zed. The man who tried everything to push me away and keep me at arm's length. He's afraid of letting people in and dropping his guard because of a lifetime of being used. But when he lets a person in, he won't

let go. His loyalty is undying, and he does anything for those he loves.

I don't know how I fit in with these three men. I'm a weirdo, an outcast, someone who has hated herself and stumbled into bleak holes that I've had to claw my way out of. But I'll never be a doormat. I'll always say what's on my mind and will refuse to back down if something goes against my beliefs.

The four of us are different, yet so similar. We're lost in a world that's forced expectations down our throats along with meaningless music. Together, we have formed a strange and unlikely alliance that makes facing the day seem possible.

"I'm not afraid of things getting difficult," I say. "I'm not easily broken, Zed. And I'm not afraid to fight for what I want."

"What do you want, Ash?" Zed pushes.

"I want to try," I say fiercely. "I don't know what the future holds, but I know that things have never felt more right than when I was singing on stage with you."

"We felt it too," Ripper says. "Your voice, our music… the way you're not afraid to tell Zed to go fuck himself. I'm glad you came tonight, Ash."

"Me too," I say, finally mustering the courage to take off the mask and feeling more naked than I did when they saw me with no clothes.

"So, does this mean you're not mad at us anymore?" Venom asks. His joking tone lightens the mood, but tension still hangs in the air.

"I didn't say that," I reply.

Ripper's phone buzzes loudly. He swears as he checks the screen, and I notice Zed's jaw clench.

Something is wrong. I don't need to ask; I feel it.

"Is it..." Zed's voice trails off as Ripper nods curtly, looking nervously in my direction.

They are hiding something.

"Who is it?" I ask, crossing my arms. Before they can make up some bullshit, I lay down the law. "Haven't you learned by now that keeping secrets doesn't always end well?"

Ripper doesn't answer. Zed looks away, and Venom plays with his fraying jumper.

"What's going on, Ripper?" I ask sharply, concern growing.

Ripper looks at Zed, who nods, permitting him to continue.

"It's Jacqueline," Ripper says bitterly, refusing to look up.

"Jacqueline?" I frown. "What does she want? Has she arranged for the Lionhearts to do something?"

He snorts and mutters darkly, "If only."

"What aren't you telling me?" I ask.

"I need a fucking drink if we're doing this," Ripper says.

He heads to the bar, grabs a bottle, and takes a long swig.

"Why don't you sit down?" Zed says, steering me over to the sofa.

What the fuck is this big secret, and why are the three of them so on edge?

"Okay, I'll just come out and say it," Ripper says finally, "she wants to hook up with me."

"What?" I stammer.

Maybe Ripper is misreading the signals. Jacqueline is a professional powerhouse. She doesn't do serious relationships according to her interviews—her career comes first—

but she's often photographed on dates with older men. Wealthy men who have invested in crazy schemes or are esteemed film producers. Why would she be interested in a guy half her age who sings in a boy band? And, out of all the Lionhearts, wouldn't Zach—the rule-following, confident frontman—be the more obvious choice?

"She wants me to go over to her hotel and fuck her," Ripper says, spelling it out for me.

"Yeah, I got that part," I snap, "but why does she want to fuck you?"

He laughs, then winks, "If you haven't noticed, I'm quite the catch."

He uses humor to hide his true feelings. Deflecting and casting shade when he doesn't want to answer.

"It's not funny, Ripper," Venom says. "You need to tell Ash the full story."

Ripper winces. Whatever they're talking about is causing him pain, and I don't want to be the reason for Ripper reliving something he'd rather forget.

"You might want to leave when you hear what I've got to say," Ripper says, avoiding my gaze and taking another drink.

"Hey," I say, "I'm not going anywhere."

"Go easy," Zed says, prizing the bottle from Ripper's fingers. "That's enough."

Ripper sits next to me, tapping his foot up and down to an erratic rhythm.

"It all started when we were at Camp Harmony," Ripper says. His eyes are vacant, and his tone is devoid of any lightness. "I caught Jacqueline's eye."

Nausea grows in my stomach, but I keep my face neutral. I have an awful feeling I know where he's going with the conversation, but I don't want to believe it.

"At first, her attention flattered me," Ripper says. "I was a young guy, and she… Well, she's Jacqueline fucking Tate. She made me feel special. She told me she could change my life and give me everything I ever wanted."

I listen without saying a word, not wanting to hear what's coming next, but Zed prompts him, "Keep going."

"I thought sleeping with her would be a one-time thing," Ripper says. "Something to tick off my bucket list. I was a stupid horny kid… but she kept wanting it to happen again."

"She's obsessed," Venom adds.

Ripper winces. "I didn't want it to keep happening, but she kept making promises."

"What promises?" I whisper.

"She promised that she'd give us a record deal and sign our band to Starnote. She said she'd make us the most successful boy band of this century if I did things for her in return," Ripper says.

"When did it start?" I ask, wondering whether it was during their final year.

"I was sixteen when it started," he admits. "It happened every summer we were there. Her requests got more and more frequent after I lost interest. She'd call me to her office if she heard about me hooking up with another girl at camp, or if she saw me getting close to someone. It got crazy toward the end."

I look at Venom and Zed. "Did you two know it was going on?"

"If we did, do you think we'd have signed that contract?" Zed spits through gritted teeth.

"I kept it from them," Ripper says. "I knew what they'd say, and I didn't want to ruin their big breaks. Signing the contract was the worst mistake of my life, but

what choice did I have? My family was broke, and I had no other options. As soon as it was in writing, I stopped seeing her and cut her loose."

"But it doesn't seem to have stopped her if she's still texting you," I say.

If I didn't hate Jacqueline before, I sure as hell do now. What kind of person manipulates a minor like that? It's abuse. She used her position for sex. If she did it to Ripper, how many other guys has she taken advantage of over the years?

"What she did to you is abuse," I say.

"It's not like that," Ripper says, shaking his head. "She never forced me to do anything. If anything, I was using her to get what we wanted."

Zed and Venom exchange concerned glances. Ripper is kidding himself, but they both understand what their relationship was.

"Did you ever tell anyone at the time?" I ask.

"You forget how powerful Jacqueline is," Zed says. "She can shut down rumors with a snap of her fingers. No one would have believed a bunch of teenage boys over someone like Jacqueline. She could ruin careers."

"There was another guy she took an interest in," Ripper says. "I can't remember his name, but after one summer, he never came back to camp. I always suspected that he rejected her or that his parents got involved. Either way, it was the end of his career."

"It's..." I can't find the word for how fucking despicable her actions are.

"I did what had to be done," Ripper says. "I wanted what she could give me, so I paid the price. It meant nothing, and it gave me everything I thought I wanted."

"You could tell someone now," I say, "you're not

dependent on her anymore. She needs you more than you need her. You can expose her."

"Do you think anyone would believe a party boy like me?" He shakes his head. We all know the answer. "I don't want other people to know about it. I'm fucking ashamed of what happened. I don't want to think about it. Zed handles all the communications with Starnote, so I don't have to see her. It's only when we're forced together like at camp and Popstarz that she reaches out. I reject her every time, but she still thinks she's got a hold on me."

"I'm sorry that happened to you," I say eventually, my voice shaking. "She's—"

"—a fucking monster," Venom finishes my sentence with enough venom worthy of his name.

Ripper's eyes are pleading as he says, "I want to forget about it, okay? I don't want to waste our time talking about her." He strokes my cheek. "You're the first girl I've met who I want to remember when I wake up the next morning."

"But—"

"Please, Ash," Ripper cuts me off, "I need you to let this go for me. I've dealt with it. I don't want to relive this. I want to move on."

"I just…" My blood boils with anger, and I want to scream. Scream because of the unfairness. The injustice. The fact a woman like her could get away with doing what she did for so long and go unpunished, then profit off the back of her abuse. "She can't get away with it."

"Let it go," Ripper says, his shoulders slump. "For me."

Zed sits on the other side of Ripper and squeezes his knee, reassuring him. They're close. Well, all three of them are, but it's different with Ripper and Zed. They share a

deeper bond and a tenderness between them. I'm glad they've had each other over the years.

I choke back the words I want to say and bite my tongue to stop myself from calling Jacqueline every terrible name I can think of. Instead, I put my hand on Ripper's other knee and say, "I'm not going anywhere."

twenty-seven

. . .

Ripper | Damon

It's all too much.

Too overwhelming.

"I don't want pity from either of you," I spit, jumping up and startling Ash and Zed.

I don't want her looking at me like I'm some kind of fucking victim. Yeah, Jacqui took advantage of me, but I got something out of our fucking deal too. A life most people would kill for.

"Ripper, wait." Zed follows me as I stalk to the bar and open a new bottle. "It's okay."

I hate it when he uses that voice. He rarely lets his softer side show, but it infuriates my rage more when he feels sorry for me.

"Don't," I snarl, squaring up to him. "Don't fucking say anything."

He puts his hand on my shoulder. A small gesture, but Ash notices. She looks away like she's seen something she shouldn't. Before that, there was something else flickering behind her eyes. Excitement?

I grab Zed's red hair and pull him in to kiss me. Venom

knows we hook up from time to time, but it's the first time he's seen us together like this. I don't care. I need something to take my mind off the conversation.

I want to change the fucking subject. I want to forget and feel good with the people I love the most.

Zed pulls away, clearing his throat. Ash's cheeks glow a rosy pink, and her pupils dilate. She fucking liked it.

"Ripper, I'm not sure this is the right time," Zed's voice is a low warning growl, but it's also full of heady lust, too.

"It's the best time," I correct him, then grin. "I think our girl wants a show."

Ash's blush deepens.

"Come on, Z," I taunt, goading him. "What're you waiting for?"

"Not like this." He steps back, and his rejection hits me like a slap to the face.

"Do you want me to stay?" Ash asks. "I can go."

"No," we all cry in unison.

I don't want to waste a second of our time alone. She hesitates, but I stroll over, locking my gaze on hers, letting her know how much I want her to stay.

Venom switches on music, the newest album of a thrash metal band, who are growing in the underground scene. The Wasted. Maybe we could collaborate with them one day when we aren't trapped under Starnote's control.

"You said you could accept us," I remind Ash, "and everything that comes with it."

Our lives are messy, complicated, and downright chaotic, but that's part of the deal.

"I know," she whispers as I step closer.

Her gaze trails to my lips, and she bites on hers, making me want to suck on them again until I coax another delicious moan from her.

Ash freezes as I move closer. She wants this, but she's holding back.

"You don't have to hold back around us, Ash," I say. "We've seen the real you, remember?"

I've seen the girl who screams with wild abandon and unleashes her emotions with a rawness that makes my heart stop.

"I-I-I…" she stammers.

I brush a hair off her cheek.

"You don't need to pretend around us, Ash," I say, resting my hands on her waist. "We like the girl we saw in Wilderton. The person you keep hidden underneath. We want all of it."

"Trying to seduce me doesn't change how I feel about what Jacqueline did to you," she says. Her brutal honesty takes me by surprise. "She can't get away with it, and we'll make sure she doesn't, one way or another."

Is that all she sees when she looks at me?

"But," she rises on her tiptoes, and her lips graze against mine for the briefest moment, "it doesn't change how I feel about you."

Relief washes over me. She knows my secret and accepts me. I want her. Fuck, I want her more than anything.

"Ash," I say. "I need you."

I grab her hair, gathering it in a ponytail to guide her face to mine. Her arms tug at the bottom of my shirt as the roars of the Wasted make my eardrums ring.

"Fuck," I groan, sliding my hands past her lower back to cup her ass.

Zed approaches, waiting patiently behind me, and Venom lurks in the shadows, watching. Ash senses them and pulls away breathlessly.

"Are you okay, Ash?" Zed asks.

Of course she's fucking okay. I want to growl. I've just kissed the life out of her.

"Yes," she replies. Her eyes sparkle as they travel down his body.

The aggressive drumbeats pumping through the bus have ignited a primal desire that makes me want to bend her over and pound into her tight pussy so hard that she screams.

I kiss Ash again and lift up her T-shirt. She doesn't object. The fabric peeling away adds to the building crescendo as I pull it over her head and let it fall to the floor, then I reach for the zipper of her jeans. She tugs them past her hips and steps out of them.

There's still time for her to run. Being faced with three guys with raging boners is intimidating, but she doesn't back away. She stands straighter like she's taking her place among us and proving she belongs at our side.

Her black lacy underwear contrasts her pale skin, and my mouth falls open.

"You're beautiful," Venom murmurs. She saunters over to where he's standing in a way that makes her hips sway and gives Zed and me a look at her peachy ass.

She runs her finger down Venom's chest, then pauses, like she's searching for something. Neither of them says anything, but a look of mutual understanding passes between them. Then he kisses her like he's afraid of breaking her.

I'm an explosion of fiery heat, while Venom is gentle, loving, and caring. She pushes him back onto the sofa and slides onto his lap. Watching her grind over his pants makes my cock ache with longing. How much sexual tension can one guy take?

Zed senses my frustration and creeps behind me. His breath heats my skin as he licks down the side of my neck, then sinks his teeth into my shoulder as his erection presses into my back.

I spin around to kiss him. His mouth and lips are firmer than Ash's and his stubble tickles my face, but our kiss is just as passionate. I tug his T-shirt off as he does mine.

I push him back to sit next to Venom. He and Ash are too busy making out to pay me any attention as I drop to my knees and unzip Zed's pants, then pull them down to unleash his massive cock.

Ash pauses and turns to watch. She grins, sliding off Venom's lap and joining me on her knees in front of him.

She looks at Venom, batting her eyelashes. "Is this okay?"

She cares about him. Venom is sensitive and gets stuck in his head a lot, but she's found a way to reassure him and cut through the noise.

"Yeah," he replies.

Of course it is. The lucky fuck is going to get his dick sucked by our girl.

My cock twitches as I watch Ash lick Venom's shaft, making him shiver and his thighs tense in desire. Her head tilts to face me as I run my tongue over Zed and take the head of his cock into my mouth.

She follows my lead, closing her lips around Venom. Does our girl want a cock sucking competition? I'd smile if Zed's cock wasn't so damn thick that I have to open wide to take all of him.

The guys moan as we pleasure them. Watching her give Venom a blowjob is fucking hot. His eyes roll back as his hands get lost in her hair to hold her head in place, and

she picks up her pace. I'd love it even more if it was my dick she was sucking.

Suddenly, Ash stops and pulls away. Spit trails from Venom's dick to her chin as she wipes it roughly with the back of her hand. My eyes follow her as she slips her panties to the side, backs up, and lowers her wet pussy onto Venom's cock. I get the perfect view of her tight hole stretching to fit him.

Venom isn't expecting it and gasps, "Fuck, Ash… a condom…"

"It's okay," she replies. "I'm on the pill."

She trusts us enough to be with us without a rubber. I doubted her commitment to us before, but I don't question it now.

I'm jealous that he's getting to enjoy her pussy first. I remember how hot and wet her tight little pussy is, but it'll be my turn again soon.

I'm entranced by Venom's cock disappearing inside her inch by inch. She bites her lip and moans, holding my stare. Our girl is fucking dirty.

Zed's breathing quickens, but I withdraw, leaving him hanging on the edge as I stand up. He sighs, "Man."

I ignore him and unbutton my jeans, facing Ash and demanding gruffly, "So it's gonna be that way, huh?"

Ash wriggles her hips in response, grinding her ass into Venom's lap.

"I don't know what you mean," she replies innocently as Venom moans beneath her, getting coated in her wetness. She's driving me fucking wild.

I approach her, grabbing her hair and pushing her mouth onto my cock. It's what she wants. I can tell from how her mouth closes around it, slurping and sucking, slathering me in her spit until it's dripping.

I yank her head back. My desire is consuming me. Venom's had enough time alone.

"It's my turn," I growl possessively.

"Hey!" Venom objects as Ash rises, slowly sliding off of him.

"It's okay," she promises, stroking his cheek. "I'm not done with you yet."

I'm not Venom. I can't wait. I take what I want. As soon as she's on her feet, I tear down her panties and grab her hips, turning her around and bending her forward, so her hands rest on the sofa.

I don't ease in gently or tease her. I enter her from behind in a hard thrust. Venom has warmed her up and her pussy is ready. Now I'm ready to take her. I unclip her bra, throwing it to the side. The wet slap of my hips slamming into her ass blend with the music's rhythm.

She arches her back, letting me see my cock vanish inside her as her pussy walls clamp down around me like a vacuum fucking seal. She moans, "Ripper."

I've dreamed about her calling my name again. It's been seconds, but I'm ready to drop my load. She wins.

I cast a look at Zed, his face clouded by building frustration. I pull out, holding onto my release and knowing it'll be even better when I finally get to spill inside her. It's Zed's turn.

twenty-eight

. . .

Zed | Zach

Ash's legs shake as Ripper pulls out. Her pussy will be nice and stretched for me. I've let the others have their fun, but it's my turn now.

Ash squeals in surprise as I scoop her up in my arms. I cup her ass in my hands as she wraps her legs around my torso. She's tall for a woman but still shorter than me. She clings to my neck, and the wet slick of her pussy rubs against my hardness.

She yelps, "Don't drop me."

"Never," I promise.

Ash doesn't look convinced until I lift her with ease to angle my cock against her and bring her down on top of me.

Holy shit. She feels incredible. Her tits press against my chest. Her nipples are hard and desperate to be touched. I enjoy having full control of her body as Ripper and Zed watch on with a front-seat view.

Ripper bites his lip, battling the urge to touch himself. I recognized how close he was when fucking her and admired his self-control. Venom's eyes fix on her perky

ass. I spread her cheeks to show him how good her pussy is at taking all of me.

"Zed," Ash cries.

"Does that feel good, Ash?" I purr. "Do you like my big cock filling you?"

"Yes. God yes," she gasps. Her small breasts bounce as her wetness leaks over me, coating my balls. She throws her head back, and I continue to take from her. Her pussy tightens around me. "Yes!"

I'm close. I lose myself in her wet heat as she holds on for dear life. She can't get away, and that's how I like it. I want to make her ours and claim her. Unlike Ripper, I have no intention of stopping.

I bounce her on my cock harder. My fingers grip her ass so tightly that it might bruise. Judging by her moans and how her hips are trying to rock against me, she doesn't mind.

My balls tighten, drawing closer to my body, and a primal roar erupts from my throat as I shoot my cum inside her. Fuck. I don't move, burying myself as deep as I can go to fill our girl with cream.

"Oh, shit…" Ripper groans, and his hand strays to stroke his cock. He can't resist. "So fucking hot."

"Zed," Ash moans, unable to contain herself. I ignore her pussy's desperate attempts to latch onto me and slide out of her. Her expression turns stormy, clouded by her desire. She's close. Her eyes burn into mine with a furious accusation. "Why did you stop?"

I grin. "Because we're gonna make you cum together."

Venom grabs a fluffy blanket and a pillow that may need to be burned later. He drops them to the floor. He cares about making sure our girl is comfortable. When we renovate Buggy, we need to look at buying a giant bed

since we made our coffins for sleeping—not incredible group sex with the girl we want to keep sharing.

"On the floor," I order her. "It's going to be worth the wait."

Ash's frustration turns to joy as she kneels on the floor and squeezes her thighs together. Ripper wastes no time.

"Spread your legs for me, baby," he says.

twenty-nine

. . .

Ash

Zed may be an arrogant ass, but he's right. The pleasure building inside me is unlike anything I've experienced before. When I let go, my world will be rocked, and I'll never come back from it.

Ripper parts my knees, spreading my legs wide to see Zed's cum leaking out and coating my inner thighs. He's not grossed out, though. Instead, he licks his lips.

"I'm gonna clean you up, Ash," Ripper promises, pushing me back gently.

Venom positions a pillow behind my head. He isn't used to sharing. I can tell from the look in his eyes that it's something he struggles with, but I spent one-on-one time with him to reassure him I wanted all of them equally. I shoot Venom a smile, and his eyes shine back in understanding. They stay glued to me, gleaming with a deep-rooted longing that makes me want to take him again.

"Oh my gosh," I sigh as Ripper's head dives between my legs. "Ripper, that feels..." I gasp as his tongue licks along the length of my slit, darting between my inner lips and eating me like I'm his favorite meal. "Amazing."

His wet tongue explores me, sliding into my hole, licking up all of Zed's cum, before circling my clit and making my inner thighs shake.

"The two of you taste so fucking good," he groans as I shiver. "I could eat you out all day."

Venom approaches, while Ripper continues his magical tongue moves. Venom pauses, not saying a word, but asking for permission with his gaze.

My moan answers his question as his unusually warm hand finds my hardened nipples. That, and Ripper licking my pussy, causes my eyes to flutter closed with the dizzying sensation.

"Venom," I moan as he catches my left nipple between his teeth. His tongue sweeps over their pebbled surface before sucking, slowly at first, and then more aggressively, making me buck against Ripper's face.

"Do you like having two men playing with you?" Zed asks. His cock is hard again. "Tell me how it feels."

I'm not sure how he expects me to make any sense when my toes are curling from the intensity of the situation, but I try anyway. "It's incredible. I'm going to—"

My building climax catches like a wildfire, building to an explosion. But Ripper pauses, drawing back, keeping me waiting for a little longer.

Is he trying to torture me? My hips jerk, begging for the release that's within reaching distance.

"Please," I plead, "I want you to make me come. I need it. Fuck, I need all of you."

Ripper wipes his mouth with the back of his hand. His chin is shining from my juices.

"What do you think?" Zed asks, tipping his head to the side and looking hungrily between my legs. "Do we give her what she wants?"

"Yes," I plead, not caring that they've reduced me to begging and forcing me to shed my inhibitions. "I need you to make me come."

Ripper shoots a sly smile at Venom and says, "She's all yours, bro."

"No," Venom corrects him with a smile. "She's ours."

"How would you like it, Ash?" Zed purrs. "Would you like Venom to fuck you while I eat your sweet pussy, and Ripper fills your mouth with his cock?"

That's exactly what I'd like.

"Yes," I moan.

Zed arches his eyebrow, teasing, knowing this will only get me off more. "Yes, what?"

"Fuck yes," I respond. If he expected me to say please, he was wrong.

Venom rolls me onto my side, carefully putting my head on the pillow so he can slip inside me from behind. My pussy is wet and even tighter from this angle, making a squelching noise as he enters me.

Venom groans as I push my ass into him and circle my hips in encouragement. He grabs one of my legs and holds it up to steady himself.

"You have no idea how fucking good you feel," he whispers seductively. The others can't hear him over the music, making the experience special to the two of us despite the horny audience eagerly waiting to join.

"What a view," Zed compliments, seeing my pussy lips part as Venom thrusts inside me.

In the meantime, Ripper is on his knees and heading straight for my mouth. A bead of pre-cum leaking from the tip of his cock shows how much he wants this. He's craving release as much as I am.

I open my mouth. It's more awkward from this angle, but I'm able to take him.

"You look so hot being filled in two holes, Ash," Zed says, working his hands up and down his shaft. "You take us all so fucking well. We're gonna make you come harder than you've ever come in your life."

I moan in agreement, making Ripper's thighs tense as the vibrations from my voice carry through his body.

Zed drops to his knees and crawls toward me. He lies on his side, and his tongue darts out to lick my clit. I gasp, but Ripper's cock pushing further down my throat stops me from making any more noise.

Being with them feels so right. Venom rocks against me from behind, and his cock puts pressure on my G-spot as Zed sucks my clit, making my toes curl. Zed's tongue must be licking against the base of his cock, but Venom doesn't seem to care.

"You're perfect for us, Ash," Venom says in a deep rumble, reminding me of his singing voice that he never shares with anyone. "Your body is fucking perfect."

His words send an electric shot between my legs, and I unravel. There's no holding it back, and none of them are going to stop. They keep going, working together like a machine with the sole purpose of delivering me more pleasure than I thought possible.

My pussy flutters against Venom.

"Don't stop," Venom says, loud enough for the others to hear. "Our girl is about to cum all over us."

Zed's pace quickens, catching my clit in his mouth and sucking gently as I come undone. I writhe and cry out as my pussy walls squeeze Venom tightly, pulsing against him.

Pleasure comes in crashing waves. A firm hand

squeezes my breast, probably Zed's, but I can't be sure as Venom tenses.

"Your pussy is so fucking tight," Venom complements. His voice is strangled, and his breath comes in short bursts. Then his hips buck, thrusting as he releases inside me, causing a sudden spray of warmth.

I moan around Ripper's cock, causing his bucking to intensify as my body feels like it's floating on a separate plane.

Ripper's thigh muscles tighten as he moans, "Fuck."

His cock twitches and salty cum slides down my throat. I swallow it all, enjoying the power this gives me and how I can do that to him. When he's quivering and done, he withdraws from my mouth, leaving me breathy and panting.

He uses his thumb to wipe a drop of cum from the corner of my mouth, then pops it into my mouth to lick clean.

"You look so hot when you're coming all over our cocks," Ripper comments appreciatively.

I'd never thought of myself as sexy before. Clumsy, awkward, non-conventional, weird—yes—but never sexy. But having these gorgeous men share my body made me feel hot.

I whimper as Venom slides out of me. The aftershocks from my orgasm are still ebbing through me as I roll onto my back. Zed stays between my parted thighs, staring at my swollen pussy like he wants to dive in and fuck me again.

I try to close my legs, but he stops me.

"What do you think you're doing, pretty girl?" Zed asks. "Did you think we were done with you?"

My body is a shaking mess. All I want to do is roll over

and fall asleep until his fingers reach out to fuck me, and his tongue returns to my clit.

I thought I was done, but my body responds to his mouth instantly. Another orgasm rolls over me unexpectedly as I thread my fingers through his hair and hold him there. Now it's my turn to hold him in place.

Ripper and Venom take a breast each, sucking on my nipples as I part my legs wider.

"You all feel so good," I moan. Good is the understatement of the fucking century. "Fuck..."

Zed sucks on my clit. The sensation borders on being too intense and makes my toes curl, but my vision blurs as my pussy grips his fingers and I come again, gushing all over him.

"Yes!" I scream. "Yes!"

Rest in peace fluffy blanket.

His tongue and the tingling pleasure from them playing with my tits combines in a mind-blowing orgasm. I can't tell how long it lasts because time seems to stretch. As soon as I think I'm done, Zed's probing fingers tease another wave of pleasure from me, leaving me unsure when one stops and another begins.

My chest heaves from the exertion. My hair is stuck to my face, and my makeup must have smudged everywhere to make me look like a panda, but none of that matters. All that does is the four of us here on this bus.

thirty

. . .

Venom | Levi

After making love to Ash, we lie panting on the floor, staring at the ceiling and letting the crushing curses and vocals of the Wasted wash over us. If we ever met them, I'll tell them we fucked to their music.

"That was…" Ash breathes, "unexpected."

Ripper laughs, propping his head on his arm, confident in his skin. I wish I had his level of confidence. Despite sharing Ash with the guys, I'm still unsure of my place and where I fit in. It makes sense for Ripper and Zed to share her because they have their own thing going on, but my link to them is only through Ash—even though it was hot watching them get her off.

"Did you ever think you'd fuck the Lionhearts?" Ripper jokes.

"I didn't fuck the Lionhearts," Ash replies without missing a beat. "I fucked the Basilisks."

She's perfect, and I know the others feel it too. Fucking her without masks was different. We showed her our true selves, and she accepted us fully.

I take her hand, running my fingers over her soft skin, and she squeezes gently, giving me the reassurance I need.

"We should get back," Zed says.

Ripper groans, "Why do you always have to put an end to a good time?"

"People may wonder where we are if we don't return from the after-party," he says. His gaze flicks over Ash's naked body. His eyes ignite with a hunger that tells me he'd stay here all night if we could.

"I'd prefer if we could stay here," I grumble.

Ash laughs, turning to kiss me. Her free hand strokes the scar on my stomach.

"We'll come back soon," she promises. "But Zed's right."

Ash sits up and stands on shaky legs, snatching her panties, and all of our faces fall. Urgh.

"We have to be careful," Zed, Mr. Sensible, says. "When we're back in the hotel, people can't find out we got back together."

"Don't worry," Ash says with a sly grin, "no one will suspect a thing. If you haven't noticed before, I'm pretty good at showing contempt for the Lionhearts."

I snicker, but we still have to work out a way to meet regularly. We'd go crazy if we had to see her every day and didn't get any time alone with her.

"We'll text you," Zed decides, reading my mind, "but this can be our meeting spot."

"That or the coffee shop," I chip in. Although, who am I kidding? If I'm gonna see Ash, I'll need more privacy than a coffee shop can provide. The owners are discreet but wouldn't turn a blind eye if I fucked her over the table.

"We're doing a Basilisks show tomorrow," Ripper says. "Do you want to come? I'll send you the details."

She hasn't left yet, but I'm already counting down the minutes until we can be together again like this. No pretenses. No complications. Just us.

"I wouldn't miss it," she says, her face lighting up. She quickly turns to Zed to add, "I'll wear a disguise."

"Good." He nods, more business-like, as he helps her zip up her dress. "And you shouldn't come here alone after dark again—not after what happened tonight."

My mouth falls open. "You'll let us travel with her?"

"I'll let you travel with her," Zed corrects as Ripper huffs. "You're her mentor. It wouldn't be strange to see you two together. You could explain it away. Either that, or we all go in disguise."

Ash's eyebrows lower, deep in thought. The others don't notice, but I do.

"Are you okay, Ash?" I ask.

"Yes, I just…" she shakes her head like she's being silly. "I just never thought I'd be here with you guys. I didn't see things turning out this way."

"Neither did we," Ripper agrees, "but I'm glad we are."

"Ash and the Basilisks," I say thoughtfully. "It has a ring to it, don't you think?"

thirty-one

. . .

Ash

I twist the door handle carefully, wincing as it creaks, and trying to be as quiet as possible.

My pussy aches after getting railed by all three of the Basilisks, but I like the feeling. It's a welcome reminder that it happened.

I wince, cursing under my breath as the door hinges screech, until…

"Okay, spill it," Cookie demands, switching the light on and making me jump out of my skin. She crosses her arms over her bright pink bathrobe. What is she doing up so late? I thought she'd be asleep. "Where have you been?"

"Nowhere," I reply unconvincingly. "The party."

She isn't convinced, looking at my disheveled clothes, out-of-place hair, and smeared makeup.

"Who is he?"

"I don't know what you're talking about," I lie, trying to slip past her, conscious that I desperately need to shower before dealing with an interrogation. "I just went to the after-party."

"Puh-lease!" She blocks my path and pulls out a chair

at the table for me to sit down. "I heard everyone else come back a few hours ago. You're not a good liar, Ash. I want all the details, and you know I won't stop asking until I get them."

Cookie has a lot of amazing qualities. Unfortunately, persistence is one of them.

"Fine," I admit, taking a seat. Dad would be proud of her interrogation techniques. "I may have made an extra stop on the way back from the party."

"I knew it," she declares triumphantly. "Who's the lucky guy?"

"No one you know," I reply, shifting in the chair uncomfortably.

"It's him, isn't it?" she says. Her piercing stare locks on mine like she's trying to see into my mind. It's a good thing she isn't psychic. I don't know how she'd react to finding out who I'm sleeping with. "It's Ripper from the Basilisks, right? You saw him again after that show, didn't you?"

"N-n-no."

She raises her eyebrows, seeing past my bullshit. My pathetic attempt at denial only confirms her suspicions as she slaps her hands on the table and says, "I knew it!"

"Okay, fine," I say, then motion for her to shush. Our rooms may be soundproofed, but I don't want to take any chances. "I went to see the Basilisks again because they're in town. Sue me!"

She smirks. "It looks like you did more than hang out."

I roll my eyes, refusing to divulge any details. "What happened doesn't matter."

"Fine." She raises her hands in surrender. "I don't need to know any dirty details, but will you be seeing Ripper

again, or is it a casual thing? I know you like him, but you don't even know who he is."

"Actually," I say, "I do."

"Hold up!" She almost falls off her chair. "You've seen under the mask, and he's not a creepy old dude?"

I laugh at her reaction. "No," I say, "definitely not a creepy old dude."

"So?" she presses. "Have you just seen Ripper or all of them?"

I shrug, keeping my lips sealed, but she reads my expression. Goddammit.

"You've seen all of them." Man, she's good. "What do they look like?"

"They look like normal guys," I say. Yeah, normal guys who are also A-list celebrities.

"Okay, you keep their secrets," she says. "But it makes me feel better that you've seen their faces. Do you know their names? I can do a criminal check on them. I have friends."

I snort at her overprotectiveness. "That won't be necessary."

Everything I could want to know about them is already in the public domain and a quick internet search away.

"If you're sure…" Her voice trails off. "But the offer is there if you change your mind."

"Thanks, Cookie," I say. "Now are you done with the questions? I need to shower and sleep before rehearsals in the morning."

"Almost," she says. "There's just one last thing…"

"Fine," I say, "but that's it."

"Will you be seeing them again?"

I try to hold back a smile, but I can't help it from spreading over my face as I answer with certainty, "Yes."

She grins. "I want you to be happy, Ash. Just let me know when you're seeing them, okay? You're on Popstarz and in the public eye now. You have to be careful."

"You worry too much," I tell her, rising from the table. My panties are still damp, and I need to wash the cum off my thighs. "But, yes," I agree, noticing her concerned expression. "I promise to be careful and tell you what's going on."

"Good," she says, breathing a sigh of relief. "Now get your ass to sleep so you can get up early."

I salute. "Yes, ma'am."

Tonight has been filled with surprises, but, as I head to bed, I'm happier than I have been in months.

I know where I stand. The connection I share with the Basilisks is mutual. Even though it'll be difficult to merge our lives, we want to try.

thirty-two

. . .

Ash

After an amazing night, I'm back to my grueling rehearsal schedule. The next show theme is female icons, and I'll be singing *Running up that Hill* by Kate Bush.

My vocal coach, Jed, is being difficult this morning. Whatever I do, he isn't happy.

"It's like you're not even trying." He slams his fist on the piano in frustration as I finish the first verse for the sixth time in a row. "Put some effort into it, Ashley. Make me believe you want to be here."

"I'm trying," I mumble, stifling a yawn. Lack of sleep doesn't help.

"Go again from the top," he orders, raising his hand.

If I could, I'd scream the chorus, but I like the tone of the song.

"No, no, no." Jed stops me, cutting the music short.

"What is it now?" I ask, my patience wavering. What more does he want? I'm doing everything I can. "What can I do better?"

"I want to feel that you're [illegible]," he says. "You're

wooden. You need to make me feel that you're singing because this is your dream."

Singing is my dream, just not singing in the way he wants me to.

"We'll loop back on this," he sighs and checks his watch. "I'll report back to Jacinta that you need extra work." He makes a shooing motion. "I have my next contestant to train. Someone who makes an effort."

I hang my head as I slouch out. Jed didn't have to say it outright, but I know he thinks I'm unworthy of my place here.

Tiffany is waiting by the door, desperate to show the full extent of her vocal range. Jed won't have a problem with her performance.

"Tough practice, Ashley?" she asks with a snide smile. "I'm not surprised that you're out of your depth. Everyone knows the only reason you're still here is because of the sympathy vote."

I take a deep breath to calm my rising anger. A reaction is what she wants. She'll use it to find a way to remove me from the competition.

"I may have the sympathy vote," I say, deciding my words are my best weapon, "but at least my family didn't pay to get me on the show."

There's no evidence to prove it, but everyone at Camp Harmony knew Tiffany's mom paid for special tuition and was great friends with Jacqueline.

Tiffany's lip twists into a snarl like a she-devil. "I earned my place here."

I should walk away. I normally choose to avoid drama, but I want to wipe the smirk off of her face, so I say, "But I'm sure Jacqueline being friends with Mommy helps."

"At least my mom supports me," she retaliates. "Yours couldn't stand to be around you, so she killed herself."

Ouch. Tiffany doesn't fully understand the circumstances around my mom's death, but her words still sting like a bitch.

I grit my teeth and step forward, seconds away from ripping out her hair extensions.

"Tiffany," Jed calls.

She shoots me a smug smile and disappears into the practice room. I stomp away, my blood boiling, and as I turn a corner, I walk head-first into a muscled chest.

"Ouch!" I rub my nose, then look up. "Ze—Zach? What are you doing here?"

"I'm a mentor, remember?" His presence is calming, reminding me I'm not alone. I have allies. He lowers his voice, his eyebrows knit together in concern as he asks, "Is everything okay? I heard you and Tiffany talking."

"I'm fine," I reply, but my voice sounds funny.

Tiffany doesn't deserve the satisfaction of her bullshit getting to me but, between the bad session and her jibes, the walls are closing in.

I sniff and blink away tears. You can't, Ash. Not in front of Zed, the king of holding everything together.

"Why don't we have lunch together?" he suggests. "I was about to grab some food."

"Lunch?" I stare at him blankly. This isn't what we agreed. We were supposed to keep our distance from each other to avoid arousing suspicion. "Are you sure?"

"Yes," he says, then loudly just in case anyone else is lurking in the corridors listening, "and any other contestants are welcome to join us."

No one speaks up, which I'm sure they would have if they were eavesdropping.

"Where do you want to go?" I ask, following him out of the studio.

"My suite," he says, slipping a room card into my palm. "I'll see you in ten minutes. We'll get room service."

I turn the card over in my hand and question whether this is a good idea. Zed is usually careful, I reason. He wouldn't put us in a precarious position unless he's confident there is no risk.

I take the stairs to their floor, panicking I'll run into another contestant who will ask where I'm going. If they do, I already have an excuse planned about hitting my step goals—not that I've ever given a shit about exercising before.

When I'm outside their door, I triple-check the number, put it in the slot, and it flashes green. I push the door open and step inside.

"Woah..." I gasp as I look around. The room is five times the size of my hotel room. In the middle of it, Zed is standing by a table with a full spread of snacks, complete with flickering candles. Who knew he was a romantic?

He looks up and smiles. "What do you think?"

I notice that all the food is plant-based. How did he know I'm vegan? He must have paid attention to what I ate in Camp Harmony, and knowing that he noticed me makes my heart skip a beat. This is like a scene people write books about.

"It looks amazing," I say, eyeballing the fresh fruit, bread, oils, and olives. "How did you pull all of this together so fast?"

It's only been fifteen minutes since we parted ways, but he shrugs like it's nothing.

"I have my ways," he replies, pulling out a chair for me to sit down.

"Who knew you could be a gentleman?" I tease.

His eyes glitter. "I have my moments."

"Are the others coming?" I ask.

He shakes his head. "They're still working with other contestants." He holds up a jug of juice. "Thirsty?"

I nod as he pours a glass and pushes it toward me. It's not the shit that comes from a carton, it's freshly squeezed.

"Are you sure this is okay?" I look around nervously, expecting a contestant or judge to jump out of a cupboard and say gotcha.

"It's not a crime to ask a contestant to eat lunch," he says. "If anyone asks, I'll say I was giving you a preview of our new remastered Lionheart album."

My heart rate slows to a more natural speed. That sounds totally plausible. The last thing I want is to get him into trouble and attract unwanted attention from Jacqueline.

"Go on," he encourages. "Eat."

I don't have to be told twice. A lot of girls I used to know lived on tiny salads, but I dig in, piling my plate high.

"What?" I ask Zed, seeing his bemused expression. I raise an eyebrow. "Are you used to hanging around with models all the time?"

Stupid question. He probably is.

He laughs. "It's not that. I'm just pleased I could do something for you. I heard what Tiffany said and thought you might need cheering up."

The tasty mouthful turns to chewy flavorless gruel as I swallow it down.

"She was just trying to get to me," I dismiss, trying to wave it off.

"It's okay to not be okay," Zed says, reaching over the table to take my hand. "Tiffany says stupid shit, but she hasn't always been like this."

I scoff. "Are you trying to defend her?"

"Fuck no," he interjects quickly. "After what she did to you at Camp Harmony, I'll never defend her again. But I know what it's like to be brought up in a family like mine and Tiffany's. Everything you do is for appearance, and they force expectations down your throat before you can talk. It turns most people into monsters."

"You have two siblings, right?" I ask, although I already know he does. "What are they like?"

"Have you been googling me?" Zed jokes, and I stuff chips in my mouth to avoid answering. "Yes, Elliot and Lacy."

"I always wanted siblings," I say wistfully. "Do you get along with them?"

He shrugs. "Lacy does her own thing. She spends most of her time with her boyfriend. Elliot, on the other hand, is a loose cannon."

"He's a good actor," I comment.

"He was," Zed replies, looking past my shoulder into the distance with a sad smile. "But he doesn't see that. He's in a bad place right now, and my mom doesn't help."

I'm not surprised. When I met Zed's mom briefly, she acted like a total dragon who wanted everything her way.

"What do you mean?" I press for information, intrigued to learn more about his background.

"Mom wants the best for us in her own way," Zed says,

"but she cares more about the family reputation than us. She wants us all to be successful without compromising the family name or damaging the foundation she's built, regardless of whether it makes us happy."

"But it's your life," I remind him. "You can do what you want with it."

"It's not always that simple." He smiles wryly. "I found success and the money that comes with it, but Lacy and Elliot still rely on her financially. She holds it over their heads to get them to do what she wants. She's a control freak. I know I have issues, but she's on another level…"

"Families are complicated."

"I'm lucky I got away," he says, "and found the Basilisks. That's what's kept me sane all these years."

"I get that," I say, deciding to open up. "After my mom died, music—your music—got me through most days. It was my release."

He nods in understanding and asks cautiously, "Were you and your mom close?"

"Super close," I reply, smiling at the memory of how she used to be the first person I wanted to tell when I had good news. "She made me believe I could do anything. She is the one who encouraged me to apply to Camp Harmony, but she just wanted me to be happy."

"My mom has never cared about me being happy, and neither has Tiffany's," he says. "People like me have never had unconditional love. Tiffany's bitterness comes from her jealousy. She doesn't know what it's like to care for someone as deeply as your mom cared about you."

I've never looked at it that way before, but it makes sense.

"Maybe you're right," I say, feeling myself let go of some of the residual anger I'm holding onto.

"It doesn't make what she said to you okay," Zed replies, "but knowing that might help the next time she says something for a reaction."

"Thank you," I mumble, touched by his effort and openness.

"I wanted to bring you here to show you I care," he says, taking a deep breath. "I don't want to be like my mom."

"You're nothing like her," I say.

Zed clears his throat to put an end to the subject.

"You know…" I say, gazing around the penthouse. "While I'm here, I'd love a tour."

He jumps up. "Of course."

As he goes to pull my chair out for me, we're both startled by a bang coming from the corridor.

"What was that?" I ask, turning to face the offending noise.

He paces to the door and looks through the peephole, frowning. "No one's there."

"It's probably one of the hotel staff dropping something on the way to Jacqueline's room," I say, grimacing as I say her name after finding out how she treated Ripper. "How can you still speak to her and pretend nothing has happened?"

Zed sighs, knowing what I'm talking about. "Ripper is complicated. The situation is complicated, and we're tied into a contract that gives us no way out. I speak to her so that he doesn't have to, but…" His shoulders tense. "It's not easy. I wish there had been more I could have done at the time, but I didn't know. Ripper didn't tell us until after we signed. If I knew, I'd never have put my name on that dotted line."

"She can't get away with it."

"No, she can't," Zed agrees. An angry inferno burns behind his eyes. He wants her to suffer. "But we can't do anything as long as we're signed with Starnote. Our hands are tied."

"It'll come out one day."

"And when it does," Zed says, "her entire house of cards will come toppling down, and I'll fucking rejoice. Until then, there's no proof anything happened when Ripper was a minor. She was smart about it. They never left a trail behind, and few people would believe him with his reputation."

"It fucking sucks," I say, deflated and at a loss.

I see the pain in Zed's face and how he holds himself. Knowing what happened to Ripper has torn him up inside, and maybe that's why he's so protective of him now. They've been through a lot together.

"The best thing you can do is to be there for him," Zed says. "You don't know the difference you've made coming into our lives. Ash, you get us. You see us for who we are. But I do have one favor to ask you…"

"A favor?"

What can I do for the guy who has everything?

"Don't hurt Ripper, Ash," Zed says. "Venom and I can deal with it if our hearts get broken. It'd fucking suck, but we can handle our emotions. Ripper isn't like us. It'd ruin him. Please, whatever happens, don't hurt him."

His words tug at my heart as I see the desperate pleading in his eyes. He's in love with Ripper, whether he realizes it or not.

"I don't plan on hurting him," I say, taking Zed's hand, "or any of you, not unless you keep a secret from me again."

He nods solemnly, satisfied with my response, then his

lopsided grin makes my stomach somersault. "So, you wanted a tour..."

He leads me to the vast living room, pointing out various artifacts and a television screen that rolls down from the ceiling. Zed is casual about it, waving it off. "If you come through here, I'll show you a painting that—"

"Actually," I catch his wrist. Seeing and hearing him open up has made me see another side to the guy who wears invisible armor by day and craves order. "I'd rather see your bedroom."

The tips of his ears turn pink in surprise. "Oh..."

He takes me through to his room, which has a giant bed with crisp white sheets and plump pillows. It's immaculate and free from any personal possessions, making it look vacant.

He hesitates before stepping inside. "You know I didn't invite you here for this."

"I know," I reply, touched by his concern, "but you've opened up to me, Zed. I want to open up to you too..."

I take his hand and lead him to the bed.

"Are you sure—"

I cut him off with a kiss that he takes as my answer, pushing me back onto the bed. We kiss deeply, his hardness pressing through my jeans. We shouldn't be doing this here, but that only heightens my need.

Zed's hand slips under my shirt and over the soft fabric of my bra, gliding across my hard nipples that are begging to be touched.

"Ash Cooper," he murmurs, "you're gonna be the death of us."

"Or the rebirth," I reply.

He moves onto his knees, tearing his shirt over his head, and I sit up to do the same.

"Skinny jeans?" He looks down at what I'm wearing and pulls a face. "You're not making this easy for me."

"Maybe that's why you like me," I tease. "I'm not like the other girls who are afraid to put you in your place."

"I'll put you in your place right now."

I squeal as his hands close around my thighs and yank me closer. He leans to kiss my neck, brushing his soft lips against me and making my body shiver. He moves down my body, leaving a trail of kisses in his wake before he reaches my waistband and undoes my zipper.

Zed's right. It's no straightforward task to get out of skinny jeans when lying down, but as soon as he's tugged them past my knees, they come off easily.

It's strange to have his full attention, and I freeze as my thoughts stray to the others.

"Will Ripper or Venom mind?" I ask.

We all agreed we'd like to keep seeing each other, but we never covered the ground rules. For someone who has never been in a relationship with one guy, I have a lot to learn. Balancing three guys is a new skill to master, and I don't want to upset anyone.

"Let me find out," Zed says, grabbing his cell.

"What are you doing?" I squeak as his fingers tap out a text. "You're not asking for permission, are you?"

"Smile," he says, leaning back to take a picture and hitting send.

"Zed." I sit up. "What're you doing?"

He shows me the photograph. It doesn't show my face, just my bare stomach with his hand lying across it with a caption.

Zed: Our girl had a tough morning.

He frowns, looking genuinely concerned that he might have upset me. "I thought you wanted me to ask them if this is okay?"

Before I can answer, he turns his phone to show me the messages.

Ripper: Show our girl a good time.

Venom: Jealous. I can't get away.

My nerves ease, even if Zed gave me a mini heart attack at thinking he sent nudes, and what could happen if his phone was hacked.

"Is this something the three of you have done before?" I ask, thinking it's a suitable time to voice what's been playing on my mind, but I've been too scared to say. "Sharing a girl?"

"No," he says, wincing like I've thrown cold water over him. "Never."

"This is all so new to me," I confess. "I've never even had a boyfriend, and you all seem so experienced…"

"You're the only girl we've ever wanted to share." Zed's features soften as he smiles and strokes my cheek tenderly. "The only girl any of us have wanted for more than a night."

"But I'm nothing special," I whisper, voicing my insecurities. "I don't get what you see in me. I'm just a normal girl from a small town and you are… Well, you are the biggest stars on the planet."

"You may be from a small town, but you're anything but ordinary," Zed says. He rolls on top of me as I part my legs to make room for him. "You captivated me with your

voice, but getting to know you drew me in even more. You don't realize how fucking special you are."

"I..." I struggle to make eye contact with him. "I don't know how to take compliments very well, either."

"I've noticed," he replies. Both of his hands rest on either side of my head. "But you better get used to it because we're gonna fucking worship you."

"But—"

"You're like us."

He puts a stop to my objections as he trails kisses down the length of my body. He pauses at my belly bar, then continues to kiss along the edge of my panties. His breath heats my skin as he kisses my pussy over the fabric. He'll be able to feel my wetness, craving his touch on my skin, but he doesn't give me what I want. Instead, his lips move to the top of my thighs and the scars covering them. There is nowhere to hide.

"You've felt pain, Ash," Zed says, kissing my scars, and running his fingers along them, almost tickling. "I want to make sure you never feel pain like that again because you'll have us."

I moan as he runs a finger down the front of my panties. My hips buck, encouraging him.

"It feels like we've known each other forever," Zed says as he strokes my swollen pussy. My panties bunch in my slit, all wet for him. "We've watched you all summer and got to know you, but now it's your turn to really see us..."

"I see you, Zed." My voice is husky. "I see all of you."

"Fuck," he groans as he pushes my panties to the side. "You're so fucking wet for me."

His index finger teases me, dipping into the pool of

wetness at my entrance and stroking it, without going inside.

"Zed," I moan, gyrating and trying to angle myself, so his finger slips into me, but he pulls away and yanks my panties off instead.

He tugs off his clothes before returning between my legs, pausing for a few seconds to look at me. We're in natural daylight—no music, no flashing lights, and no longer shrouded under Buggy's darkness. It's just the two of us. Ash and Zed. No masks.

My breathing quickens as his tongue dives in between my legs, probing and tasting me.

He slides two fingers into my pussy to stretch me. "I could eat you all day."

"That's not enough," I whine. "I need more. I need you."

I figure he'll tease me more and drag out my pleasure like he did last night. But to my surprise, he climbs up the bed and kisses me. I taste myself on his breath, and I like it.

"I want your cock inside me," I say. "I need it."

I hook my leg around his torso and push his chest to roll him over to straddle him. I sweep his red hair out of his face and notice tiny freckles under his eyes.

"I've never noticed these before," I say, stroking them.

"They come out in the sun," he replies.

Shit. I groan as the heat of his dick rubs against my pussy, warming me in the most delicious way. I reach to angle his cock and take it slowly, an inch at a time, resting my elbows on either side of his head and pressing my tits into his face. I want to make this last, tease him as he's teased me until he begs.

"Your pussy is so fucking tight," he moans as I lower

myself until I'm taking his full length. I have to be careful, avoiding vigorous motions straight away. He's bigger than Ripper and Venom, and I'm scared he'll rip me in two, but after riding him cautiously for a few strokes, my confidence increases. I don't look down, scared in case the outline of his cock is bulging through my skin—it sounds impossible, but, hey, you never know.

It also gives me time to admire Zed's body. In the sunlight, I can see every defined line and muscle. He works out and is in amazing shape, but he isn't too bulky.

"That's right, baby," Zed murmurs. "Ride me."

I get into a rhythm as he reaches to squeeze my breast in encouragement. I pop one of my fingers into my mouth to wet it, then trail it down my body to reach my clit.

I've never touched myself in front of someone else, but from Zed's primal growl and the way he's gripping my ass, I can tell he likes it.

I rock against my hand and his cock, throwing my head back. Our panting fills the silence, making a breathy melody.

"Cum all over me, baby," Zed purrs. "I want to feel your pretty pussy gush all over me."

His words are a turn-on. Reading dirty fan fiction has always been hotter than watching unrealistic porn. His dirty talk tips me to the brink of orgasm. I gasp, my cheeks flush, and my chest heaves as an orgasm makes my body shake.

I ride his cock, dripping all over him. I start to shake and collapse forward. Our skin is slick from sweat, as Zed takes control and continues to pound my orgasm out of me from beneath.

"Yes," I moan, quivering in his arms. "Fuck, yes. Zed! Like that! Yes!"

He spanks my ass, jolting my body, and he roars as he comes, spilling inside me. It's a good thing I started taking birth control.

He wraps his arms around me, holding me close. I hear his heart thundering through his skin as he stays inside me. I could lie here for hours.

Neither of us says anything until I finally prop myself up on my elbows. His smile makes me feel warm and fuzzy, a smile without pretense. Underneath the control freak, all Zed wants is someone who cares for him.

"Shit!" I notice the time on the clock on the bedside table. "I have fifteen minutes until I have to be in the dance studio."

"You'll make it on time," Zed replies, then winks. "But you've already had a daily workout."

Dancing would be a struggle after getting railed by him and the others. I'll need to make a schedule if I want to be able to walk.

I clamber out of bed, grab my clothes, and look back to see him lying across the bed like a naked statue and gulp at the size of his huge cock. How did that fit inside me?

thirty-three

. . .

Ash

"Let me do that for you," Cookie says, taking the brush out of my hands. I'm painting my face with a black-and-white candy skull design. So far, I've only completed the white base coat. "Your lines will be all wobbly."

"Thanks," I say.

The Basilisks are playing tonight, and I can't wait to take my mind off a bad day of rehearsals. Whatever I did wasn't good enough or right. Maybe it's because my whirlwind romance with the Basilisks is all I can think about. Unfortunately, my poor performance hasn't gone unnoticed by my new manager.

"And one more thing," Cookie says, drawing the lines of diamonds from my eyelids down to my cheeks. "I'm coming with you to the show."

"What?" I gasp, taking care to stay still to keep the lines straight. "Are you serious?"

"Sure am," she says, rolling her eyes. "The show is in a sketchy neighborhood. I want to make sure you're safe. Besides, it's about time I met Ripper properly, don't you think?"

"You want to meet him?" My face pales underneath the white paint. "Why?"

"Come on, Ash," she says. "You've been obsessed with him since you met. Whatever romance you've got going on is clearly on your mind, and I want to see what all the fuss is about. He needs to get your manager and best friend's approval."

I bite my tongue to stop myself from saying that she already knows him pretty well.

"You don't have to come," I say. "I'll be fine on my own."

"I've already bought a ticket," she says, ending the conversation.

"But you don't have to meet him," I say.

"Are you embarrassed by me because I'm not a hot goth chick like you?" she teases.

"No," I snort. "I'm sure you'll get along, it's just…"

"It's just, what?"

"If you're going to meet them, there's probably something else you should know…"

I haven't told Cookie yet that the relationship extends to Venom and Zed, but she's bound to find out eventually. She's not judgmental, though she might freak out about them being three times the distraction. If she wants to meet them, it'll be easier to tell her about it—even if their identities remain a secret.

"What?" She stops painting my face. "What is it?"

"I'm not just with Ripper, okay?" I blurt out. "I'm kinda… seeing the whole band."

"Hold up!" She drops her paintbrush. "You're dating the Basilisks? All three of them?"

I shrug. "Kinda."

We hadn't exactly agreed on a status yet, but from our conversations, we're exclusive.

"Kinda?" She cocks her head to the side. "You either are or you aren't."

"Well, yeah…" I say, grinning. "I guess I am."

"I knew there was a reason you were so damn happy," she declares. "Just one guy couldn't do that to you."

"You're not shocked?"

In Meadow Springs, it was a huge deal when a couple got divorced or came out—let alone admitting to screwing three guys at once.

"I don't judge," she says, "my parents are polyamorous. I'm used to them having extra boyfriends and girlfriends around."

"Wow," I say. Now it's my turn to be shocked. "How didn't I know this?"

She laughs. "It's never come up." She screws up her nose. "My parent's sex life is not something I like to think about." She has a point. Cookie retrieves her paintbrush and starts on my face again as relief washes over me. Maybe I could ask for tips if I ever met her parents. "I guess that means three guys need to get my approval."

"I'll let them know," I joke, rolling my eyes. "No pressure then."

"It's a lot of pressure," she corrects me. "I have high standards. You deserve the best."

"I think you'll like them," I say, turning my face to give her a better angle.

"If they keep making you as happy as you have been, I'm sure I will," she says, "even if I may have to take a few aspirins before the show."

I pout. "You told me you liked their music."

"I do," she says, then adds, "it's just a little more aggressive than what I'm used to."

Cookie and I are opposites. Her, always the optimist, and me, the pessimist. But we work, and it's good to know I have a friend on my side. I only hope that she likes them.

thirty-four

. . .

Venom | Levi

Where is she?

I scan the crowd. Is she here? Has she not been able to make it? Has something happened? Then I see a painted skull. Pride swells in my chest. Our girl is wearing a mask, just like us, and she isn't alone.

Her friend, Cookie, cheers by her side. Cookie doesn't seem like the type to come along to a metal gig of her own accord, so I assume she's here to look out for Ash. We can't take any chances with our girl.

It's a risky move for us to perform in the same place again. We avoid doing multiple shows in the same location as it could give our fans a clue as to where we're based. But we have to balance practicality with what we have to do for our sanity. When Ted called to say he secured a second show because of popular demand, we couldn't turn it down.

We need to blow off steam. Living in the hotel alongside the judges and Popstarz contestants makes me feel like a hamster running on a wheel. Spending a night with

Ash reminded me how it felt to be alive, and I want her to see us perform. This show is for her.

The crowd is wild, a moving mass like a living organism. People jump, bump, crash, and knock into each other like bumper cars. I try not to look at the mosh pit—a place I used to love being in the middle of. The jostling and pushing bring it all back…

Then I see Ash, roaring our words back to us. We're playing our classic crowd favorites, and they're eating that shit up. But I keep my gaze fixed on Ash, letting the surrounding chaos fade into nothingness. She is my anchor, grounding me in reality, and stopping my mind from straying to a dark place.

Ripper's pounding drums unlock the part of me I like to keep hidden. I go to the zone where I feel safe, where only our music matters. But, for once, I don't wish the show would last forever because we're meeting Ash later. Usually, the end of a show means a return to our normal lives. But I'm counting down the minutes until we finish because spending time with her will be even better.

I can tell the others are excited she's here, too. Knowing she's listening only makes us want to give the best performance and show her everything we can do.

Zed throws his head back and screams, looking like a demon sent straight from hell in his long trench coat that skims the floor. His bronze mask covers his face and has a square slit for his mouth. A copper crown nestled on his silver knee-length wig wobbles as he sings.

Ripper pounds the drum, a complicated rhythm that he makes look effortless. His mask is matte black with horns and deep grooves that morph his features to resemble a wolf. His mask is equipped with a voice changer to

deepen his tone and make it more robot-like. He looks menacing, and the fans fucking love it.

My bones rattle as Zed's roar makes the hairs on my arms stand on end. Ash whips her head back and forth, throwing her black silky hair everywhere, while Cookie jumps around in a bright pink dress that makes her stand out like a firework in a dark sky.

Our fans sing our words back to us—my words—and I wonder whether Ash has read my lyric book yet. She won't know it, but I wrote a lot of songs about her.

The lights dim, and a thunderous applause erupts, signaling the end. We leave the stage, but the crowd heckles for an encore. We always give them what they want.

"What song?" Ripper asks.

"*Underworld Calling*," I say without hesitation. The song Ash helped us with in Wilderton. "And I want to sing."

"Are you sure?" Zed presses, taken aback.

"Positive." I nod my pumpkin head with confidence. "I want to do it for her."

I want her to know the impact she'd had on our lives since she turned everything upside down. She's given me the strength to believe in myself. With her there, I can do this. I know I can.

Ripper puts his hand on my shoulder. "We're right here with you, Venom."

This isn't the same as the night I last sang metal on stage, I tell myself. I'm not alone. I have my best friends at my side. They've got my back.

"We've got you," Zed says, "whatever happens."

Despite my certainty that this is the right thing to do,

nerves flutter in my stomach. I have to channel them into excitement.

"Let's do this," I say before I can change my mind.

The audience screams as we return to the stage. My heart jumps in panic as I scan the rows of people and can't see her. Then I spot Cookie's pink dress. A wave of relief rushes through me as I spot Ash cheering along with everyone else.

"We've got a special treat for you tonight," Zed says in a deep rumble, a voice unrecognizable to those who know him as Zach Royal. "A song from our new album."

The crowd goes crazy. My palms are cold and clammy, making me cling tightly to my guitar.

Zed screams, "Are you ready?"

An overwhelming *Yes!* roars from the pit, but Zed is asking me the question. He pauses for a split second to look back at me, and I nod, lowering my head, ready to surrender to my fears.

We begin. Those first chords have haunted my head for months, but they've been repeating on a loop since Ash saw us at the recording studio.

While the fans punch the air, Ash's hands drop to her side. Cookie whispers something in her ear, but she doesn't pay her any attention. She simply stares transfixed by our act unfolding. I wish she was with us.

Heads and limbs thrash around, and flashing lights capture the dance floor like snapshots. My fingers move, the strings bringing me comfort. Playing the tune isn't a struggle, but the song builds, leading to the moment I've been avoiding for years.

My mouth is dry, my tongue feels too big for it, I try to swallow. I squeeze my eyes shut, blinking away the image of bloodied torsos falling to the floor and screams of wild

abandon turning to pure terror. I look up again and find Ash's face. I'm not singing to the audience; I'm only singing to her.

Fuck.

I miss my cue.

Zed and Ripper double back. Zed sings the last line of the first verse again. It's a new song, so the crowd doesn't know any different, but Ash freezes. She knows what's coming.

She catches my eyes, or at least tries to in my mask, and a small smile flickers over her painted face to tell me I've got this.

Her encouragement is all I need. After Zed's third repeat of the same line, I scream the lines that were written for me.

"I'm not afraid to break down the walls,
The walls of steel and wire,
Walls built to be torn down."

My voice, which I keep chained in the shadows of my subconscious, bursts out of me. My first few words are shaky, but they capture the attention of the stunned crowd. Fans pause in the mosh pit to double-check that they aren't imagining it as I continue. Every line is stronger than the last.

Where Ash should sing, Zed harmonizes with me. It doesn't have the same effect, but his voice melts into my own. His gravelly tone provides a depth to my high-pitched note that reverberates in my mask.

Ash raises her hands in the air, jumping up and down. She doesn't realize all of this is because of her. She gave me the courage to go on.

My part ends, and Zed picks up the second verse. My fear hasn't disappeared, but it's lessened. I can't stop myself from checking the exits again for any sign of trouble, but a suffocating weight has lifted from my chest, just knowing I can sing again.

When the song ends, the crowd goes wild as we take a bow and file out. My feet feel like they're floating.

Ripper's arms fly around my shoulders as soon as we're offstage. For years, I've avoided physical affection—hence why I never sought the company of women like the others. Being touched reminds me of packed crowds and being in a small area where no one can escape. But I don't flinch as he squeezes me hard.

"You killed it, man," Ripper says, pulling away.

"Not bad," Zed agrees, and I imagine he's smirking under his mask.

I shrug nonchalantly, knowing they can't see the giant smile on my face.

Ted joins us and exclaims, "You never told me you were doing vocals again, Venom."

"It wasn't planned," I say.

"That song…" Ted puts his thumb and middle finger together and kisses them. "An instant hit. How is the new album coming along?"

"It's coming," Ripper mutters under his breath.

The truth is, we're at a standstill. We have to finish the album soon, but it doesn't flow like our previous albums that came together quickly. Even though we're happy with the lyrics and composition, the songs are missing something.

"Oh, and another thing," Ted grumbles, "Ash is here along with some other chick. I told them to wait in the green room."

"Thanks," Zed replies.

"Be careful around that girl, okay?" Ted warns. "She's cool, but she's in the public's eye now. We don't want another scandal."

Ripper snorts. Poor Ted doesn't realize the irony of his comment or how he's standing with a ten time Grammy award-winning band.

"We'll bear that in mind, Ted," Zed replies seriously.

We leave him behind to meet Ash. It's not exactly the green rooms we're used to—boasting a moth-eaten sofa and a coffee machine that has seen better days.

Ash leans against the wall, straightening as we stroll in. Her black leggings have a shiny effect and her black crop top shows off her toned stomach and silver belly bar. She's done a good job with her makeup. The dark skull contour lines change the shape of her facial features, making her unrecognizable, and her eyes are lit up with unnaturally blue contacts.

"Hey!" She grins as we approach her. "You guys did great."

Cookie hangs back, narrowing her eyes suspiciously as she looks us up and down. Being in a Basilisk costume usually makes me feel untouchable, but the way she's looking at us makes me nervous. The Basilisks have never wanted someone's approval until now.

"This is Cookie," Ash introduces, "my manager and best friend."

"You must be the guys that Ash is dating," Cookie says. From chatting with her at Camp Harmony, she has a sunny disposition, but by the way she's acting now, you would never guess. She looks like she's trying to see straight through our masks, zeroing in on each of us. "Ripper, Venom, and Zed."

"Um..." Even Zed is lost for words. Ash never told us that Cookie knew about her dating all three of us.

"It's great to meet you, Cookie," Ripper intervenes in a robot voice. He holds out a gloved hand for her to shake. "We're pleased you could come to see our show."

"It's not a nice part of town," Zed says, recovering from his earlier stumble. "We didn't want Ash to come without a friend."

Cookie's frostiness thaws a little as she declares, "That's exactly what I told her."

Ash rolls her eyes. "You guys worry too much."

"We're glad Ash has someone watching out for her," Zed says.

He never gives a shit about what people think when he's a Basilisk, so it's amusing to see him using his Royal charm to win Cookie over.

"So," Ripper says, "what did you think of the show?"

"It was amazing," Ash says, then jumps straight in to give a blow-by-blow account of each song we performed, but it's hard to relax under Cookie's watchful gaze. "Venom, the last song..." Ash reaches out to touch my arm. "Your voice... it was..."

"It was amazing," Cookie finishes her sentence. "I didn't know you sang. When we saw you in Wilderton, you didn't."

"I don't usually," I confess, "but we wanted to try something different. Someone told us it would make the song better."

"That sounds like the kinda smart-ass thing Ash would do," Cookie jokes, lightening the mood. Her walls are coming down. She likes us... I think.

"Do you want to come back to our tour bus?" Zed asks. "We can get drinks and listen to music?"

"I think I'll head back to the hotel," Cookie says, a knowing smirk spreading over her face. "I'm sure you guys would like some time alone."

Ash nudges her in the ribs. "Cookie!"

"What?" Cookie asks innocently. "You've been grinning from ear to ear since your date the other night. Although I don't have personal experience, I know what a post-fuck glow looks like. I'm not gonna be a…" she pauses for a second, counting under her breath, "fifth wheel."

"You're unbelievable," Ash mutters. If her face wasn't painted, she'd be blushing. Her embarrassment only makes her more adorable.

"We'll call you a cab," Zed insists. "Our manager, Ted, will accompany you back to your hotel."

Cookie objects, "That's not—"

"Thanks, Zed," Ash says, shooting Cookie a pointed look. "She'll be happy with that. You can text me when you get back, okay? You can chat manager stuff with Ted, too."

"Okay," Cookie agrees, then wags her finger at us like a concerned parent. "Make sure you get her home at a reasonable hour, okay? She has rehearsals first thing in the morning."

Ash cringes, but Ripper holds up his hand. "Scout's honor."

"Good," Cookie says, then her smile turns stony again. Her reaction is giving me whiplash. "One more thing, if you guys hurt her, I'll track you down, and you'll have to deal with me. Got it?"

I snicker as Zed gasps. Poor guy isn't used to people not instantly liking him.

"We'll take good care of her, Cookie," Ripper says. "We promise."

"Good," she replies, now satisfied, almost skipping away. "See you again soon."

She doesn't realize how soon it would be.

"Do you think she likes us?" Ripper asks as the door shuts behind Cookie.

"I think so," Ash replies, adding with a shy smile, "Well, this version of you, anyway."

"She's a good friend," Zed says. "I'm glad you have her."

"Me too," Ash replies, although there's an underlying sadness beneath her words, "after what happened with Brick..."

Ripper's fists clench, but he stays quiet.

"Have you heard from him?" Zed asks gently.

Ash shakes her head. "He's tried to contact me, even called Cookie to apologize. But I'm not ready to speak to him yet. I know he didn't mean to give information to the journalist, and I get why he accepted money for the story, but it still doesn't make it right."

"You can't trust anyone when you're famous," Zed replies wryly, "only each other."

We've watched over the years as friendships, families, and relationships have broken down because of greed. Trust becomes much harder when you become a public figure. You can't tell when people are interested in you or want to use your celebrity for their gain.

"Let's go back to Buggy," I say. "If we sneak out the back entrance, we can swerve the fans."

Usually, Zed encourages us to stay, but he doesn't object. Our time alone is precious when we have Ash with us, and he can't keep his eyes off her ass in those leggings.

We all sneak away and jump into a waiting cab at speed. The driver shifts around uncomfortably in his seat, but Ash's presence helps relax him.

Ash sits between me and Ripper. His hand rests protectively on her knee, while she slips her fingers through mine and whispers, "I'm so proud of you, Venom."

thirty-five

. . .

Ash

Returning to Buggy is like coming home. The place where the Basilisks can be themselves, and where I can see the real them. It's where our story started.

"I think we all deserve something to celebrate," Ripper says, pouring out a row of shots. It's a post-show tradition.

"Just the one," I say shyly. "I'm already screwing up in rehearsals, and Cookie will kill me if I return drunk."

"How are you feeling about the next show?" Zed asks.

I shrug and admit, "Honestly, I'm trying not to think about it."

The other contestants are improving week after week, but I'm stuck in a state of limbo. Will the voters get bored with me? I'm never going to be an artist who sings and dances around the stage with a giant smile like Tiffany.

"How would you feel if they voted you out?" Zed asks.

"I'm not sure." I down the shot and wince from my throat feeling on fire. "Sometimes I wish I never came on the show. I'm never excited about the songs I have to perform, but it's a stepping stone—right? It's a way to

branch into other music and raise my profile, or that's what Cookie says. If I left, what would happen to us?"

I don't have a place to stay in the city, a recording contract, or a source of income, so I have two choices. I could return to Meadow Springs until I catch a break, which would be the death of my career. Or I could pick up whatever work I could and see if Cookie would want to rent an apartment with me.

"We'll work it out," Ripper says.

But we all know it won't be easy with their schedule or if they're touring in another country. I can't follow the Lionhearts around without arousing suspicions.

The main reason I want to stay in Popstarz is to be closer to them. Our arrangement—or whatever the hell it is—has only just started, and I need more time to get to know them before making any big decisions.

I nod, biting my lip, trying to push my worries away. Venom goes to take off his pumpkin mask, but I catch his wrist to stop him. I have a better idea.

"Actually," I say, "I want you to keep your masks on."

"You like us in our masks, huh?" Zed's voice is gravelly and thick with desire. Unlike when we were alone in the penthouse, he wasn't vulnerable here. Their bodies are pumping with adrenaline and the high of the performance, which I want to take full advantage of.

I smile, fluttering my eyelashes. "Maybe."

There's something hot about them in their masks.

"If that's what our girl wants," Zed says, stroking my cheek. He can't kiss me through the gap in his mask, but his touch leaves a blazing trail behind.

"Hey, no fair!" Ripper pouts. "You've already had Ash to yourself."

I freeze. "I thought you were okay with that?"

"I am," Ripper says quickly, noticing my hesitation, "but that doesn't mean I'm not a little jealous."

"Before anything else happens," I say, feeling like I'm channeling Zed's rule-abiding side, "maybe we should set some ground rules?"

Ripper tilts his head to the side. "Ground rules?"

I avoid his gaze. "Between us. You know…" I try to find the right words. "Like what we're okay with."

"What she wants to know," Zed steps in to help me out, "is whether we can fuck her one-on-one."

"That," I say, continuing to look at my boots to avoid their piercing stares, "and what 'this' even is. I told Cookie that we're dating because I didn't know how else to say it, but I don't know how you guys see this. Where you see it heading. What you want us to be."

This is all new to me. I'm not a fan of labels, but a girl needs some clarity.

"Ash, we're all here for you, baby," Ripper says with a fierceness that makes my stomach flip. "We're not just dating; we're all fucking yours."

My heart speeds up at the intensity of his words. How is this my life now?

"I'm happy for you to fuck Ripper and Venom without me around," Zed adds. Yeah, that's easy for him to say after what happened the other day.

"Venom?" I prompt. He's stayed quiet, and sharing is something he finds more challenging.

"I want you to be happy," Venom says, "and I know they make you happy. You're the only girl for us."

"So…" I pause. "You're like my boyfriends now?"

I realize how juvenile that sounds, but I want to make sure I fully understand their exclusivity.

"You can call us that if you want to," Zed says, "but

we're more than that, Ash. When I asked if you wanted out, you didn't walk away. What you are to us is more than a label. You're all fucking ours, and we're all yours. We don't want anyone else but you."

The Basilisks are mine? I used to spend hours listening to them in my bedroom. Having them swear their loyalty to me is beyond the realms of my belief.

"Is that okay with you, Ash?" Venom asks gently.

"Yes." I try to appear casual. Okay? It's fucking brilliant, but I play it cool. "That's okay with me."

"I'm glad we've settled that," Ripper says. He approaches from behind and brushes my hair off my shoulder. "Because you're looking fucking hot tonight."

"Before you undress, I've got a surprise for you all," Zed says, causing Ripper to stand back. "Get out of the way."

Ripper and Venom tilt their heads in confusion. Zed shoves us to the side and kneels alongside the sofa. He opens a compartment underneath that I've never noticed before. He pulls, and voila! The empty space turns into a gigantic bed covered with a black sheet.

"When did you get that put in?" Ripper asks. Despite his robotic tone, I sense his disbelief from his intonations. "You never told me."

"That's because it's a surprise," Zed says. "It's a thin mattress, but I did what I could with the space. What do you think?"

"It sure beats the floor," Venom replies.

"Well..." Zed steps to the side and winks at me. "Why don't we try it out?"

I unlace my boots, step out of them, and dive onto it. No more carpet burns and bruised knees. I lay out and

spread my arms and legs like I'm making a snow angel while tall guys in masks loom over me.

"Take your clothes off," I order them. "But keep your masks on."

They are quick to oblige. I've never been super assertive before, but I want to get better at asking for what I want. And what I want right now is the Basilisks.

They watch as I remove my clothing item by item, throwing them to the side until I'm in my underwear.

"Fuck," Zed compliments, "look at our girl."

My panties are already wet as his hard cock springs free of his boxers. I pat the spaces on the bed on either side of me. "Come and join me," I say.

Venom is straight to my side. He takes off his pumpkin mask to reveal a balaclava underneath, presumably in case the pumpkin falls off during performances.

I roll up the fabric to expose his mouth and kiss him as the bed dips from the weight of Zed and Ripper joining us. Venom's hands run through my hair, and I hook my leg over his torso as his hands run over the curve of my ass.

Ripper spoons me from behind, his hands moving to my bra and struggling to unclasp it. He and Venom work as a team to unclip it, then throw it away with force like they've triumphantly won a battle.

Ripper groans as his left hand moves around my side to feel my tits and hard nipples. Zed kneels near my feet, moving forward as his fingers creep up my outer thighs and keep going until he's stroking me over my panties. Their hands are all over me, and it's fucking incredible.

Everyone backs away as Venom pushes me gently onto my back. Venom pulls my panties down and spreads my legs wide for all of them to see as his head settles between them.

"Taste her, Venom," Zed instructs. "Lick her sweet tight pussy for us, and tell us how good she tastes."

Venom grasps my hips and eats me out while Ripper and Zed watch on. I grab the sheet in a fist, moaning as Venom's hot tongue laps up my wetness, and see Ripper's dilated eyes cast a longing look at Zed's throbbing cock.

"I want you to touch each other," I command. Ripper doesn't argue. He slides across the bed until he and Zed face each other. Zed grabs Ripper's wig to pull him closer still. They can't kiss through their mask, but their hands slide down each other's chests, feeling their tight, defined muscles. Ripper pauses, spitting on the palm of his hand, and takes Zed's cock in his fist.

"Do you like to watch us together, Ash?" Zed ponders as his fingers stroke Ripper's shaft.

"Yes," I gasp as Venom groans into my pussy and sends vibrations through my body. "It's so fucking hot."

"Would you like to watch us fuck?" Zed asks.

I swallow hard. "I'd love that—oh, Venom!" Two of his fingers fill me as he licks my clit while fucking my pussy in hard and fast strokes. "Fuck. Yes!"

"Keep going, Venom," Ripper encourages, working Zed faster. "Make our girl drench the sheets and cover your face in her cum."

"Fuck, I'm going to—" I scream, holding onto Venom's head as an orgasm rushes through me. I writhe against his mouth, rolling my hips as I gush over Venom's fingers. "Yes, Venom! Yes!"

Venom licks along the length of my pussy with the tip of his tongue, making my legs quiver before he pulls away.

"I have a better idea," Zed says, eyeing my pussy like

he wants to devour it. "How would you like Ripper to fuck you while I fuck him?"

I nod. That sounds incredible.

Ripper disappears into the bathroom and returns with a giant bottle of lube and condoms.

"Or," Ripper suggests, "you can take two of us at the same time while Zed fucks me."

"Two of you?" I look at their three hard-ons and question where they'll go. "How?"

"You'll let Venom fuck that wet little pussy while I fuck your tight ass," Ripper replies. My virginal asshole clenches at the thought. As hot as taking them both at the same time sounds, I'm not sure I can do it.

"I-I-I-I…" I stammer. "I've never done that before."

"I'll be gentle," Ripper promises. "We can stop anytime."

"Okay," I decide, up for trying it.

"Mount Venom, Ash," Zed says, already squirting lube over his cock. How is Ripper going to take that? "We want to see his cock disappear."

I straddle Venom, who sighs as I slide onto him. My pussy, still pulsing from my orgasm, hugs his heat.

"She's so tight," Venom says.

"Lean forward, baby," Ripper instructs from behind me and groans. "Fuck, Zed. Look at her perfect fucking ass."

I take Venom as deep as he can go, then pause as two firm hands part my ass cheeks wide. A second later, a hot tongue is probing my asshole.

"Fuck." I jump at the sensation. I never thought I'd enjoy ass play, but damn, his tongue tickles.

"That's right, Ripper," Zed encourages. "Eat her fucking ass."

Ripper eating me out while Venom fucks me is a

massive turn-on, and my previous self-consciousness vanishes as I push my ass back into his face for him to explore.

"See? She fucking loves it," Zed says, "our dirty Basilisk girl."

I grind on Venom, making him sigh as I kiss him deeply, moaning into his mouth as his tongue meets mine.

Ripper pulls back, and a wet substance runs down my ass. Seconds later, a warm finger circles my asshole.

"I'm gonna be real gentle, Ash," Ripper says as he probes my entrance and slowly eases the tip of his finger inside me. He circles and stretches, not pushing too hard too fast.

"Her pussy is getting so fucking tight," Venom groans.

"Do you like that, Ash?" Ripper asks, pumping his finger in and out of me.

I'm breathless, unable to move as I sigh, "Yes."

It's new and exciting, building to the overall intensity of the situation.

The sound of a packet tearing and a condom wrapper fluttering to the floor makes me tense. Then Ripper's wet cock rubs against my asshole.

"This may sting a little, try and relax," Ripper says as his cock presses into me. "But I'll be gentle with you, baby. I know you can take me."

"Take a deep breath," Venom murmurs. His calmness helps put me at ease as Ripper edges into me.

I squeeze my eyelids shut as I take the head of his cock. Ripper doesn't move further. He holds himself there, allowing me to stretch around him.

"You're doing amazing," Ripper says. "Your ass is so fucking tight, and it feels incredible."

I'm scared to move as his cock slides deeper. Venom's

cock twitches inside my pussy, and I wonder whether they'll be able to feel each other.

"There," Ripper says. I've taken a few more inches, but he doesn't go further as he starts slowly thrusting. "How does that feel, Ash?"

"It feels..." I pause, then moan as Venom matches Ripper's pace. There's a lot of wetness down there. "Weird."

"In a good way?" Zed asks sharply.

"Yes," I reply quickly.

I don't want them to stop.

"Good," Ripper pauses as Venom thrusts quicker, and I balance my weight onto my knees.

Venom's cock moving against Ripper's is intense. My whole body is filled.

"You feel so good," Ripper compliments, massaging my ass as his cock enters me. He'll be able to see Venom too.

I cast a look back over my shoulder.

"Are you ready to take me, Ripper?" Zed asks.

Ripper grunts in agreement and jerks into me as Zed enters him from behind. Fuck, we're all interconnected. Me and the Basilisks.

My instincts kick in as my body takes over. Instead of being worried about getting torn in two, I've proved to myself that I can take two cocks at once and relax. I close my eyes to fully embrace the moment and feel every toe-curling sensation as the pleasure builds deep inside me.

"Fuck, Ash," Ripper says, "you have the tightest little ass."

"She's so wet for us," Venom says. "Her pussy is fucking drowning me."

Their two cocks moving in tandem suspend me in a

state of pleasure. I gasp and push back, taking more of Ripper's cock. I want to take him all.

Venom's eyes meet mine, and he bites my bottom lip, making me moan. I'm trembling as a pleasure unlike any I've ever experienced takes over my body. I cry out, getting rocked to the point of no return, until…

"Holy fucking shit! Yes! Fuck! Yes! Don't stop!"

My vision blurs as an orgasm consumes me, but being filled in both holes leaves nowhere for it to go. I cling to their cocks, coming over them as my pussy and ass squeeze tightly, making time stop.

"Do you want me to fill you, Ash?" Venom asks.

"Yes," I demand. "Come in me, Venom."

He grunts and fills me while Zed's thrusts into Ripper quicken. Zed groans as Ripper plunges deeper and grips my ass hard until he releases with a raw moan.

Zed doesn't stop, though. I look over my shoulder to watch him grab Ripper's hair, and I feel Zed pounding into him. Ripper's eyes flutter closed, succumbing to the sensation as his cock twitches inside my ass that's latched onto him and doesn't want to let go.

With a gasp, Zed comes undone with one more thrust.

"That was…" My chest heaves for air. "Fucking amazing."

While we collapse in a sweaty mess, Zed hurries to collect warm towels and returns to hand them to each of us to clean up with.

"We don't have a lot of water in the tank," Zed says. "Ash can shower first."

After showering—even in a luxury tour bus like this, it's not the biggest—and washing lube and slime away, I pull on a cozy Basilisks hoodie that Zed left out.

When I return to the main room, the guys are in their underwear with no masks, watching a cartoon on TV.

"There she is," Ripper says. "Nice hoodie. It suits you."

I grin until my phone rings in my purse.

"It's fine," I dismiss. "I'll ignore it."

The vibrations continue.

"Maybe you should see who it is?" Venom suggests.

I check to see it's Cookie. There's also a flood of texts lighting up my screen that I didn't hear when we were… busy.

Cookie: Emergency. You need to come back to the hotel.

Cookie: Where are you? Pick up when you get this.

Cookie: Ash?

"Is everything okay?" Venom asks as I frown at them.

I'm about to call her when the phone goes off again and I pick up, "Cookie, what's wrong? I've seen all your messages. Are you okay?"

"I'm fine," she replies, but her tone is frantic. This isn't like her. Something is wrong. She would never interrupt a date she knew I was excited about unless she had to. "Look, I can't tell you over the phone…" There's a commotion in the background. "I know you're with the guys, but could you come back to the hotel? There's a… situation… to deal with, and we need you."

"We?"

"You'll see when you get here," she says.

"I'm on my way," I promise. "I'll be there as soon as I can."

"What's going on?" Zed asks, reading my worried expression.

"I'm not sure, but I have to go," I say. "Something's going on at the hotel, and Cookie needs me. She wouldn't call unless it was an emergency."

"But she's okay, right?" Venom asks, full of concern.

"I think so..." I answer. "She didn't want to say over the phone, but it's not like her... I'm sorry... I..."

"Go," Zed insists. "We'll get a driver to pick you up, and Venom will walk you to the car."

I nod, feeling like Cinderella having to flee after the ball with cum dripping down my thighs.

thirty-six

. . .

Ash

I clear the hotel steps, almost stumbling over my untied laces and narrowly avoiding knocking over a staff member carrying a stack of papers.

By the time I reach my room, my lungs are about to burst. I throw open the door to find Cookie sitting on the sofa with her arm draped around a crying girl's shoulders.

"Leila?"

The last I heard she was touring Europe with Conor and having the summer of a lifetime. Leila is usually chilled out and relaxed, but right now she's too distressed to speak, gulping for air.

"Thanks for coming back, Ash," Cookie says.

"I came as quickly as I could," I say, hurrying over to sit on Leila's other side.

Leila's brown curly hair doesn't look like it's been washed in a few days, and she's crying so hard that mascara is streaked down her face.

"I'm sorry," Leila manages to say between breaths, "I didn't know where else to go. I knew you were staying here, and..."

She starts sobbing hysterically again.

"Hey," I say, patting her knee awkwardly. That's comforting, right? "It's okay. You're always welcome here."

Leila collapses in on herself, putting her head in her hands, and resting it on her knees. Her gray jumper with holes in it looks five sizes too big and seems to consume her.

"Where's Conor?" I ask.

Mentioning his name only makes her wail more.

I shoot a glance at Cookie and mime, "What happened?"

"She hasn't said yet," Cookie says, "she wanted to wait until you came back to explain." She rubs Leila's back. "It's okay, Lei. Everything will be okay. We're here to help."

I look around for tissues but there aren't any.

"I'll be right back." I dash off to the bathroom and grab a bath towel. At the rate of her tear flow, it's the only thing that'll work to catch them all. I hand it to her. "Here you go."

Leila dabs her eyes with it as her bottom lip trembles. "Thanks."

"Take some deep breaths, okay?" Cookie urges.

Leila tries. After a few minutes of deep breathing, she's not hyperventilating anymore. Her eyes are red and bloodshot.

"Are you going to tell us what happened, Lei?" Cookie asks. "You're scaring me."

"It's the twins…" she says.

My mind automatically goes to worst-case scenarios. Has there been an accident? Are they dead?

"What about them?" Cookie asks. Her fingers tighten

around Leila's shoulder, telling me she's having the same thoughts as I am. "Are they okay?"

"They…" Leila's voice falters and she shakes her head, then leans to grab her purse at her feet. She ruffles around in it with shaking hands and pulls out a black-and-white photograph. "See?"

At first, I'm not sure what I'm looking at then… Holy shit.

"You're pregnant?" Cookie asks in disbelief.

"He's so angry," Leila whimpers, hugging herself in the big jumper.

"I'll kill him," Cookie says, jumping to conclusions. "He just found out and left you?"

"It's not that," Leila says, bowing her head. "Well, it kinda is. He needs some space."

I'm surprised Conor would walk out on the girl he's been secretly in love with for years because of a baby. I thought he was a decent guy, but maybe I got him completely wrong.

"He'll be scared," I say, trying to be reassuring. "Whatever he said, I'm sure he didn't mean it."

"You don't understand," Leila says, wringing the towel in her hand, plagued by whatever she's about to tell us. "I did something bad. Really bad."

"What did you do?" Cookie asks. "Leila?"

Leila's voice is barely louder than a whisper so we have to lean close to hear her say, "I slept with Declan."

"Lei!" Cookie jumps back in surprise. "What? When?"

"It happened when we were at Camp Harmony," she says, unable to meet our eyes. "The night Tiffany kissed Conor to make me jealous. Declan was so sweet. He followed me to check that I was okay, and one thing led to another. We were both high, and it just fucking happened.

We both regretted it in the morning, and when Conor found out…"

"Oh, man," I say, starting to put the pieces together. That must have been the cause of the twin's mysterious rift over the summer. It all makes sense.

"Why didn't you tell us before?" Cookie asks.

"I was ashamed," Leila says. "I never thought Conor would give me a second chance after what we did, but he got over it. He knows it was a mistake and we were never together at the time, so we wanted to make a go of it until…"

"How far along are you?" I ask, fearing I already know the answer.

"I started feeling sick when we were away," Leila says, "but I thought it was just the different food and constant travel. I never thought it could be…"

Leila's voice cracks and Cookie pulls her into a hug.

"It's Declan's baby," Leila sobs. "I went to the doctor and the dates line up. I could have lied about it. I mean, they're twins. No one would know, right? But I couldn't keep it from Conor. It's not fair. When I got back from the doctor's office, I had to tell him and, when I did, he said he had to see Declan and left. He hasn't picked up my calls since. That was three days ago."

"Have you spoken to Declan?" I ask.

"If Conor's gone to see him, then I'm sure I'll hear from him soon." She shakes her head in despair. "It's all a mess. This isn't what I expected or wanted to happen, but it's not the baby's fault."

"You're going to keep it?" I ask.

She nods, cradling her stomach protectively. Although the circumstances aren't ideal, there's a bond there already. "I never had a family growing up. I have endometriosis,

and doctors told me before that the chances of having kids were slim. I know the timing isn't great for my career… but I've always wanted a family of my own, and this might be the only chance I'll get."

"We're here for you, okay?" Cookie says. "Whatever you need."

"You can stay here as long as you need to," I say—as long as I'm still in the competition, anyway.

"Thanks, guys," Leila says with a wry smile that quickly turns to a quivering bottom lip. "I just… I don't know what to do… my parents are going to be so angry, and Conor… well… I love him. I fucking love him."

"He's a good guy," Cookie reassures her. "He just needs time. You can try reaching out in a few days—"

"He and Declan were hardly speaking when we left for Europe," Leila says. "He couldn't stand to be around his brother, knowing what we did together—even though it meant nothing. How is he going to cope with me having a baby that's going to remind him of the mistake we made every day?"

"You did nothing wrong," I say. "Everyone makes mistakes. You didn't cheat on him, and you're being honest with him now."

"He loves you, Lei," Cookie says. "He always has."

She snivels and shrugs. "Maybe love won't be enough…"

"You've been traveling all day," Cookie says. "Why don't we run you a warm bath, huh?"

"You can sleep in my bed," I offer. "I'll share with Cookie."

"You don't have to do that." Her eyes fill with tears again, but she waves them away this time. "Sorry, I'm so emotional…"

"You've got nothing to apologize for," I insist. "What you need to do is rest, okay?"

"Everything will feel better in the morning," Cookie says convincingly enough that even I believe her.

"Thanks," Leila says.

I take her arm and lead her through to my room. "I'll show you where to go."

Seeing her so fragile breaks my heart. It also makes me furious at Conor for leaving her in this state. He's hurting —but, hello! Can't he see how much pain she's in? No one planned for this to happen.

"Thank you, Ash," Leila says gratefully, throwing her arms around my neck and hugging me tightly. "You're a good friend."

Now I don't only need to stay in Popstarz to be in the same place as the Basilisks, but I need to stay until Leila manages to get some kind of support.

When I return to the living room, content that Leila is sitting in a lovely tub of bubbles, I flop down on the sofa next to Cookie, who is studying the sonogram.

"Crazy, right?" Cookie says. "Our friends are making little people."

"Crazy is one word for it…"

"It makes sense now why they were so mad at each other at camp," Cookie says, "but I want to call Conor and shake him."

"You can't," I tell her firmly. "It's not our place. All we can do is be here for Leila."

She nods, knowing I'm right. "On another note," she says, changing the subject, "the Basilisks aren't as scary in person. They get my approval, for now."

thirty-seven

. . .

Ash

It's great to have Leila and Cookie as roommates, despite Cookie spending hours forcing me to rehearse the song for tomorrow night's show. They've been taking turns doing funny impersonations of the judges, which are scarily accurate.

"Not one more," I say as Cookie claps her hands for me to continue.

"Fine." She jumps up from her seat. "It's time to show you your outfit for the dinner tonight."

"I don't want to go to another dinner," I grumble, casting a glance at the stack of menus nearby. "Can't I stay here and order take-out?"

Cookie rolls her eyes and thrusts an outfit into my hands. A black tight-fitting corset top with a purple tartan skirt that screams Avril Lavigne's grunge vibes.

Leila claps her hands and says, "Now it's time for hair and makeup."

I turned down the hair and makeup department's offer to help me get ready. Cookie and Leila would have more fun, and it'll keep Leila's mind busy. The two of them set

to work like flapping birds, talking about color palettes and blending.

Thirty minutes pass and they still won't let me look in the mirror.

"We're almost done," Leila insists.

"Are you feeling ready for tonight?" Cookie asks.

"Ready as I'll ever be," I mutter with zero enthusiasm.

Cookie holds a mirror up to show me my reflection. They've done an amazing job. Cookie smashed a sparkly purple eye—it's more colorful than my usual style, but it matches my skirt. I turn my head to admire Leila's professional French braiding skills. She's styled my black hair in a braid that goes around the side of my face and tucks behind my ear.

"Well?" Cookie prompts. "What do you think?"

"You've done a great job," I admit reluctantly.

Leila smiles. She still has black circles under her eyes, but her hair is shinier after a wash, and she hasn't cried since getting up today.

"Where are we going to eat tonight, Lei?" Cookie asks. "We need to pick a movie, too."

"Sounds like bliss," I mutter. "Wanna trade places?"

"Hell no," Leila replies. "Jacqueline Tate is the last person I'd want to see right now."

My jaw clenches. Whenever I hear Jacqueline's name, I can't help thinking about what she did to Ripper. How she coerced him and took advantage of her position.

"It'll be over before you know it," Cookie says, misinterpreting my anger and putting her hand on my shoulder, "and we'll be right here waiting for you."

"Thanks," I say, then take a deep breath.

It's now or never.

They've laid the dining room in the usual style: long tables, place cards, and overly formal seating arrangements for a casual occasion. Although this time, it looks like they have changed the seating plan.

"Now we're a smaller group," Jacqueline declares as I approach the table. She sniffs, unable to mask her disappointment at my outfit. "It's nice of you to join us, Ashley."

Meredith catches my eye and smiles apologetically. We haven't spoken recently because she's spent every hour of the day practicing, and it's paying off. I don't analyze and replay every Popstarz show like Cookie, but Meredith has been improving each week.

"I'm sorry I'm late," I lie. Although, it's only two minutes past eight. I always seem to be the last to arrive and the first to leave.

My name card is placed at the end of the table with Ripper on my side and Spark and Priya opposite. A cheeky grin plays over Ripper's lips.

"Nice of you to finally make it," Ripper mutters as I sit down. Sarcastic fucker.

He looks incredible in a pressed white shirt with a few buttons undone. He rolls up his sleeves slowly, showing off his muscular forearms. His cologne eclipses my senses, reminding me of how his naked body felt against mine last night. Give yourself a mental cold shower, Ash. I press my knees together firmly, and a blush creeps up my neck as our starters are brought out.

Piano music playing in the background gives the illusion of a relaxed atmosphere, but there's underlying tension. Everyone is making meaningless small talk and

assessing their competition, watching and waiting for them to make a mistake.

After eating the first course, people begin to relax. While Spark and Priya discuss the evolution of rap music, Ripper turns to ask, "How are rehearsals going, Ash?"

"Okay," I reply, keeping our chat light as Ripper's hand creeps onto my knee under the table. My voice elevates a pitch as I continue, "I'm trying to put the hours in."

I glare at him, but his expression stays impassive, bored even. Anyone watching would have no idea that his fingers were gliding over my thigh and delicately tickling my skin.

"There is one question I've been meaning to ask you," he says. His eyes burn into mine as his hand slides under the hem of my skirt. "What would you do with the money if you won Popstarz?"

My cheeks heat as my eyes dart around nervously. The long tablecloth hides what's going on in my lap, and the servers are busy clearing up.

"I..." I swallow hard as his fingers knead my soft flesh. I bite my lip, pretending to be deep in thought when all I want to do is moan as he slips higher. I have to pull myself together. "I... I'd like to start producing my own songs."

"Really?" Ripper pushes. "What kind of songs?"

My vision blurs as his wrist parts my legs, and his fingers stroke along the length of my panty line. The mischievous twinkle in his eyes tells me he's loving every second of toying with me.

"I've been writing songs for as long as I can remember," I babble, trying to keep my composure, "I'd love to, maybe, make an album..."

"An album," he repeats, sliding his fingers under the elastic and into my panties. The tip of his finger massages

my wet pussy, applying gentle pressure. "Tell me more about that."

Everyone else is oblivious to what Ripper is doing under the table. Two of his hot fingers find my clit and stroke it in circular motions.

"I'm not sure exactly what I want to do," I reply breathily, struggling to contain myself and biting down on my lip for a few seconds before continuing, "I have some ideas… some names… I need the songs to reflect…"

"Uh-huh." Ripper nods along as he quickens his strokes, making my toes curl. He can feel how wet I am. How much I want him. "Sounds interesting."

"I have to use the bathroom," I blurt out. "If you'll excuse me…"

Ripper withdraws for me to stand on wobbling legs. I smooth my skirt down and take a deep breath as my panties slide back over my wetness.

As I leave the room, trying my hardest to stay steady, I stop and pretend to read a sign. Zed doesn't want us to take risks, but after he fucked me, maybe Ripper has decided that all rules are off?

I have to splash my face with cold water if I'm going to endure the rest of the dinner party—that, or pleasure myself in a stall to dull the desire clawing at my insides.

I head to the nearest bathroom. This isn't like a public restroom. It's private with a marble sink and glowing lights around a mirror, plus handsoap and lotion that cost a fortune.

I grip the sink, staring at my reflection, relieved that I'm wearing enough foundation to even out my complexion.

Breathe in, Ash.

I jump at the knock on the door.

"I'll be out in a minute," I call.

"Ashley," Ripper growls back.

Holy shit. I push the door open ajar to check whether I'm not imagining it.

My eyes widen. "What are you—"

He wedges his foot in the doorway before I can finish my sentence and pushes his way into the room, clicking the door shut behind him.

"I thought we said no risks," I hiss.

"What can I say?" Ripper lowers his voice. He looks down at me like a ravenous wolf as he runs his finger over my bare shoulder. "I like a little risk."

A moment later, he grabs my hair, and our lips collide. Why does something wrong feel so fucking good? I don't want to stop.

He hitches up my skirt, squeezes my ass hard, and hoists me into the air. I wrap my legs around his torso to pull him close, feeling his rock-hard abs and the hot bulge in his pants.

He catches my bottom lip in his teeth, then growls. He kisses me urgently. A kiss that takes my breath away. I moan into his mouth as my ass hits the cold marble, sending goosebumps racing over my thighs.

"Ripper," I whimper. "We shouldn't be doing this."

He ignores me, forcing my legs open and pulling off my panties. He stashes them in his pocket and bows down in front of me.

"They'll be wondering where we are," I say, but that doesn't deter him… and I don't want it to.

"We'll have to be quick then," he says, grasping my hips and pushing my pussy into his face. "Mmm, this is all I've been thinking of eating."

I shiver as his tongue licks along my slit. I bite my lip,

willing myself not to make another sound as his tongue explores me.

"I want you so fucking bad," Ripper growls, pulling away and licking my juices off his lips. He stands and yanks me off the counter. He spins me around and pushes up my skirt to reveal my ass. "You drive me fucking crazy, Ash. Sitting next to you is torture when I can't touch you."

He unbuckles his belt, and the fabric falls to the floor. The tip of his cock rubs against me. I buck backward, and he slides into me easily. My pussy is wet and ready, even though my lips are swollen from yesterday's fuck fest. With the Basilisks, whatever pleasure they give me is never enough. They always leave me craving more.

He inches into me. I gasp, reaching to turn on the faucet in the hope the running water disguises the sound of him railing me from behind.

He takes the hint. His thrusts are brutal, hard, and fast. My ass aches from the force of his balls slapping against me with each jut of his hips, but it feels so fucking good.

"Fuck, Ripper," I gasp, gripping the counter to stop myself from passing out or falling. Explaining that I collapsed from getting pounded by a rockstar is not something I'd ever want to say to a medic.

"Come for me, Ash," Ripper commands.

His words spark a chain reaction. The frenzied friction of his cock makes my pussy jolt. An orgasm comes effortlessly like my pussy knows we have limited time. I have to come or else…

"Look in the mirror," he urges. "Look how hot you are when you come."

I see flushed cheeks, out-of-place hair, and his smirk because he knows he can get me off in minutes.

He pulls out as soon as I'm done.

"On your knees, Ash," he orders. "I'm going to give you some cream ahead of your dessert."

I sink to the floor, coming face to face with his throbbing member. My hands close around his girth. I run my tongue over the tip of his cock to lick up the white bead of pre-cum spilling out. I use both hands, working him fast and jerking him into my mouth.

He holds me there, pushing my head and making me taste myself. His cock edges deeper down my throat. My eyes water as I gag, then he explodes.

I swallow him. Every single drop. Salty, not unpleasant… but him. We can't have been longer than five minutes, right?

He pulls his pants up and winks. "I'll see you back at the table."

With that, he's gone, leaving me wondering whether I've imagined it, but my missing panties tell me otherwise.

If Zed found out, he'd lose his shit. But I can't stop a secret smile from spreading over my face at knowing what we've done. The only problem is, I'm not sure whether I'll be able to look him in the eye over dessert.

thirty-eight

. . .

Ripper | Damon

I stride back to the dinner party, exhilarated from the rush of seeing our girl come undone. My fingers stroke her wet panties nestled in my pocket, and I grin. I made her so fucking wet.

Sure, it was a risk, but the biggest danger was how I couldn't resist. I can't keep my hands off her whenever she's around. She holds my mind, and heart, in her fucking fist.

Although Zed will be pleased to hear I'm not a total moron. I overheard the staff talking about how the CCTV is broken in the bathroom corridor, so there is no evidence.

"Damon!" Tiffany steps from behind a statue of a naked man with a tiny cock. "Have you seen Ashley?"

I shrug and yawn. "No, but I think she had to take a call."

Tiffany's glowing smile makes me uneasy as she replies, "Good."

A grin that wide on a girl like her spells trouble. She falls into step beside me as we return to the dining room. I don't know what game she's playing, but the best way

to handle these situations is to pretend everything is normal.

"Are you excited about the show tomorrow?" I ask, not that I give a shit. If I had my way, the crazy bitch who tried to drown Ash would never have gotten onto Popstarz. Other contestants need to win more than her and deserve to be here.

"I'm feeling great about it," she gushes, "and even better to know we'll be seeing more of each other after the show finishes."

I say nothing, knowing she'll keep filling the silence.

"You know," she whispers like she's airing a big secret, "because of me and Zach."

"Uh-huh," I reply, not paying any attention to her bullshit.

The Lockhart and Royal families have been close since Zach and Tiffany were kids. Their moms have tried to set the pair up for years, but it never works. Tiffany is clinging to the past and buying into delusions.

No one looks up as we return to our seats. Getting accosted by Tiffany only helps to cover my absence. The next course hasn't arrived yet, but Zed's head turns, and his judgmental stare scorches me from across the room. Fuck. My fleeting break with Ash has not gone unnoticed, but facing his wrath will be worth it.

I fall into conversation with the contestant's opposite, but the hairs on my neck stand on end as another gaze lingers on me. She's watching. I've tried my best to avoid Jacqueline, but her texts are becoming more regular. She'll make any excuse to get me alone.

Ash returns to the table with rosy cheeks. No one, apart from Zed, suspects that I've just fucked her brains out.

My hands slip into my pocket to feel her panties again,

and my cock twitches at the thought of her wearing nothing under her skirt. Her pussy is my new fucking addiction, and I can't get enough. Being in her presence is intoxicating. I want to be close to her, touch her, make her moan my name…

A shrill tapping snaps me out of my reverie as Jacqueline clinks her glass to make an announcement I'd rather not hear.

Everyone spins to face her as she announces, "I have some news about this week's show. Due to scheduling on the network, two acts will leave tomorrow."

Gasps and whispers of disbelief ripple around the room.

"Two acts?"

"What?"

"It can't be!"

I know Jacqueline. This will have been the plan from the start, but she likes to throw unexpected situations into the mix and watch people scramble. Having two acts leave means there is a greater likelihood of Ash going, and if that happens… what will our next move be?

Ash grips her cutlery tighter. I'd like to reach over, stroke her soft skin, and tell her everything will be okay, but I can't. Before she arrived, others were talking about Ash's performance being inconsistent during rehearsals. Have we been a distraction?

We need our girl to get to the next round to stay near us for a little longer.

After Jacqueline's bombshell, dessert is served, but most contestants have lost their appetite. Ash pushes the cake around her plate, staying silent. Is she having the same worries I am?

After the plates are cleared, the group dissipates. The

Candy Kisses girls head to the bar, others linger to chat, while Ash and Meredith head back to their rooms.

"What the fuck did you do earlier?" Zed hisses, pulling me aside. "Don't think I didn't notice."

"I was careful," I reply, then smirk. "Don't be a hypocrite, Z."

His lip curls in disapproval. I have him, and he knows it. He can't argue with the facts.

He turns his back on me and storms away, plastering on a fake smile to speak to Jacinta, who is waving at him.

I text Ash.

Me: Shame you had to rush off...

Ash: I have to practice if I want to see another week.

Me: You're not going anywhere.

Ash: Let's hope so...

thirty-nine

. . .

Ash

The competition has taken a serious turn, heightening the tense atmosphere backstage. There are always last-minute nerves, but it's different this week. Contestants pace back and forth, singing under their breath. Two acts will be gone by the end of the night, meaning the end of the competition is in sight, and the life-changing prize fund is more real.

The crowd cheers as Meredith leaves the stage. She crushed her performance—even Jacqueline couldn't find fault in it. She deserves to win based on that song alone.

"You've got this, Ash," Cookie reassures.

I've got more riding on this song than before. At first, I wasn't sure whether I wanted to be on Popstarz, but it was an opportunity I couldn't refuse. It seemed the only viable way to potentially make a name for myself and secure a career in the industry. But now I have a real reason to stay: being closer to the Basilisks and giving Leila a place to crash during her time of need.

All of my rehearsals this week have fallen flat. I don't

know whether it's the song choice, the staging, or the fact I'm fucking trying that's making it worse.

"Cookie..." My mouth goes dry, and my words turn to nothing. I won't be on for another hour, but the wait is killing me. "I don't know if I can do this."

A voice behind me says, "Ash Cooper, you can do this."

Wait! It can't be. I must be imagining it. I spin to see Dad standing there.

"Dad?"

Cookie squeals, "Surprise!"

"Cookie called me," he says sheepishly, looking torn between whether to hug me and deciding against it. Instead, he awkwardly pats my shoulder.

"But you've got work," I say. He mentioned last time we spoke that the station was busy. "You didn't need to come."

"Cookie thought you might need to see a friendly face," he says. His face is edged with concern. "The competition's getting tough. I wanted to see that you're okay. Besides, it's not a crime to see my daughter sing on a big stage."

"It might be your last chance," I murmur darkly.

"I've read the papers," he says. "I know it's been tough on you, kiddo."

He's not wrong. When I went to grab a coffee earlier, paparazzi followed me down the street. They yelled my name and asked a string of questions about my mom and alleged high school sweetheart. Their presence is suffocating, and they drain you like hungry leeches.

"You're not a quitter, Ash," Dad says, gearing up for a motivational pep talk I'm not sure I can handle. His eyes mist over. "I'm proud of you. Seeing you out there..."

I swat him on the shoulder. “Dad!”

He sniffs and clears his throat. “Your mom would have loved to see you doing what you do best. Whatever happens during tonight’s show, you’ll be a star in my eyes.”

It’s my turn to blink the tears away.

“Thanks, Dad,” I reply, then I notice his crisp shirt. “Is that a new shirt?”

He blushes, playing with the collar. “Do you like it?”

“It looks great, Sheriff Cooper,” Cookie chirps.

“Since when do you buy new clothes?” I narrow my eyes. The more I look at him, the more small changes I see. His stubble is sculpted intentionally, not roughly shaven whenever he has a brief snapshot of time—even his black hair is shaped around his face. “And you’ve had a haircut.”

“Yeah, well…” Dad shrugs. “It’s about time I started looking after myself.”

After Mom died, taking care of ourselves was our lowest priority. Getting through another day was an achievement.

“You look great,” I say, “but if I knew this would happen when I moved out, I would have left sooner.”

A crew member hurries over and says, “You know that family isn’t allowed in the green room.”

“It’s okay, I’m leaving,” Dad interjects to stop me from telling the guy to fuck off. “I’ll see you out there. Go make me proud.”

The crew frog-marches him out.

I turn to Cookie and say, “You should have told me he was coming.”

“I wanted to surprise you,” she says brightly. “If I told

you, you'd have told him to stay home, and he'd have listened. You need him here."

She knows me better than I know myself. Seeing Dad is exactly the extra motivational boost I needed.

She winks. "Break a leg."

The camera lens follows me as I walk onto the stage, capturing my nerves in thousands of pixels. This is a big week, and I have to bring my A-Game.

I hold the microphone and close my eyes. The somber instrumentals begin. Dancers emerge from the wings and twirl around me through wisps of smoke. The big screen behind me projects a video of flickering candles and casts the faces of the audience in an ethereal glow.

The words come, but I don't feel them deep in my core —not the way I do with my own or the Basilisks lyrics. I keep my gaze ahead and avoid looking at the Basilisks or the judges, but my skin prickles from their stares.

I scan the crowd's faces, searching for Dad, then I land on… Brick?

I blink to check I'm not imagining it and waver on a note. A mistake. Shit. My faltering could cost me the competition. A camera zooms in on Brick's grinning face and a build-up of anger bubbles from the pit of my stomach. The producers will cut it to make him look like a proud boyfriend instead of my ex-best friend who betrayed me.

A renewed energy takes over me as I blast through the chorus, consumed by my fury. I think of Mom. Her cruel passing. Leaving me—us—behind. Brick selling me out. My soft tone transitions into a low growl from my throat

as I throw my head back and hold the note, throwing it into the air.

This is what I've been trying to find all week. The emotion and wild abandon that comes from not holding back. Jed would kill me for replacing my soft, controlled voice with a rasp that borders on a scream. I'm not thinking too hard. I let my instincts take over. If I'm going to leave the competition, I have to end on a high.

The music fades, and I buzz with adrenaline. I take a shaky bow, and the stage turns black.

"Did you see him?" I ask Cookie. "Brick is here."

"I told him not to." Cookie sighs and shakes her head. "Your dad told me he wanted to make amends."

"Well, I'm not ready to make amends," I say, crossing my arms in a huff. It's bad enough that we have to attend an after-show as per contract obligations—let alone have to speak to him too. "Will he be there later?"

She bites her lip.

"He will, won't he?" I sigh. "He can get a photo for the cameras and fuck off back to Meadow Springs."

"Don't you think you need to talk?" Cookie shifts uncomfortably on her feet. "He's been your best friend for, like, ever. I'm not condoning what he did, but—"

"There's no excuse," I snap. Case closed. "He broke my trust. I might get over it one day, but it's too raw right now. Everyone knows the worst thing that ever happened to me. When they look at me, it's all they see, and that's his fault."

"Why have all the guys we know suddenly turned into assholes?" she grumbles, checking her phone to see if

Leila has been in touch. "Brick, then Conor… there must be some weird shit going on with the moon or something."

"Still no news from Conor or Declan?" I ask.

Cookie shakes her head. "I've tried calling them, and so has Lei, but it goes straight to voicemail. It's like they've gone off the grid."

"Fucking assholes."

"Well, maybe not all guys," she corrects, lowering her voice. "Do the Basilisks watch the show?"

I shrug. Keeping their identities a secret from Cookie is hard when I'm surrounded by the guys all the time. But at least I expect them to be there, unlike this evening's unwelcome guest.

She nudges her head toward the green room door. "Incoming."

The crew escorts Dad and Brick in. Why has Dad forgiven Brick so quickly after his betrayal? It's not just my life he splashed over the papers. It's our family's pain.

I stomp over to them, trying to take deep breaths. We're surrounded by the crew and other contestants who could sell another story about trouble in paradise if I don't keep my cool.

"Ashley, they said they were with you," the crew member says.

"Please, Ash," Brick pleads. He shoots me his puppy-dog stare, but I'm not falling for his shit. "Give me two minutes."

His hair is messed up, and dark rings lurk under his eyes. Good. He deserves to feel guilty for what he's done.

"I've already said all that I need to," I reply coldly.

His face falls.

"Five minutes is all he wants, Ash," Dad says.

“He said two,” I point out. “Since when are you on his side, anyway?”

“I’m on your side,” Dad says diplomatically. Good choice. “But he came all this way to talk. Just hear him out, okay?”

“Fine,” I grumble. I nod to the security guard standing nearby and say, “Come back in two minutes to escort Brick out. He can’t stay.”

“We’ll leave you to it,” Cookie says, taking Dad’s arm and leading him over to a sofa to sit with the other contestants who are waiting for the votes to be counted.

“You wanted to talk, so talk,” I demand, planting my hands on my hips. “You don’t have long, so make it count.”

“I feel awful, Ash,” Brick croaks, close to tears. “I shouldn’t have agreed to take the money. It was wrong. I thought I was doing the right thing, but I never wanted it to come between us.”

He ruffles around in his pocket. He retrieves a check and holds it out for me to take. “I know money doesn’t fix everything, but I don’t want to profit from what I did. You should have the money.”

I shoot him a withering look, keeping my hands firmly at my sides.

“Your dad needs the money,” I say. The business is Brick’s future inheritance and has been a pillar in our community for years. As much as I hated him using me for financial gain, some good has to come from his mistake. “Put it into the business.”

“I’ll figure out another way to save it,” he says. “I’ll work all day and night if I have to. It won’t be easy, but I think I can do it. I can’t profit from what happened to you

and your family. It's not right. It's against everything my father and I wanted."

"Don't be stupid," I say. "Keep the money. The damage has already been done."

"No," Brick insists. "I won't."

I scowl. We're caught in a standoff that neither of us wants to break.

"You're being an idiot," I say.

"Maybe," he says. "But I know what's right, Ash."

He rips up the check and lets the paper fall to the floor.

"What the fuck did you just do?"

The security guard approaches and casts an ominous shadow over us. It's time for Brick to leave.

"I made a mistake," Brick says in a last desperate attempt to get through to me. "And I'm sorry. So fucking sorry. I don't expect you to forgive me straight away, but I need you to know that I care. You can depend on me, Ash. I'll always be there for you, whatever you need."

My heart rate quickens. He's genuine. I've always found it hard to stay mad at Brick for long, but I'm not ready to forgive him yet. His betrayal cut too deep, even if sheer carelessness caused it.

"I need time."

He nods in understanding. "I'm not going anywhere."

Security takes his arm and steers him away.

"Brick," I call after him before I can stop myself. He spins to face me as I say, "Good luck."

He'll need it if he's going to save his family business. He's choosing what's right over an easy future.

He smiles sadly. "Thanks, Smash."

A gaping hole is left in our friendship as he leaves.

Dad joins me. "Thanks for hearing him out."

If he thinks he's being let off for bringing Brick with him, he's wrong. Now it's his turn to face my wrath.

"You should have told me he was here," I say. "It spooked me when I was on stage."

"I didn't want you to get mad before the show," he mumbles, having the decency to look guilty.

I raise my eyebrows. "And you thought him showing up to surprise me would make me any less mad?"

"Brick messed up," Dad says, then adds hastily at my thunderous expression, "I'm not trying to justify his actions, but I've seen him around. He's not been the same since. He's beating himself up over it, and he's your best friend. After everything you've been through, don't you think he deserves a second chance?"

My nostrils flare as Cookie pops up between us.

"Why don't we all take a seat while we wait, huh?" she suggests smoothly. "It won't be long until Tessa announces the results."

"Fine," I grumble.

I have bigger problems to face than Brick. I have a real chance of leaving this week. Cookie shoves my backpack into my hands and purses her lips to tell me to be nice.

"You can work on new songs," she suggests.

I roll my eyes. "Yeah, like that'll distract me…"

I take Venom's lyric book out of my bag and leaf through it while Cookie chats with Dad about his cold cases. The pages are thick, and I turn them carefully. Scrawls and doodles surround sentences, even in the margins, while snatches of his thoughts and words bleed between the lines. He's a talented writer.

I trace my fingers over his words and read:

Split your heart open,

Invite the darkness in,
Let it make you whole again.

My unfinished song. He's used a red pen to cross out a few words and meld them with a song of his own:

Split your heart open,
Invite the darkness in,
Let it feed your soul,
Blacken your heart,
Fill your bones,
Ignite the fire.

Children of the night,
I call to you,
Rise from the embers.
Split her heart open,
Because I'm a vampire for her.

Reading his addition is like seeing a jigsaw puzzle slot together. He continued my song. Our song.

"What're you working on?" Cookie peers over my shoulder and frowns. "I don't know how you can read that."

Dad cranes his neck to take a peek. "That's not your handwriting."

"Alright, Dad, I didn't ask for a handwriting analysis. It's a group project," I say, shooting Cookie a warning glare.

Dad grins. "It's nice to hear you're making friends here."

"Oh yeah," Cookie replies with a devious glint in her eye. "Ash has made some really good friends."

forty

. . .

Zed | Zach

My hands clench under the table as Tessa reads their names one after the other. Four acts remain, and Ash is one of them. The show is building tension, but it's killing me. The others are just as anxious. They're trying not to show it, but I sense it from the way Ripper's knee is jumping, and Venom's back is so straight it looks like he's frozen to the spot. We're all thinking the same thing. Will she make it through?

Ash's performance was incredible. In my eyes, she stole the show, but she was different from the others. The judges commented on how she sang better than expected, but it took until the chorus for her to make an impact. Jacqueline also crucified her for dropping a note, which made me want to ram the microphone down her throat as she criticized our girl. I don't know where Ash summoned the power in her performance, but it was like someone lit a fire under her.

She stares at her shoes on the stage, waiting to hear her fate. Our fate. I want to be at her side and protect her from the scrutiny, telling her she doesn't have to do this and that

she can tour with the Basilisks forever. But life isn't that straightforward.

We have to think about what will happen next. We need more time. She has to stay for us to figure out what the hell we mean to each other and to give her a chance to think about whether she wants this.

Another name is called.

"Tiffany."

Shit.

There are three of them left now. Then Tessa says the word we've been waiting to hear.

"Ashley!"

Relief rushes through my body, and my shoulders relax. Our girl is safe for another week. We can't live in the Popstarz bubble forever, though. We must face reality and think about how Ash will fit into our lives because now we've found her, none of us want to let her go.

The rest of the show passes in a blur. Priya and Candy Kisses are the unlucky contestants with the lowest number of votes, not that it matters to me. All I want is for filming to be over for another week.

"Another great show," Jacqueline declares as soon as the cameras stop rolling. Her gaze lingers on Ripper like a hungry vampire wanting to drain him. He jumps up quickly, so fast that his leg hits the table and spills a glass of water. Jacqueline's lip curls in disappointment. "The cars are waiting to take us to the after-show party. Zachary, you'll be pleased to hear there will be a special guest waiting to see you."

My stomach drops, but I force a smile. "I can't wait."

By special guest, she means my mother.

"Do we have to go to every party?" Venom groans.

He puts his head in his hands as the limo drives us to the party.

"Yes," I reply, against all of my other instincts screaming to ask the driver to take us to Buggy instead. "We have to."

"We need to congratulate the contestants," Ripper says. Well, one particular contestant who will make attending bearable.

"Fine," Venom murmurs reluctantly.

The car parks at the end of the red carpet leading into the venue. Flashing cameras blind us as we stop to pose for a few minutes before heading inside. We've given them what they wanted. Starnote can't complain.

Her distinct sickly-sweet vanilla perfume makes my nose wrinkle before I see her. She's like a shark circling her prey.

"Darling!" My mother's shrill voice makes me wince. "It's wonderful to see you."

I greet her with air kisses on both cheeks, the way she's taught me to. "It's great to see you, Mom."

Yeah, as great as walking into your home to find someone robbing it.

"Damon, Levi!" She throws her arms in the air. "It's so good to see the two of you. How long has it been? Too long."

They both nod at her. She's never liked my bandmates. When I told her I was part of a band at Camp Harmony, she went ballistic. She wants me to be a soloist. She could never, and still isn't, able to grasp that there are benefits to sharing the spotlight. Even after all of our success, she still hopes for the band to break up and for me to become a bigger artist on my own.

"You haven't aged a day, Vanessa. You'll have to tell me the name of your surgeon," Ripper says. Mom's eyes narrow as he smirks. He hates my mom almost as much as she hates him. "We're going to the bar. Can we get you both a drink?"

"No, thank you," Mom replies in an icy tone that'd make hell freeze over. "We're fine—aren't we, Zachary? It's the perfect time for me to steal your frontman for a conversation. Don't worry, I won't keep him long. I know how much you depend on him."

I cringe at her words. She can't resist reminding them about how she sees them as second-rate citizens. She puts great importance on family connections. Ripper and Venom come from "normal" families, and she sees us as part of the monarchy.

"Be our guest," Ripper replies. "We'll catch up with you later."

Venom stays quiet. He doesn't like my mom, but he never gives her a reaction. Something that may annoy her even more than Ripper's jibes.

The two of them hurry away.

"Let's find somewhere quiet to talk," she suggests, gesturing at a nearby booth.

"You should have told me you were coming," I say.

"You should be pleased to see me. Anyone would think you've been avoiding me," she says. Yeah, because I have. "I had a break in my filming schedule, and I wanted to talk to you."

Mother isn't dropping by to have a friendly catch-up. She's not like other moms who give a shit about their kids. Vanessa Royal always has an agenda. She's here because she wants something.

"I'm all ears," I say wryly, bracing myself.

It could be a role in a film, an interview, or something to do with my siblings. Anything that'll guarantee to raise our family's profile.

"I met with Rita Lockhart this week," she begins, getting straight to the point now that we're over the fake niceties. "As you know, relationships have been fraught with the Lockharts since… the unfortunate incident." Yeah, that's one way to say that our au pair caused the breakdown of Rita's marriage because her husband couldn't keep his dick in his pants. "But Rita is a valuable friend for us to have."

By valuable, she means someone who will make eye-watering donations at Mom's upcoming charity ball and has connections to secure her the best starring roles.

"So?" I prompt.

"As you know, Tiffany is doing amazingly well in Popstarz. But the public isn't warming to her," Mom says. "We thought you could help give her a publicity boost that'll support her through the rest of the show."

It'd be easier to address Tiffany's image problem by teaching her to stop acting like an entitled brat. I bite my back teeth to stop myself from saying something I'll regret.

"What do you have in mind?" I finally ask.

Mom searches through her purse and slides a jewelry box into my lap under the table.

"Open it," she encourages.

The large diamond ring nestled inside the box makes me shut the lid fast.

"If you and Tiffany got engaged, it would help the public like her," she says. "Everyone loves you."

As if planned and right on cue, Tiffany strolls past our table.

"Oh, Tiffany!" Mom waves Tiffany over. "Come and

take a seat."

Tiffany slides into the booth next to my mother. From the way her eyes light up like a greedy child let loose in a candy store, she's already privy to our parent's plotting.

"It's fabulous to see you," Mom croons. "You're one of the family now—don't you think, Zachary?"

Their expectant eyes burn into me. But I'm not going to play along and be another pawn in Mom's games.

"I'm not doing it," I say, shattering their hopes. "It's a no."

"You need to consider your options," Mom speaks to me like a toddler throwing a tantrum. "Ignore him, Tiff. He's just having a moment."

"I am not having a moment," I sneer, clenching my fists. "I'm not doing it. That's my final answer."

Mom waves my dismissal away. "You're not seeing the bigger picture."

She's imagining the opportunities crumbling away and the effects it'll have on her reputation. She doesn't give a shit that she's treating me like a piece of meat to be traded.

"Ask Elliot," I say.

My brother will do anything to stop himself from getting cut off.

"You know Elliot has his issues to deal with," Mom snaps. Her fake smile wavers. "Besides, everyone has already seen you together. You've known each other since childhood. It makes sense."

Tiffany beams. She'll already be planning wedding dresses, and how she'll break the news to her superficial friends. She's a mini version of my mom, and it sickens me.

"I said no!" I slam my balled fist on the table, making them jump. "What part of no don't you understand?"

Their faces fall in tandem and Tiffany whimpers.

"I promise you won't regret it, Zach," Tiffany says. She's on the verge of tears. "It'll be good for our families. We're a good match. As your mom said, we're meant to be."

"We were never meant to be," I spit. My stomach churns at the thought of marrying her. "Your silly crush means nothing. Our families are friends. Nothing more."

Tiffany gasps, stunned by my bluntness. Usually, I speak with politeness, but the time for that is over.

"Zachary," Mom hisses. Her eyes dart around the room, terrified someone will have overheard my outburst. "Remember where you are."

I laugh coldly. "And remember who I am, Mother. I've played along in many of your plans and schemes, but I won't be part of this one."

I stand, desperate to get away.

Mom grabs my wrist and pleads, "At least say you'll think about it. It'll be good for all of us."

Her pathetic desperation makes my lip curl in disgust as I yank my arm out of her grasp. Even as her acting family show pony, marrying me off is a step too far.

"I am thinking of the family," I say. My nostrils flare as I slam the ring box on the table. "But I'm also thinking of me, and what I want. Something you'll never understand."

"Zach, wait," Tiffany calls after me hysterically.

I ignore her. My vision clouds from my fury. Venom and Ripper are standing close by, watching the situation play out.

"Is everything okay, Z?" Ripper asks, falling into step by my side. "What happened?"

"This party is officially over," I say through gritted teeth.

forty-one

. . .

Venom | Levi

I've never seen Zed like this. He gets angry, but now he's blinded by fury. His mother knows how to get under his skin like poison.

Ripper holds the door open to a waiting car.

"She wants me to marry Tiffany," Zed growls. "I'm not doing it."

"Of course you're not," Ripper says soothingly, rubbing Zed's arm.

Zed pushes Ripper out of the way and gets into the car. The burning inferno behind his eyes tells me he's beyond listening to reason. I've seen the same look of wild abandon in Elliot too. Vanessa Royal is a monster. It's a wonder she hasn't fucked up her kids more.

Zed is shaking with rage. "This is a step too far, even for her."

"Why don't we go somewhere you can calm down, huh?" Ripper suggests, then directs the driver, "Swing by the hotel, and then we'll be going elsewhere."

"Why the hotel?" I ask in confusion.

"We'll drop you off on the way," Ripper says.

I nod in understanding. Although we all share feelings for Ash, and I love the two of them like brothers, they love each other too. If there's anyone who can pull Zed back from the brink, it's Ripper.

"I…" Zed's voice trails away as Ripper shoves a glass of bourbon into his hand.

"Drink," Ripper orders. "It'll help."

Zed downs it and nods for a refill.

None of us speak on the drive back to the hotel. The only plus side of the bad situation is that I got to leave the party early…

"I'll see you both later," I say, then turn to Ripper, "Look after him, okay?"

He nods solemnly.

I get out and watch the car disappear down the street. My phone vibrates in my pocket. A text from Ash.

Ash: Can you talk? I can meet you in your room. I have a key card.

Looks like we aren't the only ones who left the party early. I don't know who gave her a key card, but I'm not complaining. It'll make her sneaking in more subtle. What was her reason for leaving? I don't hesitate and text back.

Me: See you soon.

I return to our room with an extra spring in my step. It's rare I have time without the others around, and I can't wait to see her again.

The penthouse door sticks as I try to open it. Weird. Something, a package perhaps, is caught between the frame and the floor. I force the door with my shoulder and

stumble in, almost tripping over the brown package on the other side.

Someone has placed it purposefully. It's too big to slide under the door. No one can enter the room but us, Ash, and the hotel staff. But it wouldn't be the first time a fan has broken into our hotel room or paid off staff.

We've had crazy-obsessed stalkers in the past, so I know better than to open something that doesn't have a label. But it doesn't stop me from turning it over in my hands to feel the outline of what's inside.

I know what it is.

I tear open the package, sending paper flying, then pull out the object inside. A mask.

It's white and smooth with small eye holes and no expression. A note flutters to my feet, and my hands shake as I pick it up.

The typed note consists of two words.

I know.

Someone else knows our secret. My throat closes up. Who wrote this note? What do they want?

I should call the others. Zed would want to know straight away. But, after seeing the state he was in, it'd only tip him over the edge.

There's a knock at the door, then the handle turns. Ash. Shit. I make a snap decision and act fast. I race to my bedroom and stash the mask in a bottom drawer. I won't tell her… not yet.

I close the drawer, sealing away the realization that our perfect double life may not remain intact for much longer. I don't know the facts. This could be someone's idea of a sick joke.

"Venom?" Ash calls. "Ripper? Zed?"

I head through to greet her, and she takes my breath away. She's stunning. Her short gray dress is covered with black lace netting that pulls in at the waist with a shiny black belt that shows off her figure.

"It's only me," I say, trying to mask my expression. "The others are… out." It's not my place to tell her what happened with Zed and his mom. "Is everything okay? Your message sounded urgent."

"I just…" Ash sighs, twirling her hair around her finger. "I wanted to speak to someone who gets it. Has someone you care about ever betrayed you?"

"Why don't you sit down, and we can talk it through," I say, nodding to a sofa that could easily seat ten people.

"Do you remember Brick?"

How could I forget? The guy the papers portray as her boyfriend; the one who looks like a model. Instead, I say calmly, "Yeah, I think so."

"He showed up at the show tonight," she says, words tumbling from her mouth. "He sold a story about me and wanted to apologize. He had his reasons and never meant to hurt me, but how can I ever trust him again after what happened? Sorry, I'm rambling…"

I want to punch the guy for causing her pain, but she wouldn't be upset if he didn't mean a lot to her.

"People sell stories about us all the time," I say. "One time, back in the early days, my mom sold a story about how I got arrested as a teenager."

Her eyes widen. "I don't remember reading about it."

"You didn't because Zed took care of it before it went to print," I say. "It was a shoplifting charge. I got caught stealing food because my mom left me for a few weeks when she disappeared with one of her boyfriends."

"Shit…" Ash's warm hand holds mine. "I'm sorry, Venom."

I clear my throat. "People sell stories all the time, but I was lucky Zed found out first and paid for it to be covered up. He made my mom sign a contract after that to never speak about me again."

"That's… awful."

"That's my mom for you." I shrug. "She never apologized. After the Lionhearts got famous and she realized she couldn't make any money off me, she gave up trying to contact me. I'm useless to her if she can't make a profit, but this isn't about me." I shake my head, pushing the memories away. "What I'm trying to say is that people make mistakes, but the reason behind why they make them is what's important."

Her brow furrows deep in thought, and she mumbles, "Brick never accepted the money. He didn't want to hurt me, but I'm still not ready to forgive him yet."

"Being famous comes at a price," I say. "You have to be careful. When you find people you trust, you need to hang onto them."

"Split your heart open… invite the darkness in," she says, then pauses, "and rise from the embers."

I grin, recognizing it instantly. "You've been reading my lyric book."

"You made my song a masterpiece."

I shake my head, putting my fingers under her chin, and tip it upward.

"No, we made the song a masterpiece," I correct her.

"It's not finished yet."

"We'll have to do something about that," I say.

"Thank you for letting me read your work," she says. "It was nice to see more of what's under your mask."

I freeze, remembering the earlier delivery.

Ash frowns. "Hey, are you sure everything is okay?"

"There's something I have to show you. Wait here."

I have to tell someone what happened.

"What is it?" she asks, squinting to get a better look at what I'm holding when I return.

I put it on the coffee table in front of us.

"I found this when I came back to the penthouse," I explain, then hand over the note. "You know what this means."

The color fades from her cheeks. I never questioned whether she was involved, but her reaction only further proves it. "But Venom, this means…"

"Someone knows who we are," I confirm.

"What did the others think?"

"They don't know," I reply.

"What? You have to tell them. They need to know!"

"You didn't see what Zed was like when we left the party," I say. "This is the last thing he needs to worry about right now."

"You can't keep it from him, Venom," she says sternly. "I know you want to protect him, but this is too big."

As much as I hate to admit it, she's right.

"How could someone have found out?" she ponders. "You've been careful."

"Not careful enough," I reply.

We took risks by playing a second show in the same place and visiting Buggy regularly. We fucked up.

"I haven't told anyone," she says quickly, worried I'll suspect her. "I wouldn't do that."

"I know," I reply, leaning and planting a kiss on her lips to erase her worries.

It's nothing more than a peck, but my cock stirs. Even at a time like this, she ignites a fire in me.

"We have to tell them," Ash insists. Her voice is breathier than a few seconds before. "Where are they now?"

"Where do you think?" I raise one eyebrow. "We'll go together."

"But what if people see us?" she says. "Don't you think the situation is risky enough?"

"If someone already knows that we're the Basilisks, we have bigger problems to worry about than us being spotted together."

I text Ripper.

Me: Something's happened. On my way with Ash.

"Are you sure you're okay, Venom?" Ash asks as we get up to leave.

I nod.

I'll be fine, but it's Zed I'm worried about. In his explosive mood, I can't predict how he's going to react to his biggest fear coming true…

forty-two

. . .

Zed | Zach

Ripper frowns at his cell. He tries to hide it, but I can read him better than anyone.

"What is it?" I question.

Anger pulses through my veins. I want to peel my fucking skin off and shed the Royal name. Screaming with Ripper has helped, but my fury still smolders like flickering embers. Buggy is more of a pressure cooker than a tour bus.

"Venom and Ash are on their way," he says. "Something's happened. I'm sure it's nothing."

I'm not convinced. Venom wouldn't interrupt us unless it was urgent.

Ripper turns up the volume of our music and hands me the microphone. "Keep singing, it'll help."

The song reaches the chorus, and I roar from the back of my throat. I let it rip, screaming until I'm sweating and panting from exertion. I collapse on the sofa, and Ripper thrusts another drink into my hands.

"Feeling better?" he asks.

I shoot him a death glare as the shutters roll up. We have company.

A few seconds later, the door flies open. Ash and Venom appear. From Venom's nervous fidgeting to the panicked look in Ash's eyes, something is wrong. Very wrong.

"What is it?" I spit.

Ash's fingers slip between Venom's, and she squeezes his palm in encouragement. My patience is waning.

I roar, "Just fucking say it!"

Has Mom or Tiffany already leaked news about a fake engagement? My refusal might not have been enough to thwart their plans.

"It's Tiffany, isn't it?" I ask.

"What?" Ash tilts her head to the side. "Tiffany?"

Venom shakes his head to signal he hasn't told her. I'm grateful for that, at least. But if they're not here about that, what else could be so pressing?

"Show them," Ash whispers.

Venom takes off his backpack and pulls an item from it. A white mask.

"What's this for?" Ripper asks, taking it from him and winking. "Are you in the mood for role play?"

Ash or Venom don't laugh. Venom holds out a piece of paper, and I snatch it from his fingers.

"Someone left the mask and this note in our hotel room," he explains.

Ripper reads over my shoulder.

Fuck. This is the moment I've dreaded since starting our double lives. I stay standing, even though my stomach lurches like I'm falling from a cliff and tumbling into the abyss.

The Basilisks ground me in reality. They keep me sane.

Without them, I'm lost in a dark pit. My mind falls into a black hole, flailing and trying to find something to clutch onto, but there's nothing to stop me.

"What did the package look like?" Ripper asks. "Any postmarks?"

Venom shakes his head. "I found it inside our room," he says. "There was nothing on the outside—"

"—which means whoever sent it has access to the building, or they paid someone to get inside," I conclude. "Whoever knows our secret is close to us."

I spin to face Ash. Our secret was safe until she came into our lives. She's the only other person who knows.

"Who did you tell?" I sneer.

She pales, taking a step back. "Wh-wh-what?" she stammers. "I didn't tell anyone."

This is why I enforced the rule about not getting close to outsiders. I knew something like this would happen. Our identities have never been compromised before, and she is the reason for everything falling apart. We are meant to be alone.

"Did you drop any hints? Leave your phone lying around? Brag to your friends?" I mock, advancing toward her. "Come on, Ash. I know it's you. It has to be."

"I swear I didn't say anything," Ash reaffirms. "I've been careful."

"We took no risks before you. Don't you think this is too much of a coincidence?" I can't stop myself. My rage takes over, and I unleash my building frustration like an erupting volcano. "Did you type the note yourself, Ash? You have access to our room. I gave you a key card."

"Do you really believe I could do this?" she whispers.

Her bottom lip trembles, but I can't stop. Words spew from my mouth relentlessly.

"It has to be you, Ash," I blast. "Who else could it be? I knew it was a mistake to get involved with you. I should have listened to my instincts. It's started going wrong for us since we met you."

Everything used to be straightforward: no feelings, no complications, and no consequences to worry about. It was the three of us against the rest of the world until she came along and put a wedge between us.

"Zed, that's enough," Venom intervenes, but I'm not done.

This isn't just about our secret being revealed, it's about taking away my reason for breathing. Ash is to blame.

Accusations catapult from my mouth like fireballs in her direction.

"Was this your plan all along?" I snarl viciously. "You came to Camp Harmony to find fame. Now that you're not doing well on Popstarz, were you trying to make more money? You don't want to go back to your old life, so you got close to us? Were you going to sell our story like your friend did? You saw how much money he could make. Did you think you could do the same?"

Her jaw drops, then her lips curl with anger, and her eyes ignite.

"Do you really believe that, Zed?" she demands, standing straighter to meet my gaze with a ferocity that matches my own. "I told you I'd never tell your secret. Isn't my word enough? Are you so fucked up that you've forgotten how to trust people? I thought we had something special. Or have you been waiting to turn on me all this time?"

"I trust the Basilisks," I spit. "I don't trust you. We hardly know you."

"You don't have to worry about me. I won't be a

problem for you anymore," she says, "and not that it matters, but I will never tell your precious fucking secret."

"Ash." Ripper tries to step in. "He doesn't mean what he's saying."

"I think he does," she hisses. "After everything, you still think I'd betray you. If you're never going to trust me, I don't know what I'm still doing here."

She tries to fight it, but her eyes glisten from the tears she's holding back.

"Don't go, Ash," Venom pleads. He tries to stop her, acting as a human barrier between her and the door. He grabs her arm. "Please, don't go."

She shakes him off like his touch burns and glares at me pointedly.

"I know where I'm not wanted," she says lowering her voice, "I'm not a Basilisk."

My words have hurt her, scorched her soul, and it's not just me she's turning her back on.

"We were kidding ourselves to think this would have ever worked," she says. Her words sting, but they echo what I'm thinking. We were never meant to be. "Zed's right. We are from different worlds. You say you want me in your lives, but you'll never let me in or trust me, not fully."

"Zed's angry right now," Ripper says. "Other things happened tonight that you don't know about."

"None of that matters," Ash says. Her voice is quiet and yet filled with resolve. "We will never work. Tonight has proven that."

"Please, Ash," Venom begs.

He will get over her.

We all will.

This is for the best.

"I'm going to leave now," she says, turning the door handle. The others step forward, but she yells, "Don't follow me."

They both jump back.

"I want to be alone," she says. "I'll leave the three of you alone to be the Basilisks, just like you always wanted."

She stomps out, slamming the door behind her. Buggy descends into silence. The words that Ash and I exchanged ricochet around the quiet bus like bullets. They wound my bandmates like soldiers caught in the crossfire. Ripper slumps into a seat, clutching his chest. Venom doesn't move, rooted to the spot, traumatized.

Ripper looks at me with glistening eyes and whispers, "Zed… what did you do?"

forty-three

. . .

Ash

I run through the streets. The bitter taste of betrayal catches in the back of my throat, and I hail the nearest cab to take me back to the hotel.

The streets stream by in a blur. I bite my lip until it bleeds, unable to stop tears from falling down my cheeks silently. I'm crying, but I'll be damned if the cab driver hears me sob.

How can Zed believe I betrayed them? I thought they understood me better than anyone else, but I'll never be one of them. I've been kidding myself and living in a fairy-tale delusion.

We couldn't live in a bubble forever. Popstarz is almost over, and the weird arrangement we have wouldn't work in the outside world.

They already have two lives to juggle, and there's no place for me. Although Zed's words were vicious, and his accusations were bullshit, there was a shred of truth in some statements.

I've been an obstacle to them. I'll inevitably end up getting hurt. How long would I have had to spend living

in the shadows? Weeks? Months? Years? I can't do that when they can't trust me.

When I return to the hotel, I storm through the lobby, ignoring the concierge's curious gazes at my makeup-streaked face.

In the hotel room, Cookie and Leila are watching a horror film. They squeal in shock when I enter like an awakened zombie and knock a bowl of popcorn over as I stagger inside.

"Ash?" Cookie squints through the darkness. "Are you okay?"

Usually, I'd storm to my room and scream into my pillow, but I don't. One look at Cookie's concerned face tells me she won't leave me alone.

"No," I mumble. "I'm not okay."

She turns off the film and switches the lamp on. I flop down on the sofa next to them, deflated and broken.

"Oh, Ash…" Cookie says. "What happened?"

"It's over," I mutter. "Me and the Basilisks."

Leila pats my back, although she's oblivious to what I'm talking about. Human contact usually makes me uncomfortable, but it's nice to be around people who care.

"I'm so sorry, Ash," Cookie says. "I know how much they meant to you."

"You know what they say…" I laugh wryly. "Never meet your heroes. It's probably for the best, anyway. It'd never have worked out between us."

Leila exchanges a look with Cookie and whispers, "She was with all of them?"

Cookie nods.

"Guys are assholes," Leila says. "One is bad enough, but three… girl, you never stood a chance. They're not worth it if they can't see how special you are."

I sniff. "Thanks, Lei."

"Do you want to talk about what happened?" Cookie asks.

I shake my head. "Can we just sit here and watch the movie?"

"Of course," she says, thrusting a chocolate bar into my lap.

"Who needs guys, anyway?" Leila says, rubbing her belly. "When you've got good friends, you don't need anyone else."

The movie plays, but I don't pay attention. The popcorn turns to cardboard mulch as I chew. If walking away is the best decision for everyone, why do I feel like I've left part of myself behind?

forty-four

. . .

Ripper | Damon

One week has passed since Zed and Ash's confrontation. Seven sleepless nights and strings of unanswered texts. Seven days spent wondering what she was thinking. Seven days of sitting between Zed and Venom who haven't spoken.

Popstarz is almost over. Ash smashed her performances at tonight's show and didn't even look in our direction once. She was so close, and yet she seemed like a stranger.

The sender of the mask hasn't been in touch again, and our secret is still safe. I always thought our identities being exposed would be the worst thing to happen to us, but I was wrong. Ash walking out of our lives was worse.

Venom has barely left his room, locking himself away to play guitar and write lyrics. He didn't appear on tonight's show, either. He refused and feigned illness.

Zed has returned to his business-like self, navigating interviews and filling schedules. His drive for survival overpowers all else. He may not show it, but he's feeling

her loss too—even if he justifies his actions by blaming Ash for someone discovering our secret.

Music plays in the background, and I lean against the bar at the Popstarz after-party. I've drunk too much, and Zed catches me as I stumble.

"I don't need your help," I slur. I'd rather fall on my face and break my nose than accept his help. "Haven't you done enough?"

"We're leaving," he says firmly. "Outside. Now."

I ignore him for the duration of the car ride. My annoyance and anger at him for pushing Ash away is growing.

When we return to the penthouse, I sense something is wrong instantly. Venom sits at the dining table, and his serious expression sobers me like a strong black coffee.

"What is it?" Zed asks sharply.

On the table, Venom has laid out an empty manilla envelope and several photographs. There's an image of me and Ash running down a street. A picture of us kissing. No one else had been around, had they?

My eyes scan the pile of shots. Images of us after the Basilisks show with Ash. Fuck, I'd give anything to see her smile at me again the way she does in those photographs.

"When did this arrive?" I ask, wrenching my eyes away because the memories are too painful. It only highlights how much I miss her.

"I don't know," Venom replies. "I was in my room and came out to find the envelope pushed under the door."

"Ash is in these pictures," Zed says, stating the fucking obvious.

"Which means she couldn't have taken them," I declare, then point at one of them. "See? There's one of us with her not wearing masks. We didn't know we were going to meet that night."

Zed's brain automatically jumps into conspiracy theory mode. "She could have arranged for someone to follow us."

"She wouldn't do that," Venom snaps. "We all know she wouldn't want to be seen dead with a Lionheart."

I scoff. "Exactly."

"Someone's been following us," Venom says. "We have to tell Ash. This affects her too."

"Was there a note?" Zed asks.

Venom nods. It's written in the same font on a piece of card:

I'm watching.

"Ash has to know about this," Venom says. "If they know about us, it puts her at risk. Who knows what they're capable of?"

"We need to keep her safe," I say. "And we need to make it up to her."

"I..." Zed stammers. His face crumples. "It made sense it was her... it..."

"It never made fucking sense," Venom insists.

"How do we tell her? She won't reply to my texts," I say. "She's pretending we don't exist. She broke up with us, remember?"

"We can't lose her over this," Venom says with determination. "Our secret may come out, but I won't let anything happen to her. You need to apologize, Zed. You're the one who accused her of betraying us."

"Maybe she's safer staying away from us," Zed says.

"Are you outta your fucking mind?" I rage. "She's got no one, and we're together. She's one of us, Zed. If they

come for her, they come for all of us. Just admit it. You made a mistake."

Zed winces. "I thought it was the right thing to do."

"We need to get her back," I say with ferocity, "whatever it takes."

I've been walking around with a gaping hole in my chest for a week. We haven't known Ash long, but she was one of us. Losing her is worse than losing my ability to play instruments. Without her, I can't think straight.

"You're the only one who can make this right, Zed," Venom pushes. "You were worried about Ash tearing the Basilisks apart, but it's not her who did that. It's you. Ash is a Basilisk. You've torn everything apart, and you're the only one who can put us back together."

"What if she doesn't want us back?" Zed whispers, hanging his head and not meeting our eyes. Zed rarely shows emotions. He sticks to his convictions, even when he's wrong. "I've ruined everything."

Zed's quiet reflection turns into a volcano in seconds. His arm sweeps across the table in a vicious motion and sends the photographs flying.

"I've fucked it all up."

"It'll be okay," I try to reassure him, glaring at Venom, who opens his mouth to agree.

Venom is right to be annoyed. Hell, I'm pissed at Zed for what he said to Ash. It was unforgivable, but Zed doesn't need to hear *I told you so* right now.

I step toward Zed and say, "We can fix this together."

"It wasn't her," Zed's voice breaks. "She didn't betray us."

I reach and stroke his cheek. Zed is a control freak governed by logic, but he has a volatile side that would do anything for self-preservation.

"She didn't, baby," I murmur. "And you have to make this right, okay?"

I stare into his eyes as he shakily nods. He's lost. Confused. Out of control. Our identities being revealed is his biggest fear because of his dependency on our double life. But he's broken right now, and there's only one girl who can fix him—even if he doesn't realize it yet.

"You have to prove you're sorry," I say. "Really fucking sorry."

He nods. "I think I know what to do."

forty-five

. . .

Ash

"How did rehearsals go?" Cookie asks. She stirs a pot of chili lovingly on the stove. As well as her many other talents, Cookie is an excellent cook. Her chili is an old family recipe.

"Mmm," Leila says, sniffing the air. "Something smells good."

It does, but I have no appetite.

"Earth to Ash!" Cookie calls over again. "How were rehearsals?"

"Great," I lie.

Last week I'd been excited to stay in the competition. But when my name was called first yesterday, I felt nothing.

Ripper and Venom have tried to reach out, but I've ignored them. The Basilisks are a package deal. Zed made his views clear and, if he doesn't trust me, there is no future for us. I'm not worth breaking up the band over. They'll get over me eventually, even if I might never get over them.

A loud knock at the door makes our heads turn.

"Are you expecting someone?" Cookie asks. "I thought Meredith said she couldn't come tonight."

"She can't," I say, dragging myself from my comfy spot on the sofa. My legs are like dead weights. I continue chatting, "But wardrobe said they'd come up tonight or tomorrow morning for my next fitting. It's—"

I freeze mid-sentence as I mindlessly open the door and see who is standing there. I'm not the only one who's shocked. Behind me, something smashes.

"Hi Ash," Conor says. Declan stands behind him. He looks over my shoulder to Leila. "We heard Lei was staying here. Can we come in?"

I block the entrance and turn to see Cookie picking up a broken mug at Leila's feet. Thankfully, the fragments bounced in opposite directions and didn't hurt her.

"Do you want to speak to them, Leila?" I ask. "I can send them away."

"Charming," Conor jokes.

This isn't the time for their cheeky Irish humor. One glare from me makes him hang his head.

"Yes," Leila mumbles, "they can come in."

At some point, Cookie must have dropped the spoon into the pot. Her arms are sprayed with red sauce, making it look like she's stepped straight out of a bloody crime scene. From her murderous expression, it may not be long until she's covered in actual blood.

"You two!" Cookie shrieks. "You—"

"I know, I know!" Conor holds up his hands in surrender. "You don't need to say it, Cookie."

Conor approaches Leila, and I put my hand on Cookie's arm to tell her silently to step down. This isn't her battle.

Leila is trembling, still clutching a blanket in her hand.

"I didn't think you'd want to see me again," she mumbles, then her gaze strays to Declan. "Either of you."

Declan buries his hands in his pockets sheepishly.

"I think we all need to talk, Lei," Declan says.

Leila didn't tell him about her pregnancy but, by now, I'm guessing Conor did.

"We should go," I say, turning off the range. "Come on, Cookie. Let's give them some space."

"No," Leila insists decisively. "I want you both to stay…" Her voice softens. "Please."

"Okay," I say. "We'll be here for as long as you want us to be."

"Yeah, we're not gonna run out on you," Cookie says. She crosses her arms and stares down the twins like she wants to string them up by their balls. I didn't know a sunshine-yellow person could possess such a menacing look.

"Can we sit down?" Declan nods to the sofa, looking more at Cookie than Leila.

"Okay," Leila says.

We all sit down. Cookie and I are on the edge, and the twins are opposite Leila.

"Leave them to talk," I whisper in Cookie's ear. "It's none of our business. They need to work it out on their own."

"Hmph," she huffs.

It's not that I don't want to give the twins a piece of my mind, but that's not what Leila needs.

An awkward silence drags on that no one wants to break. Leila wrings her hands, and Declan's eyes stray to her stomach.

"I'm sorry I walked out on you, Leila," Conor says. "I

should never have left like that. I was… shocked… I needed time to get my head straight."

"You needed time? You're a—" Cookie begins, but I nudge her in the ribs to shut her up.

"You were an asshole," Leila says. "You didn't even say goodbye."

"I know." Conor looks at his lap in shame, then up at her again. "And I'm so fucking sorry."

"You could have at least called to let me know you were okay. You said you needed time, then vanished," Leila continues. "You didn't return my texts or calls. It's like I didn't exist."

"I acted like an ass," he says. "I don't know what I was thinking. Everything was too much. I needed to get away to try to wrap my head around it all…"

"And you're sure it's mine?" Declan asks. His pale cheeks flush. "That there's been no mistakes?"

"Do you think I'd have told Conor if there was a chance I made a fucking mistake?" Leila narrows her eyes in accusation. "The dates add up."

Don't mess with a girl when her baby hormones are going crazy y'all.

"Lei…" Conor moves to sit at her side and takes her hand. She tries to pull away, but he holds on tighter. "I'm so sorry. I really am. I want to make this right."

"You've got a lot of work to do, buddy," Cookie mutters sarcastically under her breath.

"But how can you even bear to look at me?" Leila asks. Her anger has dissipated and turned to fear. "You could get over it being a one-night thing, but you said you'd never be able to live with a permanent reminder of what happened."

"I've done a lot of thinking…" Conor looks at Declan,

who nods. "*We've* been doing a lot of thinking. We're going to be here for you and the baby, Lei. Both of us."

Her eyes widen and she stammers, "What?"

"We're going to be there for you both," Declan repeats. "We're twins. We share the same DNA. It may have been me who fathered the baby, but the baby is as much Conor's as it is mine. I want to be involved in the baby's life."

"And I want more than that," Conor says. "I want you, Leila. I've been stupid. I messed up, okay? But I love you. I was angry at both of you, but I realized that the one thing worse than being angry is being apart. I want us to be a proper family."

"I-I-I…" Leila is floored. "I don't know what to say."

"You don't have to give me an answer now," Conor says, squeezing her hand. "I know you'll need time. But I promise that if you take me back, I'll never leave you both again. I want you and our baby."

I sniff and wipe my eyes quickly.

"Seriously, Ash?" Cookie murmurs, not missing a beat. "Since when are you sentimental?"

"Shut up, Cookie," I dismiss her. "I'm fine."

Leila addresses Declan, "Are you okay with this?"

"It was a shock," he admits, "but I want to be there for all of you."

"But you two…" Leila struggles to find the words. "You two hated each other because of me."

Declan shrugs. "He gave me a pretty good right hook."

"So I'd say we're square," Conor says with a grin.

The atmosphere between the twins feels lighter compared to the strained relationship they had toward the end of camp.

"I love you, the baby, and my brother," Conor says. "I

can't be mad forever. None of this is the baby's fault. I'm just sorry it took me a few weeks to realize it, and I hope you'll give me a chance to make it up to you."

Leila yelps and starts crying.

Conor puts his arm around her, pulling her into his chest. "It's okay, I'm here now." He strokes her hair. "I'm not going anywhere, okay? I've got you. Both of you."

Leila composes herself again, hiccuping a little, and pulls away. This is everything she wants to hear, but there's a reservation there.

"How can I know you're going to stick around when things get tough?" she asks. "It won't be easy. I have no fucking clue what I'm doing. I can barely look after myself—let alone a baby! My parents were barely around when I was a kid. What if I fuck it all up?"

"That's where you're lucky," Declan chips in. "The baby has two dads."

"Or double the trouble," Cookie mutters. She's still angry but thawing.

"We're not going anywhere," Conor says. "I've missed you, Lei. So fucking much."

He strokes her cheek with such tenderness that it makes my heart break a little. The guys I want to look at me like that will never be part of my life in the way I want them to be.

"I've missed you too," she whispers. A tiny smile tugs at the corners of her lips. "But you've got a long way to go to make it up to me."

"I'll be here however long it takes," he replies solemnly.

The twins spend most of their time goofing around, but they're deadly serious now. I see it in the way they look at

her with a protectiveness that shows they'd jump in front of a moving train for her and the baby.

"And I mean it too, Leila," Declan says. "I'll be there for you both whenever you need me."

She smiles. "Thank you."

Declan shuffles around awkwardly and asks, "Can I… can I see—"

"The sonogram?" she prompts.

She doesn't go anywhere without it. Even though Leila's parents were absent for most of her life, she's going to be an amazing mom.

She hands the scan to Declan. His eyes mist over as he sees the outline of his baby's face for the first time and says, "He's got our nose, Con."

"Unlucky bastard," Conor says. "Let's hope he's not ginger too."

Leila giggles. With Conor by her side, she seems happier already. The two of them complete each other.

Conor turns to me and Cookie. "Thank you for taking care of her while I've been gone."

"We'll always be there for her, but if you ever hurt her again," Cookie jabs a pointed finger in his direction to emphasize her words, "we will fucking kill you, okay?"

"Understood." He nods. "And I'd want you to. It's what I'd deserve."

"Can I have a minute with the girls?" Leila asks the twins.

"Of course," Conor says, jumping up. "We'll wait outside."

They file out like criminals being asked to leave the courtroom while the jury ponders the verdict.

"Are you sure this is what you want, Leila?" Cookie asks instantly.

"Am I stupid that I believe what they're saying?" Leila asks, running her hands through her hair. "I'm not sure whether it's just my emotions being like a rollercoaster or because I want to believe him, but I think they mean it."

"You're not stupid," I reply. "For what it's worth, I think Conor loves you. I believe what they're saying, and if they fuck up…"

"I'll be ready and waiting to cut their balls off so they can never reproduce again," Cookie says.

"Since when did you have such a violent streak?" I ask.

She flicks a purple loc over her shoulder. "No one messes with the people I care about."

"Thank you both," Leila says. "Honestly, I don't know what I'd have done without you letting me crash here."

"Anytime," I say. "Although we may not have this amazing suite for much longer."

"You'll be here right until the end, Ash," Cookie says. "I just know it."

I nudge my head at the door. "So, are you going to put them out of their misery?"

Leila smiles. "I may want to give it a go, but I'm gonna make them work for it."

"And so you should," Cookie says. She looks over at the chili and sighs. "I guess they can stay for dinner."

"Thanks, Cookie," Leila says, then hugs us both. She squeezes tightly. "Thanks for everything, Ash."

Leila meanders to the door to let them in.

"I thought you were just going to leave us camping out here," Conor says.

Leila smiles. "You've still got a lot of work to do until you're forgiven."

He nods solemnly. "I'll do whatever it takes for however long it takes—"

Leila cuts him off with a kiss. Cookie rolls her eyes. It's like witnessing a romantic movie scene. He sweeps her off her feet dramatically and kisses her like she's the air he needs to breathe.

"Jeez," Declan mutters, edging around them. "Get a room."

They break apart reluctantly and laugh, but Conor doesn't let go of her hand. Even though it'll be a difficult few months for them, the way Leila is glowing tells me they're going to be fine.

"So, who wants to eat?" Cookie asks as she starts laying out bowls.

"Me," Conor chirps.

We all sit around the table as Cookie serves up. When I first arrived, the hotel room seemed huge and empty. Usually, I'm a lone wolf—preferring my own company, but being surrounded by all the friends I've grown to love over the summer makes the room come alive. Camp Harmony almost killed me, but it gave me friends for life, which was better than anything I hoped for. But despite my happiness, an uneasy sensation gnawing at my gut tells me something is missing.

Pull yourself together, Ash. It's only been a week without the Basilisks, and it was the right thing. Zed's words proved you didn't belong in their world.

"It's like being back at Camp Harmony," Declan comments, digging into his bowl of chili.

"Almost," I say, scrunching my nose. "Let's hope Jacqueline or Tiffany don't show up to make it a full reunion."

"You've been killing it on Popstarz," Declan says.

My polite smile doesn't meet my eyes. "Thanks."

Everyone compliments Cookie's cooking and empties

their bowls. There is no chance of leftovers for lunch with the twins around.

"What's your plan for what comes next?" Cookie asks the three of them, never afraid to ask hard-hitting questions.

"We have a hotel a few blocks over," Declan says. "But we have an apartment back home. Depending on what Leila wants, we thought we could head there while we figure things out."

"You have an apartment?" I stammer.

"The perks of having rich parents who travel around." Declan shrugs. "They're in Ireland most of the time, but they like a place to stay when they come to the States."

"Parents…" Leila's voice trails off. "I have to tell mine the news."

Conor slips his fingers through hers. "We'll do it together when you're ready."

She nods, then says, "Maybe it would be better to spend some time at the apartment first."

"Whatever you need," Conor says.

Suddenly, a knock at the door makes us all jump.

"Are you expecting anyone, Ash?" Cookie asks, checking her watch. "It seems late for wardrobe to be dropping by."

"I'll get it," Conor volunteers, heading for the door. "It's the least I can do."

"If it's wardrobe, tell them to come back tomorrow," I call over. "I'll need time before they take measurements."

He opens the door and freezes. His jaw drops as a deep voice asks, "Is Ash around?"

"Um… Ash?" He looks over his shoulder nervously. "There are three people here to see you."

"Are they wearing masks?" Cookie calls.

"No," Conor says. "It's the..."

"We can come back later," Ripper says.

Fuck. My heart thunders in my chest. What are they thinking of showing up at my door without masks? Sure, dressing as the Basilisks wouldn't get them past the lobby, but this is still a bold move. Maybe they're here about something to do with Popstarz?

My heart rate slows again. That must be it. The men I know wouldn't come to my door undisguised when they're so intent on protecting their secret.

"Let them in," I mumble.

"Oh my gosh." Leila gasps. "It's the Lionhearts!"

"Hi everyone," Zed says with an awkward wave. "It's nice to see you all again."

"We didn't realize you were having a party," Ripper says.

"It's not a party," I snap. "What do you want?"

Cookie shoots me a glare and whispers, "Remember who you're speaking to."

Zed shifts on his feet and loosens the buttons on his collar. "We're here to talk."

"So talk." I cross my arms. "Anything you have to say, you can say in front of my friends."

"Ash..." Ripper's voice trails off.

I rise from the table, unable to hold my anger back. "You've shown up to my room late at night, and now you're speechless? If you want to say something, say it. If not, I'm sure Amber can pass along a message tomorrow."

"I'm sorry for Ash," Cookie intervenes smoothly, transitioning into manager mode. "It's been a long day."

I scoff and roll my eyes.

Conor squeezes Leila's hand tighter while Declan watches the situation unfold with a bemused expression.

"Can we talk alone?" Ripper asks.

"No," I say defiantly. "Anything you have to say, you can say in front of the people I trust."

Zed steps forward and clears his throat. He stares deep into my eyes, making me forget everyone else is in the room. Everything falls away. Why are his blue eyes so damn captivating?

"I'm sorry for what I said, Ash," Zed mumbles. "It was wrong of me. I was…" He pauses, turning to the others, who nod to encourage him to continue. "I was in a bad place, and I took it out on you."

"We know it wasn't you," Ripper says. "I never doubted it for a second, but—"

"I was scared," Zed admits, "of letting someone in, and now, I've made the biggest mistake of my life."

I'm stunned. He's apologizing, without costumes and makeup, in front of people? The old Zed would never have done this.

My friends are baffled.

"Do I need to file a lawsuit?" Cookie whispers in my ear, trying not to move her lips. "What did they do?"

I shush her and address Zed, "But you were right. About all of it. It'd never have worked."

"Are you following any of this?" Conor asks Lei as Cookie clears the table.

"I was wrong. We'll find a way. We can't give up now," Zed says. He takes a deep breath. "We need you, Ash. The Basilisks need you. Without you, it's not the same. Without you, there are no Basilisks."

Cookie drops the plate she's holding as realization sets in.

"You…" Cookie's voice shakes. "You are…"

"Will someone tell us what's going on?" Declan asks.

Venom takes three masks from behind his back and hands them to the others. They all put them on.

"Yes," Zed says. "We are the Basilisks."

Leila's mouth turns into a perfect-shaped O. "Holy fucking shit…"

I face the three masked guys I started falling for. They're bearing their souls and identities in front of people I care about. I want to pinch myself to make sure I'm not imagining it.

"What're you doing?" I stammer.

I trust my friends to keep their secret, but Zed was reluctant to tell me who they were—let alone a group of strangers.

"Nothing is more important than you, Ash," Ripper says, stepping forward. "We want you to know that."

"We'll do whatever it takes," Venom says.

I don't know what to say. My two worlds colliding together mean nothing will ever be the same again.

"So, the Lionhearts are the Basilisks," Cookie says aloud to make sense of it. "They are the guys you've been fucking?"

"Cookie!" I scold as Leila snorts. "Is this the right time?"

"No, you're right," she says, shell-shocked. "I'm sorry, it's just…" She glances at the Basilisks. "I just never thought…"

Zed takes off his mask to show his face. His jaw sets like he's battling his instinct to run.

"Ash," Zed says, ignoring Cookie, "I made a mistake. I shouldn't have accused you. If you haven't noticed, I'm a control freak."

"I'm pretty sure she's noticed, Z," Ripper smirks, removing his mask.

Venom follows suit, staying silent, but his gaze says a thousand words.

"I don't know what to say," I stammer. "You didn't have to do this."

"I wanted to show you how serious we are," Zed says. "I don't want to hide who we are from the people who are important to you. We may have to live a lie, but you don't have to."

"Zed…"

"You call him Zed?" Cookie chimes in.

"Not now, Cookie," Leila hisses. It's her turn to step in to hold Cookie back. "Give them their moment."

"But we come from different worlds," I say. "I don't know how we would ever work."

"We may come from different worlds," Venom says, "but we can't imagine a future world without you in it."

"Since you walked into our lives, it hasn't been the same," Ripper says.

"We want you back, Ash," Zed says. "I can understand if you don't want me. I fucked up, and what I said was unforgivable, but it's not fair on the others. They've done nothing wrong."

I'm starting to regret asking them to speak in front of an audience who are waiting with bated breath for my answer.

"I don't know what the future holds," I say to them, "or what will happen next week, or…"

"Neither do we," Zed intervenes, "but we want you in our lives. We care about you, Ash. More than you know. Please give me—us—another chance."

They're the words I wanted to hear. Words I've been waiting for. As much as my head tells me we won't work, my heart says differently. Since our argument, they're all

I've thought about. Before hearing their music, my world was a depressing pool of black and white. They pulled me out of that with their songs. Having them made me see the universe in different colors and feel things deeper than I ever had before. We had an electric connection, and maybe I'm mad, but I don't want to let them go.

I think of Leila and the twins. They're going to find a way to make it work and be a family. If they can do it, why can't we?

"I'll think about it," I reply.

"That's all we can ask," Zed says, hanging his head. "You know where to find us."

"Holy fuck…" Cookie turns to face me as soon as the door closes behind them. She plants her hands on her hips. "Why didn't you tell me, Ash?"

I shrug. "It wasn't my secret to tell."

"So, hang on a second…" Conor says. "The Lionhearts are the Basilisks? The same metal dudes we saw in Wilderton?"

"Keep up, Conor." Leila nudges him playfully. "What we're all dying to know is what Ash is going to do next."

I sit on the sofa, sinking into the plush cushions.

"I don't know," I say, exhaling a puff of air. "It's complicated."

"Seeing three guys in a metal band is one thing," Cookie says, "but the Lionhearts… damn, Ash. They're superstars."

"Not helping, Cookie," I groan.

"They must really care to say what they did in front of us," Declan says. "How do they know we won't go to the press?"

"You won't, will you?" I ask.

"Of course not," Leila says. "Their secret is safe with us."

"So, what do you call them? Zach, Levi, and Damon?" Cookie asks, trying to work out logistics.

"No." I laugh. "They're Zed, Venom, and Ripper. That's what they call each other. The Lionhearts are just a front. The Basilisks are who they really are underneath."

Cookie frowns. "But where does that leave you?"

"It'll never work between us," I say as doubt creeps in. "How can it?"

"That's what I thought about me and Con," Leila says, gazing lovingly at Conor, who kisses her forehead. "But people surprise you. And Declan's right, they must really care to make themselves so vulnerable."

"I need to talk to them," I decide.

"Right now?" Cookie asks. "Are you sure?"

I nod. "If I don't, then I'll change my mind."

"We'll be waiting right here," Cookie says.

I've never had a good group of friends before, but I've finally found my people.

forty-six

. . .

Venom | Levi

"I can't believe you did that," Ripper says.

Adrenaline pumps through me, and I pace the room. How can I sit still after that?

"Neither can I," Zed agrees. His face is ashen as he puts his head in his hands. "What if they expose us?"

Ripper rubs Zed's back. "We did what had to be done for Ash."

"If she trusts them, so can we," I say, hoping I sound more confident than I feel.

We haven't trusted other people in a long time. But we're living on borrowed time after receiving the packages. It won't be long until the world discovers our secret.

"Do you think she believed me?" Zed asks. "Have we done enough?"

"There's nothing more we can do," Ripper says.

Zed's apology should have shown how badly we want her in our lives, but that doesn't mean she has to accept it.

"What have I done?" Zed mumbles, more to himself than to us. "I've fucked up everything."

I don't know whether he's talking about him accusing her of betraying us or his apology tonight.

"You did the right thing," I say."

The hotel room door opens, startling us, and Ash slinks inside. Her cheeks are slightly flushed, her hair is out of place, and her oversized T-shirt over leggings makes her look damn huggable.

Zed rises, almost knocking over the coffee table. He needs her reassurance the most. He didn't realize how much he fucking needed her until she was gone.

"Ash," he says. "What are you—"

She holds her hand up to silence him.

Instead of talking in her usual calm voice, she explodes, "You fucking idiot." She marches over to Zed and jabs a finger into his chest. "Why did you have to say all of that?"

It's the first time I've seen Zed truly lost for words.

"You didn't have to tell them your secret," she says. "I thought keeping your secret was everything to you."

"It was," Zed replies, "until we lost you."

"You're infuriating," she rants, blowing a loose strand of hair out of her face with a huff.

"That's what I keep telling him," Ripper adds cheekily.

"Why are you here, Ash?" I ask. I don't want to get my hopes up, but she draws my body toward her like a magnet.

"I…" She looks at me, Ripper, and Zed. "I… I just want to say this quickly before I change my mind. I'm still pissed at what you said, Zed. I'd never betray your trust, and I thought you knew that. But I never expected you to tell my friends the truth. I know how important your privacy is, so it shows me how much you care… and I'm fucking scared, okay? I don't know what this is between

us, but ignoring you has been fucking killing me inside, and…"

She gulps for air after the words come in a rushed babble.

"Ash, we're not giving up on us, okay?" Ripper ignores her request not to be interrupted and puts his hands on her shoulders. "We want you. All of us do. We'll do whatever it takes."

"Really?" she whispers.

"Yes," I say.

Her gaze turns to Zed. "And what about you?"

"I want this, Ash," Zed confirms. "I fucked up, and I know I don't deserve a second chance, but I won't let you down again. I'm scared of what will happen if people find out who we are, but some things—you—are more important."

A small smile tugs at her lips, making my heart melt. I love her smile and the way she does a terrible job of trying to hide it.

Ripper tucks her hair behind her ear. "We've missed you, Ash."

They share a hypnotic stare until Ash breaks the trance and says, "I've missed you, too. All of you."

Zed simply nods, but his shoulders slacken in relief.

"Can I kiss you?" Ripper asks.

His pupils dilate like crazy. His entire irises are eclipsed in lusty blackness. She swallows hard, then nods. He wraps his arms around her waist, pulling her close and kissing her like they're the only two people in the world.

Watching them makes my cock tingle as she moans into his mouth. When they pull away breathlessly, Ash's eyes find mine. She doesn't speak, but I know what she's asking. We communicate without words. She's the only

woman who can tell what I'm thinking with a single glance, like an invisible thread ties us together.

She moves from Ripper to me. Her hand strokes the front of my chest and rests on my beating heart for a few seconds, feeling it race under my skin… for her.

I put my hands on her waist, thinking about how fucking lucky we are. Now we've found Ash, we won't let her go. She is one of us. We belong together.

Her chin tips up as she stretches on her tiptoes. My lips tingle as hers softly brush against mine, until I swoop in to claim her. I don't hold back. I fill my kiss with hunger and promises. A promise that we'll do whatever it fucking takes to be together.

I slide my hand underneath her shirt to meet her warm lower back. She isn't wearing a bra, and her nipples harden, pressing into my chest.

She reluctantly pulls away. She doesn't want to stop. Her swollen lips and eyes darting down my body tell me that. But there's something she has to do first.

She turns her back on me. Her round ass rubs against my erection like a form of torture.

"Zed," she beckons him over.

Time slows as his eyes light up in surprise. Zed's family has never wanted him for who he is. He finds it hard to comprehend that people care about him without a hidden agenda.

He joins us and tilts his head, looking at me for approval. I nod. He knows I've been pissed at him for how he treated our girl, and he has to do better.

This is new for all of us, and showing vulnerability is a struggle for him, but when he leans to kiss Ash, I can almost see another side to him as his guards come

crashing down. She sees all of us for who we are. She is exactly what we all need.

Ripper is like a scorching fire—obsessive, passionate, and unrelenting. When he finds someone he wants, he makes them his entire world and will never let go. He has a crippling fear of being used and getting hurt, but Ash reassures him. She cuts through the bullshit, isn't afraid to say what she thinks, and gives him security.

Zed likes to be the puppet master, pulling the strings of others around him—it's what the Royal family has taught him. Losing control, or giving it to someone else, is his biggest fear because he's used to being treated like a prop. But Ash shows him he is more than that. They both favor loyalty above all else and are ready to do whatever it takes for those they love. His relinquishing control by sharing the Basilisk's true identities with Ash's friends shows how much he cares for her.

I live in the shadows, avoiding attention, and hoping people won't notice me. Feeling truly alive is scary, and guilt about being happy keeps me up at night. But Ash pushes and challenges me. She sees my fear, takes my hand, and teaches me how to face it. She makes me want to be a better person because I want to be the man she deserves. Our experiences of loss and pain have drawn us together, and we're pulling each other through to the other side.

"I'm so sorry, Ash," Zed says. "I mean it."

She hesitates and then kisses him again. He isn't forgiven fully yet, but she's willing to look past it because she knows how big a deal Zed's earlier revelation was.

"I don't deserve you," he says as she pulls away.

"None of us do," I agree, stroking her hips and sandwiching her between us.

"I don't know what's going to happen next," Ash says, "but I want to see what does."

"You have us, Ash," Zed says. "You're ours, and we won't let you go."

"Does this make me a Basilisk now?" she jokes.

"Oh no," Ripper chimes in from his spot on the sofa, watching us with hungry eyes. "You're much more than that. You're our Ash."

Zed kisses her again as I move her hair to one side, kissing down her neck and breathing in her scent that I'm beginning to associate with home. She's right where she belongs.

forty-seven

. . .

Zed | Zach

I never expected her to forgive me, but having her in my arms again is better than any feeling I've had from performing on stage. She is a buzz I want to keep chasing. Music has always been my reason for living, but now it's because I want her to hear it.

If the situation was reversed, I don't know whether I'd have forgiven myself. I got it wrong and pushed her away, just like I push away everything when it gets too close. I see now that I was wrong. Ash was never a threat or a danger. She's always been the fucking solution.

I slip my tongue into her mouth, kissing her deeply and wanting to swallow her whole. Her tight body is feverish, responding instantly to my touch as I slide under her tee. My hands move over her stomach to cup her breasts. I catch her pointed nipples between my fingers, rubbing and rolling them back and forth.

I want to claim her again and show her how fucking sorry I am, but Ripper clears his throat.

"Why don't we take our girl somewhere more comfortable?" he suggests.

I step back and Ripper comes in like a superhero. He puts one arm around her back and the other under her knees to scoop her into his arms.

He carries her to his bedroom—of course—and drops her in the middle of his giant bed. She squeals, and her hair fans around her head like a fallen angel. She sits up, drawing her knees to her chest, and watches the three of us expectantly, wondering what'll happen next.

Ripper is eager. He wastes no time in pulling his shirt off, displaying his perfect body and carved muscles.

"Are you sure this is what you want, Ash?" Ripper asks as he crawls toward her. He likes to check she's okay. He cares about people, putting them before himself, and a surge of love pours from me.

Fuck. Love… is this how it feels?

Ripper pulls Ash onto his lap. She straddles him as she pulls her T-shirt over her head. Her dark hair trails down her front, covering her breasts. Seeing the pair of them together tugs at something deep inside me. Am I in love?

"You're beautiful, Ash," Ripper says, running his fingers down her spine. "So fucking beautiful."

He pushes her off his lap, lays her back onto the pillows, and yanks down her leggings and panties until she's lying naked before us. A few months ago, this situation would have intimidated her. Now she turns her head toward Venom and me, then smirks.

"Are you just going to stand and watch?" she teases.

We don't need to be asked twice, eagerly undressing quicker than we have in our lives to join them on the bed.

Ripper parts Ash's legs, kissing her soft inner thighs and faded white scars. She's stunning—what other people see as imperfections only make her more perfect. Her pussy is pink and swollen, ready and dying to be tasted.

I take her nipple in my mouth. Ash moans, writhing as Venom heads to the other side to knead her other breast and suck her nipple. I slide my tongue over the pebbled surface, playing and sucking.

Ash's body jerks and she cries out, "Fuck."

I glance down to see Ripper feasting on her cunt. I'm jealous. I know how fucking good she tastes, and I can't wait for my tongue to slide between her lips and fuck her insides.

The three of us work as a team. Her legs shake, and a flush creeps over her white skin from her chest and up her neck. Our mouths are all on her at once, working to give her the best fucking orgasm she's ever had.

"You're so wet for us, baby," Ripper compliments. He pulls two fingers out of her, shiny with her juices. He holds it out. "Taste her, Zed."

I abandon her nipple for a second and suck her wetness off his finger.

"Fuck," I groan, licking my lips.

"That's so hot," Ash moans.

Is she remembering Ripper sucking my cock? She enjoyed watching us together, which is another reason why she's perfect for us.

I taste her sweetness on my tongue, then get back to her nipple. My hands run down her body until they land on Ripper's head. I hold him down. I want him to eat our girl better than he's eaten any pussy before.

Ash's chest heaves as her breathing grows erratic. When her orgasm comes, it takes none of us by surprise. Her body jerks, and I bite her nipple, making her cry out as Ripper laps up her cream.

"You guys..." she murmurs. The aftershocks make her shudder. "You're the fucking best."

"We know," Ripper replies. "And we're not finished yet."

Ripper withdraws and gives Venom a *you first* look. Venom doesn't argue. He positions himself between her legs and slides his throbbing cock inside her. She wraps her legs around him to draw his body close.

"Fuck our girl good, Venom," I encourage. "We need her nice and wide for me and Ripper."

"Do you think your pussy can take two guys, Ash?" Ripper asks.

"Fuck." Her nails claw Venom's back, rocking her hips to match his movement. "Yes!"

I beckon Ripper closer and kiss him. His manly body pressed against mine after feeling the soft satin of Ash's skin is alluring. We can share a special moment while Venom warms our girl up for us.

"I don't know if she'll be able to take us," Ripper says to me. Ash moans too loudly to hear us. "She's so tight."

"We'll make her nice and ready. She can do it," I say, trailing my hand over his abs, then down to grip his hard cock. I pause and spit on my hand, then coat his shaft with it.

He groans, biting my lip hard. He grabs my ass and squeezes.

"Don't," he growls in warning, as I go to play with his balls. His cock is already close to bursting. "I want to make this last."

"I want to feel you when we're inside, Ash," I say. "I want to feel your hard cock rubbing against mine while we fill our girl."

What could be better than fucking the two people I love the most at once?

forty-eight

. . .

Ash

My breasts wobble as Venom's cock plunges in and out of me. Over his shoulder, I watch Zed and Ripper touch each other. I never thought watching two guys together would be such a turn-on, but my god, it makes me wetter.

I rock my hips against Venom, feeling another orgasm approaching. I like how it's just the two of us for now.

He whispers in my ear, "I've missed you."

I sigh, pushing against him to force his cock deeper, desperate to take him as far as he can go. "I've missed you, too."

My pussy is still contracting from my first orgasm. My walls squeeze his hardness as another wave of pleasure creeps up on me, and I moan.

"Fuck, Ash," Venom groans, quickening his pace. "I'm going to come."

"Fill me, Venom," I demand.

Our skin glistens with sweat as we move together, and his tongue assaults my mouth to let me know how much he wants this. My nails tear into his skin like I'm possessed by a

wild animal. My pussy clamps down on his cock tightly as he rocks me to another orgasm and shoots a burst of warmth deep inside me, marking me in the best possible way.

Being desired by the Basilisks is surreal, but I love it. It's better than any other feeling in the world—even the euphoria I get from singing with them on stage.

Venom pulls out, leaving a trail of cum dripping from his cock. I shakily struggle to my knees and lick his cock clean. Venom's thighs shudder, and I take my time, knowing Zed and Ripper have paused to watch the show. Finally, I slide my tongue over the tip of his cock and lick the last drop of cum away.

"Lie down, Ripper," Zed instructs. His eyes burn with pure lust. "Ash, I want to see you ride Ripper's cock while facing me."

I'd usually reply with a snarky feminist comment about not taking orders from men, but Ripper's cock is too irresistible. I mount Ripper, facing away from him, and lean back. To accommodate the curve of his dick, I rest my arms on either side of his torso.

"Holy fuck," Zed says. He's holding a bottle of lube—he must have got it when I was busy with Venom—and squirts it over the front of my pussy.

He watches with fascination as I slowly ease Ripper into me. Zed uses his hands to rub lube over Ripper's cock, then ventures to stroke my swollen clit that's still begging for attention as I spread my legs wider. I have no limits with the Basilisks.

Zed coats two of his fingers, then strokes the base of Ripper's shaft. Then he takes me by surprise as he slides his finger into my pussy, too. I'm stunned, but my pussy opens up to the sensation. She's hungry for more.

"It's okay, Ash," Zed promises. "I won't do anything that'll hurt you."

"I'm doing all I can not to come right now," Ripper growls from behind.

"Just stay real still," Zed says. His fingers are long and shapely. He parts my pussy lips wide, and he slides another finger inside me alongside Ripper's cock.

This is different to getting fucked in two holes. Vaginas stretch, but how far will I be able to go?

Venom returns to the room. With all the additions of cocks and fingers, I didn't notice that he disappeared to clean up, but he's back again. He sits next to me, grabs my chin, and turns my head to kiss me. His presence keeps me rooted and calms me. While Zed is moving his fingers inside me against Ripper, Venom's slightly cold fingers find my clit. The change of temperature from the slippery hot lube is incredible.

"How does that feel, Ash?" Zed asks.

He slides a third finger inside me. I gasp at the sudden fullness, but I'm so wet, and my pussy is stretching. His fingers work their way in, right to his knuckles, and I relax into it. I like how the two of them together put pressure on my G-Spot—even if it's a little ticklish.

"I feel…" I struggle to vocalize the sensation. "Full."

"Good, that's just how we want you to be," Zed praises.

He withdraws his fingers with a squelchy pop and lubes his shaft.

"I want you to turn around now, Ash," Zed says. "I want to see that cute fucking ass of yours before I join Ripper in your tight little pussy and make it stretch."

My toes tingle with nerves and excitement as I climb off Ripper and spin around. Part of me is pleased I won't

have to see him entering me. Seeing Zed's monster cock is enough to terrify anyone. I don't know how I'll be able to fit the two of them, but Zed's confident tone tells me it will work. I'm in safe hands.

Venom watches with intrigue as I position my pussy over Ripper's cock again. His legs are pressed together, locked in place. He fits with no problem at all. My pussy is loosened up, almost craving an addition of something more after Zed's fingers. I arch my back then, and Zed approaches from behind.

His slippery cock brushes against me.

"Stay still, Ripper," he orders. "I'm gonna make all three of us feel good."

He covers us with more lube. Poor Ripper's sheets need burning after this. I don't move as Zed's cock probes my wet entrance. I gasp as his head pushes in, but he's gentle.

"You can take both of us, Ash," Zed purrs. "Your pussy is desperate to be filled with two cocks. I can feel it."

His words of reassurance help me relax as his tip edges into me. He hesitates, not moving. Ripper twitches and groans, sending vibrations through me.

"How is that?" Zed asks.

"Intense," I reply.

"Do you want me to stop?"

"No," I insist.

I want to see what my body can handle. I want them to push me to my limit. And more than that, I want to take two guys who love each other at once.

Zed squeezes in another inch or so. It stings, and I squeeze my eyes shut, but I don't want him to stop. I will my pussy to open and take a few deep breaths.

I'm doing it.

I'm really fucking doing it.

It's only a few more inches, but it feels like I deserve a medal.

The initial pain subsides as Zed moves back and forth. He and Ripper are stretching me wide. The friction of their two cocks rubbing against each other is driving Ripper wild, too. His deep moans tell me how much he's loving it, and it makes me want Zed deeper.

"Deeper," I order. "Zed, I can take it."

"I don't want to push you," he says.

"I said, I can take it," I insist, moving my hips to make a point.

Zed growls. He grasps my ass hard. I turn to look at Venom. His cock is hard again, and he's pleasuring himself. One lusty glance in his direction has Venom moving closer for me to get a better view.

Zed's thrusts are restrained—I'm probably only taking half of him, but that's enough. He and Ripper are rubbing together to create a building heat inside me.

"Holy fucking shit," Ripper says. "This is the best… I can't control myself…"

"How does it feel, Ash?" Zed asks as his cock slides against my walls and Ripper's cock, making us both moan in tandem.

I can hardly speak. I've never experienced anything like this before. It's all-consuming, taking over my entire body, and making me dizzy. I have zero control. My body is being used in the best possible way, and I can't think straight.

Pleasure consumes me and renders me speechless. I can only moan, gasp, and make primal noises that I didn't know were within my vocal range.

Zed speeds up, making me wetter than I've ever been before.

"I'm going to..." I don't speak but scream in pleasure as my vision blurs and my knees quake. Every wave of my orgasm pulses against the two of their cocks, amplifying the feeling. My whole body trembles but Zed keeps me held in place.

Ripper grunts as he explodes at the same time, while Zed gasps as he nears release. His body jerks like a bomb's gone off inside me and stolen our air. We're a sweaty, gooey mess.

I look up to see Venom about to come. I open my mouth, unable to speak, but asking for him to fill it with my lustful gaze.

He angles his cock close to my face as salty semen spills out. I open my mouth wide, but he misses, spraying over my cheeks, chin, and tongue. Ripper doesn't care that some drops fall onto him. Our three bodies are inexplicably connected and linked forever.

forty-nine

. . .

Ripper | Damon

Sex with Ash is incredible. It always has been, but nothing compares to the feeling of her taking me and Zed at the same time. Me and the man I love are inside the woman who sets our souls alight while Venom spills down her throat.

Zed is careful, gently pulling out first as Ash collapses onto my chest. Despite the best orgasm of my life, my cock clings to its erection because it wants to be inside her for a little longer.

Venom, the least sticky of the three of us, dashes to my ensuite. He returns with towels for us. Ash rolls off of me, lying in a state of pure bliss at my side.

"That was…" she breathes. "Something."

I roll over to stroke the side of her face. "It was certainly something,"

What have we done to deserve her? A girl so unique and perfect for each of us.

"You're incredible, Ash," Zed says, collapsing onto his front at my other side with a satisfied groan.

We could all sleep for days after the exertion.

"I really should get going soon," Ash says. "In case you didn't notice, I had visitors..."

"Come on," I tease. "Can't you stay a little longer?"

"I wish I could," she says, then grins. "But then I won't be able to walk tomorrow."

"Are you hurt?" Venom asks sharply.

"No," she says, smiling and reaching to take his hand. "But there's only so many times I can fuck three guys in one day. I'm only human."

"Superhuman to us," I confirm. Corny, but I can't help it. When she's around, I revert to being a horny teenager.

She groans as she sits up, and her hair falls over her face.

"I'm gonna shower," she says. My cock twitches at the thought. She smirks and looks down at it, then adds, "Alone. I'm serious about needing to walk tomorrow. I have dance rehearsals, and I don't want to look like I'm doing Michael Jackson's *Thriller* because I can barely move."

I pout. "Fine."

We all watch as she hobbles from the bed. I check out her ass from behind. She's perfect and comfortable in her skin around us.

"Well, that went better than I expected," Zed says. His tone is lighter, less weighed down by worries. After we roughly clean up, Venom dresses quickly as Zed and I throw on robes.

"We still have to tell her about the photographs," Venom says over the sound of the shower, bursting our euphoric rush.

"I thought Zed was the killjoy of the band," I mutter. Venom glares at me, and I sigh. "I know you're right."

We leave Ash's clothes out on the bed for her and wait in the living room until she's finished.

When she joins us again, her nervous smile takes my breath away. How is it possible she looks even more radiant than before?

"I should go," she says, nudging her head at the door. "It's an early start."

We all exchange glances with each other. None of us wants to ruin the good night we've shared, but we have to tell her.

Venom is the bravest and says, "Before you go, we have to show you something."

Her eyes narrow in suspicion. "What is it?"

Venom goes to the table where the envelope is and tips the photographs out. "We received this earlier…"

"Shit," she murmurs, picking them up and studying them. "They know about us, too."

"It looks that way," Zed confirms, "or know about you and Ripper, at least."

"News like this would make headlines," Ash says. "Why are they sitting on it?"

Zed's hands curl into fists. "Because they want something."

"But they haven't made any demands," she points out.

"Yet," he mutters darkly. "If they've not acted, it's because they want to spook us first."

"You have to be careful, Ash," Venom says. "Whoever is leaving these messages isn't just watching us. They're watching you too."

It's not the first time we've had stalkers. Hell, we probably have a handful of obsessed superfans at any single given time for both bands. But this feels different. A superfan wouldn't ordinarily leave cryptic clues. If you

upset them, they're prone to leaving threats, but it's unclear whether the leaver of the messages has malicious intent.

"You shouldn't go anywhere alone, especially after dark," Zed says. "At least until we figure out who is behind this. You should tell your friends about it."

"No stalkers will get past Cookie," Ash mutters.

"They're toying with us now, but they'll have to act soon," Zed says. "Popstarz is ending soon, and we don't know what their end game is."

Ash nods in understanding.

"I'll be careful," she says. "I promise."

fifty

. . .

Ash

"It's weird without them around, isn't it?" Cookie says wistfully.

Leila and the twins left a few days ago. It's eerily quiet without them here—not that I can enjoy it. Cookie accompanies me everywhere after learning about the weird packages the Basilisks received.

"It's strange," I say, "but I'm happy for them."

Leila promised to keep in touch and let us know how she's doing. She and Conor are determined to make a go of it, with Declan around for support. One thing is for sure, their baby will grow up with the coolest lullabies. If their parent's musical abilities are anything to go by, the kid will probably have a number-one hit before they're in high school.

"Speaking of visitors," Cookie says, checking her cell. "Claudia is going to be in the city for a few days. She has a guest spot at a fine-dining restaurant for a night. I've got us a reservation."

"That sounds great," I say. "When is it?"

As good as the hotel food and Cookie's home-cooked meals are, I miss Claudia's cooking.

"Tonight," Cookie says, then wiggles her eyebrows. "Your guys are going to be there too."

Cookie still can't get over how the Basilisks are the Lionhearts. It's nice to not have to keep it a secret. Although, it'll take a while for her to get used to swapping their names depending on what scenario they're in.

"Oh, yeah," I say, remembering an earlier text Venom sent. We've all been so busy that we've not seen each other for a few days, but the guys stay in regular contact. They're even more obsessed with checking in on me than Cookie. "They mentioned something about an exclusive dining event."

"Isn't it weird to pretend you don't know them?" Cookie asks.

"I guess." I shrug. "But it's not weird if we speak to each other in public. Everyone knows they were mentors at Camp Harmony and are on Popstarz. Besides, the guys they have to be in public aren't the same guys I spend time with behind closed doors."

"When the show is over," Cookie says, "I'd like to get to know them more."

"I'm sure you will," I say, "but only if you get over that star-struck look in your eyes whenever you talk about them. So, tell me about tonight."

"There will be a load of famous people going," she says. "Claudia is rocking it. She got us a last-minute table because someone dropped out. I can't wait to see her again."

It'll be nice to get out of the hotel for a night. My rehearsal schedule is grueling with the semi-finals coming

up. Plus, the Basilisks won't be able to worry about my safety when they'll be in the same restaurant.

We get a cab from the hotel. I feel over the top in a tight red dress that Cookie insisted I wear because the invitation called for formal attire.

Her deep purple dress makes her complexion pop and matches her freshly dyed blue locs that are piled on top of her head and styled with butterfly clips.

"I don't know how I'm going to eat in this thing," I curse, pulling the hem down.

"You'll be fine," Cookie says. "We'll probably have to stop for pizza on the way back, anyway. Fine-dining restaurants have tiny portions."

"Are you sure this is it?" I ask, looking at the nondescript entrance.

The restaurant is hidden away and hosts various pop-up events for up-and-coming chefs. Tonight, we're promised a fully raw, plant-based eating experience.

"Yep," Cookie says as we descend the stairs to the basement entrance.

"Can I take your coat, Miss?" a guy at the door asks as soon as we step inside.

I look at Cookie for guidance. She's been to places like this before, but I'm out of my depth.

"Of course," she says, taking hers off. "Here you go."

"Thanks," I mumble, handing over my jacket and feeling very exposed with my spaghetti straps.

The interior is like a grotto, with vines and trees climbing over the walls. Fairy lights twinkle among the

foliage. It can seat around one hundred people, I'd guess, so it feels small and cozy.

We're shown to our table, and a server thrusts a tasting menu under our noses. I glance around and don't see the Basilisks yet. The first of the twelve courses will be served soon, so I'm sure they'll be here any minute.

"Look over there." Cookie nudges her head to a pair of famous actors. "And look behind them."

Faces that I recognize from movies and the news fill the room. This is different from the Meadow Springs diner.

I catch the scent of Ripper's cologne before I see them. Desire shoots up my thighs like they've conditioned my body to respond whenever they walk into a room.

They're smartly dressed. Ripper is in a crisp white shirt rolled up to his elbows with suspenders over the top and a suit jacket he would never choose himself slung casually over his shoulder. He belongs in a Burberry ad. Next to him, Zed wears an impeccable sleek black suit and Venom trawls behind them. He looks uncomfortable in an oversized blazer, and his hair flops over his eyes to hide his face.

"Woah." Cookie winks. "You've snagged some good ones there."

"Shh," I hiss as my cheeks heat. No one can see me blushing with the dim lighting and flickering candles.

"Look who it is." Cookie points at Claudia on the other side of the restaurant.

Claudia wears her chef whites, her hair is pulled into a ponytail with a load of flyaways, and she's absolutely glowing. I've never seen her so happy. She does the rounds, shaking hands with important diners and introducing herself. I guess it's a way to make them feel important. Finally, she reaches our table.

"You guys," she says. "I'm so happy that you could make it." She drops her voice. "I'll hug you later. I have to be professional, you know."

"We're so glad we could come," I reply.

Claudia was a big support in Camp Harmony, and it's great to be here for her now.

"So, where is he?" Cookie asks, looking around. "Your mystery man?"

"You've met someone?" I ask. This is the first I've heard of it, but Cookie keeps in touch with her more regularly.

"He's around here somewhere," she mumbles. Her smile wavers for a minute—maybe I'm imagining it, or maybe she's just nervous.

"When can we meet him?" Cookie asks.

"I'm not sure. He's not really social," she says, then makes eye contact with the diners at the next table. "We'll catch up later. Enjoy the food."

"Was it just me or was that weird?" Cookie asks.

I shrug. "Maybe she's dating someone famous and is keeping it a secret."

"Well, she wouldn't be the only one," Cookie says knowingly. She looks at my guys sitting in the corner of the room. We're not the only ones who are staring at them. The Lionhearts attract attention wherever they go, and half the women in the room are checking them out.

The evening passes with amazing food that's surprisingly filling. The dishes are expertly constructed and have a perfect combination of flavors. They're also displayed beautifully with edible petals and glitter, and there was even a bell pepper carved into the shape of a rose.

After eating three miniature cheesecakes—that were all heavenly—there's no way we'll be stopping for pizza.

"That was the best meal I've ever eaten," Cookie declares. Her eyes dart around before swiping her finger around the rim of the plate to not waste any delicious strawberry sauce.

"I second that," I agree. "If I'm ever rich and famous, I'll be hiring Claudia as my personal chef. She was wasted in Camp Harmony."

We aren't the only ones who are admiring her talents. Many of the surrounding tables are leaving gigantic tips with compliments to their chef alongside their numbers. I overhear a couple discussing how they want her to do the catering for their wedding for an eye-watering amount of money.

"I'll be right back," I say, rising from the table. "I need to go to the bathroom."

As I make my way through the restaurant and pass the Basilisk's table, their eyes are on me. My cell vibrates in my purse. I read the message.

Ripper: That dress is beautiful… but it'd look even better on your floor.

I smirk, resisting the urge to laugh, and respond.

Me: Really? Is that the best you got?

I'm too busy texting that I pay no attention to where I'm going, and almost stumble into someone.

"Sorry," I say, full of apologies, then freeze as I get a proper look at the man wearing a nice suit. I blink again, making sure I'm not imagining it. "Dad? What are you doing here?"

His face turns crimson. "Ash," he says, loosening his collar. "I didn't expect to see you—"

"Hey, Jack!" Claudia rushes out of the kitchen doors at that exact moment. "What did you think of—"

Her smile drops as she looks between us, then back to my dad. Hang on a second. How do they know each other?

"Why are you here, Dad?" I ask again, trying to keep my voice level.

"I-I-I…" He can't get out the words and looks at Claudia for support.

She joins him at his side, putting her hand on his arm. It's an intimate move. Something you'd only do if it was someone you knew well. Too well.

"Ash, we were going to tell you," Claudia says.

I ignore her. All the amazing food is now swirling around in my stomach like a washing machine as I taste the bitter pang of betrayal.

"She's not much older than me," I point out like a petulant child.

"There's a bit of an age gap," Claudia says, "but age is only a num—"

"Dad!" I cut Claudia off and narrow my eyes. "How long has this been going on?"

"You introduced us at Camp Harmony at the final show, then…" he trails off, burying his hands in his pockets and looking down like he wants the floor to swallow him. I wish it would. "I was going to tell you soon."

"We're at the same fucking restaurant," I exclaim. "Didn't you think I'd notice you were here?"

His face turns stern. "Ashley Cooper, there's no need to swear."

Claudia hangs her head. "You weren't supposed to see each other. Jack was supposed to be staying with Kelly in the back."

"How long were you planning on sneaking around, huh?" My anger boils over. "You're dating someone almost half your age, Dad. Someone who was my friend! You should have told me."

"Ash—" He reaches out, but I step away.

"No." I shake my head. "I don't want to hear it."

Dad follows me as I turn my back on them, but I spin around and say, "Don't even think about following me. Stay and support your new girlfriend."

Saying the word makes me feel sick. It's not that I don't want Dad to be happy or move on one day, but it feels too soon. And I never expected him to shack up with someone like Claudia.

I storm back to my table. Dad knows me well enough to leave me alone when I'm in a mood.

"What's wrong?" Cookie asks.

"We're leaving," I say. "Now."

"What's happened?" Cookie looks quizzically around the restaurant, oblivious to the fact my father is cozying up with another woman.

"I'll tell you on the way," I say. I push my chair in with a loud screech, causing a few diners to turn and stare, but I'm too angry to give a shit.

"Okay, okay." Cookie jumps up to follow me. "I get it. We're leaving."

She hurries after me, having to take two steps to one of my long strides. Thankfully, a cab is already waiting.

Fuck this.

"What the hell is going on?" Cookie asks as soon as

we're speeding away. "Did something happen with the guys?"

I scoff, still unable to collect my thoughts. If I say it aloud, it makes it real.

"Hello?" Cookie waves her hand in front of my face. "Is anyone home? What is it?"

"It's my dad," I say.

"Oh my gosh." Cookie's face falls. "Is he okay? Has there been an accident or did something happen at work?"

"He's just fine," I say through gritted teeth, "but I found out he has a new girlfriend."

Her expression softens in sympathy. "Oh, Ash…"

"It's Claudia," I say, putting an end to her pity. "I ran into him in the restaurant, and they told me. They're dating. They met at Camp Harmony."

"Woah…" Cookie exhales slowly. "I didn't see that coming. I guess that explains his new haircut."

Yeah, his new haircut, new clothes, and new fucking life.

"Why her, Cookie?" I ask. "It's not that I don't want him to be happy, but she's so much younger. What about Mom? I never thought he'd be single forever, but…"

Mom and Dad used to say they were soulmates. After she died, he said he'd never find someone else who compared and made him feel the way she did. Yet, he's traded her in for a younger model at the first opportunity. It's a betrayal.

"And they lied about it," I continue, curling my hands into fists and savoring the feeling of my nails digging into my skin. "They weren't even planning on telling me tonight. I only found out because I ran into him."

"It's a pretty new relationship, right? I guess they

thought they were doing the right thing, keeping it quiet until they knew where it was going."

I glare at her. I'm not in the mood to listen to reason right now.

"It was still wrong of them to lie to you," she adds hastily.

"What does she see in him, anyway?" I ask. "He's forty-two! He works all the time! He barely leaves the house. It's not like he's loaded or anything. The guy can't even cook for himself."

Cookie presses her lips together, avoiding saying anything to make things worse.

"He lied to me," I say. "Is this how it's going to be from now on?" My voice crumbles, but I try to keep myself together. "He said we were going to be a team."

Me, him, and Mom were a team. They were young when they had me and didn't want more kids. They liked it being the three of us. Where does that leave Dad now? Will he have more kids? Would Claudia and Kelly move into our house and take over my bedroom? There wouldn't be space for me in his life anymore. I'll be pushed out.

My cell buzzes. I whip it out, ready to hurl it out of the window if it's Dad.

Venom: Are you okay? You left in a hurry...

Nope, Dad can't be bothered to text to apologize. He's too busy sneaking around and forgetting to fill me in on any big life changes.

My shoulders shake from the anger and shock. There's only one thing that'll make me feel better. I need to scream.

Me: I'm heading to Buggy. Emergency. I'll meet you there.

The cab pulls up outside the hotel. Cookie gets out, but I don't move.

"Aren't you coming inside?" Cookie asks.

"No," I growl. "I'm going… somewhere else."

"You shouldn't be on your own," she says. "Remember what they—"

"I know full well what they said," I explode, then look away in shame. I shouldn't have snapped at her. She's only trying to help. I force an apologetic smile. "Sorry, Cookie. But I need this, okay?" I hold up my purse and wave it. "I've got pepper spray."

She looks like she wants to argue, but she's already out on the sidewalk. I shut the door and lock it, so she can't get back in again.

"Ash," she warns sternly.

"I'll text you," I say, then give the driver directions.

I'll have to walk a short distance, but if anyone tries anything tonight, I'll blind them with spray.

fifty-one

. . .

Venom | Levi

I make the table rattle as I jump up. "She needs us."

We're only halfway through our desserts, and they're the best I've ever tasted, but she's more important than anything else. Ripper shoves two cheesecakes into his mouth at once, making his cheeks bulge like a famished hamster. He's ready to go.

"Fuck," Zed curses, checking our schedule on his cell calendar. We have to make an appearance later at a new bar opening. "Venom, you go. We'll stay behind."

"But—" Ripper objects with his mouthful.

"We all want to be there," Zed says, "but we're treading on thin ice. We can't arouse any more suspicion, okay? Not when someone is watching us. Besides, no one is going to miss Levi at the opening."

I roll my eyes sarcastically. "No offense taken."

He's telling the truth. The cameras live for shooting them. I'm nothing more than an extra accessory at their side.

"Go," Ripper says, swallowing down his food. "Let us know she's okay. Take our car."

I nod and hurry out. Ash fled the restaurant like a hurricane. I don't think I've seen her so angry before. Whatever happened upset her, and if she's anything like me, anger might be a trigger to hurt herself. I want to make sure she doesn't.

She can't be too far ahead of me, but I don't want her waiting out in the cold. I ask my driver to go to the top of the street where the garage is. What does blowing our cover matter when our girl needs me?

I call her as soon as I get out, breaking into a run toward the garage. She picks up.

"Where are you?" I ask.

Then I see her. Her back is pressed against the wall of an alleyway, hidden from view, and she steps out of the darkness.

Flickering streetlights and rubbish blowing in the wind give the empty street an unsettling atmosphere. She says nothing as we head to Buggy.

"The code is 2-7-4-5-3-9," I say, pressing the buttons on the keypad. "In case you ever need to meet us, or just want to get away from the hotel for some space."

The keypad beeps in approval, and I cast a quick look behind us as the shutters roll up. No one's around.

"What is it, Ash?" I ask as soon as we're inside.

She paces the length of the bus. Her back is rigid, her shoulders tense, and a deep frown lines her face.

"What happened?"

"It's my dad," she says, almost spitting the words. "He's dating Claudia."

It's a good thing I've come along. I'm pretty sure Ripper would have responded by giving her dad a mental fist bump. We've met Ash's dad before—he's in good shape and is attractive in a rugged way.

"Okay," I say, taking a seat. The news has come as a shock to her. "So…"

"So, they lied about it," she blasts. "I found out by accident because I stumbled into him after dinner. He said he'd never find anyone else. He said he and Mom belonged together and that no one else would compare. Then he hooks up with a younger woman—my friend. What does that say about their relationship? What would Mom say?"

"Ash." I stand, stopping her from taking her next step, and put my hands on her shoulders. Pain is etched into her features. This isn't pain about betrayal—or even pain about her dad moving on—this is about something deeper. "What's really bothering you?"

"I told you," she erupts. Like Zed, anger is one of her first responses. "They lied about it!"

I take her hands and unfurl her fists. Thankfully, her nails are short, but I see the angry pink marks. She shakes me off and continues to pace.

I block her again. "Ash," I say, looking into her eyes and wanting to do anything to take away the pain staring back. I hate to see her hurting. "This is about more than that."

"I don't want to talk," she snarls. "I need to sing."

I nod in understanding.

"How about we sing our new song together?" I suggest.

She pauses a second, forgetting her anger. "Our song?"

I rummage around in a drawer that is filled with loose papers. While Ash has had my lyric book, I've still been writing songs. It's been a long time since I've been this inspired. Ash is my muse, and the words keep coming… but there's one song I keep coming back to.

The one I originally read in her book and finished. I know the words by heart. They're burned in my brain. I hand her the paper.

"You know all the words from memory?" she asks.

I shrug like it's nothing, then say, "What do you think? A duet?"

"But we don't have music."

"Actually…" I say, heading to the CD player. "We do."

It's a track I wanted to be included in the next album. Something I wanted to do to surprise her. I produced it myself. It's rough around the edges, but I recorded myself playing all the instrumental individual parts and edited them together. The Starnote producers didn't notice me using their equipment when I had time to kill in the studio over the last few weeks.

I hit play, and her eyes flicker closed. The opening plays—a crashing emotional beat that courses through my body. That's our cue. She picks up on it instantly. She doesn't open her eyes but starts singing. She memorized the song too. Perhaps it means as much to her as it does to me.

Her voice is a deep growl, filled with fury. I watch in awe as the words come from her. Her tight muscles relax as she sings, giving me a private show.

The drums quicken and pound against the surface. Then, the chorus comes. I take her hands again, and a surge of energy passes from her body to mine as I join her.

"Split your heart open,
Invite the darkness in…"

Her voice wavers, then she opens her eyes, and we sing to each other. There's no one else in the world but us. The

last time we sang together, her voice elevated and carried mine. This time, I summoned all of my power, rooting her to reality and giving her the strength to keep going. Then she lets go of my hands, throws her head back, and screams. A scream so perfect it stuns me to silence.

Buggy's door flies open, and Ripper and Zed come inside. They don't interrupt, just stand and watch as we continue with the song. They must have gotten out of the club appearance somehow. If Ash has noticed they've joined us, she doesn't react.

We reach the final chorus, the peak of the song, the heart-wrenching moment it all comes together. I pass Ripper and Zed the lyric sheet.

They don't join in, but follow along, nodding their heads. Zed sings the lyrics under his breath as Ash blasts through the last line.

"We rise together."

She falls to her knees. Tears run down her cheeks as the music stops. She looks up at us like we are anchoring her to the world. I want to be the one who can take her pain away.

I don't offer her a hand to help her up. Instead, I kneel at her level and pull her into my arms to cradle her. The others sit down as her body folds into itself, curling against me.

"We're here," I say, stroking her hair. She's safe in my arms. "We're not going anywhere."

"You were right, Venom," she whispers. "It's not about them dating. It's about my mom. Sometimes it feels like I'm the only one who remembers her."

After the story leaked, we all knew about Ash's mom's

death, but it's different to have her open up about her struggles.

"Why don't you tell us about her?" I say.

She smiles, her anger dissipating. "Really?"

"What was she like?"

"She was my best friend," Ash says, wiping her eyes. "She was a singer and had a beautiful voice—even though she sang country. Dad never understood me, but Mom? She always knew what to say…" Her face crumples. "I miss her."

"Of course you do," I say.

Zed smiles wistfully. "She sounds great."

"She was," Ash remembers. "She really was, and then she got sick. She knew things were getting worse, and she wouldn't be around for much longer. She didn't want us to watch her suffer or forget who she used to be, so she ended it all…" She shudders, causing me to hold her tighter. I can sense her pain. It's so deeply etched in her psyche that it's changed and become part of her. "I found her."

"I'm so fucking sorry," Ripper murmurs.

What else can we say? Nothing will bring her mom back.

"The pain was… unreal," she explains. Her voice takes on a monotonous quality as if she's entering a different space in her head. A safe space that allows her to talk about something so hard. "I didn't just lose mom, but a part of me. I wanted her to be there for the big moments, like being there for my graduation or watching me on this stupid show. She's the person who I thought would never leave me behind. I… I… just wanted the pain to stop…" She's still talking but nuzzles into my chest. Her heart quickens. "I took pills one night. A load of them. What-

ever I could find. If Brick hadn't found me when he did..."

For the first time, I'm grateful she had a model-like football player in her life.

"I wanted it all to end, you know," she says. "I couldn't take it anymore."

"I get it." I nod slowly. "You needed it to stop."

"I didn't die," she says, "but the pain helped. Cutting took it away. It gave me something else to think about. When my world was falling apart, it was the only thing I had control over. My dad was different. He became a shell. He kept going, but I could see he wasn't okay."

I understand. It's the reason why my body is covered in scars. We listen silently, giving her the space she needs to let her emotions out.

"He lost the love of his life," Ash says. "They'd been each other's first and only loves. He said he'd never find someone else and couldn't imagine it. But now, he's moved on like it meant nothing. He lied to me. What if he forgets about her?"

Ash's earlier outburst at the restaurant isn't about her dad moving on; she feels like she's losing her mom again.

"He'll never forget her, Ash," I say.

"She sounds like she was an amazing woman," Ripper says. "If she's anything like you, she'll be impossible for him to forget."

"How do you think he's feeling?" I ask.

She bites her lip, stopping to think and hitting the brakes on her emotional whirlwind.

"I... I..." she stammers. A tear slides down her cheek, and I lean to kiss it away. "I know he has to be hurting too."

"I can't pretend to know exactly how you're feeling,

Ash," Zed says. Sometimes I question whether Zed has any emotions at all, but his eyes are full of care and worry. "I've never had a good relationship with my family like you had with your mom, but it sounds like she cared about you a lot. She gave up the little time she had left because she wanted you to only have the good memories. She was strong, Ash, just like you."

"She'd want you to be happy," Ripper says, "both of you."

"I know she would," Ash sighs. "But I don't want her to be forgotten."

"No one will forget her," I say. "She's part of you."

The silence stretches for a long time, each of us lost in our thoughts.

fifty-two

. . .

Ash

I know the guys are right, but it doesn't make it any easier. I've been used to seeing my parents together. The two of them. A team. Soul mates. Lovers. I expected them to spend their lives together and watch them getting old, but now...

I remember what it was like after Mom died. Dad's smile never met his eyes. He's never been good at talking about emotions, but that only got worse. When I left for Camp Harmony, I worried because there was no one around to cook for him. I panicked that the house would fall to ruin without me keeping on top of things. Is that the life I want him to have because I'm stuck in the past? Would I be happier if he died alone with a broken heart, pining over a woman he'll never see again?

"You're right," I mumble. "Mom would have wanted him to be happy. Claudia is a good person. I know she is. I know she'll care about him, but it doesn't make it less weird."

I never expected him to be with someone young and successful like Claudia. What do they have in common?

He's set in his ways, devoted to his work, and she… well, from what I know about Claudia, she cares about her job but cares about her family more. She's kind-natured, takes good care of her brother, and she was always there when I needed her at Camp Harmony. On paper, she has everything I'd want for him in a partner.

The last few times I saw him, I noticed he'd been taking better care of himself. He seemed different, happier. Isn't that all that matters?

"It'll take time," Venom's soothing voice keeps me calm.

I lean against his chest, listening to the steady thud of his heart and counting each beat.

He's right.

"I need to speak to him," I say, recalling how Dad's face fell in the restaurant. Guilt stabs me in the gut. They caught me off-guard, but I still acted like a brat. "I have to apologize."

"Speak to him tomorrow," Venom says, "when you've both had time to sleep."

"Can I stay with you guys tonight?" I ask, adding quickly, "only if you don't mind."

Venom wipes smudged mascara from under my eyes with his pinkie finger.

"Of course," Zed answers. "I'll call Cookie to let her know where you are, otherwise, she'll worry."

He's not wrong.

"How did you get her number?" I ask.

He laughs drily. "Your friend is very persistent."

"That's one way to describe her," I say. The mood is lighter, and Ripper picks up the lyrics sheet from earlier, so I ask, "What did you think?"

I need to focus on something else. Music is the only

way I ever learned to handle my emotions healthily, without blades.

Ripper's eyes sparkle as he says, "I thought it was the best fucking song we've ever had."

My heart skips a beat. "Really?"

"Really," Zed confirms, returning from his brief call with Cookie. "It was amazing."

Venom squeezes my shoulder as if congratulating me.

"Maybe you can put it on your next album?" I suggest. "I can help you with it and make sure it sounds good."

"I don't think we can do that," Zed says, sitting down on the floor next to us again and leaning against the sofa.

"But I thought you said you liked it?"

"The song is perfect," Zed says, "but we can never sing it without you. You're part of that song."

"You don't need me," I dismiss hastily, but Venom's arms squeezing tighter around me must disagree. "You'll do an even better job without me."

Ripper laughs and looks at the others. "She doesn't get it, does she?"

"Hello," I say, returning to my snarky self. "I'm still in the room."

"Don't you understand there are no Basilisks without you, Ash?" Ripper says. "You're one of us now."

I frown. "What do you mean?"

The three guys shoot each other various looks as if they're communicating through expression alone.

Zed rises and holds out his hand for me to take. I let him pull me to my feet while Venom heads to the CD player and hits play on our song again.

"We want you to join us, Ash," Zed says.

I don't know if I'm understanding what he's saying.

My mouth goes dry, and I stammer, "You mean… join the band… become a Basilisk?"

Zed shakes his head, glancing at Venom and Ripper who nod in agreement.

"No," Zed says. "You're so much more than just a Basilisk. You're Ash."

"But what…"

"Ash and the Basilisks," Zed says. His eyes sparkle. "Doesn't that have a ring to it?"

I laugh, thinking I've misheard him and missed the cue for the song's first verse.

"You can't be serious," I say as my head spins.

"Everyone knows who you are, Ash," Ripper says. "They know you've sung with us before. People would know who you are from your voice, even if you wore a mask."

"You don't have to join us, if you don't want to," Venom says hastily. "We'll understand if you want to start a solo career."

This is beyond anything I could have hoped for. Being a contestant on Popstarz already felt like living in a parallel universe, but being asked to join the Basilisks? That's mind-blowing.

"We may have to hide who we are half of the time," Zed says, "but I don't want the real us to have to pretend or hide."

Fuck.

"You don't have to give us an answer now," Ripper chips in. "You can think about it."

I don't need to think about it. I already know what I want to do.

"Yes," I breathe.

Venom's eyes light up.

"Really?" Zed asks, almost in disbelief, blinking hard, like he's trying to wake himself from a dream. "Do you mean it?"

"All I ever wanted is to produce music that means something," I say. "Your music makes me feel things I never have before. It's gotten me through tough times when I couldn't see another way out." I take a deep breath before continuing. "After I tried to overdose, I went to therapy, but it was you guys who got me through each day. Your music is the reason I got up in the morning. If I can be part of the Basilisks, it'd be the biggest honor. I don't know how it'll work, or what your fans will think, but—"

"They'll love you," Ripper interrupts. "Can't you remember the applause you got when we sang together at the Smoker?"

"But we can make it a gradual transition," Zed says. "You'll still feel the heat from Popstarz for a while. You can sing with us in a few shows here and there—just like in Port Valentine—then we can make an official announcement."

I nod, dazed. Is this happening? I have to be sure.

"But are you sure this is really what you want?" I ask.

"Do you think we'd joke about this?" Ripper chuckles. "She still doesn't believe us, guys."

"You make our music better, Ash," Venom says. "Don't you feel it when you sing with us? The electricity?"

Of course I do. The air fizzes with energy, but I thought that was natural when singing with my favorite band.

My mouth falls open. "You guys feel that, too?"

"We do," Zed confirms.

"Our music has grown over the years," Venom says,

"but we can't evolve if you're not part of us. We need you."

Ripper steps in to hold my face in his giant hands and kisses me. His kiss is soft, filled with a thousand words and promises that make the pit of my stomach flutter. Are these the butterflies people talk about?

I break away, still suspended in a state of disbelief about their offer, but Ripper kisses me again. This time, with more urgency and passion, full of hopes and dreams. I respond hungrily, wanting to prove how much I want this… how much I need them.

He presses his body against mine, pushing my breasts into his chest, allowing me to feel his heartbeat. Our hearts pound in sync.

Ripper pulls away and Zed takes his place. His kiss is harder, desperate even. His tongue battles with mine, fighting for power and control. Then he relinquishes, succumbing as I bite his bottom lip, and he groans.

He reluctantly steps aside for Venom to kiss me. His eyes meet mine in a stare that tells me everything I need to know. His gaze speaks of reassurance, safety, and want. He doesn't play games. Our noses brush together, and it makes me smile. Then his mouth seals our fate and binds us together.

"You're one of us now, Ash," Venom whispers.

The Basilisks slow my racing thoughts. All my other worries fall away as I think about how fucking lucky I am.

I unzip the side of my dress slowly. Zed's Adam's apple bobs as the teeth come undone, revealing my skin inch by inch as the fabric falls away.

"Ash," Ripper murmurs, "you don't have—"

"I want to," I snap, glaring at him. I've had a tough

night, but my want for them supersedes all else. It's not just a want. It's a need.

My dress drops to the floor, leaving me in nothing but panties and combat boots. I bend down to undo the laces, but Zed growls, "Keep them on."

As I stand, he pulls me into his arms. His hands smother me in a hot squeeze as his desperate mouth finds mine. I barely come up for air, leaving me light-headed and panting for more.

Another hand slips between my legs from behind, caressing my pussy through my panties. From the smell of his cologne, I know it's Ripper. I moan into Zed's mouth as Ripper pulls my panties down my hips and over my thighs.

My lips tingle for more, but I pause and step out of my panties. I'm unsteady on my feet, but Zed's muscled arms stop me from wobbling.

"Why am I the only one naked?" I question.

Zed smirks. "Because that's how we like it. Now, why don't you get on your knees for me, pretty girl?"

I do as he asks, moving down his body and stopping to undo his belt. His cock strains under his pants, but I intend to tease him. I take my time, rubbing his erection, before undoing his zipper. I may have listened to his orders, but I'll carry them out in my own way.

He drops his pants and pulls out his cock. I look into his eyes, batting my eyelashes, as I slide my pointed tongue up his shaft.

"You're killing me here," he moans.

The tip of my tongue glides over his head, but I'm not putting all of him in my mouth. Not yet.

I look at Ripper, who is standing next to him, and reach

for his cock too. He blinks, taken aback, but eagerly pulls off his T-shirt and undresses until he's naked.

Zed's cock jabs my cheek in frustration, but I'm not giving him what he wants. Mr. Impatient has to learn to wait—not everything is under his control.

Venom watches from the sidelines as I wrap my lips around Ripper's cock. He gathers my hair into a ponytail and watches his length disappear into my mouth. I create a tight seal as I suck, making him moan.

"Hey!" Zed objects in dismay. "That's not fair."

I ignore him, continuing to enjoy Ripper's cock as he moves my head to set the pace.

"You look so fucking good sucking my cock, Ash." Ripper smirks. "Doesn't she, Zed?"

Zed's frustration is boiling over, and that only makes me take Ripper deeper. His cock slides down my throat, and I gag, coating him in spit as my eyes water. When Ripper's thigh muscles tense, I pull away.

"Venom?" I turn to him. He might feel left out sometimes because of the bond Zed and Ripper share, but I need him to be part of this. He grins as I say, "I want to taste you."

Before, Venom would have been hesitant, but there is no reluctance as he strips. He's gradually becoming more comfortable being naked in front of the other guys and sharing me with them.

I want to show him how much I appreciate that, appreciate him, and all of his thoughtful understanding.

His throbbing cock stares me in the face, and I bow before Venom. I gaze up at the quiet guy who lived in his head for years and is slowly starting to come out.

I feel his veins beneath my tongue as I twirl my tongue around him. From the corner of my eye, I spot Ripper

reaching down to touch himself, and I use my hand to reach out and slap him away. I want to be the one in control today.

"Fuck, Ash," Ripper groans. "You're unreal."

I lick and suck Venom, edging his cock into my mouth. The heat of his erection warms my tongue, and I use my hand to assist, wrapping my fingers around his shaft, then moving up and down. His hips buck into me. He likes it.

I use only my mouth now and reach my hands for Zed and Ripper, who stand on either side of him. I take their cocks in my fist and match the pace to my head bobbing.

This evening has been a rollercoaster of emotions, but the Basilisks have proved they will be there for me. No matter what happens, I'm one of them.

Ash and the Basilisks…

They don't want me to be a temporary feature in their lives. Popstarz doesn't signal the end of us. It's only the beginning.

In my vigor, Venom's cock falls out of my mouth. My wetness drips down my inner thigh.

I stand to kiss Venom, letting Zed and Ripper spring free. Ripper creeps behind me, rubbing his cock between my ass cheeks, then sliding to my pussy. His head strokes against the wetness pooling there.

He edges inside me, and I'm ready to take him. I angle my hips, leaning forward slightly, and balance my hands by gripping Venom's shoulders.

Ripper grasps my hips, jerking them back onto him. Venom's eyes light up as Ripper pushes deeper inside me, so deep I can feel his balls tickling my ass.

"You look so beautiful when you're getting fucked," Venom purrs.

"Move," Zed grunts at him, bossy and dying for a release.

I would correct him for being impolite but, by his standards, he's already been patient enough.

Venom moves as Zed drops to his knees. He parts my legs to watch Ripper enter me from beneath, then… shit! His tongue finds and probes my clit, making me shiver.

"Eat her pussy, Zed," Ripper encourages. "It makes her tighten all over me."

For a change, Zed does what he's told. His hands lay over Ripper's on my hips as his wet tongue slides across me, lapping at the base of Ripper's cock too.

"Yes," I moan as pleasure rushes through me.

I wobble on my feet, but they don't stop. Venom senses my unsteadiness, and stands behind Zed, allowing me to bend slightly and steady my hands on his shoulders again. He's an anchoring force in the chaos that is getting fucked by two of his bandmates at once.

My tits bounce as Ripper quickens, pushing my pussy into Zed's face.

"We're going to make you come, Ash," Ripper says in a low and seductive growl.

A high-pitched strangled sound comes from the back of my throat as the first wave of my orgasm races through my body.

I tighten my grip on Venom as Zed catches my clit with his mouth, coaxing my orgasm further. A second wave comes, stronger than the first, almost blinding me as a gush of wetness squelches between my legs.

"Fuck yes," Ripper groans. He takes advantage of the opportunity, sinking deeper. "You're so fucking wet for us, baby. Drench me, Ash. Come all over my cock."

His voice sends vibrations through me, heightening the

sensation, as Zed reaches from beneath to pinch my nipple hard. The sudden pain intensifies my pleasure, making me cry out so loud that it makes me pleased we're in a garage on a quiet street.

Ripper shudders, gripping my ass hard as he shoots his load to claim me. I hardly have time to think as he pulls out, and Zed moves at the speed of a superhero to take over fucking me.

Zed is girthier than the others, but my pussy is ready. He's unrelenting, pounding into me in hard and brutal strokes that makes a slapping noise around the bus.

"You're right, Ripper," Zed says. "Her little cunt is so fucking wet and tight for us."

He's an animal, unleashing all the pent-up frustration from earlier. He takes from me, making my pussy ache from the brutal intensity, but I love it at the same time. He's fucking me so hard that even my tiny tits feel like they're about to be torn from my chest.

Suddenly, he roars. His hips jerk and twitch as he grasps my hips and spills his load.

"Fuck," he cries. "You're all ours now, Ash."

My legs shake as he withdraws. A sheen of sweat coats my skin from the exertion, and their cum runs down my thighs.

Venom puts his arm under my shoulder to steady me.

"I'll help her clean up," Venom offers, leading me to the bathroom.

It's a small space, but there's just enough room for the two of us to fit inside. The water tank on the bus is small, so showers can't be long.

"Hey," I say, eyeing his erection. My body may feel like a train has run over it, but I still want him. "Why don't you join me?"

"Are you sure?" he asks.

I grin. "Positive."

I can't help but giggle as we squeeze into the tiny cubicle together. The cool flow of water runs over us, a refreshing change from the heat of our skin.

I wrap my arms around his neck and draw him close. His wet hands cup my breasts, kneading my flesh and rolling my nipples between his fingers.

Then his hands move to my back, dancing over my spine and to my ass. I moan into his mouth, succumbing to my pussy's desire—she can't get enough.

Venom has long fingers, an advantage for playing instruments. He strokes the curve of my ass and slips between my legs to meet my slick entrance from behind.

He pulls away from our kiss. "I'm supposed to be cleaning you up."

"And you will," I promise. "After you've fucked me."

With that, he pushes me backward, raising one of my legs and hooking his arm underneath my knee.

"What if I—"

"You're not gonna fall, Ash," he says, reading my mind. "I've got you."

His cock slides effortlessly into me. He's gentle, unlike the hard and desperate urgency of the others. He takes his time, moving torturously in and out of me in sweeping strokes. My moans echo around the space over the running water.

"You feel amazing," I say, watching his cock vanish, which turns me on more. He slides out of me, so far that I can see his tip.

"No," I beg. "Please, don't stop."

I'd buck my hips, but I'm too scared moving will make me fall and break a leg.

"I won't," Venom says in a deep, seductive rumble. "I told you, I've got you."

I gasp as he plunges in again, and again, and again. My walls contract against him. They're still pulsing from my previous orgasms, but another peak rises again—slower, more gradual—like a warm rush and an outpouring of affection.

He doesn't want to hurt me, but as he speeds up, his forearm muscles tense. I scratch his back, wanting to leave my mark behind, as he tips me over the edge.

That's all the encouragement Venom needs. With a final thrust, he cums as I do. Tears spring to my eyes as my pussy holds him inside me like I never want to let him go.

I shudder as he slips out. His wet hair is stuck to his face, and water droplets glitter over his tiny freckles. I'll never understand why he gets overlooked by the Lionheart fans. He's fucking gorgeous.

"Now," Venom says, reaching for the soap, "I promised to clean you up."

I nod shakily as he lathers it up in his hands.

Is this what life is going to be like from now on?

fifty-three

. . .

Ripper | Damon

Last night was incredible. After sharing Ash with Zed and Venom, sex with any other woman wouldn't compare. She slept between me and Venom, curled up with her back against his chest and one arm draped across me. I struggled to drift off, overcome with adrenaline, but I watched her. She's part of us now, and we'll never let her go. How could we? No one else could ever make us feel the same way… and even better, she agreed to be ours.

Zed is still working out the logistics, including how to break the news to Ted. But Ash wanting to join the band is the first step and has given me the reassurance I've been waiting for.

I'm sitting in the hotel restaurant where they have a constant stream of drinks and snacks throughout the day. I have spare time before I have to help with Tiffany's singing lesson. Having to listen to her squawk is my idea of a nightmare, but knowing it won't be long until we start our new life with Ash makes being around a spoiled brat like Tiffany more bearable.

I watch a chef meander around the dining room. I frown. This isn't the same woman, but I've seen her before.

Claudia... that's it... the chef from Camp Harmony who ran the pop-up last night.

I frown. I can understand why Ash was upset, but seeing her now troubles me for other reasons. I watch Claudia check everything is okay with the pastries, and my brows furrow.

I know her from somewhere. I had the same feeling the last time we spoke on the night Ash almost froze to death on the lake. Had she come to a Lionheart concert? Was she one of our superfans? No...

Her curly hair bounces around her chin. It's brown with natural-looking highlights, but... then I remember.

"Casey?" I say aloud.

Her head jerks like someone poked her with a cattle prod. It is her. How didn't I see it before?

She pales, looking at me, then quickly checks to make sure no one else is around. She turns to inspect the cakes, but it's too late. I've already seen her reaction.

I'm already on my feet and moving across the room, but I don't want to scare her away. I clear my throat, close behind her, making her jump and almost drop the tongs she's holding.

"What are you doing here, Casey?" I ask.

"My name's Claudia," she says. If I wasn't sure she was lying, I'd believe she was sincere. "You must have confused me with someone else."

"You don't have to lie to me. I remember you," I whisper. "Why didn't you say anything before?"

"I don't want to talk about it," she says. "People call me Claudia now. My life has changed."

She looks different now. I remember her as a young

and naïve sixteen-year-old with platinum blonde waist-length hair.

"I didn't mean to scare you," I say, reaching out to comfort her. She flinches, and I drop my arm to the side.

"Look, I've got a new job now," she says. "I'm only here for a few days, and the hotel needed someone to cover last minute. I'm not here to cause any trouble. I'm here to work because I've got to look after my little brother, okay?"

"I don't want to take any of that away from you," I say. My expression softens at the look of pure fear on her face. "I thought I recognized you at Camp Harmony over the summer, but I couldn't place you..."

I'd been too concerned about Ash catching hypothermia over the chef who looked familiar. Apart from that, I hadn't seen her all summer. Maybe she'd been avoiding us.

"Yeah, well," she says, backing away, "you have now."

"I won't say anything," I say.

Her shoulders sag in relief, but her eyes narrow in suspicion.

"I want to forget what happened, okay? I don't want to be reminded of the past," she snaps, ending the conversation. "I have to get back to work."

Casey was a final-year camper at Camp Harmony when we started. She didn't sing but was a skilled musician. Piano, I believe, but my memory is hazy.

Casey was a favorite, like me. At the time, another producer from Starnote called Thomas Whitton used to help around camp. Rumor said he had a thing for young girls, girls who looked like Barbie, girls like Casey.

I didn't see Casey a lot, but I recall having a meal with her, Thomas, and Jacqueline in Jacqueline's office. They

portrayed it as an evening dinner for our development, almost like a mentorship. This was before Jacqueline and I had sex, but during that time, she dropped hints and flirted. Zed calls it grooming.

Casey hardly said a word during the meal, but I remember how he looked at her, like a starved hyena readying to devour his prey.

If Jacqueline took advantage of me, I'd bet all the money I earned from being a Lionheart that Casey—Claudia—had a similar arrangement with Thomas.

My stomach sinks, remembering how Casey left Camp Harmony shortly after that dinner. It wasn't until my final year that Thomas left. Drugs and alcohol have blurred a lot of my memories, but now I remember who she is, I can picture the dinner more clearly, leaving no doubt that it was her.

Why did Casey change her name? Maybe I wasn't the only person who was keeping secrets and had suffered at Starnote's hands…

fifty-four

. . .

Zed | Zach

After spending the night on the tour bus, I don't have long to get ready for a busy day, which includes a teleconference with a journalist and a meeting with Jacqueline about what events she has lined up for us after Popstarz.

We still have ten years left on our Starnote contract, and its ending can't come soon enough. Signing our souls to a monster organization that abuses their artists is the worst thing we've ever done.

It's funny how many kids dream about being famous, but I never wanted it. Growing up in the Royal family makes fame inevitable, but even with my background, no one explains how hard it is. It's portrayed as something to aspire for. Everyone will know your name, want to be your friend, and want to be you. But it doesn't come with a manual.

No one tells you that being a celebrity means having no rights. The public thinks they own you. By buying your music, coming to your shows, and getting cheap merch, they think that entitles them to know everything going on

in your life. Privacy is non-existent. People stop seeing you as a person.

Ash isn't like that. She sees beyond our names. I don't know how her joining the Basilisks will work, but I'll do everything within my power to make it happen because there's no other option.

Since she's come along, all our shows as the Basilisks have fallen flat. Combining her voice and ours is like a final puzzle piece slotting into place. She belongs with us.

Ripper has already left for breakfast, and Venom has holed himself up in a Starnote recording studio. He prefers being there to the hotel—no windows, fewer interruptions, and it's easier to fake that he's working.

I tidy up around the kitchen, filling the basin with hot soapy water. Ripper and Venom are slobs. They've gotten better over the years, but there's not a vast improvement from when we all shared a cabin at Camp Harmony. There are staff members who come to clean, but I enjoy it. It's therapeutic. Soothing, almost.

The door buzzes. I frown and dry my hands before going to answer it. I see Tiffany through the keyhole and consider not answering it, but that'll only make my mom angry if she hears about it.

I open it. "Hi, Tiff."

"Are the others around?" she asks, looking over my shoulder.

"Not right now," I say, but remain in the doorway. "What can I help you with?"

"Can I come in?" she asks.

"Sure," I reply, although that's the last thing I want. I step aside to let her pass. Her perfume makes my nose wrinkle. It's the same as my mother's. "Take a seat."

I take my time to close the door behind me, checking

the corridor to make sure no one is lurking with a camera. When I turn around again, Tiffany's coat is on the floor, and she's wearing nothing but lingerie.

"I thought we could get to know each other better, Zach." She smiles and saunters over, walking her fingers up my forearm. "I know you weren't keen on your mom's idea, but I thought I could persuade you. A Royal and a Lockhart together make sense."

I tear my arm out of her grasp and turn my back on her. "Put your coat back on, Tiffany."

"But Zach!" Her whine grates on me. "We have to get married. Think of what the media will say. It'll be well worth your while." Her heels click over, and she leans to whisper in my ear, "I'll do anything for you and, I mean, anything…"

My stomach lurches. Can't she take a fucking hint?

"I said, put your clothes back on, Tiffany," I insist, firmer this time.

She huffs. I don't turn around again until I hear her pick the coat up. When I do, she's pouting, but at least she's dressed.

"Are you playing hard to get?" she asks.

"It's never going to happen, Tiffany," I snarl.

"Why?" She crosses her arms. "We can help each other out. People will love us together. We look like we belong together."

That's exactly why I'd never want to be with someone like her, who cares more about image and what other people think than connection. She can't comprehend there might be more to a relationship than what the media will say. She's blinded to anything but fame.

"Looks aren't everything," I snap coldly. "I won't tell you no again."

"Why are you doing this to me, Zach?" she wails as her eyes fill with tears. "Us getting married has been a deal since we were kids. Think about how happy it'll make your mom."

I struggle to wrestle with the anger building inside me but keep my cool.

"I'm not interested, Tiffany," I say. "There is more to a marriage than keeping your parents happy and what's printed in magazines."

Her eyes widen in shock. She's not used to people saying no to her after a lifetime of getting everything she's ever wanted.

"There's someone else, isn't there?" She jumps to conclusions. "You're making a big mistake, Zachary Royal."

"I'm saving both of us from making a big mistake," I correct. "You'll understand one day."

Her incredulous expression tells me she doesn't believe it.

"You're going to regret this," she warns. She flicks her hair over her shoulder and pulls her coat tighter around her body. "You'll see."

I head to the door and hold it open. "Have a nice day, Tiffany."

She flounces away, and I slam it behind her. A threat from Tiffany doesn't scare me, but the prospect of losing Ash does.

fifty-five

. . .

Ripper | Damon

I send a message to the Basilisks group chat, texting quicker than my fingers can even keep up.

Ripper: We need to talk. Hotel room. Ten minutes.

I hurry from the dining room after hearing Claudia's revelation about her identity.

I run into Venom in the foyer. His cheeks are flushed from rushing from the studio next door. He cocks his head to the side quizzically, but I shake my head and mime, "Upstairs."

We don't speak in the elevator, but my mind buzzes. Is there something we can do with the information that could help take Starnote down?

When we reach our floor, Tiffany storms past us, tears running down her cheeks. She narrows her eyes at us as she pushes past Venom, knocking into his shoulder.

"Ouch." He rubs his shoulder. "She'd make a good football player."

Inside, Zach is washing up—aside from singing, it's his favorite way to calm down.

"We just saw Tiffany—" I begin.

"Don't ask," he growls in response, smashing his fist into the bubbles and sending them flying. "What's so urgent you have to speak to us now?"

"It's Claudia…"

Venom frowns. "The chef dating Ash's dad?"

"That's the thing," I say. "Her name isn't Claudia, it's Casey."

"Casey…" Zed repeats. "Should that sound familiar?"

"She went to Camp Harmony with us," I say, "for the first year."

"I didn't recognize her," Venom says.

"Neither did I," Zed says, drying his hands to fully pay attention.

"There were lots of people at Camp Harmony that none of us would recognize from that first year," I say.

We spent most of it partying and, when we weren't, we were so focused on our music that there was no time for anything else. Casey wanted to blend into the background. Back then, the camp was more separated. Vocalists and instrumentalists used to take breaks at different times, and it wouldn't have been difficult to slip under the radar.

"She went to one of Jacqueline's special dinners as Thomas's guest."

Venom is still confused, but Zed understands what it means instantly. "You think that he and her…"

"You should have seen her face when I brought it up," I say. "I think something happened to her. Something bad. Something she wants to forget. Do you think it's a coincidence that she gets a job as head chef at Camp Harmony a few years later?"

Being a chef at Camp Harmony isn't the same as working in a school cafeteria. It gives opportunities.

Zed rubs his chin. "So you think she blackmailed Jacqueline into getting a job?"

I shrug. It'd certainly help catapult her career, but Claudia didn't seem like the type of person to do that. "Either that, or it was part of Jacqueline's offer for her silence."

"We all know what the rumors said," Venom mutters darkly.

Thomas used to hold their hand for a little too long, helping them to "position" their bodies to give them better form. He was in his forties, charming, and handsome, but something about him gave me the creeps.

"We don't have any proof anything happened with Casey—Claudia—and Thomas," Zed says. "But if it did, she could be a second witness."

"Hold up," Venom says, "what am I missing?"

"It means," Zed begins, his voice rising the way it does when he has an idea and gets excited, "we might have a way to take down Starnote and get out of our contract for good. It gives us leverage."

"Oh…" Venom mumbles as the dominoes fall into place.

"That depends on whether Claudia is happy to talk," I say. "She seems to have gotten a lot out of an arrangement so far. She might have signed NDAs."

"But if something happened to Claudia," Zed says, "there's nothing to say someone else who was at Camp Harmony at the time couldn't make an allegation against them. With Ash and Tiffany now on Popstarz, Camp Harmony applications are higher than ever. A scandal would ruin everything."

"We have to tell Ash," Venom says. "If anyone can get Claudia to talk, it's her."

When we signed on the dotted line, we signed the best years of our lives away to a record label. We're like zoo animals locked in cages. If we can terminate the contract early, I wouldn't have to see Jacqueline again.

"We need to speak to Ash soon," Zed says. "She'll understand."

"I'll do it," I say. "It should come from me."

"But we can't get her hopes up," Zed says. "Claudia might not want to help."

If Claudia went through a similar thing with Thomas to what I did with Jacqueline, it might be too traumatic for her to talk about. I don't want to reopen an old wound and remind her of a bad time in her life.

fifty-six

. . .

Ash

My heart sinks when Ripper tells me his theory about Claudia's past. It was risky for him to visit my room between rehearsals, but he insisted it was necessary. My simmering anger from last night fades.

"And you think Thomas did something to her?" I ask. "It's a big accusation to make."

"I have no evidence." Ripper shrugs. "And I can't be sure, but if it's true and Claudia shares her story, we might be able to leave Starnote… and Jacqueline."

I want nothing more than to get Ripper away from the woman who used him and exploits her power.

My cell buzzes as my mind whirs.

"It's my dad," I say, looking at the screen.

Dad: Can we talk? Dinner tonight? I'm leaving tomorrow.

I show Ripper the text.

Me: Invite Claudia along too. It's time we all

spoke.

"There," I declare. "I'll talk to her later."

"Are you sure, Ash?" Ripper asks. "You don't have to do this. I know that it's a little—"

"It's fine," I cut him off, then sigh. "I need to face them again sooner or later."

I can't stand arguing with anyone—let alone Dad. He replies quickly, giving me the name of the restaurant and the time. I wave my cell and say, "It's done."

Dad suggested we meet at a small Italian place, not far away from the hotel, but somewhere I'd never noticed before. I suspect it's a recommendation from Claudia, which means it will have fantastic food.

I wipe my clammy hands on my jeans, then tuck them into my pockets. My nerves are rising. After being confronted by Dad and Claudia last night, I'm not sure how I'll feel seeing them together again, and somehow, I also have to speak to Claudia alone.

I'm last to arrive and spot Dad straight away. He plays nervously with the buttons on his shirt, frowning in worry. Claudia is next to him, placing her hand on his arm in reassurance, and his body relaxes. Seeing them as a couple is strange, but the age gap doesn't seem as pronounced. You wouldn't look at them and think he was her father.

Candles flicker on all the tables, creating a warm glow and a homely vibe. It smells of freshly made bread, garlic, and juicy tomatoes—three of my favorite things.

Claudia sees me first. Her eyes widen with nerves or panic. After last night, she might be worried I'll cause another scene. She gives me a nervous smile and raises her hand in an awkward wave.

I'm not at the point where I can beam at the two of

them yet. They still lied to me. But I push through those feelings and go over to join them.

Dad stands, almost knocking over the table and sloshing a glass of overfilled water over the sides.

"Ash," he exclaims. "You made it."

I nod, managing a small smile. He looks like he wants to hug me, then decides against it and awkwardly pats my arm instead.

We all sit down. Dad's eyes dart toward the door like he'd rather be anywhere else. He and I both.

Unlike the two of us socially awkward Coopers, Claudia breaks the silence and says, "Thanks for coming, Ash."

I shrug nonchalantly. "It's fine."

Another tense silence stretches out. I glance at the clock on the wall behind them. Is time passing slower than usual? We're all relieved when a server places a bread-basket on the table, and we thank them before returning to our strained silence.

I fidget with the tablecloth, playing with the frayed hem, and Claudia nudges Dad in the ribs.

"So, Ash…" Dad clears his throat. "I know last night was… a shock… I…"

It's painful listening to him trying to apologize. It's like hearing a child learning to read, stumbling over every word, and trying to sound things out.

"Why didn't you tell me?" I ask, getting straight to the point.

"Well…" He runs his hand over his face and loosens his top button. "I thought… I… I was nervous."

"Nervous?" I arch an eyebrow. "Dad, this is me you're talking to."

"I never thought…" His voice fades. This is killing him.

"I never thought someone like Claudia would be interested in me. She's younger, talented… I didn't want to say anything in case it didn't work."

"Oh, Jack…" Claudia's eyes soften as she shakes her head.

She looks at him like she really cares. I only thought Mom would look at him that way. I feel a pang of pain, not because I don't want him to be happy or to be loved again, but because I'll never see Mom looking at him like that again.

"I didn't want to upset you or tell you before I was sure it was serious," Dad admits, squirming in his seat.

"And is it?" I ask. "Is this something that's going to last?"

Dad looks hopefully at Claudia. If it wasn't my father, it'd be sweet. No one wants to see their dad with puppy-dog eyes like he's back in high school.

"I care about your dad, Ash," Claudia says. "I know it probably seems weird to you. I get that there's an age difference, but that doesn't matter to me. When we first met, we just clicked…"

"At Camp Harmony?"

I recall how they left together after the final show.

"Yes." Claudia blushes. "I asked for his number after that."

Dad smiles fondly. "I thought she was joking around."

"Then I covered myself and said I'd send him a recipe because I didn't think he felt the same way I did," she says. "And then we started texting more…"

"You can text?" I ask Dad. "More than a few words?"

"I'm getting better at it," he grumbles.

"Says the guy who used to be scared phones would brainwash you," I mutter.

The atmosphere lightens as Claudia laughs at Dad's sulky expression.

"I get why you didn't want to tell me straight away," I say, "but I wish you told me sooner or at least told me you were dating."

"I never wanted you to find out the way you did," Claudia says quickly. "We wanted to meet you and tell you together, but someone couldn't stay at the table I reserved."

"I got lost," Dad says sheepishly. "I'm sorry you had to find out like that, Ash. Claudia's right. It's not what I wanted. I know it'll be hard for you to see me with someone else after your mom, but it'll never change how much I loved your mother—how much I'll always love her. But Claudia makes me happy, Ash."

My gaze softens. "I want you to be happy, Dad. I'm not mad you've found someone else... It's just..."

"Something that will take time to get used to?" he suggests, finishing my sentence.

I nod and fiddle with my napkin.

"You don't have to stay," he says. "If you need space, that's okay—"

"I want to stay," I interrupt. As the initial shock is wearing off, I see Claudia cares about him as much as he cares about her. I grin at Claudia. "But I'll never call you stepmom."

Claudia laughs, sounding more like the person I came to know at Camp Harmony. Her shoulders relax as she winks. "You can count on that."

"So, we're okay?" Dad asks hopefully.

"It'll be weird for a while," I reply, "but I want you both to be happy. If you think you've found that with each other, I don't want to stand in your way."

Dad beams. After Mom died, he aged ten years overnight. But now, in his new clothes, he looks younger again.

"Plus," I add cheekily, "your new clothes suit you."

His ears turn pink.

Claudia tips her head to the side. "What new clothes?"

Dad gives me a *thanks for nothing* look.

"I just got some… new clothes… that's all," he stammers.

"You picked them by yourself?" I ask, now genuinely shocked.

Dad's cheeks flush, and he mumbles, "Brick helped me."

My stomach drops at hearing Brick's name. "Oh, right…"

"He feels awful for what he did and how things are with you, Ash," Dad says. "He wants to make it right."

"It's too late for that," I say.

From my tone, Dad knows it's best not to push me, and our server returns to take our order and end that part of the conversation.

We keep the conversation light-hearted for the rest of dinner. Claudia tells me about her plans to cater for events while Kelly is in school.

"How is it going to work with the two of you?" I ask.

Claudia will be traveling all over the country, Kelly's in school, and Dad has to stay in Meadow Springs for work.

"We'll find a way," Claudia says confidently. "We can make it work."

"If you'll excuse me," Dad says, getting up to go to the bathroom and leaving the two of us alone for the first time.

This might be the only chance I get to ask about her past.

"Thanks for being so understanding, Ash," Claudia says as soon as he is out of earshot. "I need you to know I'm serious about this. I won't hurt him."

"I'm glad," I say. I picked up on their cute—if a little vomit-inducing—vibes throughout dinner, and I believe her. Their personalities complement each other. She pulls Dad out of his introverted shell, and he gives her the stability she craves. "If you don't, you'll have me to deal with."

"It's still early days," she says, dropping her voice to a whisper, "but I think this could be something special."

"I hope it is," I say, conscious our time is running out. As much as I'd like to continue to vet her as my father's new girlfriend, I have to ask her about what happened at Camp Harmony. I have my guys to think about, too. "While we're here, there's also something else I want to talk to you about…"

"Shoot," she says, digging her spoon into a decadent chocolate mousse.

"What happened when you were at Camp Harmony?"

Her arm freezes halfway to her mouth.

"What do you mean?" she asks cautiously. "I've worked there for the last few summers. It's a good job."

"I'm not talking about when you worked there," I say. "I'm talking about when you were a camper and used to call yourself Casey."

The color drains from her cheeks.

"Who have you been talking to?"

"You were there one summer, right?" I push gently.

"H-how did you find out?" she stammers. "The only person… did Damon tell you?"

Who's Damon? Shit… it's Ripper she's talking about.

"Fuck," she mutters, rising panic creeping into her voice. "If you know, then other people will find out."

"Hey!" I try to calm her down. "It's only me, okay? No one else will find out. I've not told anyone. But I think, if I'm right about why you left, you may not be the only person who was affected. Your story could help other people."

"Ash, you don't know what you're asking," Claudia murmurs. "I can't talk about it, okay? You don't understand what'll happen if I do."

"There are people I care about who can help you," I say. "Did something happen with Thomas?"

She flinches at the mention of his name, and her whole body shudders. She doesn't have to answer for me to know Ripper is right.

"It happened years ago. Why are you asking about this?" she asks. "Does your father know?"

"No," I say, "of course not."

"What happened is best left in the past," she says, "for everyone."

"You're not the only person who Starnote took advantage of at Camp Harmony," I say, deciding not to ask her any more questions. "The corruption goes all the way to the top. People in positions of power have exploited other kids there."

"What exactly did Damon tell you?" Claudia is smart. Her eyes narrow. "And why did he tell you?"

I decide to throw a curve ball into the mix. She won't tell me anything unless I give her something in return, and she knows why I care.

"We're together," I say, deciding I'll ask Ripper for forgiveness later—even though he'll probably be delighted.

"You and Damon Archer?" Her mouth falls open. "Does your dad know?"

"No," I blurt out. "And I don't want him to, either."

She nods, biting her lip. At that moment, Dad returns to the table.

"Have I missed anything?" he asks.

"No," I lie.

"Would you be able to get us another drink at the bar?" she suggests, noticing there's a long line.

"Got it," he says, taking the hint. "I'll leave you to have more girl talk."

I smile. "Exactly."

"How long have you been a thing?" Claudia leans across the table. "You and Damon?"

"We met at Camp Harmony, and it went from there…"

That's not a fabrication—apart from admitting that when I first met him, I didn't know he was Damon Archer at all.

"And he told you he recognized me, right?"

"And I don't need you to tell me what happened," I say quickly, "but Damon mentioned the dinners. What happened to you with Thomas happened to him with Jacqueline." I hope he won't mind me sharing this, but there's no other way to gain her trust. "Who wouldn't do anything for a record deal?"

"It was the same with me," she whispers, wringing her hands. "Thomas… he…" She swallows. "When I reported him to Jacqueline, she paid for my silence. Not many people knew, but I had a scholarship to Camp Harmony, and it was my only chance. After playing piano, I always liked to cook, so she sent me to culinary school and paid for it all, then gave me a job after. All for keeping my

mouth shut. I didn't know what else to do. I was desperate and needed the money."

I shake my head as my lip curls in disgust.

"Damon's story is similar, and he's stuck," I explain. "The Lionhearts signed a Starnote contract, and there's nothing they can do to free themselves."

"I thought there was something wrong at the time." She wrings her hands. "But I never said anything to him. Maybe I should have."

"None of it is your fault," I say.

She nods, and her expression hardens in determination. "What do you need from me?"

"Truthfully," I say, "I don't know yet. If they tried to leave, it might help to have someone to corroborate their story."

"I signed all sorts of waivers." Claudia chews on her bottom lip. "I was young and didn't know what I was signing. All I knew was Jacqueline would give me a better life and more opportunities than I could have hoped for. I just got custody of Kelly, and I couldn't risk losing him either. Jacqueline told me they might take him away if I pressed charges. She said no one would believe me over someone as powerful as Thomas. The narrative would have been turned around, and I'd look crazy. I couldn't take the risk. Then I changed my name to Claudia. Whenever someone said Casey, I could hear *him* saying it." She shudders. "Claudia was my grandma's name, and I always liked it. I needed a fresh start and wanted Casey to disappear."

"We don't want you to get in trouble," I say, "and the Lionhearts won't want that either. But it might help them bargain if Ri—Damon—can mention he knows what happened to you. That way, you don't have to say

anything and won't be breaking any rules. But they'll never mention your name without your permission."

"I..." Her voice trails off. She's conflicted. "I don't know what I'd do if I had to see Thomas all the time. I thought Jacqueline covered up what happened to me because she cared, and now... She's been covering her ass this whole time."

"You couldn't have known," I say.

"I'll help in whatever way I can," she says. "I'm stronger than I used to be. I'm not a scared camper, and I don't need Jacqueline's help to make a name for myself. I don't want my success to be at the expense of someone else's suffering. You have my number. Just let me know what you need."

Dad rejoins us with glasses of wine for them and an orange juice for me. Claudia and I exchange a look of mutual understanding.

I don't know what's coming next, but maybe the Lionhearts can find a way out of Jacqueline's clutches after all.

fifty-seven

. . .

Venom | Levi

"Ted?" I answer his call. "What's up?"

It's unusual for him to contact us outside our pre-agreed hours.

His words come out in a nonsensical string. "Mom's house… package… threat…"

"You need to talk slower," I say.

He catches his breath and says, "I got a letter under the door. It…"

"What did it say?" I ask sharply, covering my other ear to hear him because Ripper and Zed are watching a loud zombie movie. I wave my hands to catch their attention and put a finger to my lips. "What did the letter say?"

I put the call on speaker, and they gather around.

"It says they'll kill me if I keep working with you," Ted says. He's an introverted guy who lives in his mom's basement. Death threats are not unusual to the Lionhearts, but this is the first time we've had one as the Basilisks.

"Is that all?"

"No…" He gulps. "There's a picture of Ash, and it says they'll kill her too."

Ripper is already putting on his jacket.

"Is there anything else in the envelope?" I ask.

"No," he says. I hear him shaking the paper. "Actually, there is one other thing. A match."

"A match," Zed mumbles to himself.

"We need to get to Ash," Ripper says, jumping straight into valiant knight rescue mode.

"She's out with her dad tonight," Zed hisses, trying to calm her. "She'll be fine. He's a cop. He'll protect her."

Ripper's nostrils flare. I can't say I don't feel the same way, but Zed's right. She won't be in danger with her dad around.

"Just stay calm, Ted," I tell him. "It'll be fine. Someone's trying to scare us."

"How did they get my address?" he asks. "Look, my ma is freaking out. This isn't what I signed up for, Venom. I love your music—you know that—but I don't want to be involved if you've got a crazy-ass stalker. I'm not down for that shit."

"It'll be fine, Ted," I reassure him, although I don't feel entirely confident. Whoever is watching us has crossed the line. "This kind of stuff happens all the time. It's just words. It doesn't mean anything."

"If you say so," he says, although he doesn't sound convinced.

"Let us know if you get any other letters," I say.

We end the call, and I turn to the others. "What next?"

"I'm going to speak to Cookie," Ripper says. "She'll be able to tell Ash what happened when she gets in. She has to know."

I nod in agreement. "Let me do it."

"But—" Ripper argues, and Zed raises his hand to stop him.

"It makes sense," Zed says, "Venom is Ash's mentor. It'll be less suspicious. We all have to be extra careful now. We don't know what this person is planning next."

"Fine," Ripper groans, slumping into a chair and crossing his arms. "But we need to figure this out…"

I leave the two of them to speculate and head for Ash's room. Cookie answers within seconds. An amazing smell wafts from inside and makes my stomach rumble. She brushes a freshly dyed pink loc out of her eyes. "What're you doing here?"

"Can I come in?" I ask, glancing over her shoulder nervously, then speak louder for the benefit of anyone who may be listening. "I want to run over a few things ahead of Ash's next performance."

"Sure," she says, picking up on my weird choice of words.

I sniff the air as she closes the door behind me. "Something smells good."

"I've made pizza," she says, "I made enough if you want to stay?"

I shake my head, despite my rumbling stomach trying to argue.

"You know Ash isn't here, right?"

"Yeah," I say, "but something happened."

"Did you get any more mysterious packages?" she jumps straight in.

"Whoever is threatening us is escalating," I say. "Ted got a death threat, and he wasn't the only name mentioned."

"Ash?"

"We want to make sure she's protected," I say. "It might only be words, but…"

"I'll speak to the producers to see if she can get extra

security," Cookie says, stepping into action. "I'll tell them she's received threatening comments online, and I'm worried about her safety. It's not exactly stretching the truth. Trolls are everywhere these days."

Damn, she's good.

"Thanks, Cookie," I say. "We appreciate it."

I turn to leave, but she calls after me, "Lev—Venom, there's one more thing."

"Yeah?"

I spin to see her brandishing a pizza cutter like a weapon. "If any of you do anything to hurt her, I'll cut your balls off. Lionhearts or not."

I gulp. "Yep."

"Good." She smiles sweetly and returns to sawing through her pizza. "Are you sure you don't want a slice?"

"Actually," I grimace, "I'm not feeling that hungry anymore."

fifty-eight

. . .

Zed | Zach

"What now, Ted?" I answer my cell in an angry roar. My patience is dangerously thin. If he's whining like a little bitch about death threats again, I'll lose my shit. After rebuffing Tiffany's advances, finding out about Thomas and Claudia, then hearing about Ash's life being threatened, my bad day limit has been reached. I won't soothe his fucking ego like Venom. "I don't have time for—"

Ted is hysterical, blabbering, and making zero sense. I didn't think a grown man's voice could be that high-pitched, but he could hit serious notes with that range.

"It wasn't an empty threat," he wails. "It's Buggy! I've just gotten a call from the guy we're renting from. The fire department has just left. They've spent an hour trying to track me down. The whole thing… burned down… the match… and someone was inside."

"Someone was inside?"

Venom is downstairs with Cookie. Ripper is next to me. I hang up the phone and call Ash. My heart races as it goes straight to voicemail. Could she have gone over there?

"We have to go," I roar. "Buggy now!"

"What's happening?" Ripper asks, running to keep up with me.

We fly down the stairs, racing along the corridor to Ash's room, where Venom is leaving.

"Is she here?" I demand.

Venom frowns. His eyes widen in alarm. "No, why?"

I've heard enough. We can't wait for the elevator, so I sprint and take the stairs. I call her again. Nothing. No answer. Fuck.

"What the fuck is going on?" Venom pants.

We race from the building, and I push past the photographers shoving cameras in our faces.

"Get out of my fucking way," I roar. Their camera flashes go crazy, but I don't care about what the headlines will read tomorrow… *Zach goes on a rampage. Is the pressure getting to Zach?* Fuck it all. Fuck them.

A cab is conveniently waiting, and I jump inside.

"Pick up already," I scream, hoping she'll answer and wasn't stuck in the blaze. Nothing!

I bark instructions at the apprehensive cab driver. Ripper and Venom are looking at me like I've lost my fucking mind.

"There's been a fire," I tell them, not caring about our usual protocol about breaking cover. It wouldn't make sense to the cab driver, anyway. "Buggy's destroyed."

"A fire?" Venom asks. His voice is cool and measured, the calm anchor in the center of a storm.

"Yes, a fucking fire. What do you think I meant, dumbass?" I bark. "Ted called."

"The match…" Venom murmurs under his breath. "It makes sense. The same person who sent the packages…"

"Someone was inside the garage when it went up in flames," I say.

"What?" Ripper's knuckles turn ghostly white from how tightly his hands ball into fists. "Ash…"

"She's not picking up," I growl, hitting redial again and again. Nothing. Why won't she answer?

"She's with her Dad," Ripper reasons. "She can't have gone to Buggy without us. Without the code to the door, she couldn't have gotten inside."

"She knows the passcode," Venom admits, hanging his head, unable to meet my eyes. "I told her when we went there alone. I wanted her to know it in case she met us there or if she needed some space."

"Fuck!" I kick the passenger seat in front. The driver casts a nervous look over his shoulder but stays quiet. He knows who we are. I can imagine him speaking to journalists and how they'd spin the story…

Zach Royal is on the loose.
Where it all went wrong for Zach Royal.

We all try to call. Nothing.

"It's me," Venom says, getting through.

We all pause.

"Is it her?" I ask. "Venom. Is it her?"

Adrenaline has taken over my body. My heart is thumping so hard that I don't know whether I want to smash something or throw up.

"It's Cookie," he replies, then into the phone, "Is Ash back yet? She is? Uh-huh, she just got in? Great thanks."

We sigh collectively in relief. I slump back in the seat. She's safe. Our girl is safe. But for how long? Being associated with us puts her in danger.

Venom turns on the speaker phone, and Ash's voice fills the car. "What's going on?"

A massive weight lifts at hearing her voice again. I take a deep breath in, letting the air fill my lungs, but it doesn't help calm me down. Ripper squeezes my knee, sensing my struggle.

"Guys?" Ash asks. "Can you hear me? What's happened? You freaked Cookie the hell out."

"It's Buggy," Venom says. "There's been a fire, and we're heading over to check the damage."

"I'll meet you there."

"No," I growl. "Stay at the hotel where you're safe."

"You can't tell me what to do," she reminds me. Why does she have to be so goddamn difficult? "Buggy is like a part of the family. I'll bring Cookie with me too."

She hangs up before I can argue.

"Can't we go any fucking quicker?" I snarl at the driver.

Ripper takes my hand and says, "You've gotta calm down."

But I can't. Knowing Ash is okay is the most important thing, but my chest aches for what we're going to find at the garage.

Buggy may be a vehicle, but it's the heart of the Basilisks. Our safe place. The tour bus has been our sanctuary for years, the one place where we can truly be ourselves. It's kept our secrets and been there for us when no other person has. I never felt my family's house was somewhere I belonged, but Buggy? It was our fucking home.

When we arrive a few blocks away, I jump out.

"Wait." Ripper tugs me back as the cab hurtles away, pleased to be rid of its passengers. "We need to cover our faces."

How could I be so stupid? I'm not thinking clearly. My

control is slipping. Ripper must have grabbed a backpack on our way out and takes out three masks, handing them to each of us. We always carry them in case of emergencies.

"When did you—" I ask.

"I'm not completely reckless," Ripper says. "I've learned from the best."

I fasten the mask, pull my hood up and tuck my hair in. The smell of fire greets us, and smoke hangs in the night air, dancing underneath the streetlights.

We head down the street. Ted has parked at the edge of the yellow police tape. A few onlookers mill around, curious about what's happened, but arson is another standard activity in this neighborhood.

Ted perches on the hood of his car, hunched over and holding his head in his hands. The guy doesn't handle stress well.

The fire department is still on the scene, but they have put the blaze out. The metal shutters are blackened from the flames. Judging by the gasoline stinging in my nostrils, nothing will be salvageable.

"What's happening, Ted?" I ask as we join him.

"It was a girl," Ted explains. "They found her over there." He points opposite the garage. "Apparently, the blaze threw her back. It got out of control fast."

"Who was she?" I ask.

"They don't know, but she was blonde…" he says, and his entire body shudders. "Or half of her head was, at least. She got burned pretty badly. I saw them put her in the ambulance when I arrived." Ted heaves like he's about to throw up and croaks, "I need to take a walk."

He walks further up the road, clutching his stomach, and I turn to address the others. Even though I can't see

the faces, they'll be having the same thoughts as I am. Who else could it be?

"Tiffany," I confirm.

It makes sense. She had an obsession with wanting to be perfect. She was furious at my rejection. How long has she been watching and following us around?

"Guys!" Ash's voice comes from behind us. Cookie trails behind her as she runs down the street into Ripper's open arms. He squeezes her tightly, refusing to let go as she spins to stare open-mouthed at the garage and the charred remains of Buggy. Her voice is choked. "Are you okay?"

"Holy shit," Cookie comments. "That looks…"

"Unsalvageable," I say.

"Does anyone know what happened?" Ash asks.

"A girl set it on fire," I reply coldly. "A blonde girl willing to do anything to get what she wants."

"Tiffany." Ash covers her mouth with a shaking hand. "But how can you be sure?"

I raise my eyebrows, even though she can't see it. At that moment, my cell buzzes. I check the caller. I don't have time to speak to my mom right now. I send it to voicemail, but then she calls again, then a string of incoming texts flood in:

Mom: Zachary! Pick up your phone right now!

It seems to buzz more aggressively when it's her messages coming through.

Mom: Emergency.

Mom: Answer your phone.

"I have to take this," I say grudgingly and step away from the group to take the call. "Mom, I'm kinda in the middle of something right now…"

"Where are you?" she snaps. "It sounds loud."

"If this isn't important, I can hang up—"

"No!" I hold the cell away from my ear as her high-pitched screech almost deafens me. "I've just received some bad news."

My fingers tighten around the phone. "What news?"

"Rita Lockhart has called," she says. "Tiffany has been rushed to the hospital. She's been in an accident—a fire, they're saying. It's going to be announced on the news soon."

"What fire?" I ask. "What happened?"

"They don't know yet," she says flippantly. "I'm telling you all I know."

"Is she going to be okay?"

There's a pause. "I assume so, as Rita is already asking if you can go over to the hospital. It'll be good publicity for you to run straight to her bedside, don't you think, darling?"

My hands shake in anger at her sheer audacity. "You can't be serious right now."

I'm never going to be Tiffany's number-one fan, but it doesn't mean I'll exploit an injury for the fucking media.

"Don't be so melodramatic, Zachary," she scolds. "I'm just saying that—"

I end the call. I don't want to hear any more of her bullshit. That toxicity drove Tiffany to become a monster.

"It was Tiffany who started the fire," I tell the others. "My mom called to let me know she's in the hospital."

"Fuck," Ash sighs, slumping back into Ripper. "She was the one behind it all? The letters? The threats?"

"It looks like it."

"But why would she do that?" Cookie asks.

"Because our families want us to get married," I explain, "I think all of this was part of a bigger plan that went wrong."

"That means Tiffany knows who we are..." Ripper says.

"As long as she thought she had a chance with me, she wouldn't have told anyone," I say.

Everything clicks into place. Tiffany would have used the knowledge to negotiate. My earlier rejection must have tipped her over the edge. She needed serious help and hours of therapy.

"We should get outta here," Venom says. "There's nothing we can do."

I nod in agreement, but where do we go from here? Buggy burning down hasn't only cost us a place to live, but the flames have stolen years of work.

We filled Buggy with masks and costumes from all our previous shows, along with our memorabilia. With it, a part of us has died too.

As everyone turns to leave, I hang behind. Ash whispers something in Ripper's ear, then breaks off. She returns to slip her fingers through mine and says, "This isn't the end."

But if it isn't, why does it feel like it is?

fifty-nine

. . .

Ash

We return to the hotel in different cars. Cookie and I arrive first, then the guys are due to follow later. We arrive at the back of the hotel and sneak through the kitchen. News has leaked about Tiffany's accident, and the main entrance is swarming with paparazzi.

"This is crazy," I mutter. How could this have happened? "Do you think she'll be okay?"

"It's too early to tell," she says, madly scrolling through social media. She's been glued to the breaking online news for the entire journey, reading various articles and snatches of information. So far, no details have been released.

When we reach the hotel lobby, I immediately sense that something is different. The place is a ghost town, apart from Amber impatiently tapping her heel on the floor.

"Where have you been?" She sniffs the air. "You smell like smoke."

"We went to a BBQ," Cookie lies smoothly, "and the

last time I checked, Starnote doesn't keep its contestants prisoner."

Amber's lip curls. "All contestants are required in the dining room. The hotel is on lockdown until further notice."

"Is this about Tiffany?" Cookie presses. "I saw the news."

Amber blocks Cookie from following me.

"She's my manager," I say, standing my ground. "She goes where I go."

"Fine." Amber sighs in exasperation. "Jacqueline has gathered everyone together to speak to them before the press conference."

Cookie and I exchange nervous glances. It won't be long until the Basilisks get back, either.

"Hurry up!" Amber clicks her tongue impatiently, jostling us into the dining room. When we're inside, she slams the door shut behind us.

Meredith comes to join Theo and me.

"Have you heard about Tiffany?" Meredith asks. Her eyes are bloodshot like she's been crying. Even though they aren't friends, she's the type of kind person who cries whenever something sad happens. "It's awful."

Tiffany is a victim of her selfish desires. The fire wasn't a freak accident. She'd purposefully set Buggy alight and had stalked the Lionhearts for weeks. After what she did to me in the summer and whatever involvement she had in Riley's accident, it was only a matter of time before her actions caught up with her, but it doesn't mean I wished for her death.

"We'd better sit down," Cookie says as Jacqueline sweeps into the room.

Jacqueline doesn't look concerned. If anything, she has

an extra spring in her step. She'll be thinking about how this will affect the viewing numbers.

"Take a seat, everyone," she says. "I have some news."

We all sit down, and she continues.

"You may have read about an incident that happened earlier this evening with Tiffany Lockhart," she says. "Unfortunately, I can confirm these stories are true. Tiffany was involved in a fire. She's now receiving urgent medical care."

"Will she be okay?" Theo asks, his voice hoarse from crying. He's been pining after Tiffany since we arrived and looks devastated by the news.

"She is in a stable condition," Jacqueline answers, "but she has suffered serious burns that will require surgery."

"Where was the fire?" Meredith asks. "Was it near here?"

"I heard from the Lockhart family that Tiffany was visiting a friend earlier this afternoon," Jacqueline says. "Early reports suggest there was a gas explosion. She was in the wrong place at the wrong time."

How much did it cost the Lockhart family to pay off the cops and keep the story under wraps? When you have enough cash, it's no problem to cover how Tiffany started the fire. There was no question it was arson, but her family would wonder why Tiffany took a sudden interest in that garage. It won't be long until they find out what she knows.

"After speaking to the Lockhart family directly," Jacqueline says, "we will continue with the show, and Popstarz will air this weekend. As Tiffany will no longer be able to participate, this will be the finale."

"What?" I stammer, unable to hold my tongue. "You're kidding, right?"

Jacqueline narrows her eyes. "The Lockharts have assured me it's what Tiffany would have wanted. The competition must go on."

I resist the urge to scoff.

"That means..." Jacqueline claps her hands. "You'll all need to work on an extra song to perform with the Lionhearts."

Theo, Meredith, and I look at each other in stunned silence. What should be a celebration feels more like a funeral, but as Jacqueline said, the competition must go on...

sixty

. . .

Ripper | Damon

After hearing about the Popstarz finale, I text Ash.

Ripper: We're on our way to your room now.

"I can't believe they're going ahead with the show," Venom says.

"Jacqueline would never cancel the show riding on the tails of a media feeding frenzy," I mutter.

"It'll be good for the Lockharts too," Zed says. "They'll want to paint Tiffany as the perfect victim and milk the situation for all it's worth."

Cookie answers the door, and we pile inside. "Just come right on in." She rolls her eyes and calls to Ash, "We're gonna need a bigger hotel room to fit all three of your boyfriends."

"You've heard the news then?" Ash asks. "The show is going ahead, and we have to sing together."

"What a fucking day," Zed growls. He's in a grumpy mood and collapses onto the sofa next to Ash

"You're telling me," I say. "The spawn of Satan almost sends herself back to hell, then Ted quits."

"Ted quit?" Ash frowns. I take a seat on her other side, making myself comfortable. It's nicer than the one in our suite—probably because ours came from an old museum.

"The fire freaked him out," Venom says, sitting at the table next to Cookie.

"And the icing on the cake is we have to sing for the nation and dedicate it to the psycho who burned our home down," I joke, trying to make light of the situation.

"We have to do it," Zed says. "We have no choice."

He's drained and looks like he's done ten rounds in a boxing ring. I've never seen him lose control in front of the press like he did today. But I was there to lift him up again. It's what we do. He's spent years protecting the band. Now it's my turn to step up.

"Maybe we do have a choice," Venom says. "But I'm not sure whether you're going to like it."

"What're you thinking?" I ask, noticing his eyes sparkle in the way they do whenever he has a good idea. It's the same sparkle when he's penning the most incredible lyrics. "What if we perform with the contestants, but do it our way?"

"You mean, out ourselves as the Basilisks?" I burst out laughing. "No fucking way. We'll be dead."

"It won't be long until Tiffany talks," Venom says. "Our days in hiding are numbered. We all know it. Our secret is going to blow up in our faces just like Buggy did. Wouldn't you rather we do it our way?"

"Jacqueline would sue us," Zed says. "Either that, or she'd pay for a hit. It goes against everything we signed in our contract."

"A contract we can't get out of," I murmur bitterly.

"Actually," Ash chips in, "you may have extra leverage to work with."

"You spoke to Claudia?" Zed sits up straighter, like she's given him an adrenaline shot to the heart. "What did she say?"

"She confirmed Ripper's theory." Ash nods slowly. "And she'll help however she can."

"We could get out of the contract," Zed says, "and end the Lionhearts for good."

The cogs in his mind are whirring. This is the smart guy I fell in love with, the one who plots and schemes his way out of any situation.

"But are you ready to do that?" Cookie asks. "Do you understand what you're giving up? You're the biggest boy band on the planet. How do you think people will react when they find out you're the Basilisks? The impact will be huge. It could jeopardize everything you've ever built and end both bands."

"It's going to fall apart regardless," Venom says. He's already made his mind up. This is what he's wanted for years. It's exhausting to live your life like an actor. "We wanted to start over with Ash, anyway. Ash and the Basilisks, remember?"

Cookie turns on Ash. "When were you planning on telling me this?"

"Hey." Ash holds up her hands in surrender with a sheepish smile. Damn, she's cute with a guilty grin on her face. I look away before my mind jumps in with dirty thoughts about what I'll do to her next time we're alone. "We've been busy. Besides, I wanted to make sure that… the guys didn't change their minds."

"There's no going back if we do this for any of us," Zed says. "And, in case you've forgotten, the Basilisks don't have a manager anymore."

Cookie clears her throat. "I have an opening."

Ash's eyes light up and she gushes, "Cookie is the best."

Her enthusiasm is enough to sell it to me.

"That works for me," I say, propping my feet up on the coffee table.

Zed won't be so easily convinced. "What actual experience do you have?" he asks, raising one eyebrow.

Cookie snorts. "I'm one of the few people who know your true identities now, and I haven't told anyone. Doesn't that say enough about who I am?" She flips her hair over her shoulder. "I'm Ash's manager already. You're Ash and the Basilisks, remember?"

"We may not even need a manager after all this goes down," Venom mumbles.

"Are you kidding?" Cookie scoffs. Her passion is infectious. "You're gonna need one more than ever. I'm already thinking of all the shows I can line up for you—I have connections everywhere. Think about all the new fans you'll convert to metal music. I've already done enough research—"

Zed raises his hand to stop her from continuing and says, "If we get out of our Starnote contract, then we'll talk."

The fact he hasn't said no tells me he's open to the idea.

"Deal," Cookie says. "And if this works out, we'll need to talk about the constant sexual tension in the room."

Zed splutters. The sheer shock on his face makes me snicker. Maybe Cookie will be the best manager we've ever had.

"But are you sure about this?" Ash asks. Her deep brown eyes are full of concern. "You'd be coming out on live TV to the world. There's no going back anymore. There'd be no hiding."

"I'm done hiding," I say. "I'm sick to fucking death of being a Lionheart. You've shown us we can be brave, Ash."

"You can't do this for me," Ash says firmly. "You have to do it for yourselves."

"And we will," Venom says.

"Whether we want to accept it or not, the Basilisks are over in the way we know it," Zed says, his voice shaking. He pauses to gather his thoughts, then nods decisively. He's made his decision. "It's time."

"But what about your family, Zed?" Ash asks.

His muscles tense. This will be the hardest for him. The fallout will be unreal.

"We've made enough money as the Lionhearts for us to live comfortably for the rest of our lives," he says. He's not saying it to brag, it's simply a fact. "If my family never speaks to me again, that's their call to make."

"This isn't the same as Camp Harmony," Cookie reminds us. "When Lei, the twins, and I hijacked the final show, we knew everyone. We called in every favor we had. Popstarz is so heavily produced and monitored, it won't be as easy to pull off."

I grin. "Leave that to me."

I know most of the staff. Sure, they won't willingly want to be part of this. However, if we give them a backing track and request certain instruments to be present on stage, there's nothing they can do when the cameras are rolling.

"What song will we sing?" Ash asks.

"Easy," Venom says. "*Vampire For Her*."

"Who knew you were a romantic?" Zed mutters as Venom glares at him.

Our lives will change by the end of the week and, for the first time in years, I'm excited about what's coming…

sixty-one

. . .

Ash

Jacqueline has forced all contestants to pay Tiffany a hospital visit. The clinical smell of disinfectant and the long windowless corridor makes me want to claw at my skin.

Journalists were waiting outside, primed to take photographs of our show of solidarity for the girl who should have won—or at least that's what social media is saying. They're wrong, but Tiffany will be happy with the headlines.

"Do you remember the scene in *Mean Girls* where Regina gets hit by a bus?" Cookie whispers in my ear to lighten the mood. "It feels just like that."

I snort. She isn't wrong. We're in a private room waiting to be called one at a time to deliver a gift to Tiffany's bedside. I'm clutching a bunch of roses that have scratched my arm. They're like Tiffany—beautiful on the outside but hiding sharp thorns.

A nurse trots in and checks the list of names on the clipboard. "Ashley Cooper, you're next."

Theo's shoulders slump in disappointment. He'll be seeing her last. I got the impression he was an arrogant asshole, but Tiffany's accident has seriously affected him. Dark rings under his eyes signal he hasn't slept, and according to Meredith, he's hardly left his room.

"Wish me luck," I murmur to Cookie, who isn't allowed to join me—not that she'd have wanted to.

I follow the nurse down the corridor. No one likes hospitals, right? Bad news and death slither between the walls, and the bright lights trick you into losing your sense of time.

Being here brings back bad memories. I remember being pushed along on a hospital bed, looking up at the spinning ceiling. Brick and Dad were at my side, telling me it'll be okay. All I felt was anger that I hadn't been able to finish the job properly. I didn't stay in the hospital for long after my overdose, but if I had, it'd have been enough to make me want to tip more pills down my throat.

"She's had a full day of visitors," the nurse says, pausing by Tiffany's door. The blinds are drawn. "Before you go inside, I have to warn you that Tiffany might look a little different from what you remember."

I nod. Jacqueline has briefed us on Tiffany's burns, but I'm not prepared for what I see when the nurse pushes open the door.

Half of her face is covered in bandages, and they've had to shave most of her hair on the right side away. She stares vacantly at the clock on the wall, not acknowledging me as I step inside.

"Look, you have more friends here to see you," the kind nurse says to her. I would use the term friends loosely. "I'll be back soon."

I place the flowers on a table. It's hard to find space as it's already full—the entire room is. Gifts are everywhere: flowers, stuffed animals, chocolates, and cards.

"Uh... hi," I say, not sure where to begin. Tiffany doesn't reply, and I sit down in a chair to count down the minutes until I have to leave. "You've got a lot of cards."

She sighs. "Why did you come, Ashley?"

Even though her mouth has escaped the worst of the burns, there are a few blisters, and every word is an effort for her to say as it pulls her skin.

"To see if you were okay," I say, although we know that's a lie. "And because Jacqueline told us too."

"You must think I deserve this," she croaks.

"No one deserves this," I say, "not even you."

She's been punished enough without being reminded of the dangers of playing with gasoline and matches when she doesn't know what she's doing.

She sniffs. "I don't want your sympathy."

"Fine," I reply.

"Good," she snaps.

I twiddle my fingers and check the time. It's not even been a few minutes yet.

"Everyone is treating me like a victim." She barely moves her lips, but I can decipher what she's saying. "But you know the truth, and so does my mom."

"She knows the full truth?"

Tiffany winces. "She thinks I'm a pyromaniac. It's not the first time I've been involved in accidents."

"Your mom loves you."

Tiffany laughs, but it's hoarse. She groans and stops.

"My mom will love the attention of a burn victim for a daughter," she mutters.

She has no reason to tell me this. For the first time since we met, this is her talking from the heart about how she feels.

"That sucks," I reply lamely. What else can I say?

"You must hate me," she says.

"You're not exactly my favorite person in the world," I say, deciding she has enough people kissing her ass.

"At least you're honest," she says. She painstakingly turns her head to meet my eyes. "I've always been jealous of you."

"Jealous of me?" I splutter. "You're the girl who has everything: fame, success, an incredible voice. Most people want to be you."

"Zach didn't want me," she says. "You don't care about the rules. Maybe that's why he likes you."

"Some people aren't meant to be," I say, trying to steer the conversation away from the subject.

She's plugged with so many drugs that, even if she told anyone what she thought was going on with me and the Basilisks, they wouldn't believe her—at least not until after the show.

"I don't care about that now," she says. "No one is going to want me now. Just look at me. I'm a monster."

"There's more to love than looks," I say.

"Not for me," she mutters. "I'm a bitch. I tried to drown you, remember? You don't have to be nice."

"Everyone deserves another chance," I say, "even the bitch who tried to drown me."

"My career is over," she says. "I should have died in the fire. It's what I deserve."

"Hey," I object, standing and moving closer to her. "I know from experience that life gives us second chances."

"Easy for you to say when you have everything."

"You should know better than anyone that appearances are deceiving," I say.

"But no one is going to look at me the same again."

"You're not a victim, Tiffany," I say firmly, cutting off her train of thought. "You're a survivor, and you're going to get through this the same way you get through everything—the good and the bad. You'll do whatever the fuck it takes."

She has no answer to that, but I swear a small smile crosses her face.

"Good luck in the finale," she mumbles. "I'll be watching."

Tiffany would never apologize, so that's the best I'll get. One accident doesn't change a person overnight, but there's a shift in her.

Tiffany's door bursts open, and Theo stumbles inside.

The nurse is close behind him and raises her voice in disapproval. "I told you, no more than one person in the room at once."

"I couldn't wait anymore," Theo says, dropping his bouquet to the floor and rushing to Tiffany's side. He takes her uninjured hand.

"I don't want to see you like this," she says.

"Tiff…" He squeezes her hand. "I'm not going anywhere. I've not slept since I heard because I've been so worried."

A machine beeps as her stress levels rise. "But look at me."

"You're as beautiful now as you were the first day I saw you," Theo whispers.

I've seriously underestimated him…

"I'll see you outside, Theo," I say.

Tiffany's actions may not have landed her the guy she wanted, but maybe she can find redemption and love after all.

sixty-two

. . .

Venom | Levi

Rehearsals have plagued every hour of our days since Tiffany's accident. As well as dealing with Popstarz, we've had to deal with logistical arrangements to sort out what's left of Buggy.

The Popstarz finale is tomorrow. Ash and Cookie are celebrating with their friends, Leila and the twins, who have come to watch the show. Usually, Popstarz does a pre-show party, but it wasn't appropriate after what happened to Tiffany. It hasn't stopped Jacqueline from arranging a post-show party, though.

The Basilisks are spending the last night of our old life together, just the three of us.

Ripper pours each of us our second drink. A somber mood hangs in the air like we're at a funeral.

"So this is it..." Zed says, raising his glass. "The last night before everything changes."

We clink our glasses together and down the amber liquid. Ripper refills them.

"Can we do this?" Zed asks, doubt creeping in. "Are we ready?"

"It's time now," I say. "We've spent years living in the shadows. We can't do it anymore."

"I spoke to a lawyer earlier," Ripper says, "although Claudia can't make an official statement, we should have enough grounds and supporting evidence to get out of our contract with Starnote—if they even want to keep us signed to their label after what happens tomorrow."

"She won't want us after the show," Zed says definitively. "None of the big labels will."

"But we'll have Ash," Ripper says with a grin. She has come into our lives and turned everything upside down for the better. "There'll be no more sneaking around or having to wear masks everywhere."

"True," I say, "but they're still part of who we are."

My heart plummets, remembering all our memories have turned to ash. The masks, the costumes… everything that made us the Basilisks is gone.

"You're right." Ripper smirks. "Dressing up is way too much fun not to do."

"It won't be the same after this," Zed mumbles, "but every band must evolve. Deep down, I think I knew it would come to this eventually."

He's right. We've had close calls. Many times when we've wondered if someone spotted us. Having to change cars, venues, hotels, appearances… it's exhausting and unsustainable, even though we were damn good at it.

"Why don't we share some of our favorite Basilisks stories?" Ripper suggests. "Is it time for us to know the story behind your pumpkin mask?"

"Maybe it's a good thing that one burned," Zed jokes, "it was gathering a cult following."

Ripper snickers.

"You don't remember?" I ask. From their blank expressions, they have no idea what I'm talking about.

"It's from our first full moon party at Camp Harmony," I explain. The night got messy and out of control, as most of them did. But it was the night I found my people, guys who would become my brothers. "We decided to dress up..."

"Oh, yeah." Ripper slaps his knee. "I went as a ghost and made out with too many chicks under that sheet."

Zed scowls and shushes him, nodding for me to continue.

"Anyway," I continue, "I didn't have a costume, and we found a pumpkin in the canteen. I spent ages carving it and wore it to the party. When we got back to the cabin, it was just the three of us..."

It was a chilly night. We staggered back after getting lost in the woods and taking a few wrong turns. We talked about possibilities for the future and what we wanted to achieve with our lives.

"We were wasted," Ripper recalls.

"But we got chatting about metal..."

I shared my love for metal music with them. It's not something either of them had listened to before. Ripper liked Black Sabbath, but Zed had only been exposed to mainstream garbage.

"And we asked you to sing for us," Zed adds, remembering now.

"I was nervous," I say. It was intimidating to sing for the most talented guys in the camp. It was a weird fluke that I ended up sharing a cabin with them. After getting scouted through busking and securing a scholarship, the camp was already over-subscribed, so they had to put me somewhere. "I thought you'd laugh at me."

"You were terrified," Ripper says, "but—"

"But I had my pumpkin mask," I remember fondly. "I said I'd only sing for you if I could put it on..."

"And that changed everything," Ripper says.

I nod, taking a swig of my drink. That performance opened their eyes overnight. From then, we spent our spare time listening to metal, and it set us on a journey. We started experimenting with our voices and finding our inner screams together... but it was about more than the music. It brought the three of us together and bonded us for life.

"You brought the band together, Venom," Zed says.

"I may have brought us together," I murmur, "but you kept us together."

Without their encouragement, I would have never returned to Camp Harmony or tried to make music again after what happened at the open mic at the end of our first summer.

"We've been through a lot," Ripper says, "but our biggest challenge is coming."

When we unmask ourselves, there's no going back.

sixty-three

. . .

Ash

"Before we go onto the next round of songs, we'd like to invite a special guest to the stage to say a few words," Tessa says. We watch from the screen in the green room as Rita Lockhart heads onto the stage. "As we know, Rita's daughter, Tiffany, was involved in a tragic accident earlier this week and had to leave the show."

"Thank you, Tessa," Rita says, taking the microphone. "I speak for Tiffany, and the entire Lockhart family, when I say the show must go on. It's what Tiffany wants. My daughter is a strong woman. We know she'll make it through this, and she's watching right now from her hospital bed."

The camera zooms in as Tessa speaks directly to the camera, "Well, Tiffany, we have compiled clips of your best Popstarz moments for you to look back on. And here they are..."

A thematic song plays over a moving montage, projecting clips of Tiffany's performances and some behind-the-scenes clips. They've done a great job to make

her look like a popular and well-liked contestant—rather than the bitch who everyone, apart from Theo, avoids.

"We all wish you a speedy recovery, and we know you're going to do amazing things," Tessa says, closing the section off. "I'm sure Tiffany is as excited as we all are about the contestant's final performances coming next. Our finalists will all be singing with our very own mentors, the Lionhearts."

The studio goes wild, clapping and cheering. Little do they know this is going to be the last time the Lionhearts perform if everything goes according to plan.

My palms are so sweaty, I'm not sure I'll even be able to hold a microphone. Thankfully, Meredith and Theo are going first.

"I don't know if I can do this," I murmur to Cookie, my knee jumping up and down.

"You've got this, Ash," Cookie reassures. "Just keep watching the show."

Meredith is incredible. Despite the Lionhearts supposedly being the stars, she overshadows them. Her voice gives me goosebumps as she sings a power ballad. There's not a dry eye in the house.

Theo is next. He wavers on a few notes but gets a giant round of applause, likely because magazines have reported him as being Tiffany's doting boyfriend. People love that shit.

"Fuck," I say, wringing my hands in my lap. "I don't know if I can do this..."

Popstarz is aired live. There are no do-overs. The world is watching, and they're going to find out who the Lionhearts really are.

"It's going to be fine, Ash," Cookie says, taking my shaking hands in hers. Her tone is so convincing, I almost

believe her, but she can't know for sure. "The guys know what they're doing."

"Do they?" I ask. "I haven't heard from them since Zed texted this morning."

We talked through a rough plan, but there were still a lot of details I wasn't sure of. Will they go through with it, or will they change their minds at the last minute? If they do, I wouldn't blame them for it.

The guys have sung flawlessly with the other contestants—well, as flawless as you can be when you're singing on auto-tune. It's weird to hear them perform as the Lionhearts. They sound flat, devoid of the complex layers of emotions that go into the Basilisk songs.

"What if it all goes wrong?" I mutter, getting up and pacing the room. "What if—"

Cookie stops me and puts her hands firmly on my shoulders.

"You can do this, Ash Cooper," she says. "You're the bravest and strongest person I know."

"I don't feel like it," I mumble, wanting to throw up.

"Think of your mom," she says, "think about how proud she'd be. Your dad and Claudia are in the audience watching. We're all behind you, cheering you on. You're not alone."

A crew member comes over. "We're ready for you, Ash."

Thank fuck I'm slathered in makeup so people can't tell my skin is a shade of gray.

I take a deep breath.

This is it.

The moment that will change our lives forever.

sixty-four

. . .

Zed | Zach

Ripper, Venom, and I gather in a circle like a sports team about to go onto the field for the biggest game of their lives. Venom is strangely calm, accepting of the inevitable. Ripper's body is buzzing with nervous energy and excitement. And me? I'm trying not to think at all because, if I do, I'm scared I'll run.

"This is it," I say, mustering my courage. "There's no going back after this."

Us singing with Ash is the last performance of the evening.

"We all know the plan, right?" Ripper asks. "We've got this."

Before I perform, I'm normally brimming with confidence and accustomed to putting on a show. But this time, nerves consume me. My hands shake, but I try to hide it. I need to hold it together for the others.

Tonight, people will see who I really am. Not the show pony. Not the masked metal star. The real me… and that is fucking terrifying.

"We all know what to do," Venom confirms, and I simply nod.

Ripper coordinated our performance well, orchestrating a clever ruse.

"You're up," the producer's voice speaks to us through the earpiece.

We stand on the right wing, ready to head back out. On the left side of the stage, through the curtains, Ash stands alone.

I see her. Her long black dress sweeps the floor and has a slit up both sides, showing her legs but not going high enough to reveal her scars. It has a plunging neckline that's fucking hot, but she makes it look elegant too. Her black hair is perfectly poker straight with bright red lips, reminding me of a younger, sexier Morticia Addams.

She must sense me watching as she looks over and catches my eye. She smiles, and all my worries dissipate. We're doing this for us, but we're doing it for her too. For our girl.

"They're all here," Ripper whispers triumphantly, "all the instruments we requested."

"And last but not least," Tessa's voice booms, "we have Ashley Cooper, who is singing *Hold Me Tightly* with the Lionhearts. You may remember she covered this in an earlier week."

Tessa exits, and swirling smoke fills the stage. The audience plunges into darkness and cameras pan along the front of the stage, ready to capture every moment of our last performance as the Lionhearts.

"Let's do this," I growl, undoing the collar on my shirt.

There's no going back now.

sixty-five

. . .

Ripper | Damon

The lights hit us as we stride to take our places to applause. Apart from the judge's table, everyone else is in darkness. It's better that way.

Ash walks out from the other side of the stage, meeting us in the middle. I sense her nerves, but I meet her gaze and nod.

I've got you, and we've got this. Everything is going to be okay.

Ash moves to her starting spot where she's been told to stand during rehearsals. It made sense to choose to sing *Hold Me Tightly* after Ash's earlier cover. Plus, it was slower, and with a few extra instrumental additions, it played into my plan perfectly.

Ash's fingers close around her microphone as Zed moves to stand by her side. I slide behind the drum kit, and Venom grasps his guitar.

A few seconds pass, then the music starts. The melody to *Hold Me Tightly* plays, but we miss our cue. The production crew [illegible] fast, looping back and restarting the song

We miss our cue again, staying silent and staring into the darkness.

Zed clears his throat as Jacqueline shuffles in her chair. Her nostrils flare. This isn't what she expected.

Jacinta speaks to Jin. I read her lips, and she asks him, "What's happening?"

"We have a special surprise for you today," Zed says. Jacqueline's eyes narrow into thin slits. Now she's fucking furious and out for blood. His voice shakes, but he stands strong. "We're going to sing a new song tonight. A song you won't have heard before."

Zed looks at Ash, and she smiles to reassure him. We've got this. She's our rock.

Ash may be one of our reasons for doing this, but it's not just because we want to be with her. She's shown us what our lives could be like.

Now we're fucking ready to step into the unknown.

sixty-six

. . .

Venom | Levi

"We've kept a secret from you all," Zed says as the song continues to play in the background. He looks straight into the camera lens in a piercing stare. "A secret we'd like to share with the world."

We're doing this. I don't need to check to know the production team is panicking.

"We've been hiding who we are and living a lie for years," Zed announces. Whispers ripple through the audience. "You've known us as the Lionhearts, but we're actually a band called the Basilisks." Zed pauses and grins at Ash. "Now Ash and the Basilisks."

The audience and judges don't understand what's going on. Why would they? None of them have heard of an obscure metal band, or if they have, it's because they watched a video of Ash performing with them in the summer.

Jacqueline talks rapidly into her earpiece, but she can't shut it down. It's too late. She can't cut the feed. Whether she likes it or not, our faces are being streamed all over the world right now by hundreds of companies.

I don't know what's going to make her more furious: the fact we're the Basilisks and have kept it from her, or that we're stealing her finale.

Ripper hits his drumsticks together and screams, "One, two, three."

He smashes the drums, and I play the guitar. It's the first time I've performed without a mask as a Basilisk.

Zed throws his head back and releases a scream that echoes through the studio, stunning the audience into silence. It's primal, raw, and fucking perfect. The Basilisks Wiki boards will be going crazy right about now.

Then Ash steps in. She doesn't hold back, embracing her true raspy voice. Her singing makes the hairs on the back of my neck stand on end as she harmonizes with Zed.

sixty-seven

. . .

Ash

The dizzying high of an adrenaline rush replaces my earlier fear.

This is the biggest Basilisk performance to date, and we're fully exposed. It's just us and the music. Using the backing tune of *Hold Me Tightly* was a stroke of genius. It gives a gentle, almost lullaby-like quality to the song, and it's a nod to what they're leaving behind.

Ripper pounds the drum surface. Out of the corner of my eyes, I see him thrashing around, throwing his hair. The wild abandon on his face as he lets go is one of the sexiest things I've ever seen.

Venom thrashes his guitar strings expertly—fingers I know are equally talented in other ways. As a Lionheart, he avoided the camera. He was the spare part. But now he looks right at home. Comfortable, at ease, and finally happy to be in his skin.

Then there's Zed. His voice tugs at my heart and soul, making me wish I could stay in this moment and listen to him forever. I hear it all—his pain, anger, frustration, and sadness. All of his emotions fall from his lips and strike a

chord deep within me. He's faced his fear tonight, and he sounds fucking incredible.

I sing by his side, unapologetically myself. I don't manipulate my voice to fit their mold, and I don't hold back. As we reach the chorus, I lean into my natural gravelly tone and unleash my growl.

My whole body shakes from the sheer power of the four of us colliding. Singing alone on a big stage gives me a buzz, but singing alongside the Basilisks takes it to another level.

I take a breath between the lines and, at that moment, I fully realize what I've known all along.

I love them.

All of them.

Zed, Ripper, and Venom.

This isn't a fling. What they've done tonight shows me it's more than that. How we'll do whatever it takes to be together.

I'm in love with the Basilisks, and knowing that sends my voice to crashing heights I didn't know I could reach.

Mine and Zed's voices feed off each other, building and stretching, pushing our limits like we're in an exhilarating chase.

We meld as one and roar the ending line:

> "Split her heart open,
> Because I'm a vampire for her."

Zed knocks the microphone to the floor as soon as the music stops, making a screeching noise. We're not met with applause, only silence. The power is zapped, and the lights above our heads are extinguished.

Zed's hand finds mine in the darkness, and he pulls me

with him off the stage. I focus on putting one foot in front of the other.

Everything rushes by like we're in a dream as we move through the corridors. The crew gapes as we pass them. They're all frozen to the spot and open-mouthed as if time has stopped. I bite my lip to stop myself from laughing at their bewilderment. Haven't they heard metal before?

"You guys did it." Cookie runs toward us, throwing her arms around my neck, then opens her arms wider for the guys to join in a group hug. "You all killed it!"

"We have to get outta here," Zed says nervously, glancing over his shoulder at the approaching army of security and producers. What are they going to do? It's not like we committed a crime. "I'm not ready to face the fallout tonight."

"That's already sorted," Cookie says. She thrusts a backpack into my hands. "All of your cell phones are in here. This way, follow me."

We follow her as the producer finds us and starts asking questions. None of us answer him. All I can focus on is Zed's warm palm, and how he is my anchor to reality.

Cookie takes us to a fire exit and hurries us out the back. Now it's my turn for my jaw to drop.

"What the…"

Dad, Claudia, and Brick are standing in the parking lot. Zed's grip tightens when he sees Brick, and I squeeze him back in reassurance.

"What are you all doing here?" I stammer.

"Cookie told us something might happen," Dad says.

"I figured it was best for everyone to leave together," Cookie says matter-of-factly. She thinks of everything. "It won't just be you that the press will want to speak to."

Claudia's gaze strays to me and Zed's interlocked hands. She raises her eyebrows mischievously and says, "It looks like we've got a lot of catching up to do."

Dad and Brick are less impressed.

"Ash…" Brick steps forward. "I wanted to be here to support you—even if I'm the last person you want to see right now."

Actually, he's wrong. He's exactly who I needed to see to prove this is happening. Brick made a stupid mistake. But if the Basilisks could shed their Lionheart identities, I can move on from what happened.

I grin. "If you ever do something like that again…"

"I won't," Brick promises. "I've got your back, Smash. You know I do."

"Thanks for coming tonight."

He didn't have to come to the finale, especially when he expected a frosty reception. We've still got a long way to go until our friendship is back to where it used to be, but I don't want to hold on to any grudges.

"And you're with…" Brick's eyes widen. "The Li... and you're…"

"The Basilisks," Zed growls.

"So you're the band my daughter has been listening to for years," Dad steps in, crossing his arms.

Unlike Brick, who was a secret Lionheart fan, Dad doesn't listen to much outside of grunge and eighties metal.

"She's part of the band now," Ripper says, extending his hand. "It's great to meet you, Sir."

Dad grasps his hand, squeezing so hard that Ripper's fingers click.

"Let him go, Dad," I hiss. He does, reluctantly, and poor Ripper massages his fingers. I nudge my head

toward a barrier that's holding back a flock of paparazzi. "Look, Dad, while I appreciate you wanting to do the whole protective thing, can you save it for later? We all need to get out of here."

"Fine," he grumbles, side-eyeing the guys. "We have to talk. Soon."

"Come on." Cookie opens one of the two waiting car doors. "Ash and the Basilisks in this car, everyone else in the other. Chop, chop!"

"But what about you?" I ask her.

"I'll hold down the fort here," she promises, then winks. "I'm your new manager, remember? I've got it covered."

I let go of Zed's hand to hug her.

"I couldn't have done this without you," I whisper. "Thank you for everything."

"You can thank me when you're not at risk of being murdered by Jacqueline," she says, squeezing me back so tightly I struggle to breathe. "Now go already."

We jump into the car and keep our heads down as we drive out. Flashing cameras light up the tinted windows. As soon as we're a few blocks away, we can relax.

"Don't you think we should have stayed for the winner's announcement?" Ripper asks cheekily.

His suggestion is so ridiculous that I burst out laughing. Zed and Venom start too, and now that we've started, we can't stop. We laugh so hard that tears roll down our faces.

This is the moment we'll remember forever as being the beginning of Ash and the Basilisks.

sixty-eight

. . .

Ripper | Damon

"Where are we?" Ash asks, pressing her nose against the glass as we drive through unfamiliar streets.

"We have one last surprise for you," I say, something I spoke to Cookie about ahead of time.

"Don't you think we've had enough surprises for one night?" Ash asks, raising an eyebrow.

"You'll love this one," I say as the car comes to a halt on a nondescript street. I take a blindfold out of my pocket and wave it in front of her face. I've come prepared. "Turn around. I don't want you to see ahead of time."

"Seriously?" she groans but turns around anyway.

Zed and Venom know what I've been planning, but it's a surprise for them, too. I'm super pumped for them to see it. I place the silky fabric over Ash's eyes and tie it in a tight knot behind her head, being careful not to catch her hair.

"No peeking, okay?" I say as the car stops a few minutes later. "We'll guide you."

When we've navigated Ash out of the car, Zed and

Venom take her arms to steer her around the back of a building.

"You better not be taking me to a serial killer's lair," she grumbles. "How much further do we have to go?"

"Just a few more seconds," I say.

As we turn the corner, Venom's eyes widen. "Woah…"

"Are you ready, Ash?" I ask, sneaking behind her to wrap my arms around her waist.

"Uh-huh."

I untie the blindfold to reveal my surprise.

"Holy shit," she exclaims. "Is this what I think it is?"

We stand in front of a giant tour bus. Mechanics have been working around the clock to get it ready. After Popstarz, I figured it'd be good to have a place to stay until we found something more permanent.

"It's all ours," I say proudly, taking her hand. "Do you want to see inside?"

She nods, dumbstruck, as I guide her to the door. The bus is black. Instead of having orange flames over the sides like Buggy, a white snake slithers across the paintwork.

We pause at the steps, and I bow, "Ladies first."

The interior's not fully decorated yet. I want us to personalize it together, but it still has everything we need. A living area with black sofas that convert to a giant bed, a kitchen area, with a nice bathroom and an extra-large shower. It has fantastic speakers alongside a cinema screen that rolls down from the ceiling, and of course, no tour bus of ours is ever complete without a bar.

"So…" I nervously watch her look around. "What do you think?"

"It's…" Her voice trails off, then she turns and throws

her arms around my neck, almost knocking me over. "It's perfect."

"We want the best for you," I say. "And we're gonna give you it."

"You've already done enough," she says. "All of you have."

"You're everything we could want, Ash," Zed says. "You're a Basilisk now."

"And we wanted to show you how much we love you."

Shit. Did I really say that? It came out so easily. Ash freezes, and so do the others.

"You love me?" she whispers.

"Um…" I rake my hand through my hair, feeling like a total ass. "I-I-I—"

"Of course we do." Zed steps in to save me. He always knows what to say when I don't. He cocks his head to the side and grins a Hollywood smile that melts hearts. "Didn't you know that already?"

"I…" An adorable blush creeps over her cheeks—yet another reason why I'm so fucking in love with her. She can't hide how she feels. "No one's ever said that to me before."

"You better get used to it," Venom says. "Because I love you, Ash. We love you."

Her eyes fill with tears as she replies, "I love you too, all three of you."

sixty-nine

. . .

Ash

The sound of my pounding heart fills my ears. It's deafening, louder than any drumbeat.

The Basilisks love me.

And I love them too.

Everything falls away and fades to background noise: Starnote, Popstarz, Tiffany… none of it matters.

Ripper moves closer and kisses me. It's tender and deep, putting all of his emotions into it and making me feel like the most special person in the world. He pulls away breathlessly to let Zed take his place. His kiss is harder and more passionate like he has something to prove. It takes away any doubt that he means it. He bites my lip and steps back for Venom to step forward.

I've never been in a position where I'm unsure about what's going to come next, yet so confident in knowing everything will be okay.

"We love you, Ash," Venom says, stroking the hair around my face. His eyes burn into mine, making me lose myself. "I think we have from the moment we met you."

"You're…"

How can I explain how much they mean to me? The men who pulled me from the pit of depression. The men who ignited a fire and a passion for music that's kept me going. To listen to the Basilisks is a privilege, but to be loved by them… I can't find the words.

"I don't know what to say…"

"You don't have to," Ripper murmurs, standing in front of me and running his hand down my side. "We're not going anywhere. We're in this together. Ash and the Basilisks."

Ash and the Basilisks…

How did we get here?

I lock eyes with Ripper. A primal rush takes over me as I reach for him. He responds in kind, kissing me as I claw at his clothes, desperate to feel his skin on mine. He pulls his T-shirt off as Venom slides up the slits in my dress from behind.

I moan into Ripper's mouth, desperate for more, while Venom squeezes my ass and yanks my panties down.

Zed approaches from behind Ripper, already naked. I don't know when his clothes came off, but I don't care. I want him. I want all of them more than I've ever wanted anything.

Zed kisses Ripper's shoulder, then bites the sensitive skin where his neck meets his shoulders, making Ripper groan and break our kiss.

Zed's arms slide around Ripper. His gigantic hands stroke his torso, pushing me back a little to give him space. I watch as Zed's hands stroke Ripper's pecs, abs, his delicious V-lines until Ripper whimpers as Zed strokes the tip of his cock.

Meanwhile, Venom's fingers slip between my thighs from behind, moving around the floaty fabric. He strokes

my heat—I'm already dripping for them. Two fingers push inside my wetness, making my body shudder with pleasure as they fuck me.

"Fuck," I cry. "I need you. I need all of you."

Ripper smirks, his pupils dilated like crazy. "And we need you."

The animalistic drive to be filled with all of them at once consumes my body. I can think of nothing but our bodies colliding, just as our music had. The connection we share is deeper than sex. I feel it in the heavy longing deep in my core that draws me to them like flowers to the sun or werewolves to the fucking moon.

Venom withdraws as Ripper helps me take off my dress.

"Get on your hands and knees for us, baby," Ripper demands.

Zed throws the cushions off the sofa, making it deep enough for me to get on all fours comfortably.

"Like this?" I ask, arching my back and wiggling my ass.

"Just like that," Ripper says, approaching me from the front as Zed disappears into the bathroom to retrieve something.

Ripper steers his cock into my mouth. He throbs against my tongue, begging to be sucked, and I'm happy to oblige.

The sofa dips as Venom comes from behind. He grasps my hips as his silky head rubs against my entrance, where his fingers have been.

I moan over Ripper's cock and push back onto Venom to push him deeper.

Zed re-enters with a grin. He smirks, enjoying the

show as he squirts lube and slathers himself with it. "She looks so fucking good taking you both."

Ripper threads his fingers through my hair, guiding me, and pushing my head further down his cock. I slather him with my spit as he slides in and out.

"Her pussy is so wet for us," Venom says. He parts my ass to get a better view of him entering me, and Zed chuckles. "And so fucking tight."

Venom thrusts into me hard, filling me and making the room spin as I arch my back.

"I hope your ass is as tight as Ash's pussy," Zed purrs.

I look up to see Zed taking his position behind Ripper. He's going to take him as Venom's taking my mouth, and it's fucking hot.

I slow down, moving to lick and suck on Ripper's balls while Zed squirts lube over his ass. After all his planning, he deserves a special treat.

"Are you ready?" Zed whispers seductively in his ear.

Ripper nods as I wrap my lips around his shaft. His thighs tense, and he sighs as Zed edges into him from behind. I stay still, letting Zed's gentle thrusting move Ripper into my mouth.

"I fucking love you guys," Ripper groans.

As we fuck on our tour bus, and a toe-curling orgasm builds inside me, I can't help wondering… Can life get any better than this?

one year later...

. . .

Ash

"How are you feeling?" Ripper asks.

He sneaks up behind me, kissing my neck and sending a shiver of longing down my spine. I yank my mind out of the gutter because we have zero time to think about sex right now—even though it's what we spend most of our time doing when we're not working on the new album.

"Excited," I reply. His cock hardens against me, and I wiggle to tease him. My faux leather skirt hugs my ass and leaves nothing to the imagination. "But it seems like I'm not the only one."

He groans, licking down the side of my neck. "Are you sure we don't have time?"

"No, we don't," Zed says firmly, entering the room. He smirks. "Well, definitely not enough time for what I'd like to do to her."

My pussy heats at the thought.

I turn to face him and pout. "Is that a promise?"

"You know it is," Zed replies with a wink.

I sigh and return to the mirror to fix the final touches

on my makeup. I'm donning black lipstick and a heavy smokey eye. Why not go all-out, right?

I run a brush quickly through the fiery red ends of my hair. I finally let Cookie dip-dye it, and I love what she's done. The new color reflects how our life has changed in a year. A fire Tiffany set caused our life to spiral in another direction, and now we're rising from the ashes.

"Why are you all hiding back here?" Venom asks, poking his head around the dressing room door. "Cookie will lose her shit if we don't go out soon. The crowd is wild."

"Let them hang on a little longer," Zed says. "The best things come to those who wait."

"Exactly," I agree, rubbing my lips together. Perfect. "Has Cookie heard any more from the lawyer?"

It's been a long legal battle, but we finally received notice that Starnote has released the Lionhearts of all obligations. It leaves a country of mourning Hearties wondering what went wrong and what happened to the band they used to love so much.

I've read all the conspiracies. Some people think I'm a bad influence—an evil woman who corrupted innocent guys. Others blame Ripper and his wild antics. Some claim we've joined a cult. None of their comments get to me anymore.

"Yep," Venom declares. "The paperwork is all done. We're finally free."

It's been hard, but we've helped each other get through it. Since the Popstarz finale, we've spent most of our time on the road, traveling across the country—even stopping at Meadow Springs to see Dad and Claudia.

"It's about time," Ripper mutters. It's taken its toll on him, but he's coming through the other side.

My cell buzzes with a message from Claudia. It's an image. I open it to see her, Dad, and Kelly crowded around a laptop to watch the live stream of our first show of the tour together.

I flip the phone around to show the guys. "Look who's rooting for us."

Claudia and Kelly moved in with Dad a few months ago. She doesn't miss city life, and it's given her the home she's always wanted for Kelly. In fact, she's looking to open a new restaurant in town.

She isn't the only one who messaged.

Brick: Good luck, guys. Go smash it!

Brick wants to enjoy the single life for a while. He's interrailing around Europe to find himself. A bigger company bought his dad's business and ensured his parents would always be comfortable. Its sale gave Brick a chance to reconsider what he wants now that his future isn't mapped out. Hopefully, he finds what he's looking for.

Even Meredith texted to wish us luck. After she won Popstarz, we kept in touch. She's currently on a Popstarz revival tour with other contestants, including Theo and Tiffany, who are now officially an item. Funnily enough, Jacqueline never asked me to take part.

"Okay." Cookie bursts in with a clipboard in hand. Her love of lists has only grown, and we keep her busy. She's great at keeping the guys in check. They've grown to love her as much as I do, even if they collectively groan whenever she walks in. "If you guys are busy screwing in here, I swear I'll—"

"We're coming out in a second," I promise.

"Before you do," she says, "we have some VIPs for you to do a quick meet and greet."

The guys look just as confused as I do. It's the first we've heard about it.

"Cookie," Zed says, "we never agreed to—"

He stops talking as the door flies open, and we're greeted by the joyful gurgle of a baby.

"Surprise!" Conor cries. He carries a gorgeous baby boy in his arms. "We wanted to be here to congratulate you on your first show."

Leila follows behind him. She's glowing.

"Oh my gosh!" I rush over.

I'm not a baby person, but this little guy is the cutest.

"Say hello to Finn," Leila says, squishing his chubby cheeks and making him giggle.

He has Leila's nose and, like the twins, has a sprouting of ginger hair.

"You know we'll definitely be late on stage now, right?" Zed says to Cookie.

"He's perfect," I say.

"We wanted to surprise you," Leila says. "You did so much for us when things were tough. We wanted to be here for you, too."

"This is the best surprise ever," I say, looking more closely at what Finn is wearing. "Oh my gosh, is he wearing…"

"We all are," Leila says.

She unzips her jacket and proudly shows us the Ash and the Basilisks band T's they're wearing. They have our new logo on them—a snake coming out of a skull. Dily, an awesome UK designer, made it for us, and she captured our vision perfectly.

"He's your youngest fan," Conor declares proudly.

"We'll come back after the show," Leila says, taking the hint from Cookie, who is tapping her watch impatiently. "We'll catch up properly then, okay? Declan's waiting in the car, so he can take the little man back to the hotel and watch him for the night."

"He can take his turn to change nappies for a change," Conor says.

"Nappies?" Venom frowns.

"He means diapers," Leila says, rolling her eyes. "Good luck."

They're doing a great job of co-parenting. Conor and Leila live in the twin's parents' house permanently, while Declan works all over the country. He pops by to see them every other weekend.

"Now, you really need to get out there," Cookie says, giving me a small push. "You can't keep your fans waiting."

Although many people were upset when the Lionhearts wanted to follow their metalhead dreams, there is a minority who followed them too. They found our music and felt seen and understood. For all the complications it brought, including Zed being disowned by his mom, it put metal music back on the map.

"Elliot's in the crowd, right?" Venom asks Zed as we head out.

Although his mom hasn't forgiven him for his faux pas, Zed's brother and sister have been supportive. Part of me thinks it's because it takes the pressure off them. Finding out their perfect brother isn't so perfect after all has given them the power to be themselves.

Since getting out of rehab and being six months sober, Elliot has been busy working on a new movie, while Lacey is happy taking more of a backseat from the public eye.

"This is our first tour as Ash and the Basilisks," I say. "We have to remember this."

For old times' sake, the guys are wearing masks, but they only cover their eyes. They're made from silver metal and look like winding snakes.

"Break a leg!" Cookie shouts after us.

We'll be sharing songs from our new album, *Metamorphosis*, for the first time tonight. We've put our heart and soul into the lyrics, sharing our story through music and turning it into art. It encapsulates us and everything we stand for.

Cheers from the restless crowd grow louder as we near the stage, but I'm not afraid. Why would I be? I'm part of the Basilisks now.

We step onto the stage and Ripper roars, "Are you ready to make some fucking noise?"

authors note

So many thank you's go into this series. Writing a book is a team effort, and I'm fortunate to have so many amazing people around me.

Thank you as ever to my beautiful beta readers, Ria and Kyla — you are the freaking best! Thank you to Dily for an amazing logo that matches the band perfectly. For the band names, thanks to Leanna Silvia and Lydia King for your imagination.

Finally, thanks to all the readers who've come along on this crazy ride with me. I appreciate you more than you know.

Artwork by Dily Iola Designs

about the author

Holly Bloom has a degree in English Literature, but don't let that fool you... she would pick a steamy romance over a Shakespeare play any day!

Holly writes contemporary romance - the dark, gritty and twisty kind. She loves creating badass babe characters, who aren't afraid to speak their minds, and writing about the men who can handle them - often, there is more than one! Why choose, right?

When she isn't working on her next project, Holly spends an unhealthy amount of time watching true crime and roaming around the woods near her home in the UK.

As well as gooey chocolate brownies, Holly's favourite thing in the world is hearing from her readers - her characters may bite, but she doesn't! Promise!

**Find out more and sign up to Holly Bloom's newsletter to receive a free book at:
www.hollybloomauthor.com**

Printed in Great Britain
by Amazon

21341447R00280